ANARCHISM

ANARCHISM
Old and New

by Gerald Runkle

DELACORTE PRESS / NEW YORK

66285

Library of Congress Cataloging in Publication Data

Runkle, Gerald.
  Anarchism, old and new.

  Includes bibliographical references.
  1. Anarchism and anarchists. I. Title.
HX833.R83   320.5′7   76-39671

Grateful acknowledgement is made to the following publishers for the use of material under
their control:

ARLINGTON HOUSE PUBLISHERS, for material from *The Conservative Mainstream* by Frank S.
Meyer. Copyright © 1969 by Arlington House, New Rochelle, New York. Used by permission.

ATLANTIC-LITTLE, BROWN AND COMPANY and EYRE & SPOTTISWOODE (Publishers) LTD., for
material from *The Anarchists* by James Joll. Copyright © 1964 by James Joll. Used by permission.

BENJAMIN BLOM, INC., for material from Kropotkin's *Revolutionary Pamphlets*, Benjamin
Blom, Inc. 1971 edition. Used by permission.

LITTLE, BROWN AND COMPANY, for material from *Democracy and the Student Left* by George
F. Kennan. Parts I and IV copyright © 1968 by George F. Kennan; Parts II and III copyright © 1968 by Little, Brown and Company. Used by permission.

THE MACMILLAN COMPANY, for material from *The Political Philosophy of Bakunin* edited
by G. P. Maximoff, copyright © 1953 by The Free Press; and for material from *Reflections on
Violence* by Georges Sorel, copyright © 1950 by The Free Press, a Corporation. Used by
permission.

NEW DIRECTIONS PUBLISHING CORP. and LAURENCE POLLINGER LIMITED, for material from
Nausea by Jean-Paul Sartre, translated by Lloyd Alexander. Copyright © 1964 by New
Directions Publishing Corporation. All Rights Reserved. Used by permission.

OXFORD UNIVERSITY PRESS, for material from *What Then Must We Do?* and *A Letter to
Engelhardt* by Leo Tolstoy, translated by Louise and Aylmer Maude. Published by Oxford
University Press. Used by permission.

PHILOSOPHICAL LIBRARY, INC., and METHUEN & CO. LTD., for material from *Being and
Nothingness* by Jean-Paul Sartre. Copyright © 1956 by Philosophical Library, Inc., New
York. Used by permission.

RANDOM HOUSE, INC., for material from *Danger on the Right* by Arnold Forster and Benjamin R. Epstein, copyright © 1964 by the Anti-Defamation League of B'Nai B'Rith; for
material from *Crisis at Columbia* by Archibald Cox *et al.*, copyright © 1968 by Random
House, Inc.; and for material from *The Year of the Young Rebels* by Stephen Spender,
copyright © 1968, 1969 by Stephen Spender. Used by permission.

RUSSELL & RUSSELL PUBLISHERS, for material from *The History of the Haymarket Affair* by
Henry David. Used by permission.

VANGUARD PRESS, for material from *Now and After: The ABC of Anarchist Communism* by
Alexander Berkman. Used by permission.

Contents

PART ONE. *THE OLD ANARCHISM*

6. *The Good Society*

7. *Evaluation of Anarchism*

PART TWO. *THE NEW ANARCHISM*

8. *The Student Left*

9. *The Radical Right*

10. *Existentialism*

11. *Conclusion: Confessions of a Liberal*

PART

THE OLD ANARCHISM

ONE

1

The Nature of Anarchism

THE MEANING OF ANARCHISM

Liberty

The essence of anarchism is individual liberty. To the degree that an individual favors a society in which the lives of its members are directly controlled by their own decisions, to that degree does he espouse anarchism. Anarchism thus opposes authority in all its forms: governmental rule, social constraint, religious domination, and moral compulsion. The anarchist, as Proudhon proclaimed, accepts no master, recognizes no sovereign.

The classical statement on liberty was made by the anarchist William Godwin, two generations before John Stuart Mill's well-known essay. Man, argued Godwin, is rational. He is thus entitled to a "sphere of discretion" in which his reason can operate. But although he is reasonable, he is also fallible. It is important, therefore, that he learn from experience, that he profit from his successes and failures. Man "must consult his own reason, draw his own conclusions and conscientiously conform himself to his ideas of propriety. Without this, he will be neither active, nor considerate, nor resolute, nor generous." [1]*

The individual's liberty does not extend, however, to the control of others. Even if he were infallible or had an "infallible criterion," he would be wrong to impose his judgment on others, for to do so would cut them off from the same kind of development he prizes

---

* SEE NOTES, GROUPED AT END OF EACH CHAPTER.

4 THE OLD ANARCHISM

for himself. In any case, to impose one's judgment on others is in the end to rely on force—which is always an alien factor when truth is at stake. Godwin wrote: One "may advise me, moderately and without pertinaciousness, but he must not expect to dictate to me." [2] Argument and expostulation are acceptable; coercion is not.

The greatest enemy of liberty is the state. "Countries, exposed to the perpetual interference of decrees, instead of arguments, exhibit within their boundaries the mere phantoms of men." [3] "Whenever government assumes to deliver us from the trouble of thinking for ourselves, the only consequences it produces are torpor and imbecility." [4] According to Godwin, government necessarily does these things. It makes laws and establishes punishments. It therefore directs conduct. Its subjects thus do not act according to their own insights; they do not rise to the dignity of rational beings.

The fact is that man is a very complex being, and each man is unique and different from every other man. An American anarchist wrote: "The individualities of such a being are utterly immeasureable, and every attempt to adjust the capacities, the adaptations, the wants or the responsibilities of another human being, except in the very broadest generalities is unqualifiedly futile and hopeless. Hence every ecclesiastical, governmental or social institution which is based on the idea of demanding conformity or likeness in any thing, has ever been, and ever will be, frustrated by the operation of this subtile, all-pervading principle of Individuality." [5] Anarchists will necessarily disagree among themselves in the areas of ethics and religion. When they are consistent with their basic principle, however, they will refrain from prescribing codes of conduct for men in the good society. They agree that individuals must voluntarily select their own norms of conduct. The individual could not really be said to *have* an ethics or a religion if it were imposed upon him. He has himself to choose the ideals according to which he will govern his life.

Authority

The anarchist is beguiled by neither the practice nor theory of democracy. That political decisions are based on the popular will does not mean that these decisions express *his* will. That laws are made democratically does not mean that they are his laws. That magistrates exist means that he is subject to the domination of others. A collective action, no matter how democratically arrived at, is not an individual action. Democracy can exist only to thwart the individual.[6] Even in the freest and most democratic countries, wrote Bakunin, "the people really obey not laws which they make themselves, but laws which are made in their name, and . . . to obey these laws means nothing else to them than to submit to the arbitrary will of some guarding and governing minority or, what amounts to the same thing, to be freely slaves." [7]

The social contract, by which Rousseau and Locke supposed that men exchanged their natural liberty for civil liberty, is at best a myth. The anarchist does not believe that it ever occurred. And if it did occur, any individual is privileged to reject it. Acceptance of this myth is forced on men by their governments and by tradition. The first step toward freedom is to explode the myth. The second step is to realize that no government now in existence is based upon the present consent of its individual subjects. That a person *accepts* his government does not mean that he tacitly gives consent to it; it means only that he finds it easier to submit than to revolt or emigrate. Government, as Godwin said, "is a question of force, and not of consent." [8]

"Anarchy" means, in its etymological sense, "absence of rule." Since the most obvious kind of rule is political rule, anarchism historically has been directed most eloquently and most forcefully against governments. The advocates of anarchism in the eighteenth and nineteenth centuries were those who found the authority of government most oppressive: the peasants and working classes. Bourbon France, parliamentary Britain, constitutionally monarchical Italy, czarist Russia, republican United States, and absolutist Spain—all these states were denounced as tyrannical. Their governments were unacceptable to anarchists, not because of their form, but because they were governments. When a society is organized as a state, it becomes subject to attack from anarchism simply because *it is a state*. From this point of view George Woodcock's definition of anarchism is a good one: "A system of social thought, aiming at fundamental changes in the structure of society and particularly— for this is the common element uniting all its forms—at the replacement of the authoritarian state by some form of non-governmental co-operation between free individuals." [9]

When a government and a society are united in their aims, power may be exercised on behalf of a great many social, religious, and moral purposes. Such a state is not the only power the anarchists must oppose. Authoritarianism and threats to individual liberty are to be stamped out whatever their source. Anarchism insists that man be free from the coercion of custom, religious dogmas, and moral codes. All social institutions must be scrutinized. Nothing is to be imposed from above or from outside. Government is the first target simply because its authority is so clearly based on force: it has its policemen and judges. But the other, more subtle forms of domination of the individual spirit must be resisted, from whatever aspect of society they derive.[10]

Chaos

Despite the fact that virtually everyone who has written on the subject has pointed out that anarchism is not equivalent to chaos and nihilism, the popular belief persists that anarchists attack the social order because they prefer disorder. There is doubtless a tendency among some people to regard *any* alternative social form as chaotic and disorderly. Republican government, for example, as Malatesta pointed out, was virtually synonymous among some monarchists with disorder and confusion.[11] The earliest anarchists, however, opposed government because they preferred a different *kind* of social order. The Epicureans and Cynics withdrew from society in order to pursue a way of life structured in terms of their own conceptions of human nature and morality. Zeno of Citium, the founder of Stoicism, held that men should be subject only to the moral law and consistently viewed the state as superfluous (if not harmful) to the goals of individual virtue and social harmony. Anarchists ever since have argued that ordinary governed society is, in a deeper sense, more chaotic and nihilistic than their own. The use of compulsion by people who would dominate others constitutes disorder and provokes more; the natural result of individual freedom is order.[12] Tucker put it this way: "Just as truly as Liberty is the mother of order, is the State the mother of violence." [13] A slogan of mid-nineteenth-century anarchism was: "Anarchy is order: government is civil war." [14]

But after saying this, the anarchist will admit that order is not always an unmixed blessing. "As to the beneficial effects of order, the kind of order that reigned at Naples under the Bourbons surely was not preferable to some disorder started by Garibaldi; while the Protestants of this country [Britain] will probably say that the good deal of disorder made by Luther was preferable, at any rate, to the order which reigned under the Pope." [15] "Order" is not good in it-self, when liberty is absent or when it conceals basic tensions and animosities within society. Anarchists *are* revolutionists, and while not prizing *disorder* in itself, are willing to subject society to it in order to bring about a higher "order" or harmony.

Anarchism would permit the individual to enter into whatever voluntary relations he chooses with others. Free cooperation and mutual aid are emphasized. Rules imposed from outside are to be replaced by natural expectancies of conduct firmly grounded in human nature. Men may associate as equals without some being subject to others. Even today, in modern states, "millions of trans-actions are made without the slightest interference of government; and those who enter into agreements have not the slightest inten-tion of breaking bargains." [16] Kropotkin's point is that in most actions of ordinary life government is not needed. With the destruc-tion of the state there will be a reconstruction of society. There can be peace without a peace-keeping body, possession without laws upholding property, marriage without legal contract, production without wage-slaves, and leadership without coercion.

Forms of association and production freely entered into are con-sistent with anarchism. Kropotkin offered many examples of asso-ciations formed by men for common aims, of "societies" already found in the modern state: scientific associations, societies for gymnastics, shorthand writing, study, games, sports, cultivation of the arts, philanthropy, etc. They are voluntary, they do not depend on the state, and they get things done.[17] Ethical and religious be-liefs are also compatible with anarchism, as long as they are genu-inely grounded in private conscience. These beliefs, like voluntary associations, produce order in the lives of individuals and society.

Socialism

The relationship between anarchism and socialism-communism is a curious one. Although Proudhon had early (1840) and clearly distinguished his theory from communism, it was widely believed in the nineteenth century that anarchism and socialism-communism were about the same thing. The most famous anarchist was Bakunin, and his criticism of bourgeois society was very similar to the one made by the socialist Karl Marx. Moreover, the revolutionary strategies of Marxists and Bakuninists, while significantly different, had important similarities. The new society that both Marx and Bakunin looked forward to was based on collective ownership. And for both the ideal was the elimination of the state.

But, as is well known, Bakunin turned against Marxian socialism, and thousands of people in the First International Workingmen's Association followed him in his rejection of the critic of capitalism from whom he had learned so much.

> I detest communism because it is the negation of liberty and because I can conceive nothing human without liberty. I am not a communist because communism concentrates and absorbs all the powers of society into the state; because it necessarily ends in the centralization of property in the hands of the state, while I want the abolition of the state—the radical extirpation of the principle of authority and the tutelage of the state, which, on the pretext of making men moral and civilized, has up to now enslaved, oppressed, exploited and depraved them.[18]

Like its predecessors, the next generation of anarchists rejected the Bolshevik form of Marxism.[19] United against the bourgeoisie, often fighting side by side, Marxists and anarchists are nevertheless inspired by different conceptions of means and ends. Experiences during the Spanish Civil War once again demonstrated that the great radical doctrines, Marxism and anarchism, are irreconcilable. Anarchism is unalterably opposed to any form of state socialism, whether the Marxist form, in which the proletariat class exercises a dictatorship over other classes, or the democratic form, in which the majority enacts laws for the general welfare. In democratic socialism, wrote Tucker, "the community, through its majority expression, will insist more and more on prescribing the conditions of health, wealth, and wisdom, thus impairing and finally destroying individual independence and with it all sense of individual responsibility." [20] Tolstoy, in his fear of industrial socialism, struck a new note by questioning whether it is ultimately beneficial to raise the standard of living. In exchange for loss of liberty and healthy labor, the people will get more and more junk—harmful or inane commodities—as well as a constantly growing appetite for more of it.

Some modern socialists (who are not *state* socialists) look with nostalgia to the partnership that existed in the past between anarchism and socialism. Despite the Marxian and Fabian forms that socialism has taken, Arthur Lewis could write: "Contrary to popular belief, Socialism is not committed either by its history or by its philosophy to the glorification of the State or to the extension of its powers. On the contrary, the links of Socialism are with liberalism and with anarchism, with their emphasis on individual freedom. . . ." [21] Anarchists and socialists march together on May Day. The existence of May Day as an occasion for celebrating the solidarity and achievements of labor goes back to the events of 1886, events in which the anarchists were especially conspicuous. [22] And the anarchists supplied the martyrs. Kropotkin regarded the anarchists as the most dedicated and resolute elements of the working classes; he called anarchism the left wing of socialism.

In conclusion, it may be said that although anarchism is incompatible with any form of *state* socialism, it is not incompatible with socialism itself. Anarchists disagree greatly on the *degree* of socialism the new society should have. This disagreement ranges from extreme individualism to complete communism.

It is time now to distinguish the various forms anarchism has taken.

VARIETIES OF ANARCHISM

Never organized into a disciplined party, never held to a rigid body of dogma, but stressing always the freedom of the individual, anarchism has necessarily taken many forms since man first challenged authority. All of these forms or varieties were revolutionary in the sense that they called for the elimination of existing governments and a fundamental alteration of the societies on which they were based. On what the methods of revolution should be there was extensive disagreement. Most theories of anarchism, furthermore, called for more or less definite forms of society after government had been eliminated. On what the form of society should be there was also extensive disagreement.

There were other disagreements in the various theories of anarchism. There was disagreement on the nature of human nature and on the principles of morality and religion to which human nature was subject, in the analysis of royal, constitutional, and democratic government, and in the description of the economic and other social institutions of the day. And there was disagreement on the tactics and strategy of direct action.

If, however, we can regard as fundamental the differences in the new society and in the choice of revolutionary methods by which to bring it about, a twofold classification can be made.

Differences in Goals

The first classification is on the basis of the bonds that are to obtain among the individuals in the new society. Are human relations external and adventitious, or are they internal and definitive of the life the individual will live?

One extreme answer, issuing from the right, is what we will call Individualistic Anarchism. This viewpoint opposes all kinds of socialism and envisions a society composed of reasonable and/or resourceful men. Each man works and asserts his own being, respectful of others but in no sense dependent upon them. "I . . . want the liberty which will enable each to live according to his ideal. I want to be let alone, I want to be spared from any demands that may be made in the name of 'ideal of humanity.' " [23]

Somewhat to the left of individualism is Mutualism. This viewpoint welcomes free association and mutually beneficial contracts. Communes and federations may come into being, and groups can enter into larger federations with others. Its earliest inspiration came from peasant groups that opposed the growing power of the bourgeoisie and the development of an industrial society.

The third variety may broadly be termed Collectivistic Anarchism. Here people are more deliberately brought together for resistance to oppression and for the satisfaction of their economic needs. Sub-varieties are syndicalism, based on the collective power of the trade unions; collectivism (in the narrow sense), which insists on possession of the means of agricultural and industrial production by society as a whole, but guarantees the full fruit of his labor to the worker; and communism, which, while opposing Marx, will have some kind of authority to enact the principle of "from each according to his ability, to each according to his needs." All these forms of collectivistic anarchism seek to remain faithful to the basic libertarianism of the creed, but emphasize the importance of widespread and systematic cooperation among workers. The collectivistic anarchist speaks of "administration of things" rather than "dominion over persons." [24] He believes that only collectivism marks an advance over liberalism, and he argues that modern society with its complex interrelationships and scientific production has already socialized man.[25] To seek to abstract the isolated individual is not only "bourgeois" but reactionary; it represents a non-fraternal attitude and is a sign of society's decadence. Progress lies in the direction of association and cooperation. Bakunin, discussing solidarity, spoke of "the inherent collective nature of man, in virtue of which no man is free if all the men who surround him and exercise the least influence, direct or indirect, on his life are not so equally." [26]

The anarchist's attitude toward private property obviously parallels his position on the issues of the first classification. The individualist defends private property; the collectivist does not. All anarchists are committed to the elimination of the state: the rightist abolishes it in order to *preserve* property, while the leftist abolishes it in order to *suppress* property. The state is thus viewed as both the enemy and the defender of private property—which, of course, it is.

Differences in Means

Cutting across the preceding classification is one having to do with methods. Methods for the same end may differ, and some anarchists are more concerned with clarifying themselves on the methods they favor than on the ends they wish to achieve. Indeed, many anarchists, almost as a matter of principle, refuse to discuss ends at all, believing that authoritarian society is so bad that anything free men create will be much better than that which has been destroyed.

At one extreme in a classification by method would be the anarchism that employs the method of violence as often and as widely spread as possible. The force of tyrants is to be met by the violent force of revolutionaries. Where revolutionary force can be organized openly it will be. Where it cannot it will be secret and conspiratorial. If revolutionary violence cannot take place on a broad scale, it may simply aim at the seizure of a factory or the capture of a city. Where this is impossible anarchists can instill terror in their enemies by individual acts of assassination or "propaganda by the deed." In its most extreme form anarchism makes common cause with criminals: laws are bad, so law-breaking is good—especially murder.

At the other extreme is pacifistic anarchism. Abhorring the violence of the state, the pacifist will meet it with love. Triumph by force over force is neither possible nor desirable. "Triumph of the conscience" is always possible, although it may take place only in the soul of the individual. The pacifist tries to convert others to his view by example and persuasion. He may compromise his basic principle of concord by acts of deliberate disobedience, but these acts are always peaceful. His resistance is passive. He will endure whatever the state subjects him to, but he will not permit himself to be implicated in its nefarious policies and practices. And he will not oppose it physically by returning evil for evil. Pacifists may choose to retire from society in order to live in colonies of their own.

Between these two extremes are many forms of violent and non-violent revolutionary action. Near the second extreme is the general strike, a tactic in which the masses of workers simply stop working. Near the first extreme is the destruction by the workers of the factories and machines. Most anarchists will seek to drive away the officials of government by whatever degree of violence (or intimidation) is necessary.

The typical anarchist is not a pacifist. He is an activist who has chosen to act in as direct and decisive a way as possible. While the assassins and bomb-throwers are only small minorities in historical anarchism (and many were not anarchists at all), the pacifists too are a minority. Revolutionary violence of one kind or another has characterized the mainstream of anarchist theory.

The "Old" and the "New"

There is a further distinction made in this volume between kinds of anarchism.

Part I deals with the "old" anarchism: those ideas expressed by men and movements in Europe and the United States in the period of time centered in the nineteenth century. This was the heyday of anarchism, and its exponents are the famous names in the history of the movement. For purposes of convenient organization I have chosen to call the theories of this classical period expressions of the "old" anarchism.

One can, of course, find anarchistic thought earlier than the eighteenth and nineteenth centuries. While believing that "anarchism as a developed, articulate, and clearly identifiable trend appears only in the modern era of social and political revolutions," Woodcock can cite, in all consistency, the Diggers in revolutionary seventeenth-century England and their great leader, Gerrard Win-stanley.[27] Less convincing cases can be made for the sixteenth-century German Anabaptists and the early Quakers. Still earlier Christian sects may be cited for their resistance against the state: the Waldenses, the Albigenses, and the Hussites. Some anarchists claim that the real founder of anarchism was Jesus and that the first anarchistic community was the company of apostles. The anarchism of Cynicism, Stoicism, and Epicureanism has already been cited.[28]

Part II deals with the "new" anarchism. The student left, the radical right, and existentialism seem, at least superficially, to be contemporary forms of anarchism. The "new anarchists" are not, however, presented as adherents of the old ideology. The old tradition laid down fundamental principles of anarchism, as well as some qualities of anarchism that may or may not be essential. Some of these ideas found their way into contemporary radical thought and some did not. Some were refuted and some were ignored. How this came about is not the concern here. Actually, of course, distrust of political authority is endemic in Western culture. Both the old and the new anarchism draw on a common libertarian tradition.

The "new" anarchists are not, then, presented as the contemporary inheritors of the "old" anarchistic thought. They have points of view of their own, and if they are anarchists at all, they are so in their own distinctive ways. The conservers of the classical anarchist tradition are today a small and hardly visible remnant. Despite their contemporaneity, their views belong more appropriately in Part I under "old anarchism" than in Part II under "new anarchism."

There is no attempt here to show that the "new" developed from the "old," to deny that the "new" developed from the "old," or to indicate the nature and scope of the historical debt that the "new" owes to the "old." The specification of any temporal connections that may exist will be left to the historian, sociologist, and psychologist.

But although I am not concerned with tracing the particular influences of men and movements on other men and movements, I do wish to emphasize the many interesting similarities and dissimilarities between the old and the new anarchism. The ideas of both the old and the new are worthy subjects for examination. The reason for dealing with them in the same volume is to provide an occasion for noting these logical relationships. Moreover, analysis and criticism of the old and the new may indicate how far libertarian thought has advanced and how far it has failed to advance.

NOTES

1 William Godwin, *An Enquiry Concerning Political Justice and Its Influence on Morals and Happiness* (Third Edition), F. E. L. Priestley, Ed. (Toronto: The University of Toronto Press, 1946), Vol. I, p. 168.

2 *Ibid.*

3 *Ibid.*, p. 178.

4 *Ibid.*, Vol. II, p. 230.

5 Stephen Pearl Andrews, "The True Constitution of Government," in *The Science of Society* (Second Edition), (New York: Fowler and Wells, 1852), p. 20.

6 "The essence of government is control, or the attempt to control. He who attempts to control another is a governor, an aggressor, an invader; and the nature of such invasion is not changed, whether it is made by one man upon another man, after the manner of the ordinary criminal, or by one man upon all other men, after the manner of an absolute monarch, or by all other men upon one man, after the manner of a modern democracy." Benjamin R. Tucker, *Instead of a Book: By a Man Too Busy to Write One* (Second Edition) (New York: Benjamin R. Tucker, 1897), p. 23.

7 Mikhail Bakunin, *Marxism, Freedom and the State,* K. J. Kenafick, Trans. (London: Freedom Press, 1950), pp. 46–47.

8 Godwin, Vol. I, pp. 225–226.

9 George Woodcock, *Anarchism* (Cleveland: The World Publishing Company, 1962), p. 13.

10 "Social norms or laws, like political authority and coercive moral codes, are forms of government. For the anarchist, they too must be abolished to allow for the individualization of ethics." Leonard I. Krimerman and Lewis Perry, Eds., *Patterns of Anarchy* (Garden City, New York: Doubleday & Co., 1966), p. 560.

11 It is interesting to note that the term was used in a derogatory sense by the Marxists for the anti-authoritarians in the International Workingmen's Association. After the split in 1872 the anti-authoritarians accepted the term; they called themselves "anarchists" but insisted that it designated its literal meaning as simply *absence of government.*

12 "Anarchism means voluntary cooperation instead of forced participation. It means harmony and order in place of interference and disorder." Alexander Berkman, *Now and After: the ABC of Anarchist Communism* (New York: The Vanguard Press, 1929), p. 188.

13 Tucker, p. 442.

14 Woodcock, p. 276.

15 Peter Kropotkin, *Revolutionary Pamphlets,* Roger N. Baldwin, Ed. (New York: Benjamin Blom, 1927), p. 62.

16 *Ibid.*, p. 64.

17 See *ibid.*, pp. 66–67.

18 Bakunin, quoted in James Joll, *The Anarchists* (New York: Grosset and Dunlap, 1964), pp. 107–108. For an extended criticism of Marx and Marxism, see

Mikhail Bakunin, *The Political Philosophy of Bakunin*, G. P. Maximoff, Ed. (London: The Free Press of Glencoe, Collier-Macmillan Limited, 1964).

19 Some examples: Peter Kropotkin, *Letter to the Workers of Western Europe;* Alexander Berkman, *The Bolshevik Myth;* Emma Goldman, *My Disillusionment in Russia.*

20 Tucker, p. 8. Tucker then expressed fear of such ultimate consequences of socialism as a state religion, a state morals code, elimination of all private schools, controlled and regulated breeding, etc.

21 Arthur Lewis, quoted in "Moving With the Times . . . But Not in Step," *Anarchy* 3 (May 1961), p. 66.

22 See pp. 27–29.

23 John Henry Mackay, *The Anarchists: A Picture of Civilization at the Close of the Nineteenth Century,* George Schumm, Trans. (Boston: Benjamin R. Tucker, 1891), p. 139.

24 The individualistic anarchist retorts that "administration of things" inevitably *becomes* "dominion over persons."

25 "Can anyone," asks a modern collectivistic anarchist, "lay his hands upon an integrated product of the labor of millions of men and declare it his own?" Senex, "Whither the Libertarian Movement?" *Vanguard* 1:5, p. 37.

26 Bakunin, *Marxism, Freedom and the State,* p. 53. The paragraph concludes: "This truth is to be found magnificently expressed in the Declaration of the Rights of Man drafted by Robespierre, and which proclaims that *the slavery of the least of men is the slavery of all.*"

27 See Woodcock, pp. 39, 43–49.

28 It should also be noted that anarchistic thought is not limited to the western world. Lao-Tse may be cited. Bertrand Russell quoted him on the title page of his book on socialism, anarchism and syndicalism: "Production without possession; action without self-assertion; development without domination." See also, in the same volume, Russell's excerpt from Chuang Tzu: *Roads to Freedom* (Third Edition) (London: George Allen and Unwin Ltd., 1949), pp. 50–51. See also Robert A. Scalapino, *The Chinese Anarchist Movement* (Berkeley: Center for Chinese Studies, Institute of International Studies, 1961).

2

Spokesmen for Anarchism

EUROPE

A complete list of articulate spokesmen for anarchism would be very long, thus testifying not only to its widespread appeal, but to the variability of its forms. Anarchism, it almost seems, can be about anything the anarchist wishes it to be. Communism has its Marx and democracy has its Locke and Rousseau. There are in the history of anarchism no towering figure or figures, people whose ideas must always be taken into account by the lesser lights. Proudhon, Bakunin, and Kropotkin are indeed important to the movement, but hardly in the way that Marx is important to the communist movement. Individual freedom is the starting point. Precisely what it is and how it may be achieved and maintained are questions to which no final and uniform answers may be found.

In this chapter various European and American spokesmen for anarchism are cited and briefly identified. The inclusion or exclusion of certain names may be subject to controversy, but no claim to completeness is offered. In the countries chosen for discussion names are left out. And some countries that have had their spokesmen for anarchism also are omitted (*e.g.,* The Netherlands, Sweden, Mexico). In the case of the United States, the attempt will be made to place the spokesmen in some kind of historical context.

France

In France the name of Jean Meslier (fl. 1735) has an honored but obscure place.[1] Meslier was a priest in the village of Etrepigny who denounced authority of all kinds—ecclesiastical, economic, social, and political. At his death he left a *Testament* for the peasants of his parish in which he called for violent revolution against the nobles who oppressed them. Voltaire and d'Holbach appreciated his anti-clericalism, and Proudhon was later to commend his demand for free association of peasants.

Many anarchistic ideas were expressed during the period of the French Revolution. The most uncompromising voices were those of the *Enragés*. Opponents of the Girondins and of the Jacobins who succeeded them, the *Enragés* denounced the governments that replaced Bourbon tyranny with other forms of tyranny for the purpose of enforcing economic injustice throughout the land. Jacques Roux (d. 1794) advocated direct mob action, especially seizure of goods, in order to rectify social injustice. "Freedom is but an empty phantom if one class of men can starve another with impunity." [2] The high point of his life occurred when he escorted Louis XVI to the scaffold; the low point was his death by suicide in one of Robespierre's prisons. Jean Varlet (fl. 1793) survived Robespierre and criticized the Directory.[3] Having witnessed so many forms of government in those turbulent years at the end of the eighteenth century, he condemned government in principle. Justice and equality are incompatible with political rule: under any government, the people lose.

Later anarchists could find in the views of the Jacobins, including Robespierre himself, some ideas of value: Robespierre's vision of independent and cooperating peasants, his insistence on equality and fraternity in social life, and his ruthlessness toward the defenders of the privileged orders. Marat also provided inspiration: "The lot of the poor, always downtrodden, always subjugated and always oppressed, can never be improved by peaceful means." [4] Babeuf, executed during the Directory, has been claimed by many later revolutionists for his belief in the usefulness of conspiratorial methods. The French Revolution in general serves the anarchists as the great prototype of the successful uprising against government, even though in the end its aims were not realized. The next revolution will succeed not only in deposing the existing government but in bringing in a new social order that requires no government.

Charles Fourier (1772–1837),[5] a revolutionist, but not a violent or conspiratorial one, is always listed as a utopian socialist. In his ideal societies, in which membership is wholly voluntary, cooperation and harmony are to prevail. While not an egalitarian, Fourier was an anarchist in his conviction that society requires no government in order to be just and happy.

One of the people influenced by Fourier was Pierre-Joseph Proudhon (1809–1865),[6] the greatest of the French anarchists. Proudhon rejected both private property and communism. He opposed all political authority, but would preserve free association through law. He was a spokesman for the free peasant and a foe of industrialism and the bourgeoisie. His thought is elusive and self-contradictory, but he had many followers among the anarchists.

Other French anarchists were the journalists Sébastien Faure (1858–1942),[7] Jean Grave (fl. 1895),[8] Anselme Bellegarrigue (fl. 1850),[9] and Emile Pouget (fl. 1895); Fernand Pelloutier (1867–1901),[10] the leader of the Fédération des Bourses du Travil; the exiles Ernest Coeurderoy (1825–1862)[11] and Joseph Déjacque (fl. 1860);[12] the mutualists Henri Tolain (1828–1897) and Charles Limousin (fl. 1865); the collectivists Eugène Varlin (1839–1871), Benoit Malon (1841–1893),[13] and Jules Guesde (1845–1922); and, to varying degrees, a host of painters and literary figures.

Finally, the name of the great syndicalist Georges Sorel (1847–1922)[14] should be cited. Sorel held many views in his long life, but he always regarded himself as a follower of Proudhon. Contemptuous toward the bourgeoisie and rationalism, he sought liberation for the proletarians in industrial syndicates, advocated direct action, and believed in the purifying effects of violence.

Great Britain

When we turn from France to Great Britain, we encounter fewer native anarchists. With its more permissive laws, however, Britain served as sanctuary in the nineteenth century for anarchists from all over the world.

Thomas Paine (1737–1809)[15] is claimed by some anarchists as a forebear. His distrust of government was genuine. Like Denis Diderot (1713–1784), his French contemporary, he contrasted a happy and harmonious state of nature to a society corrupted by wealth and power. "Government, like dress," wrote Paine, "is the badge of lost innocence; the palaces of kings are built on the ruins of the bowers of paradise."[16] In *The Rights of Man* he not only extolled the natural rights that no government can abrogate, but pointed out man's natural propensities for free cooperation: "mutual dependence and reciprocal interest" inspire and make possible mutual aid.

Among those influenced by Paine was the first unmistakable British anarchist and the most systematic one: William Godwin (1756–1836).[17] A resolute rationalist and equalitarian, Godwin espoused a theory of society composed of individualists and based upon a "true" psychology. He was opposed to force in the good society and to violence in working for it. Democracy was acceptable to him, but only as a transitional stage to a society without government at all.

Other spokesmen for anarchism in Britain hardly existed until the last two decades of the nineteenth century. This was an active period of anarchist endeavor, but dominated by foreign visitors. "The rumor that an international conspiracy of assassins was directed from London headquarters was hard to dispel." [18] Henry Seymour (fl. 1885), influenced more by Proudhon than Godwin, edited a journal called *The Anarchist*. William Morris (1834–1896), the artist, socialist, and journalist, was active in and around anarchist circles. Oscar Wilde (1856–1900) [19] was another literary figure who expressed anarchistic ideas. While espousing socialism, he consistently demanded individualism—especially for the artist. Art is not for him (as it was for Proudhon and Tolstoy) a means for the good society; it is the end.[20] Favoring creativity and free imagination, Wilde naturally favored rebellion also—rebellion against public opinion, poverty, law, and government.

The syndicalist movement in Britain was not notably anarchistic. Tom Mann (1856–1941) and Guy Bowman (fl. 1912), however, sought to express syndicalism in anarchistic or quasi-anarchistic terms.

Germany

The most conspicuous figure in German anarchism is Max Stirner (1806–1856).[21] Of no influence during his lifetime, Stirner (or Johann Caspar Schmidt, which was his real name) celebrated the ideal of the complete individual, the egoist, absolutely unique, who creates his own values, who takes what he can without apology, and who rebels but does not deign to make revolutions. The self-realization that Stirner talked about is not of the rational form that Godwin emphasized but is rooted in the passionate and instinctive will.

Wilhelm Weitling (1808–1871) [22] is a name often encountered in connection with major figures like Marx and Bakunin. His anarchism was of the communistic variety, and he sought to arouse the downtrodden and exploited (those who have nothing to lose) to revolution. Weitling's real antecedents were the French utopians. "The perfect society has no government, but only an administration, no laws only obligations, no punishments only means of correction." [23] His search for the perfect society led him after the revolution of 1848 to the United States, where he spent his declining days trying to establish utopian societies.

Later German anarchists were Rudolf Rocker (1873–1958) [24] and Gustav Landauer, anarcho-syndicalists. Quite unlike these intellectuals was Johann Most (1846–1906), [25] a revolutionary of the most violent kind. Devoted to conspiracy and terrorism ("propaganda by the deed"), he did much of his "work" in the United States.

Russia

Among the men influenced by Weitling was the great Russian anarchist Mikhail Bakunin (1814–1876). [26] Bakunin seemed always to be aroused by ideas: those of Fichte, Hegel, Proudhon, Marx, Weitling, and many others. His enthusiasm for these ideas did not induce him to create a new anarchistic theory of his own. It is in the area of action that Bakunin made his name. Always ready to support insurrection anywhere and everywhere, he was until his death an active and militant foe of the establishment. His vast influence rests not on his philosophy but on his temperament, on his passion for conspiracy and revolution. This influence far outweighed that of such lonely theorists as—to take the opposite extreme—Max Stirner. The anarchist movement in Italy owes much to Bakunin, and the movement in Italy, France, and Switzerland was inspired by his memory long after he died. Yet he did manage, finally, to distinguish in his own mind and in the minds of his followers the fundamental differences between his own collectivism and that of Karl Marx. This division in thought was to become important in the history of revolutionary movements, in the division between the "Red" International and the "Black" International.

Another important Russian anarchist, also born to an aristocratic family, was Peter Kropotkin (1842–1921). [27] Dropping the title "Prince" from his name at the age of twelve, he was early interested in liberal and radical causes. His first arrest for revolutionary activity was in Russia in 1874. Two years later he made a dramatic escape to England via Sweden. He lived for five years in Switzerland, where he stayed with the workers of the Jura Federation, encountered the ideas of Bakunin, and wrote articles for *Le Révolté*. After being expelled from Switzerland he returned briefly to England before going to France. There he was arrested as a result of the Lyons riots and served three years in prison for being a member of the International Workingmen's Association. He returned again to England in 1886 where he pursued his scientific and political studies until his return to Russia in June 1917.

Recognized as the successor to Bakunin as the leader of international anarchism, Kropotkin, with his scholarly and saintly ways, so opposite in temperament to the flamboyant and legendary Bakunin, almost brought respectability to the movement. He sought to harness moral principle and social evolution. He was a brilliant geographer (and had been invited to join the British Royal Geographical Society) and was widely read in many other areas of science. He sought to apply the methods of natural science in the social sciences and to show that anarchism was thoroughly scientific in nature and inception and was grounded on a scientific study of nature and society. He sought to remain a consistent revolutionist, however, for fundamental and decisive changes in society must finally be made—peacefully if possible, violently if necessary. The society to emerge must be communistic.

Leo Tolstoy (1828–1910) [28] is the best example of pacifistic anarchism. Utterly dedicated to the Christian teaching of love, he would not resist force with force, no matter what evil that force supported. The state was clearly such an evil, for it exploited and demoralized its subjects. True brotherhood is possible only in a society in which men live simply and naturally. Property, classes, taxes, and wars must finally give way to a free society in which men live simply and naturally as brothers. Tolstoy taught that one should not permit himself to be implicated in the state in any way. When the state commands, one should simply disobey.

There were other Russian anarchists. One of the first was Alexander Herzen (1812–1870),[29] who introduced Proudhon's ideas to Russian radicals and gave financial support to Bakunin. Herzen was an exile. So too were Emma Goldman (1869–1940) [30] and Alexander Berkman (1870–1936),[31] who did much of their work in the United States until they were deported. Finally, there was Nestor Makhno (d. 1935), the great peasant military leader. In the last year of World War I he inflicted great injury on the armies of the Central Powers in the Ukraine; later he defeated forces of the White Army; finally, he was repudiated by the Bolsheviks and crushed by overwhelming Red forces. "On the day when Makhno fought his way across the Dniester into exile, anarchism as a vital force ceased to exist in Russia." [32]

Italy

The first anarchist influence in Italy was Proudhon, whose ideas were disseminated by Carlo Pisacane (d. 1857), a collectivist and federalist who also advocated what later was called "propaganda by the deed." There were soon a great many articulate and resolute anarchists in Italy. The greatest foreign influence, however, was Bakunin, not Proudhon.

The most important Italian spokesmen were two aristocratic leaders who linked their own ideas with those of Bakunin: Carlo Cafiero (fl. 1880) and Errico Malatesta (1853–1932).[33] But Malatesta went beyond Bakunin in his collectivism; he opposed the state but would defend collective regulation of things. People everywhere must liberate themselves: little revolutions produce big revolutions. Direct action, small or large, would educate the masses for the final violent blow against property, church, and state. For syndicalism Malatesta had contempt, not only for its class bureaucracy and class bias, but for its tactics. He sought to unmask the myth of the general strike:

> The general strike is pure utopia. Either the worker, dying of hunger three days on strike, will return to the factory hanging his head, and we shall score one more defeat. Or else he will try to gain possession of the fruits of production by open force.[34]

Active with Cafiero and Malatesta in the Bakunin-dominated International in Italy was Andrea Costa (fl. 1874). Costa, however, drifted away from the conspiratorial violence of Malatesta, discounting the effectiveness also of propaganda by the deed. Believing that a true social revolution required mass organization and mass propaganda, he finally turned to political action and became a respectable socialist.

Spain

In Spain as in Italy the successive influences of Proudhon and Bakunin were felt. The first important Proudhonist in Spain was

Pi y Margall (fl. 1870),[35] who favored federalism but not necessarily by means of a sudden destruction of all political power. "I shall divide and subdivide power; I shall make it changeable and go on destroying it." [36]

The leaders who first brought Bakunin to Spain were Giuseppe Fanelli (1827–1877), an Italian, and Anselmo Lorenzo (fl. 1871). More than anyone else Lorenzo set the stamp of puritanism on Spanish anarchism.

More recent spokesmen for Spanish anarchism were José Sánchez Román (fl. 1901), Buenaventura Durruti (d. 1936), García Oliver (fl. 1937), Juan Peiró (fl. 1933), and Federica Montseny (fl. 1933).[37] The men were all uncompromising apostles of violence, including Oliver, who served as Minister of Justice during the Civil War. Montseny commanded widespread respect for her honest and intellectual power; she too was a minister during the war.

THE UNITED STATES

Native American Individualism

Although a case could be made for the existence of "native American" anarchists before the nineteenth century,[38] the earliest unmistakably anarchistic American thinker was Josiah Warren (1798–1874).[39] After an instructive experience with Robert Owen's utopian society at New Harmony, Warren departed in order to establish societies of his own. Here individualism would be practiced more uncompromisingly than Mr. Owen would have permitted. Some of Warren's colonies were Village of Equity (1834), Utopia (1846), and Modern Times (1850), which were moderately successful. Warren's concept of "sovereignty of the individual" had to exist side by side with the concepts of mutualism and cooperation. Earlier in his career, acting on the principle that the individual was entitled to the full fruits of his labor (but no more), Warren had established a "Time Store" in Cincinnati: labor notes were to serve as the medium of exchange. Like Proudhon (whose work he did not know) and unlike Marx, Warren refused to accept community of property as the logical consequence of the proposition that labor is the source of all value. Modern Times, which finally dissolved after the Civil War, had as its motto "mind your own business."

Important followers of Warren were Lysander Spooner (1808–1887) [40] and Stephen Pearl Andrews (1812–1886).[41] Like Warren, Spooner was concerned about banking and currency and their relation to human freedom. Always critical of the economic follies of government, Spooner finally called into question its very existence. Andrews was a tireless worker for many liberal causes, but is perhaps most remembered for his defense of individual freedom in sexual matters.[42]

Standing apart from these individualists was the most famous American individualist of all, Henry David Thoreau (1817–1862).[43] He addressed himself to solitary souls, not organizations, and believed that modern life conspired against freedom on a variety of fronts: political, economic, racial, moral, and artistic. Thoreau's great injunction is to disobey when the state (or social pressure) commands against conscience. Like Emerson and perhaps Jefferson, he believed that government is only an expedient at best, and that its demise rests on the return of humanity to its natural perfection. Although himself a passive rebel, he defended the deeds of the activist John Brown.

Benjamin R. Tucker (1854–1939) [44] was another native American individualist. He associated himself with the Warren tradition rather than with the tradition of Thoreau of transcendentalism. The ideas of Proudhon, so similar to Warren's, had been introduced to America at mid-century,[45] and Tucker, much impressed, sought to popularize them. He translated and published at his own expense two of Proudhon's basic works. Tucker's anarchism was intended to be the final synthesis of Stirner, Warren, and Proudhon.

Opposed to state socialism and communism, Tucker defined anarchism as "the doctrine that all the affairs of men should be managed by individuals or voluntary associations, and that the State should be abolished." [46] When Most derisively called his position nothing more than "consistent Manchesterism," Tucker answered, "Well, what better can a man who professes Anarchism want than that? Yes, genuine Anarchism is consistent Manchesterism, and Communistic or pseudo-Anarchism is inconsistent Manchesterism." [47] Tucker never advocated violent revolution, but as a gesture of principle refused to pay his poll tax—for which he was jailed. He finally gave up the struggle for truth in America in 1908, after his printing press and books were destroyed, and migrated to France to spend the last thirty years of his life. No more spirited journalist had ever devoted his considerable talents to the anarchist cause.

One last native American individualist should be mentioned: John Beverley Robinson (1853–1923). A college professor and noted architect in St. Louis, Robinson published an important work in Proudhonian economics in 1916: *The Economics of Liberty*. His translation of Proudhon's *General Idea of the Revolution in the Nineteenth Century* appeared seven years later.

Internationals: Red and Black

The basic notions of native American anarchism were overwhelmed in the years after the Civil War by ideologies carried here by radical immigrants from Europe. American anarchism took on a much more collectivistic or communistic character, as well as a more violent one. Not even the industry and eloquence of Tucker could preserve the spirit of individualism and peaceful change.

Four million Germans immigrated to America between 1850 and 1890, bringing with them the alien ideas of class consciousness and socialism. Aware of the ineffectiveness of individualism and utopian societies, a small fraction of the immigrants would meet the evils of inhuman American capitalism by class solidarity and revolution. The growth of socialism was interrupted by the Civil War (in which many of the radical immigrants served as Union soldiers), but resumed afterward. From the beginning, however, the movement was split in ways reflecting the split in Europe. Early immigrants, Wilhelm Weitling, Joseph Wedemeyer, and Friedrich Sorge, were all disciples of Marx, but were Marxists in different ways.

The International Workingmen's Association with Marx as leader and London as headquarters was formed in 1864. The Association had a branch in the United States called the North American Federation. Under the leadership of Sorge it sought to unite all workers against capitalism and to exploit the potential of American trade unions. The International in Europe and America was rent by two great issues. One, to oversimplify, was whether the members were to function as a political party and to make common cause with "radical bourgeois" groups for the sake of political (*e.g.*, legislative) gains, or whether they should concentrate their efforts in the trade unions for material gains and education for revolution. On this issue the followers of Ferdinand Lassalle of Germany chose the first alternative; the more faithful followers of Marx (including Sorge) chose the second. Both groups were committed to the end of replacing the bourgeois state with a socialist state under proletarian leadership. The other issue was whether the International was to be directed in an authoritative way and whether the eventual socialist society would exist as a state with a government and laws. On this conjunctive question the followers of Marx and Lassalle answered in the affirmative, while the followers of the anarchist Bakunin answered in the negative. Marx, in order to frustrate his European enemies, caused the headquarters of the International to be moved to New York in 1872. After a few more years of dissension it was officially dissolved in July 1876.

These dissensions were reflected also in the Socialist Labor Party of North America, which was founded in 1877. The Lassalleans remained in power until 1889. Some members seceded in protest to form other parties and trade unions.[48] The SLP under the leadership of Daniel De Leon in the 1890s sought to return to the principles of Marx to formulate a revolutionary program that would utilize politics and unions without being deflected by work for liberal political goals or short-term economic goals. Its decline began at the turn of the century when moderates under the leadership of Morris Hillquist withdrew to form the Socialist Party of America. De Leon's death in 1914 further weakened the first important Marxist party in America.

Socialist parties had some success in the depression of the 1870s, participating in the great riots and railroad strike of 1877 and in electing some of its members to local office; improved economic conditions, however, all but destroyed them. The workers turned to labor unions and short-term goals. An SLP leader lamented: "The plundered toilers are rapidly being drawn back to the old paths, and are closing their ears to the appeal of reason. They are selling their birthright for a mess of pottage by rejecting the prospect of future emancipation in their greed for the trifling gains of the present." [49] The more extreme socialist leaders "demanded something more virile than election campaigns. For this group it was the union, rather than the franchise, which was the fulcrum for revolution." [50]

In 1881, at about the time when the national trade unions were being organized, the Revolutionary Socialist Labor Party was established in Chicago. Certain leaders of the Socialist Labor Party of North America, Albert Parsons (1848–1887) and G. A. Schilling, had brought their many followers into the new group. Recent socialist arrivals from Germany (which had passed anti-Socialist laws in 1878) also joined. Declaring that the ballot was "an invention of the bourgeoisie to fool the workers," the new revolutionary group adopted a communist-anarchist ideology.

Johann Most, a fugitive in England from Germany's anti-Socialist laws, was arrested in 1881 for praising the assassination of Czar Alexander II ("propaganda by the deed"). Released in 1882, he came to New York and soon made himself the leader of Eastern radical socialists and anarchists. Most's ideas seemed to be more violent than even those of the Chicago group. Parsons and August Spies of Chicago sought to bring the East and the West together. In October 1883 delegates met in Pittsburgh to form a branch of the International Working People's Association.[51] This American "black" International formulated a manifesto that was theoretically confusing but solidly anarchist. Some excerpts:

> The struggle of the proletariat with the bourgeoisie must have a violent, revolutionary character. We could show by scores of illustrations that all attempts in the past to reform this monstrous system by peaceable means, such as the ballot, have been futile, and all such efforts in the future must necessarily be so. . . . Knowing that from them [our masters] no good may be expected, there remains but one recourse—FORCE!
>
> What we would achieve is, therefore, plainly and simply: *First:*—Destruction of the existing class rule, by all means, i.e., by energetic, relentless, revolutionary and international action. *Second:*—Establishment of a free society based upon cooperative organization of production. *Third:*—Free exchange of equivalent products by and between the productive organizations without commerce and profit-mongery. *Fourth:*—Organization of education on a secular, scientific and equal basis for both sexes. *Fifth:*—Equal rights for all without distinction of sex or race. *Sixth:*—Regulation of all public affairs by free contracts between the autonomous (independent) communes and associations, resting on a federalistic basis.[52]

Most, the violent anarchist of the East who had published his notorious pamphlet on explosives shortly after reaching the United States, now had allies in the West. Albert Parsons himself printed articles in his paper *Alarm* extolling the virtues of dynamite.

The Haymarket Affair

The series of events that was to bring the anarchists into national prominence and inspire widespread fear and persecution occurred in Chicago in 1886 and has been called the Haymarket Affair. The issue behind it seemed innocuous enough: the eight-hour day. The eight-hour day had been demanded by liberals and radicals of all denominations. When the anarchists finally joined the movement, they did so with vigor. In Chicago they propagandized indefatigably. A strike had been called for May 1 at all establishments where the eight-hour day had not been granted. When that day arrived, hundreds of thousands of workers refused to work.

It was on May 3 that real trouble occurred. At McCormick Harvester in Chicago, where management had locked out its employees three months before, strikebreakers were brought in under police guard. The strikers assembled near the factory to hear a speech by August Spies. During the speech the working day ended and hundreds of strikebreakers poured out of the plant. A battle ensued. Bystanders, including women and children, contributed to the general confusion. When police arrived and were taunted by rocks and insults, they fired into the crowd. Six people were killed and dozens were wounded.

The anarchists, striking a stance of righteous indignation, used this outrage for all that it was worth. The headline in *Die Arbeiter Zeitung* was: "BLOOD! Lead and Powder as a Cure for Dissatisfied Workers—This Is Law and Order!" Circulars in German and English read: "Revenge! Workingmen to Arms!!!" [53] They scheduled a protest meeting in Haymarket Square on May 4. About three thousand workers and their families appeared to hear speeches by Spies and Parsons. The program was carefully observed by a large force of police. The speeches themselves were not especially incendiary. The crowd thinned out as rain began to fall, and there were perhaps five hundred people still in the square when a police captain ordered them to disperse. At that moment a bomb was thrown from an alley near the platform, exploding within the area held by the police. The policemen panicked and began firing wildly. It is possible that some workers fired also.[54] Seven policemen and four civilians were dead or dying, and possibly a hundred people were wounded.

The identity of the bomb-thrower was never established, but Americans throughout the nation demanded arrests and speedy justice. After the riot authorities arrested hundreds of workers and conducted illegal searches. Police Captain Michael J. Schaack took the leadership. "Bombs were discovered all over Chicago. The newspapers published details of impossible plots and conspiracies which Schaack, the master-detective, had uncovered. Most of the bombs were either non-existent or had been planted by the police, and the conspiracies were manifestly the product of the heroic captain's imagination. Tales, which at any other time would have been laughed down as preposterous, gained credence." [55]

Ten leading anarchists in Chicago were indicted within a fortnight. One escaped and one turned state's evidence. Eight were brought to trial: Albert Parsons, August Spies, George Engel, Samuel Fielden, Adolph Fischer, Louis Lingg, Oscar Neebe, and Michael Schwab. The selection of the jury was manifestly rigged, the judge and the prosecutor were allies, and the newspapers kept public opinion at a murderous pitch. Although it was impossible to link the defendants to the bomb, judge and prosecutor argued that they had made the bombing possible by their spoken and written words. It was further argued that the defendants, being anarchists, were opposed to law and order, and thus were enemies of society. "Gentlemen of the jury," said the prosecutor, "convict these men, make examples of them, hang them and you save our institutions, our society." [56]

They were all found guilty of inspiring to murder. Neebe was sentenced to fifteen years, the other seven to death by hanging. Lingg committed suicide. Fielden and Schwab pleaded for mercy and had their sentences reduced to life imprisonment. On November 11, 1887, Engel, Fischer, Parsons, and Spies were hanged. They died bravely and eloquently.[57] Four martyrs had been created for the anarchist cause.[58]

It was not until six years later that this travesty of American justice was corrected. The newly elected governor, John Altgeld, commissioned a full inquiry. The result of the inquiry was the release of the three imprisoned men. This action was not, according to Altgeld, a pardon, for the men had not been fairly convicted in the first place.[59]

Decline of Anarchism

The great upsurge of anarchism the condemned men expected did not occur. Anarchism in America had already reached its crest. It was not merely that prosperity had returned. The anarchists were distrusted by other radical groups. The Socialist Labor Party, seeking to dissociate itself from anarchism, issued a pamphlet in 1886. Some excerpts:

Socialism . . . is an antipode of Anarchism.

Socialism is the most decided enemy to both the Anarchism of the capitalistic class, and the Anarchism of those revolutionists who have been rendered more or less crazy by the cruelties and revolting injustice of our present "law and order." In fact, this latter class of Anarchists hate us more than they hate the other class of Anarchists, *or anybody.*

We do not in the least deny that we have little hope for an entirely peaceful renewal of society and politics, and that we may have to fight for the redemption of the working class from the threatening thraldom. But that war must be forced upon us—we try our best efforts to avoid it, and though this may be impossible in most of the European States, we must and do consider it possible in the United States, and wherever freedom of speech and of the press, the right to peacefully assemble and organize, and universal suffrage (inclusive of women) are not curtailed by existing laws.

We, therefore, protest against being confounded and in any way identified with Anarchists of any type; we are the implacable enemies of all anarchism.[60]

Most workingmen opposed the senseless violence with which anarchism was now associated and distrusted foreign ideologies. They were interested in improving their living and working conditions. And how, even discounting the risks of the enterprise, would destroying the government help in these concerns? There were dozens of radical groups offering panaceas. The anarchist voice was neither loudest nor clearest.

Although after 1886 anarchism was no more violent than many other radical movements, two more violent and senseless (and well-publicized) events occurred within fifteen years. These further discredited anarchism and fixed it in the public mind as fanatical and insanely violent. Once again immigrants were involved.

The first event occurred at Homestead, Pennsylvania, in 1892. Andrew Carnegie's steel mills near Pittsburgh had made some concessions to strikers in 1889. Now, in 1892, Carnegie directed Henry Clay Frick to reduce wages by about 25 percent. The workers refused to accept the cut and were locked out. The Pinkerton Agency was hired to bring in and protect strikebreakers. The workers attacked them, a pitched battle ensued, and a dozen people died. Carnegie and Frick were not to be denied. With the help of the National Guard "scabs" were installed in the plants. Legal proceedings were instituted against strike leaders, charging them with riot and murder.

Two weeks after the governor called out the Guard a young an-

archist forced his way into Frick's office and shot him with a re-
volver. The bullet, meant for the head, entered Frick's neck—a
serious but not fatal wound. The would-be assassin was seized, tried,
and sentenced to twenty-two years.

Frick's assailant was Alexander Berkman, who had come to the
United States from Russia in 1887. Influenced by Johann Most in
New York and a good friend of Emma Goldman, Berkman was an
educated and sensitive idealist whose act of violence cannot easily
be explained. Grieving for the steelworkers and their families and
feeling helpless against the colossal forces of Carnegie, Frick, and
government officials, he deliberately set out to perform an act of
"propaganda by the deed." He served fifteen years of his sentence
and returned to society to write several important defenses of communistic anarchism.

The other event was also an assassination attempt—this time a
successful one. In 1901 a young Pole, Leon Czolgosz, shot President
McKinley. He claimed to be an anarchist but was not known as one
by any anarchist group. At his trial and execution, in the anarchist
tradition, he bore himself bravely. He died believing that he had
performed an act of "propaganda by the deed" against the hated
system personified by McKinley.

European immigrants were always important to the anarchist
cause. In addition to the Germans, the ranks had been swelled by
Russian refugees from repressive czars (Berkman and Emma Goldman are examples), Italians (Carlo Tresca is an example), and Jews
from Eastern Europe. One consequence of the McKinley assassination was an end to the American policy of granting asylum to all
political refugees: in 1903 a law was passed forbidding the entry of
foreign anarchists. While the foreign-born continued to dominate
anarchist thought in the early part of the twentieth century, the
movement was in decline. The Black International had fallen apart
and *Die Freiheit* vanished with the death of Johann Most in 1906.
The history of anarchism is now one of individuals rather than
periodicals, parties, and congresses.

Industrial Workers of the World

One association of workers was conspicuous for a brief period and
drew some of its support from anarchists. The Industrial Workers
of the World was formed at a convention in Chicago in 1905. A
leading group in attendance was the Western Federation of Miners,

which had broken with the AF of L for what it believed was poor support during the bloody battles with capitalists in places like Cripple Creek and Leadville. "Big Bill" Haywood (1869–1928), its leader, was an authentic hero from the West, a fearless strike leader, and a defender of illegality. Revolutionists of all stripes were present, including De Leon (with some supporters from the Socialist Labor Party and the Socialist Trade and Labor Alliance) and Eugene Victor Debs (with some supporters from the Socialist Party). From its beginning the history of the IWW was turbulent. Haywood, a syndicalist, retained his charismatic popularity. Debs, interested in democratic political action, resigned within a year. De Leon tried to follow Marx, saying that "the political expression of labor is but the shadow of economic organization."[61] But De Leon was, after all, a leader of the SLP, and political action was implied by its very name. For a time De Leon was influential, and short-term union gains were sacrificed to the aims of militant class struggle.

A shift in Haywood's direction took place in 1907–1908 when a species of radicalism similar to French anarcho-syndicalism achieved power. The syndicalists succeeded in expelling De Leon from the IWW in 1908. The following tenets of American syndicalism were decidedly anarchist in nature: unions should engage in "direct action" rather than politics; strikes are more effective than ballots and the general strike is most effective of all; the worker should be subject to his syndicate (association of his co-workers) rather than to his government; sabotage is more effective than negotiation; willingness to defy repressive laws may embarrass the authorities by filling up the jails.[62]

The IWW was always ready to help the downtrodden when more respectable bodies backed off. It achieved a brilliant success in a strike in 1912 against the woolen industry in Lawrence, Massachusetts. Usually, however, the "Wobblies" failed—gloriously. "As a result of its heroic defeats the IWW acquired a romantic aureole which continued to glow, particularly in the eyes of the Eastern radical intellectuals, until it was extinguished during World War I."[63] It is probable that the IWW, for all the headlines that it made, never exceeded one hundred thousand members.[64]

War and Repression

World War I, a trial of basic convictions for socialists all over the world, was a difficult time for American anarchists as well. Involved were the questions of pacifism (are our real enemies foreign nations or domestic capitalists?) and the Bolshevik Revolution (is this the beginning of the new society we have been seeking?). On the first issue the IWW was steadfastly pacifist—even after the United States entered the war—and they suffered under the repressive action handed down by legislators and prosecutors to all radical elements thought to be traitorous or obstructive to the war effort. The infamous Espionage Act of 1917 is one example. Another is the prosecution of radicals Thomas J. Mooney and Warren K. Billings in 1916 in California for exploding a bomb during a patriotic parade in San Francisco. The "evidence" against these two men was ridiculous, the trial a mockery.[65] Mooney was a friend of Berkman. An attempt was made to extradite Berkman and charge him as an accomplice, but the Governor of New York would not permit it.

Hundreds of IWW members (including Haywood) were convicted of violating the Espionage Act, several more were arrested, raided, and harassed. After a raid on the headquarters of the Socialist Party, John Reed wrote: "In America, the month just passed has been the blackest month for freedom our generation has known. With a sort of hideous apathy the country has aquiesced in a regime of judicial tyranny, bureaucratic suppression and industrial barbarism which followed inevitably the first fine careless rapture of militarism." [66] Berkman and Emma Goldman were arrested in 1917 for obstructing the draft—they had helped form a "No Conscription League"— and were fined and given two-year sentences. Eugene Debs was arrested in 1918 for uttering "profane, scurrilous and abusive language" about the government; he was sentenced to ten years.

When the Bolshevik Revolution occurred, all radicals were immensely heartened. The ruling classes *somewhere* had been toppled. Russia immediately made peace with her foreign enemies, and the workingman at last seemed to be in control of his own destiny. The Revolution, however, was the occasion for a second wave of repression in the United States. Attorney General A. Mitchell Palmer, deeply fearful of the Bolshevik threat in America, took drastic and unprecedented steps to protect "law and order." Thousands of "suspects" were arbitrarily arrested and hundreds of alien radicals were deported. In 1919–1920 Berkman and Emma Goldman, with 247 other Russians, were shipped to Russia.[67] It was, however, the anarchists (and Goldman is the best example) who, of all radical groups, most promptly and most clearly recognized the true nature of the new authoritarianism in Russia.

The twenties was a time of prosperity and languishing left-wing causes. "Normalcy" meant weak unions, strong management, and continued repression. The IWW was practically defunct, the Socialist Party had 7793 members in 1928, and the Communist Party had 9642 members in 1929.[68] Jewish and Italian anarchists continued to print their papers for small audiences.[69] The anarchists were an obscure presence in American life; they talked mainly to themselves.

In this decade, however, the anarchists acquired their most famous martyrs: Nicola Sacco (1891–1927) and Bartolomeo Vanzetti (1887–1927).[70] These anarchist revolutionists were arrested in Boston in 1920 while distributing circulars announcing a meeting to protest the treatment of a friend of theirs who had been arrested in one of Palmer's raids. They were charged with a murder that had taken place during a payroll robbery three weeks earlier. Once again it was anarchism on trial. Judge Webster Thayer told the jury that Vanzetti was "morally culpable, because he is the enemy of our existing institutions." [71] And once again the "evidence" was inconclusive and the witnesses self-contradictory. Felix Frankfurter wrote: "The district attorney invoked against them a riot of political passion and patriotic sentiment; and the trial judge connived at—one had almost written cooperated in—the process." [72] All appeals failed. The two innocent [73] men were executed in 1927. Radical, liberal, and fair-minded men everywhere were outraged. While the Sacco-Vanzetti case may be taken as "a symbol of the frustration shared by the forces left of center," [74] it is also a symbol of the lengths to which fearful officials can go in repressing liberty. The twenties was indeed "the lost decade."

Down to the Present

The depression of the thirties did not inspire much interest in anarchism. Most concerned people believed that the government should be stronger, not weaker. Several strong-government panaceas were put forth, including state socialism. Communism grew much stronger in America in this decade. Although many young anarchists, the discontented children of the depression, joined the Communist movement, the dedicated and principled anarchists had long since gotten over their brief infatuation with this kind of collectivism.

Several articulate anarchists have appeared on the contemporary scene. Ammon Hennacy (b. 1893) [75] was imprisoned as a pacifist in

World War I. Later he worked with Dorothy Day and *The Catholic Worker*. Paul Goodman (b. 1911) [76] is the best known of the contemporary anarchist thinkers. His writings are extensive and are on a wide variety of subjects: sociology, psychology, city planning, economics, criticism, and linguistics; he is also a poet and novelist. "He regards himself as a creative artist reshaping traditional anarchism." [77] The poet Karl Shapiro (b. 1913) [78] has frequently expressed anarchistic ideas. In 1961 he wrote: "Throughout the world, the human right of insubordination against industrial society, colonialism, militarism, and against the entire cult of the Western Tradition (religious, sexual, esthetic) is making itself felt in a thousand ways. The governments are losing their young. The lifeblood of history is flowing away from the centers of force. Patriotism is having its long-awaited nervous breakdown." [79]

Murray Bookchin (b. 1921) [80] is a contemporary representative of communist anarchism. In an article in a 1969 issue of *Anarchos,* he wrote: "Men do not remove their ties of bondage and become fully human merely by divesting themselves of social domination, by obtaining freedom in its *abstract* form. They must also be free *concretely:* free from material want, from toil, from the burden of devoting the greater part of their time, indeed the greater part of their lives, to the struggle with necessity." [81] Martin Duberman (b. 1930),[82] a professor of history at Princeton, has sympathetically discussed anarchism and its relevance for the "new left." In 1966 he wrote: "The Anarchist belief in the harmonious possibilities of human development—and the threat to that development posed by a hostile environment—is neither utopian nor outmoded. . . ." [83]

Other important contemporary American writers whose work has been at least sympathetic toward basic anarchist ideas are Frank Lanham [84] and Sam Weiner,[85] who have discussed freedom and authority in union organizations. Irving L. Horowitz [86] is a sympathetic and brilliant expositor of anarchist ideas. Karl Hess,[87] actively for Goldwater in 1964, has moved from a conservative position in recent years to an extremely individualistic point of view that he proudly calls anarchistic.

These men, presently or recently on the American scene, preserve the tradition of anarchism and are thus regarded as spokesmen for the "old" anarchism. They and their ideas exist side by side with quite different ideas that also seem to be, in some sense, anarchistic. Mature and educated men, they know what they are about; concerned with the present, they yet link up with the past.

The views of the student left, the radical right, and existentialism will be discussed in Part II as possible expressions of a "new" anarchism.

NOTES

1 See Alain Sergent and Claude Harmel, *Histoire de l'Anarchie* (Paris: Le Portulan, 1949), pp. 24ff.

2 Quoted in Joll, p. 43.

3 *Explosion,* by Varlet, was published in Paris in 1793.

4 Quoted in Joll, p. 45.

5 *Selections from the Works of Fourier,* Charles Gide, Ed., Julia Frankton, Trans., was published in London in 1901.

6 *Oeuvres Complètes* was published in twenty-six volumes in Paris in 1867–1870. *Qu'est-ce que la Propriété?* (1840) appeared as *What Is Property?* in 1876, Benjamin Tucker, Trans.; *Système des Contradictions économiques ou Philosophie de la Misère* (1846) appeared as *System of Economic Contradictions: or, the Philosophy of Misery* in 1888, Benjamin Tucker, Trans.; *Solution du Problème Social* (1849) appeared with other writings in Proudhon's *Solution of the Social Problem* in 1927; and *Idée Générale de la Révolution au XIXᵉ Siècle* (1851) appeared as *The General Idea of the Revolution in the Nineteenth Century* in 1923, John Beverley Robinson, Trans. Other important works are: *Les Confessions d'un Révolutionnaire* (1849), *De la Justice dans la Révolution et dans l'Eglise* (1858), and *Du Principe Fédératif et de la Nécessité de Reconstituer le Parti de la Révolution* (1863).

7 Faure published *La Douleur Universelle* in Paris in 1895 and edited *L'Encyclopédie Anarchiste* in Paris.

8 Grave's works, all published in Paris, include *La Société Mourante et L'Anarchie* (1893), *La Société Future* (1895), *L'Individu et la Société* (1897), *L'Anarchie, Son But, Ses Moyens* (1899), and *Le Mouvement Libertaire sous la Troisième République* (1930).

9 Bellegarrigue published *Au Fait! Au Fait! Interprétation de l'Idée Démocratique en 1848* (Paris and Toulouse).

10 Pelloutier's *Histoire des Bourses du Travail* was published in Paris in 1902.

11 Coeurderoy's *Jours d'Exil* was published in Brussels in 1854.

12 Déjacque's *La Question Révolutionnaire* was published in New York in 1854; his *L'Humanisphere* in Paris in 1899.

13 Malon's *Histoire du Socialisme* was published in Paris in 1882–1885.

14 From the long list of Sorel's books one may select: *Les Illusions du Progrès* (Paris, 1909) and *Réflexions sur la Violence* (Paris, 1908), translated as *Reflections on Violence* by T. E. Hulme and J. Roth (Glencoe, Ill.: The Free Press, 1950).

15 *Common Sense* was published in 1776, *The Rights of Man* in 1791–1792.

16 Thomas Paine, *Common Sense and Other Political Writings,* Nelson F. Adkins, Ed. (New York: The Liberal Arts Press, 1953), p. 4.

17 Godwin's chief work is *An Enquiry Concerning the Principles of Political Justice and Its Influence on Virtue and Happiness* (London, 1793).

18 Krimerman and Perry, p. 16. In fact, of course, England was much freer of anarchist violence than the other European countries and the United States.

19 Wilde published *The Soul of Man Under Socialism* in London in 1891.

20 See Woodcock, p. 449.

21 Stirner's one important work, *Der Einzige und sein Eigentum,* was published in Berlin in 1845. It was translated into English as *The Ego and His Own* by Steven T. Byington.

22 Weitling's important works are *Die Menschheit wie sie ist und wie sie sein sollte* (1838) *(Humanity as It Is and as It Ought To Be), Garantien der Harmony und Freiheit* (1842) *(Guarantees of Harmony and Freedom),* and *Evangelium eines armen Sünders* (1845) *(Gospel of a Poor Sinner).*

23 Weitling, quoted in Joll, p. 55. (Kropotkin, however, regarded Weitling as "strongly authoritarian," and would cite Moses Hess and Karl Grün among the Germans instead. See *Revolutionary Pamphlets,* pp. 161, 292.)

24 Some of Rocker's works are: *Johann Most: das Leben Eines Rebellen* (Berlin, 1924), *Anarcho-Syndicalism* (London, 1938), *Nationalism and Culture* (Los Angeles, 1937), *Pioneers of American Freedom* (Los Angeles, 1949), *The London Years* (London, 1956).

25 Most's most famous work is a pamphlet called "Science of Revolutionary Warfare: A Manual in the Use and Preparation of Nitroglycerine, Dynamite, Gun-Cotton, Fulminating Mercury, Bombs, Poisons, Etc. Etc." (1885).

26 Collected works of Bakunin were published in Russia, Germany, France, and Argentina after his death. His most important single work is *Statism and Anarchism,* which first appeared in 1873. The most useful book in English is the selection edited by G. P. Maximoff, *The Political Philosophy of Bakunin.*

27 Among Kropotkin's works are: *The State: Its Historic Role* (1898), *Fields, Factories and Workshops* (1899), *Mutual Aid: A Factor in Evolution* (1902), *The Conquest of Bread* (1906), and *Modern Science and Anarchism* (1908). Most of these were published in London. His autobiography, *Memoirs of a Revolutionist,* was published in Boston in 1899. The unfinished *Ethics: Origin and Development* was published posthumously in New York in 1924.

28 Some of Tolstoy's important political works in English are: *The Kingdom of God Is Within You* (London, 1894), *What Then Must We Do?* (New York, 1899), *The Slavery of Our Time* (London, 1900), and *What I Believe* (London, n.d.).

29 Herzen's *My Past and Thoughts* (1924–1927) and *From the Other Shore* (1956) were published in London.

30 Goldman wrote *Anarchism and other Essays* (New York, 1911), *Living My Life* (London, 1931), *My Disillusionment in Russia* (New York, 1923), *My Further Disillusionment with Russia* (New York, 1924).

31 Berkman wrote *The Bolshevik Myth* (New York, 1925), *Prison Memoirs of an Anarchist* (New York, 1912), and *Now and After: the ABC of Anarchist Communism* (London, 1942).

32 Woodcock, p. 424.

33 Malatesta's *Scritti Scelti,* Zaccaria and Berneri, Eds., was published in Naples in 1947.

34 Malatesta, quoted in Joll, p. 205.

35 Pi translated many of Proudhon's works into Spanish. His own first book was *La Reacción y la Revolución* (1854).

36 Pi, quoted in Woodcock, p. 357.

37 Montseny's *Militant Anarchism and the Reality in Spain* was published in Glasgow in 1937.

38 See Eunice M. Schuster, "Native American Anarchism," in *Smith College Studies in History* 18 (October 1931–July 1932). Nineteenth-century American anarchism was not *entirely* native. It was inspired by the writings of Thomas Paine and William Godwin and by French and English utopian socialists.

39 Important works of Warren are *Equitable Commerce* (New Harmony, 1846) and *True Civilization* (Boston, 1863).

40 Spooner wrote *Poverty: Its Illegal Causes and Legal Cure* (1846) and *Natural Law, or the Science of Justice* (1882).

41 Andrews is the author of *The Science of Society* (1851).

42 Andrews edited *Love, Marriage and Divorce, and the Sovereignty of the Individual: A Discussion by Henry James, Horace Greeley, and Stephen Pearl Andrews, Including the Final Replies of Mr. Andrews Rejected by the Tribune* (New York, 1853).

43 Thoreau wrote *On the Duty of Civil Disobedience* in 1849. *The Writings of Henry David Thoreau*, in twenty volumes, appeared in 1906.

44 His most important book, *Instead of a Book: By a Man Too Busy to Write One*, was first published in 1893. He edited *The Radical Review* (1877–1888) and *Liberty* (1881–1907), printing many of his own articles.

45 William B. Greene (1819–1878) was the first to bring Proudhon's ideas to America's attention. Active in a great many radical movements in his lifetime, Greene had a genuine streak of anarchism in his outlook. His works on economics and finance (*e.g., Mutual Banking*, 1850) are thoughtful and scholarly.

46 Tucker, p. 9.

47 *Ibid.*, p. 404.

48 The International Labor Union was formed in 1878, the American Federation of Labor in 1881. Originally militant and revolutionary, such groups soon toned down their goals in order to work for economic ends—"pure and simple" unionism.

49 See Albert Fried, *Socialism in America* (Garden City, New York: Doubleday & Company, 1970), p. 186.

50 See Sidney Lens, *Radicalism in America* (New York: Thomas Y. Crowell, 1969), pp. 163–164.

51 The International Working People's Association, the "Black International," had been formed in London in 1881. Several Americans had attended.

52 See Henry David, *The History of the Haymarket Affair* (New York: Collier Books, 1963), pp. 95–96.

53 See Lens, p. 168.

54 A handbill calling the meeting had instructed them to arm themselves.

55 See David, p. 191. For a revealing insight into the personality of Schaack, read his own version of the Haymarket Affair: *Anarchy and Anarchists* (Chicago, 1889).

56 See Lens, p. 170.

57 See David, p. 387. The speeches delivered in court by the anarchists were printed by Lucy Parsons in *Anarchism: Its Philosophy and Scientific Basis* (1887). For excerpts from those of Spies, Schwab, and Parsons, see Fried, pp. 221–229.

58 May Day, as a labor festival, really goes back to the opening of the struggle for the eight-hour day. The deaths on the streets of Chicago occurred two and three days later, and the executions over a year later. The early anniversaries of May 1 reiterated the need to struggle for the eight-hour day. But the publicity and drama of 1886 were supplied by the anarchists, and their martyrdom so impressed itself on popular thought that many people assumed that *this* was what was being commemorated on May Day. Today, of course, May Day is observed in honor of the general history and solidarity of the international labor movement.

59 The St. Louis *Globe-Democrat*, already on record with the slogan "there are no good anarchists except dead anarchists," now pronounced: "There is practically but one opinion throughout the whole country as to the action of Governor Altgeld. . . . It is condemned everywhere as a gross abuse of the pardoning power, and not a word is said in its defense except by the enemies of society. . . . The use of the pardoning power to defeat the ends of justice in such a case cannot be too severely condemned." See David, pp. 187, 414.

60 Alexander Jonas, *Socialism and Anarchism.* See Fried, pp. 231–232. In fairness it should be pointed out that the SLP did attack the judicial machinery that condemned the defendants; it called the executions "foulest murder." There was, of course, widespread confusion of socialism and anarchism in the public mind. For many years after the Haymarket riots "anarchist" was a popular smear word.

61 See Joll, pp. 219–220.

62 The degree to which the IWW was genuinely anarchistic can be debated. Its factionalism perhaps makes the debate pointless. Berkman and Goldman tended to support it—they would *always* support free speech, agitation, and direct action. But the IWW was really too centrally organized for their tastes and for the tastes of all anarchists who agreed with Berkman's comment that "no organization of independent and self-reliant workers is thinkable without complete local autonomy." See Joll, p. 221.

63 Fried, p. 452.

64 By contrast, the AF of L (its union rival) had a membership of 2 million in 1914, and the Socialist Party (its political rival) polled almost a million votes in the Presidential election of 1912. See Lens, pp. 241–242.

65 It was not until 1939 that Governor Olson released Mooney and Billings from prison.

66 See Lens, p. 253.

67 Emma Goldman had come to the United States in 1886 at age sixteen. A fearless fighter, effective speaker, writer, and organizer, she thrust herself into the forefront of many unpopular radical and liberal causes. She edited *Mother Earth* from 1906 to 1917. She campaigned for birth control (for which she was imprisoned). After her deportation she carried on her fight in Europe against repression. Eventually she fought on the side of the anti-Franco forces in Spain. She died in 1940 while touring Canada to raise support for the Spanish anarchists and republicans. She is buried in Chicago near the graves of the Haymarket martyrs. Her autobiography, *Living My Life,* appeared in 1931. For a fuller account of her life, see Richard Drinnon, *Rebel in Paradise: a Biography of Emma Goldman* (Chicago: University of Chicago Press, 1961).

68 See Lens, p. 296.

69 For example: *Freie Arbeter Shtimme* (Jewish) and *L'Adunata dei Refratteri* (Italian).

[70] M. D. Frankfurter and G. Jackson have edited *Letters of Sacco and Vanzetti* (New York, 1928).

[71] See Lens, p. 280.

[72] See *ibid.*, p. 281.

[73] "Innocent" because not proven guilty. Opinion today is that Vanzetti in fact was innocent, but that Sacco may indeed have been guilty. See Francis Russell, *Tragedy at Dedham* (New York, 1962).

[74] Lens, p. 282.

[75] His *Autobiography of a Catholic Anarchist* was published in New York in 1954 by The Libertarian Press.

[76] Among Goodman's works are: *Communitas* (New York, 1960), *Community of Scholars* (New York, 1962), *Drawing the Line* (New York, 1962), *Utopian Essays and Practical Proposals* (New York, 1962), and *Like a Conquered Province* (New York, 1966). He edited *Seeds of Liberation* (New York, 1965).

[77] Krimerman and Perry, p. 53.

[78] See Shapiro's "On the Revival of Anarchism," *Liberation*, February 1961.

[79] See Henry J. Silverman, Ed., *American Radical Thought: The Libertarian Tradition* (Lexington, Mass.: D. C. Heath and Company, 1970), p. 255.

[80] See Bookchin's "Post-Scarcity Anarchy," *Anarchos*, Spring 1969.

[81] See Silverman, p. 322.

[82] See Duberman's "Anarchism Left and Right," *Partisan Review*, Fall 1966.

[83] See Silverman, p. 263.

[84] See Lanham's "Two Kinds of Unionism: Some Basic Ideas," *Why?*, April 1947.

[85] Weiner is the author of *Ethics and American Unionism* (New York, 1958).

[86] See Horowitz's valuable introduction and postscript to *The Anarchists* (New York, 1964). He also wrote *Radicalism and the Revolt against Reason: the Theories of Georges Sorel* (London, 1961).

[87] Examples of his recent work are "The Death of Politics," *Playboy*, March 1969, and *The Lawless State* (Lansing, n.d.).

3

Human Nature and Conduct

NATURAL MAN
AND NATURAL SOCIETY

Natural Man

Modern man in civilized society lives under political authority. This all but universal condition of man is not, however, according to the anarchist, man's natural condition. The attitudes, habits, patterns of behavior, and customs that characterize man in a civil state have developed over a long period of years; they conceal man's *true* nature from all but the most careful observer. Behind the artificial is the real. What is it like?

The Christian tradition, of course, finds the natural in Eden before Adam's fall. The naturalistic anarchist, such as Bakunin, finds the clue for natural humanity in man's kinship with animals rather than in some myth of primordial divine intention.

> In all the animal species, with no exception, but with a great difference in development, we find two opposed instincts: the instinct for preservation of the individual and the instinct for preservation of the species; or, speaking in human terms, *the egoistic and the social instincts.* From the point of view of science, as well as from the point of view of Nature itself, those two instincts are equally natural and hence equally legitimate, and, what is even more important, they are equally necessary in the natural economy of beings.[1]

The presence of two such strong and complementary drives in man, and their failure to produce inflexible and rigid behavior patterns, make a vast number of kinds of human society possible.

The account by Diderot of the unspoiled life of the Tahitians in the eighteenth century was well known to later anarchists. The old patriarch addresses the departing Europeans:

> We do not want to barter what you call our ignorance for your useless civilization. Everything that is necessary and good for us we possess. Do we deserve contempt, because we have not known how to develop superfluous wants? When we hunger, we have enough to eat; when we are cold, we have wherewith to clothe us. You have been in our huts; what is lacking there, in your opinion? . . . Go to your own country to agitate and torment yourself as much as you like; leave us in peace. Do not worry us with your artificial needs nor your imaginary virtues.[2]

Some anarchists profess to find remnants of natural man surviving in the peasantry. Many peasants, further removed from the complications of modern life than either their aristocratic neighbors or their proletarian brothers, have managed to preserve their natural sentiments. They are relatively content with the simple life; they have simple needs and enjoy simple satisfactions. And most important, they can live together as friends. Respecting one another, helping one another, and equal to one another, they do not seek domination over one another.

Man, whatever his status or class, has a natural propensity for justice, both to know it and to follow it. Men instinctively protest against action that seems unfair. Despite their differing conceptions of right and wrong, despite the different conditioning they have had in various societies, and despite the brutalizing effect that domination has had on them, they nonetheless, then and now, can recognize injustice and feel great indignation. This impulse is the ideal and constant element of human nature.

Human nature is maligned, say the anarchists, by the argument that justice requires for its recognition and enforcement a political apparatus backed by force. Justice is not *made* by instituting government and passing laws. At best it is reflected in these enterprises; at worst it is corrupted by them.

Thomas Hobbes's belief in the inevitability of a social contract instituting government is incorrect, for the simple reason that his concept of human nature was distorted. If it were the case that man is basically egoistic, driven by competition, diffidence, and glory, then perhaps it would also be the case that without government his life would be "solitary, poor, nasty, brutish and short." Hobbes's theory of the state is a desperate remedy for a fancied disease. John Locke, whose conception of human nature was more optimistic than Hobbes's, nevertheless came to a similar conclusion, for Locke believed that government could more efficiently and more fairly enforce adherence to natural law than could individuals. Locke's theory gives the state the authority to interpret this law for all people and to defend their natural rights. Jean-Jacques Rousseau, whose celebration of the simple life and whose praise for the natural goodness and equality of man make him a hero of sorts for many anarchists, is nevertheless a flawed hero. For not only did Rousseau believe that the deterioration of natural man had proceeded so far that to contract a government was the only reasonable expedient, but he also described a state in which the general will swallowed up everything, even the theoretical natural rights preserved by Locke. The notion of natural law, which on the face of it would exclude the necessity for manmade law, was perverted by three of its most notable adherents into doctrines of political oppression.

History

Man at one time did not have government; he has it now. Something happened. Was it instituted by force or by fraud? Or did he willingly create a power to which he would submit? Kropotkin regarded the state as of fairly recent origin. The modern centralized state in Europe arose in the sixteenth century and was made possible by the defeat of the free medieval communes. The alliance of lord, priest, merchant, judge, soldier, and king annihilated all free unions—"of village communities, guilds, trades unions, fraternities, and medieval cities." [3] "It was by massacre, the wheel, the gibbet, the sword, and the fire that church and State established their domination, and that they succeeded henceforth to reign over an incoherent agglomeration of 'subjects' who had no more direct union among themselves." [4] Whether men willingly gave up their natural liberty is not nearly so important to anarchists as the propriety of such an action. If it happened, it was a bad bargain, made long ago by our ancestors. We are not bound. Since humanity does not require for its security and happiness an external organized authority, men should regain for themselves the freedom they have lost. The state is, after all, merely "a transitory historic form, a passing form of society." [5]

Bakunin, however, with his consistent materialism, had no illusions about a perfect past. Humanity was a long time in emerging from animality: cannibalism, slavery, serfdom, and capitalist exploitation precede it. Man also had to break the various chains that bound him to his natural environment—the need for food and shelter, threats of danger, pain, and privation. He must always work and he must always think, but the quality of both activities changes as he exercises more conscious control over nature. Humanity is something won over a period of time; it results from a process in which man liberates himself from the external rule of the natural and social environments. He wins bread and leisure.

In achieving his humanity, the individual discovers a natural solidarity that links him with others. Universal love and brotherhood signify his furthest development from his bestial beginnings. The individual is not fully human until he recognizes the equal right of others to the free development and exercise of their various faculties. The moralist Bakunin and the amoralist (self-styled) Tucker can say in unison: "The freedom of every human individual should be limited only by the liberty of all other individuals." [6] But Bakunin elevated the idea to the level of ethical humanism: "Respect for the freedom of others is the highest duty of man. To love this freedom and to serve it—such is the only virtue. That is the basis of morality; and there can be no other." [7]

The positive point the anarchists make is that before there were states there were societies. Man does not *choose* his society; he is born into it. His character is fixed from the beginning as a social animal.[8] Man is the product of society. What humanity he achieves, he achieves through society. One cannot even speak of contracts or constitutions or national states without assuming a society of people with a common language and common aspirations. These societies could not, by definition, have been based originally on domination. They were based on more concrete and human principles of mutual dependence and advantage. For ages men lived without written law. "Human relations were simply regulated by customs, habits and usages . . . acquired by each person in childhood, exactly as he learned how to obtain his food by hunting, cattle-rearing, or agriculture." [9]

Kropotkin, who adapted the theory of evolution to his purposes, could point out (as Darwin himself occasionally did) the survival value of such tendencies as cooperation and accord for many species, including the human. Societies have evolved, and each society that emerges marks an advance over its predecessors. If further evolutionary development is to take place, smoothly and progressively, society must remain open and flexible. The kind of rigidity and petrification induced by governments and rigorous custom leads to social stagnation. Society and its development are natural (and therefore good); imposition of controls from above is artificial (and therefore bad). Just as society preceded the state and laws, so too will it endure after these impositions have disappeared. And, being more natural, it will be better.

The Future

Anarchism looks both backward and forward for natural man in a natural society. There are rather wistful references to a golden age in the past—perhaps to a simple agrarian community before the filth and misery of industrialization. Like so many theories of history, that of many anarchists takes the form of: paradise, paradise lost, paradise regained. But the hope is in the future. And one of the first steps is to rediscover the natural man beneath the grotesque individuals of modern times. It is on him that the future depends. There is a sense of progress in anarchist literature, but this progress differs in significant ways from that of rational liberalism. It is progress *back* to fundamentals: the past must be recovered for the future. The purpose in looking backward is simply to establish that man can live in a good society because he has already done so. The future will be even better.

There is also a sense of utopia in anarchist literature, a vision of an almost perfect society. But there is usually a notable reluctance to spell out the details. The anarchist society is never completely described. A blueprint would impose patterns, a plan would be too directive, a full description would be an affront to individual freedom. Marxists criticize the utopians for being "unscientific" in their means; anarchists criticize them for being too concrete and too detailed in their ends. They prescribe, they regiment. "There is no intellect that can devise a social organization capable of satisfying each and all." [10]

The path, whether conceived as going backward or forward, will be difficult. Modern Europeans are even more corrupted than were the Tahitians after Bougainville's visit. Moreover, in their realistic moments anarchists see problems in human nature itself. "Man," wrote Proudhon, "is a tyrant or slave by his own will before he is made tyrant or slave by fortune; the heart of the proletarian is like that of the rich, a cesspool of babbling sensuality, a home of filth and hypocrisy." [11] Often he spoke like a Calvinist about man's divided nature, his "original sin." Even the rationalistic Godwin was aware of the strong irrational drives in man. Achievement of the good society, then, requires not only fundamental changes in the political and social environment, but internal changes in man himself. The individual must recreate his ideal in himself.

The latter is so important, that whatever outward success one may have, he will by his inner strength have gained a great victory. Life is a moral drama, "a drama in which individuals are pitted against social systems." [12]

Free Will

Many anarchists believe that man has free will. He can, if he so wills, do all that is necessary. His destiny does not rest on the decisions of an omnipotent God, on the inexorable working of social laws through history, or on the gradual enlightenment brought by education. If paradise is to be regained or the heavens stormed, men must do it themselves as conscious and deliberate agents of their own purpose. "Because we are the products of evolution we are not therefore to be its puppets. On the contrary, as our intelligence grows, we are to be more and more its masters." [13] Philosophical determinism, whether Hegelian or Marxian, fatalism, and predestination—all are doctrines of conservatism. Though their proponents accept change, they do so *in its own good time,* not as something wrought by free men. They thus echo the Stoicism of Marcus Aurelius: "Everything harmonizes with me, which is harmonious to thee, O Universe. Nothing for me is too early or too late, which is in due time for thee." [14] Anarchism once again opposes kings.

After saying this, it must be admitted that anarchism, centered as it is in the nineteenth century, has more than a little of that century's respect for science and the lawfulness of nature. Bakunin endlessly repeated his denial of free will. Man does not have an autonomous and unconditioned soul that can, *in vacuo,* direct his efforts. Rather, he is born with a natural endowment that is then subject to a host of physical and social influences that make him what he is and determine his actions. "All men, with no exceptions, at every moment of their lives are what Nature and society have made them." [15] Regardless of their present primitive state, sociology and history are in essence sciences.

This inclusion of man in the pattern of universal causality does not for Bakunin or any other anarchist serve the cause of fatalism. In the first place, the importance of external conditioning factors implies that many of them can be changed—according to the most intelligent prescriptions of social science. If men behave badly, the cause more often than not is to be found in their social environment. Not only is the misery of man attributed to the conditions under which he is forced to live, but so too is his "immorality." Advocates of the state defend it as a necessary evil for dealing with man's viciousness. But man's viciousness is often *caused by* the state: it would not exist unless the state preserved the social conditions that lead to viciousness! [16] In the second place, no individual man knows precisely what he is determined to do. Bakunin himself pointed out that while such sciences as psychology and physiology are incomplete, hidden ("accidental") factors may be of enormous importance.[17] So success is always possible. The Puritan was not less zealous for believing in predestination, nor the Marxist for believing in the inexorable stages of history. The anarchist even more can have a *sense* of free will in the context of natural determinism, for the future lies in man, in individual men who find their own emancipation and can work for the emancipation of others. Godwin, a determinist, wrote in his old age: "We can never divest ourselves of the delusive sense of the liberty of human actions; it is not desirable that we should do so." [18] Finally, actions that proceed from the conscious will are determined only in the technical sense of the word. Godwin was as concerned as anyone to develop a science of human nature, but in his deterministic scheme there is room for a distinction between the voluntary and the involuntary, between actions determined by deliberate rational judgment and those determined by custom and passion.

Equality

There is among the anarchists a widespread belief in equality. The stratification of society into social classes does not correspond to anything in human nature. The position of privilege occupied by some is not based on any kind of natural superiority. The anarchists recognize, as all must, that there are differences among individuals: some are strong, some are weak; some are wise, some are foolish. But these differences seem to us to be greater than they really are: some have been magnified by modern society; others are supposed to exist where they do not exist at all in order to justify purely social distinctions; and some are the result of civilization. Godwin argued that the real differences in the "uncultivated state of man" were in fact much less than the differences that exist today:

> Diseases, effeminacy and luxury were little known; and, of consequence, the strength of every one much more nearly approached to the strength of his neighbour. In the uncultivated state of man, the understandings of all were limited, their wants, their ideas and their views nearly upon a level.[19]

Bakunin put it this way: "We believe that these natural differences are now quite exaggerated and that most of them should be attributed not to Nature but to the different education which has been allotted to each individual." [20]

Intellectual and moral qualities, which are of such great importance, are in great measure the product of the environment in which one lives and matures. Moral qualities especially are developed in the context of social forces. That some men have faulty characters, wrote Bakunin, "lies not with them nor with their nature, but with the social environment in which they were born and have been developing." [21]

In any case, whatever the differences in men may be—now, then, or in the future—they are not so great that they justify some men's holding dominion over others. Men may have to live under some kind of law or agreements, but not under other men. Virtually equal in aptitude or endowment, men must finally also be equal in freedom.

There is another important sense of equality, which is based on the foregoing: equality of *treatment*. All human beings, virtually equal in natural endowment and freedom, should receive respect and consideration from their societies. No one is to be deified and no one is to be brutalized.

> We are partakers of a common nature, and the same causes that contribute to the benefit of one, will contribute to the benefit of another. Our senses and faculties are of the same denomination. Our pleasures and pains will therefore be alike. We are all of us endowed with reason, able to compare, to judge and to infer. The improvement therefore, which is to be desired for one, is to be desired for another. We shall be provident for ourselves, and useful to each other in proportion as we rise above the sphere of prejudice.[22]

Much more on this point will be said later, in the discussion of the good society.[23]

The anarchist's commitment to equality goes beyond the borders of one society. He espouses the brotherhood of man; he opposes nationalism and racism.

> The State then is the most flagrant negation, the most cynical and complete negation of humanity. It rends apart the universal solidarity of all men upon earth, and it unites some of them only in order to destroy, conquer, and enslave all the rest. It takes under its protection only its own citizens, and it recognizes human right, humanity, and civilization only within the confines of its own boundaries. And since it does not recognize any right outside of its own confines, it quite logically arrogates to itself the right to treat with the most ferocious inhumanity all the foreign populations whom it can pillage, exterminate, or subordinate to its will.[24]

The similarities that all men bear to one another are far greater than the incidental differences that modern states have permitted to split the community of the human species.

The natural basis for a living society consists of the common traditions, habits, interests, and aspirations of its members. Such a society is a real unity, not the artificial and abstract unity imposed by a state. Social unities are the foundation for "federations," which ultimately may culminate in a union of all people. Bakunin's version of federalism was to start with "the organization of the lowest nucleus" (communes and workers' associations), then to proceed upward. With the disappearance of states, regions can achieve "beneficent unity," then nations, eventually continents, and finally the "unity of all the peoples of the earth . . . will unfold itself in all its majesty, not divine but human." [25] Union will be voluntary and secession will be permitted. Everything will be natural and nothing will be imposed, for true federalism is based not on political concepts, but on genuine social relations.

RELIGION

Harmful Institution

Neither man's nature nor his proper conduct can be understood without taking religion into account. Is there a supreme being?

If there is, what is man's relation to him? How is man's nature qualified or enhanced by such a presence, and what special obligations will he have? If there is not a supreme being, how should man deal with the widespread belief that there is? In either case, what place do churches have in the society?

Anarchists unanimously agree that religious *institutions* are harmful to man and are usually allied with the government in imposing the power of the state on individuals who should be free. Churches have consistently supported slavery, serfdom, and economic bondage. "OBEY! that is the eternal cry of church and school, no matter how vile the tyrant, no matter how oppressive and unjust 'law and order.' " [26] Religion is still a powerful institution. Its officials either direct the state or support it, thus keeping mankind in intellectual, moral, and political slavery. When the church does not openly support the state, it at least teaches resignation and submission; the people meanwhile have another world, a more hopeful one, to which to flee. "So long as the masses of the people are sunk in religious superstition, they will always be a pliable instrument in the hands of all despotic powers leagued against the emancipation of humanity." [27] How people are governed and whether they are exploited are unimportant. What is the state of their *souls?* The state and its religious partner can endure the unhappiness and poverty of the people (concern for which would be crassly materialistic) while assuring themselves that they are providing them with the means for eternal spiritual blessedness.

Institutions have seldom remained faithful to their original inspiration. Proudhon passionately proclaimed the degeneration of Christian teaching. Jesus, calling himself "The Word of God," had preached some very good things: "that the world was about to experience a new birth; that the priests were vipers, the lawyers ignoramuses, and the philosophers hypocrites and liars; that master and slave were equals, that usury and everything akin to it was robbery," etc.[28] However, "the truth of Christianity did not survive the age of the apostles." [29] The Gospel became loaded with pagan fables, corrupted by theology, and finally exploited by tyrannical priests. Kropotkin pointed out that religious movements, especially reform movements, often had an anarchist basis. Early Christianity, in opposition both to Judaism and to Roman immorality, and Anabaptism, in opposition to Luther and his princely allies, are examples. The latter was crushed by its enemies, while the former "degenerated into an ecclesiastical movement, modeled upon the ancient Hebrew church and upon Imperial Rome itself, which killed the Anarchistic germ, assumed Roman governmental forms, and became in time the chief bulwark of government, slavery, and oppression." [30]

Proudhon discussed "the corruption of morality by religion." [31] Religion speaks of God as "a being who is essentially anti-civilizing, anti-liberal, anti-human." [32] Proudhon abhorred the idea that man wallows hopelessly in sin unless the deity deigns to rescue him. Man admittedly has erred and does err. He is ignorant. But against the doctrine of sin and the distrust of human instincts, Proudhon would simply say that man is "reasonable and free, susceptible of education and improvement." [33] Progress toward truth is possible, provided that man rejects the Christian idea of God. Most important of all, he must understand the nature of justice and fight for its realization. Religion either misconceives justice, or else banishes it to another world while opposing it in this one.

Thus Proudhon opposed the *idea* of God. Having lost faith in God, he developed a renewed faith in humanity. Proudhon, it would appear, was a provisional and somewhat reluctant atheist.

Naturalism

There was nothing provisional or reluctant in Bakunin's view of the matter. He is an excellent example of an anarchist who sought to remain within the limits of nature alone. Man, he believed, is a natural being living in a natural universe. Beyond this there is nothing. "Man forms one whole with Nature and is but the material product of an indefinite quantity of exclusively material causes." [34] That the belief in the supernatural is so ancient and widespread does not prove it to be true; many absurdities (*e.g.*, that the earth is the center of the universe) have enjoyed this kind of mass support. Religious belief can be given a naturalistic explanation; when this is provided, the concept of God turns out to be man's creation in which are crystallized and magnified all his notions of goodness and power. The result of this process, begun and completed in pre-scientific days, is that the created becomes the Creator: man is enslaved and degraded by his own imagination. God appears to man "as the absolute master, as thought, will, the source of every-thing—as the creator and regulator of all things." [35] Eventually the moral values invested in God become no longer applicable to man, or even respectable. "Did there ever exist in the world a being more atrociously jealous, vain, bloody, and egoistic than the Jewish Jehovah or God, the Father of the Christians?" [36] The "reasons" for the belief no longer seem cogent, but the religion itself is absolute and demands unquestioned assent and obedience. Earthly life is disdained, for everything is owed to God and heaven is the goal and reward. "Heaven is translated into contempt for the earth, and adoration of divinity into disparagement of humanity." [37]

Transcendent egoism is cultivated: "Let him save himself who can." Love of fellow man is not necessary; love of God is sufficient. The second commandment is derivative and corrupting. We are to love others, not for their own sake, but for God's. And we are to treat them as slaves of God. The first commandment, then, enjoins a humiliating and slavish "love" for a great master who has our fate in his hands; the second enjoins us to implicate others in the same debasing posture. "If God really existed," said Bakunin, "it would be necessary to abolish him." [38]

For Bakunin and others a much more natural and humane morality exists than the one espoused by religion. This morality is based on man—his natural endowment and its potential development on earth. The basis of religious controls, like the basis of political controls, is the alleged depravity of man. Both church and state "are essentially based upon the idea of sacrifice of life and natural rights, and . . . both start equally from the same principle: the natural wickedness of men, which, according to the Church, can be overcome only by Divine Grace, and by the death of the natural man in God, and according to the State, only through law and the immolation of the individual on the altar of the State. Both aim to transform man—one, into a saint, the other, into a citizen. But the natural man has to die, for his condemnation is unanimously decreed by the religion of the Church and that of the State." [39] If man were properly appreciative of his natural goodness, he could dispense with both state and church.

Theism

In contrast to the views of Proudhon and Bakunin are those of Leo Tolstoy. Believing that Jesus was man's greatest teacher, Tolstoy espoused a "pure" form of Christianity, a religion without complex dogma and institutions. The kingdom of God is within you; it is universal brotherhood and is ruled by the spirit of self-sacrificing love. Mutual help is a fine thing, but the genuinely reasonable man will love his comrade—which is even better. Justice may dictate the destruction of an oppressor, but love, as Jesus taught, gives the other person *more* than he deserves.

Utterly opposed to the social and political conditions of his day, Tolstoy nevertheless believed that concrete gains by direct action would not compensate for the harm they would do to the soul of the revolutionist. For Tolstoy, unlike so many other Christians, violent action in defense of others does not justify harming oppressors. The usual release from pacifism ("I will never use force on behalf of myself, only for others") does not suffice for him.

While Tolstoy's acceptance of theism is exceptional among anarchists, his commitment to the doctrine of love is not. No anarchist, however, was so consistent and so dedicated to the literal requirements of this doctrine. And, Georges Sorel might add, very few non-anarchists.[40]

Atheism

Some mention should be made about the place of religion in the thought of individualistic anarchists. Obviously, no religion that teaches the self-effacing virtues of humbleness and sacrificial love is acceptable. Stirner shared with the other anarchists the view that one's relations with the "so-called God" is his own affair and that God, in any case, does not exist. For himself, he banished all the "spooks" of the "spirit-realm." But this is not enough. A mere "change of masters" must also be avoided. For example: "To expel God from his heaven and to rob him of his *'transcendence'* cannot yet support a claim of complete victory, if therein he is only chased into the human breast and gifted with indelible *immanence.*" [41] Moral faith, too, must be avoided, for it "is as fanatical as religious faith!" [42] And finally, Stirner rejected the notion that humanity should take for itself the values it had hitherto invested in God. Value, according to Stirner, is found not in the essence of man, but only in the individual, and it is of his own choosing. The command to serve non-religious values is as oppressive to the individual as the command to worship divine values. "Moral people skimmed off the best fat from religion, ate it themselves, and are now having a tough job to get rid of the resulting scrofula." [43] Their attitude remains a religious one. Stirner was thus a foe of the moral teachings of Jesus, of the transcendent ethics of Kant, of the ideal religion of Hegel, of the social morality of Proudhon, and of the humanitarian religion of Ludwig Feuerbach. "The divine is God's concern; the human, man's. My concern is neither the divine nor the human. . . . Nothing is more to me than myself." [44]

After a few years in the ministry, Godwin, another individualist, became an atheist. Only by eliminating the Calvinism of his youth could he embark on his great project of education. Man's moral character is neither good nor bad; it develops through experience. External (environment) and internal (reason) factors are decisive. "The vices and moral weakness of man are not invincible: Man is perfectible, or in other words susceptible of perpetual improvement." [45]

It is arguable whether one can accept the authority of the will of God and still retain his anarchist credentials. Bakunin maintained: *"For if God is,* he is necessarily the eternal, supreme, and absolute Master, and if such a Master exists, man is a slave. Now if man is a slave, neither justice, nor equality, nor fraternity, nor prosperity is possible for him." [46] Tucker spoke contemptuously of the wavering infidel who finally capitulated to religious superstition, saying, "There may be, after all, a God, or a Christ, or a Hell, or some damned thing or other." [47] On the other side, one can argue that religion is compatible with anarchist ideals provided that one accepts God of his own free will. Acceptance of a supernatural authority might, as the Catholic anarchist Dorothy Day maintained, make one a better rebel in the natural world. This, of course, was abundantly proved by the heroic resistance of the religious sectaries in the later Middle Ages and the early Protestant era. Ammon Hennacy argued that religious faith helped one make the great sacrifices anarchism requires and called Jesus the "true rebel." [48]

ETHICS

Most anarchists reject the principle that ethical action consists of obedience to a supernatural being; they also reject the principle that ethical action consists of obedience to a categorical imperative. Ethics is not based on absolutes imposed from above. Ethical behavior develops in natural society, in its first instance within the family itself, and ideally extends to the entire human race.[49] Kropotkin warned, however, that moral sentiment is conditioned through history by a host of institutional factors and that only a careful anthropological examination can untangle man's real ethical sensibilities.

Justice

Justice is the most important concept of ethics. Indeed, Godwin used the term "as a general appellation for all moral duty." [50] Justice is the central theme of at least two of Proudhon's books.

> Nothing takes place between men save in the name of *right;* nothing without the invocation of justice. Justice is not the work of the law: on the contrary, the law is only a declaration and application of *justice* in all circumstances where men are liable to come in contact.[51]

The sense of justice, for Proudhon, is immanent in man, but he becomes conscious of it only after living in a "natural group." Justice is based on a sense of equality, the recognition that other men are equally important. Unless men have the experience of mutually helpful association, they will develop the sense of neither equality nor justice. Conditions of modern life have almost obscured the sense of justice so lively in happier times.

It is easier for the reformer to point out instances of injustice than to explicate justice itself. There is no justice, for example, in the protection of ownership in land and capital for those who do not work. Proudhon's most famous aphorism is "property is theft." Only possession for *use* can be defended, and then only when the prospective user has himself worked to exploit the natural resources and brought a product into existence. Even here there is a reservation, for the whole earth belongs equally to those who inhabit it. Since man is a usufructuary of the world's natural goods, he is responsible to all for the way he appropriates them. It is unjust for any individual to take or control at the expense of others.[52] There is enough for all—provided that none is greedy and all are willing to work.

Work in the writings of Proudhon and others is not simply a condition for possession. It has a positive value. Proudhon called work "the first attribute, the essential characteristic of man." [53] Work testifies to the dignity of man. Work is not punishment from God, nor is idleness a divine privilege. Bakunin regarded work as "the supreme condition of human happiness and dignity. Human morality recognizes that only by working does man reach the stature of man." [54] Tolstoy wrote: "A man who regards labour as the business and the joy of his life will not seek to lessen his labour at the cost of other people's work." [55]

Modern conditions of work degrade men where they should elevate them. For Proudhon, of course, agricultural work and the work of the craftsman and artisan are preferable to toil in industrial factories. There is disagreement among the anarchists on the distinction to be made between the kind of work that is dull, routine, and stupefying and the kind that is truly ennobling.

Returning now to justice, it may be noted that Godwin's theory does not espouse the equalitarian kind taught by Proudhon and most other anarchists. Godwin, as a utilitarian, was interested far more in the *amount* of goodness produced for society as a whole. He wrote: "I am bound to employ my talents, my understanding, my strength and my time, for the production of the greatest quantity of general good." [56] This general good is pleasure or happiness, but more specifically, enlargement of the understanding and incitements to virtue.[57] Special duties based on particular relationships, debts, or need, are hardly recognized by Godwin. Everyone, indeed mankind in general, has a claim on the agent's efforts. Godwin's theory is not simply altruism, however, for the agent himself is to count the same as others. The only principle to determine the direction in which benefits are to flow is the one Godwin called *equity*. "The treatment to which men are entitled is to be measured by their merits and their virtues." [58] A scholar is to be helped before a chambermaid, a philanthropist before one's father. Since justice consists of contributing to the general welfare, especially to those particulars in atomistic society that have most merit, it is important that real merit be given the opportunity to be developed and recognized. "The thing really to be desired, is the removing as much as possible arbitrary distinctions, and leaving to talents and virtue the field of exertion unimpaired." [59]

Bakunin, while expressing justice in terms of *equal* rights,[60] agreed with this last point. Among the rights every man has equally is that of having "the material and moral means to develop his whole humanity." [61] Bakunin preferred to speak of human rights instead of political rights, for "equal political rights" is a contradiction in terms. When some have political power and some do not, there can be no equality. Kropotkin agreed with Proudhon and Bakunin when he wrote: Anarchism "aspires to *Justice* (a term synonymous with equality) more than any lawgiver in the world. . . ." [62]

Love

What is the role of love in anarchist ethics? It is praised by Proudhon ("the joys of self-sacrifice are ineffable"), but equality remains the main concept. Equality generates friendship and full regard for all. But "benevolence degenerates into tyranny, and admiration into servility." [63] Bakunin also praises love but, like Proudhon, he has reservations:

> The love of the superior for the inferior is oppression, effacement, contempt, egoism, pride, and vanity triumphant in a feeling of grandeur based upon the humiliation of the other party. And the love of the inferior for the superior is humiliation, the fears and the hopes of a slave who expects from his master either happiness or misfortune. [64]

A general regard for one's fellows may move one to create the conditions of equality. Then genuine love between individuals may develop in a society of equals. [65]

Of all the anarchists, Leo Tolstoy was most concerned to pass beyond the claims of mere justice and to celebrate the beauty of universal and undiscriminating love. Love is to start now and apply to all; it is to characterize every specific human relation.

> Instead of love being merely one of the virtues, [it is] a supreme law . . . an absolute rule of conduct. . . . It is this law of love and its recognition as a rule of conduct in all our relations with friends, enemies, offenders, etc., which inevitably brings about the complete transformation of the existing order of things. . . . You will be preserved from evil and you will acquire the real good, not by looking after your interest, not by envy, hatred, anger, ambition; not even by a sense of justice, or above all by the care of organizing the life of others; but, strange as it may seem, only by the work of your own soul. . . . The real love, which denies self and identifies its "ego" with another is synonymous with the awakening in the soul of the superior, universal principle of life. This love is the true, and gives all the good that it can give when it is only love—that is to say, free of any personal interest. And it is this kind of love that must be felt for the enemy or the offender. [66]

The demands of love are not in conflict with the nature of man. On the contrary, "this faith, far from being artificial, exceptional, inculcated by education, is in human nature; we cannot do without it any more than birds who have lost their wings can fly." If, in the so-called Christian world of today, man's true nature has been obscured, "this abnormal situation is temporary, has happened by chance, bred of special conditions in which men are living; this state is as exceptional as that of men who live without working." [67]

Evolutionary Ethics

The most philosophical discussion of ethics in the anarchist literature is contained in Kropotkin's unfinished book, *Ethics: Origin and Development*. For him, as for Proudhon, justice is the major theme; but while Proudhon expressed his ideas in a kind of pseudo-Hegelian dialectic, Kropotkin expressed his against the backdrop of late-nineteenth-century natural science and evolution. Man "can derive his ideals from Nature," wrote Kropotkin, "and he can draw the necessary strength from the study of its life." [68] Kropotkin's approach is evolutionary in several senses: (1) man has evolved from other animals and shares with them certain attributes; (2) societies and social institutions evolve, and so do the values they conserve; (3) ethical thought evolves; most philosophical systems have made contributions to the more perfect understanding of ethical truth. But ethical science will never be fully constituted, because "new factors and new tendencies will always have to be taken into account in proportion as mankind advances in its evolution." [69]

Kropotkin was concerned to correct the common misinterpretation of Darwin in which nature is viewed as an immense battlefield upon which organisms seek to survive at the expense of others, a place of continual conflict and violent struggle. A poet may describe nature as "red in tooth and claw," but a philosopher-scientist, said Kropotkin, should examine the facts—or at least Darwin's own writings. In *The Descent of Man* Darwin emphasized the importance for survival of mutual support among animals of the same species. [70] Many examples of mutual aid in the animal world are provided in the pages of Kropotkin's books—and these citations go far beyond the many obvious cases of maternal love. [71] Kropotkin concluded that mutual aid is "the predominant fact of nature," that it is the best means for combatting the dangers to life, that it makes possible *progressive* evolution (in contrast to struggle, which sometimes leads to regression), and that it is indeed necessary for the preservation of the human race. [72] Possessing such survival value, the tendency toward mutual aid has become a permanent instinct in all social animals, especially man. Cooperation, not belligerence, is the lesson of evolution.

As the character, institutions, and societies of man develop, so too do his conceptions of right and wrong. At the root of the latter is the tendency or instinct toward mutual aid. Together with his tendency to sociality, man possesses an individualistic tendency. This latter moves a man toward an increase of intensity and happiness in his *own* life. Given these two natural bases, human ethics must express itself somewhere between the extremes of Christian self-abnegation and Hobbesian egoism.

Kropotkin found this obligatory center in the concept of justice. Some actions have the character of reciprocity. Such actions are "absolutely necessary" for life in a society. Justice consists of equity and equalitarian self-restraint. "The personal rights of every individual are as unassailable as the same rights of every other individual." [73]

If the sense of justice is the first development from the sense of mutual aid, altruism is the next. Although actions of altruism—*i.e.,* actions done on behalf of others with no hope or thought of compensation—are not imperative or obligatory, they do constitute a higher stage of morality; they are praiseworthy. But ethics in the broader sense must also recognize individual initiative. The individual can and should take heed of his own development and happiness as well as the similar interests of society.[74]

In an earlier work Kropotkin had also recognized something more than "golden rule" equality, something that encompassed the call both to altruism and to self-realization. In characterizing this human quality, he used expressions like "large nature overflowing with tenderness, with intelligence, with good-will," "fertility of mind," "superabundance of life," "exuberance," "expansion of life," and "the struggle to live." This active force that is found in the wholly developed individual is the perfection of his own nature and is of the greatest service to the whole human race. "Be strong. Overflow with emotional and intellectual energy, and you will spread your intelligence, your love, your energy of action broadcast among others! This is what all moral teaching comes to." [75]

All this was involved in the "empirical" ethics of Kropotkin. Being an empirical ethics, it does not require supernatural support in the commandments of God, rationalistic support in the transcendent imperatives of Kant, or political support in the Leviathan of Hobbes.[76] Ethical theory does not have to impose something on man from without; its support is in nature itself. Rather than holding that man is naturally inclined to do ill, Kropotkin held with Darwin that the check to man's egoism is found in man himself. "Darwin, who knew nature, had the courage boldly to assert that of the two instincts—the social and individual—it is *the social instinct which is the stronger, the more persistent, and the more permanently present.* And he was unquestionably right." [77] Finally, ethics is not a subjective matter or an exercise in defining words. "The conception of 'virtue' and 'wickedness' are zoological, not merely human conceptions." [78]

There is a normative element in Kropotkin's outlook. The natural instincts do in fact lead to a richer and happier life. Man and his society can progress, and they *ought* to progress. They have not always done so; there have been regressions ("temporary illnesses of the social organism"). But there is "the tendency of always widening the current conception of human solidarity and justice, and of constantly improving the character of our human relations." [79] "Good" and "evil" are, whether we like it or not, social conceptions. "Once this or that rule was established by the tribe, the individual submitted to it, no matter how hard it was to abide by it." [80]

The bulk of Kropotkin's book consists of analyses of ethical systems from the time of ancient Greece to the present. According to him, there is something true in all of them, and except for Darwin's Guyau's, and his systems, there is also something false. The errors are based on perversions, misinterpretations, or ignorance of the nature of man and his natural surroundings.

The Greeks, for example, sought to disentangle ethics from religious mythology, from the counterfeit authority supplied for social customs by the sorcerers, priests, and prophets. Their success was only partial. Plato, believing that ethics is neither conventional nor supernatural, resorted to "Ideas" beyond the universe. Aristotle remained within nature and man's inherent possibilities, but had a most conservative notion of the meaning of justice. Epicurus did much to liberate man from fear of the gods and of death, but his conception of happiness was too narrow and his genuinely social life was belied by his counsels to egoism. The Stoics rightly taught life in accordance with nature, the importance of justice, and (some of them) social responsibility, but not knowing how to find the normative principles of nature, they too often turned to a rationalistic Logos or outright religious revelation.[81]

Christian ethics made a great contribution in teaching "justice for all . . . recognition of the equality of men . . . love for all, friends and strangers alike, and finally . . . *forgiveness of injuries,* contrary to the general rule of those times of the obligatory revenge for injuries." [82] These fundamental principles were, however, quickly rejected by the followers and preachers of Christianity.[83] And worst of all, "the movement which began as a protest against the abominations of the ruling power, now became a tool of that power. The blessing of the Church not only forgave the rulers their crimes,—it actually even represented these crimes as the fulfillment of God's will." [84] And finally, the moral element in man is consistently asserted to originate from beyond man—in that very divine will which created him evil. Christians and non-Christians for centuries have fallen victim to the delusion that "nature can give us only lessons of evil." [85]

Kropotkin presented discussions, sometimes acute and sometimes superficial, of a great many major figures in ethical philosophy: Hobbes, Cudworth, Cumberland, Spinoza, Locke, Shaftesbury, Grotius, Bacon, Hutcheson, Leibniz, Descartes, Hume, Helvétius, Diderot, d'Alembert, Holbach, La Mettrie, Montesquieu, Voltaire, Rousseau, Smith, Kant, Hegel, Fichte, Bentham, Mill, Schopenhauer, Comte, Feuerbach, Proudhon, Spencer, Huxley, Guyau, and many others. It would appear, then, that ethical theory is a subject for study not only by anthropologists but by philosophers as well. In what aspects and with what degree of adequacy does a theory justifiably set forth the nature of justice and morality? How indeed do its injunctions lead man, individually and collectively, to a rich and happy life?

Kropotkin recognized the importance of reason in several places in his book. For example:

> With the help of reason we create out of our innate feelings and tendencies that which we call moral conceptions, so that the moral element in man is at once inherent and the product of evolution. We come into this world as beings already endowed with the rudiments of morality; but we can become moral men only through the development of our moral rudiments. Moral tendencies are observed also among social creatures, but morality as the joint product of instinct, feeling, and reason, exists only in man. It developed gradually, it is

developing now, and will continue to grow,—which circumstance accounts for the difference in moral conceptions among different people at different periods.[86]

Kropotkin himself, presumably, had rationally discovered the general end of social man and its connection with his natural endowment. How man is to make this goal more specific and how he is to approach closer to it must now be subjected to reflection. Some of this has taken place, but much more remains to be done.[87]

Kropotkin continually acknowledged the *ethical* acuity of Darwin. His own views are derived directly from *The Descent of Man.* It is no accident that the *biologist* who knew most about man's nature and its relation to the rest of the animal kingdom should also have been most perceptive about man's *ethical* ideals.

The essence of Kropotkin's ethical theory is the deduction of the "golden rule" from the "solidarity" and "mutual aid" displayed in nature. "By an unprejudiced observation of the animal kingdom, we reach the conclusion that wherever society exists at all, this principle may be found: *Treat others as you would like them to treat you under similar circumstances.*" [88] This is the principle of equality, the basis for justice. I do not want to be ruled, therefore I will not rule anyone else. I want food when I am hungry, therefore I will feed the hungry. I want reward for my work, therefore I will reward others for theirs. I don't want to be lied to, therefore I will be truthful to others. Does it ever become ethical, then, to resist by force those who would oppress us? "Yes, certainly! Because we ourselves should ask to be killed like venomous beasts if we want to invade Burmese or Zulus who have done us no harm. We should say to our son or our friend: 'Kill me, if I ever take part in the invasion!' Yes, certainly! Because we ourselves should ask to be dispossessed, if giving the lie to our principles, we seized upon an inheritance, did it fall from on high, to use it for the exploitation of others." [89]

Egoism

It may be observed here that the mutualistic and collectivistic anarchists stressed the social aspects of ethics, while the individualistic anarchists stressed the personal aspects. Proudhon and Kropotkin are good examples of the former, while individualists like Godwin, Tucker, Warren, and Andrews, who were more concerned with the dignity of the individual, the growth of his own person, and the deliberate choice of his own ethical norms, represent the latter. In either case, whether the anarchist emphasizes duties to others or duties to himself, he refrains from issuing a *carte blanche.* That the individual chooses his ethical values does not mean that they may be anything at all, for the individual chooses those which *appear* to him to be most valid, most deserving of his support.

The exception to this is the case of Max Stirner. Stirner's views stand in marked contrast to Godwin's rationalistic theory and Kropotkin's collectivistic one. Stirner emphasized instinct and will, and he carried individualism to its furthest limits. What is even more important, he is unique among the anarchists in appearing to deny completely the significance of ethics. Unless the injunction "do as you please" be regarded as an ethical imperative, and the completely unbound and unprincipled individual be regarded as an ethical ideal, Stirner has indeed transcended (or subverted) morals.

Stirner, recognizing no moral law, no duty to others, feared only "weakness from conscience." He repudiated justice. "In considerations of right the question is always asked, 'What or who gives me the right to it?' Answer: God, love, reason, nature, humanity, etc. No, only *your might, your* power gives you the right." [90] The individual is to realize himself, and at the expense of whoever gets in his way. "I do not demand any right, therefore I need not recognize any either. What I can get by force I get by force, and what I do not get by force I have no right to. . . ." [91]

The egoist finds his greatest enemy in the state, which he must oppose with all the power he possesses. Stirner attacked all versions of political and social control, but none more furiously than liberalism.[92] With all the equality and rights and respects accorded, liberalism fatally eliminates the unique elements in the individual and thus destroys him. Humanity gains, humans lose. Men become citizens; they serve humanity and lose their souls.[93] The appearance of freedom is given in order that real freedom ("ownness") may be forgotten. "Given (chartered) freedom is no freedom, since only the freedom one *takes* for himself, therefore the egoist's freedom, rides with full sails." [94]

Just as he recognizes no rules in his dealings with other individuals, the egoist will be unrestrained in his rebellious acts. Crime, violence, and destruction are all done with contempt for the state and in celebration of the strength and integrity of the free and sacred individuality. This struggle against the state and society may or may not be in association with other individuals: one freely enters and separates from associations. While strategy and tactics may seem important, they were not to Stirner—practical matters never were. The individual will assert himself and glorify himself in any case. The action is one of personal morality, not social organization; it is *his* action, not a historical development. The fact that the egoist *rises* against oppressors, *exalts* him—whatever other consequences there may be.

Stirner's egoist does not seek domination over others. To need to subordinate others is a sign of weakness. Just as the unique individual does not need others at all, he does not need them as servants. Nor does he need great property. His own liberated great soul is his most precious possession. Grudging respect he may pay to other free souls. A society of egoists would not, according to Stirner, be a bad place at all. Each is independent, each goes his own way, and each defends himself. A "union of egoists" can exist where no one has a claim on anyone else and where each member sees it as his instrument.

There is much Stirner in the theory of Benjamin R. Tucker.[95] Over and over Tucker denied inherent rights and duties. He went to great dramatic lengths to avoid moralizing. He called himself an egoist in the "farthest and fullest sense." [96] He specifically denied that a person was morally obligated to keep promises or agreements—though others may *force* him to honor his word. If right means anything, it means what might can impose. Tucker did, however, recognize the value of expedience. On utilitarian grounds men fare better when they decide to respect the liberty of others. Equality of liberty, therefore, can become a social convention. It is at this point that Tucker's egoism becomes mutualism:

> My neighbor is not my enemy, but my friend, and I am his; if we would but mutually recognize the fact. We help each other to a better, fuller, happier living; and this service might be greatly increased if we would cease to restrict, hamper, and oppress each other. Why can we not agree to let each live his own life, neither of us transgressing the limit that separates our individualities? [97]

Tucker's mission in life was to convince people of the expedience of a social contract for equal liberty and the inexpedience of any other social contract. Speaking as if the contract had already been made, he heaped scorn on invasion and tried to educate people on the means of defense. And he did all this with great concern for others and with unctuous earnestness! "I regard liberty as the chief essential to man's happiness, and therefore as the most important thing in the world. . . ." [98]

Personal Morality

There is a great deal of disagreement among the anarchists in specific areas of personal morality. Some anarchists are quite permissive, while others tend to be conservative and even puritanical.

As an example of the former tendency one can cite the demands by Bakunin for equality in political, economic, and social rights for women, the elimination of marriage as a civil action, and the weakening of marriage by abolition of inheritance and by recognition by society of its right to rear and educate children. Benjamin R. Tucker wrote: Anarchists "acknowledge and defend the right of any man and woman, or any men and women, to love each other for as long or as short a time as they can, will, or may. To them legal marriage and legal divorce are equal absurdities. . . . Love relations between . . . independent individuals shall be as varied as are individual inclinations and attractions; and . . . the children born of these relations shall belong exclusively to the mothers until old enough to belong to themselves." [99] Sexual relations are natural; individuals should not be regulated by narrow-minded and morbid puritans.

The most prominent proponent in the anarchist movement for women's rights was Emma Goldman, who fought the Philistines on three continents. "The demand for equal rights in every vocation of life is just and fair; but, after all, the most vital right is the right to love and be loved." [100] Modern "marriage is primarily an economic arrangement, an insurance pact. . . . If, however, woman's premium is a husband, she pays for it with her name, her privacy, her self-respect, her very life, 'until death doth part.' " [101] "Can there be anything more outrageous than the idea that a healthy, grown woman, full of life and passion, must deny nature's demand, must . . . abstain from the depth and glory of sex experience until a 'good' man comes along to take her unto himself as a wife?" [102] "Free love? As if love is anything but free!" [103] "Few children in wedlock enjoy the care, the protection, the devotion free motherhood is capable of bestowing." [104]

At the other end of the spectrum is Proudhon—who would not have gotten along with Emma Goldman. Detesting female writers, he held that woman's place is in the home, dutifully performing the role of wife and mother. The family must be preserved, for it is the basis of all society. His view was not simply "petty bourgeois"; it was often puritanical: hard work is good because it reduces the sexual urge, luxurious living is corrupting, homosexuality is an abomination that society should punish, and so on. The puritanism of certain Spanish anarchists in the nineteenth century is well known. "The really serious anarchists, especially in Andalusia, neither smoked nor drank, while their sexual morality was often extremely prudish." Austere, simple, and dedicated leaders like Fermin Salvochea and Anselmo Lorenzo were their heroes.[105] The views of Georges Sorel are another example of the conservatism of some anarchists in the area of family life.

What is perhaps the most significant moral commitment of the anarchist is that of bringing about—one way or another—the end of government and existing social conditions. To some degree all anarchists share Sorel's conviction that the most splendidly heroic ethical action one may perform is to strike a blow for the good society. In obedience to this moral imperative he will suffer privations but at the same time justify his existence. The tactics and strategy of revolution and their justification will be discussed in Chapter 5. It is sufficient here to note that for most anarchists the highest kind of moral integrity is that which is displayed in revolutionary effort.

NOTES

1 Bakunin, *The Political Philosophy*, p. 146.

2 Denis Diderot, "Supplement to Bougainville's *Voyage*," in *Diderot: Interpreter of Nature*, Jonathan Kemp, Trans. (New York: International Publishers Co., 1963), p. 155.

3 Kropotkin, *Revolutionary Pamphlets*, p. 131.

4 *Ibid.*, p. 132.

5 Bakunin, *The Political Philosophy*, p. 144.

6 *Ibid.*, p. 163.

7 *Ibid.*, p. 341.

8 "The appearance of societies on the earth preceded the appearance of man." Kropotkin, *Ethics: Origin and Development*, Louis S. Friedland and Joseph R. Piroshnikoff, Trans. (New York: The Dial Press, 1924), p. 152.

9 Kropotkin, *Revolutionary Pamphlets*, p. 201.

10 Bakunin, *The Political Philosophy*, p. 299.

11 Proudhon, quoted in Joll, p. 67.

12 Irving L. Horowitz, *The Anarchists* (New York: Dell Publishing Co., 1964), p. 19.

13 Tucker, p. 49.

14 Marcus Aurelius, *Meditations*, IV, 23; in Whitney J. Oates, Ed., *The Stoic and Epicurean Philosophers* (New York: Random House, 1940), p. 511.

15 Bakunin, *The Political Philosophy*, p. 101.

16 "Whatever depths his intellectual and moral degradation may reach at any particular moment, unless he is congenitally insane or an idiot . . . his human character, amid the most monstrous deviations, still exists in him, in a very real manner, *as a possibility, always present with him so long as he lives, that somehow he may become aware of his humanity if only a radical change is effected in the social conditions which made him what he is.*" *Ibid.*, p. 147.

17 "The concurrence of special circumstances, an unforeseen event, an accident insignificant in itself, the chance meeting of some particular person, and sometimes a book falling into the hands of an individual at just the right moment. . . ." *Ibid.*, p. 154.

18 Godwin, *Thoughts on Man* (1831), quoted in Woodcock, p. 73.

19 Godwin, *An Enquiry* . . . , Vol. I, p. 144.

20 Bakunin, *The Political Philosophy*, p. 153.

21 *Ibid.*, p. 147.

22 Godwin, *An Enquiry* . . . , Vol. I, p. 146.

23 See Chapter 6.

24 Bakunin, *The Political Philosophy*, p. 138.

25 *Ibid.*, p. 273.

26 Berkman, *Now and After*, p. 48.

27 Bakunin, *The Political Philosophy*, p. 119.

28 Pierre Joseph Proudhon, *What Is Property? An Inquiry into the Principle of Right and of Government*, Benjamin R. Tucker, Trans. (New York: Howard Fertig, 1966), p. 28.

29 *Ibid.*, p. 30.

30 Kropotkin, *Modern Science and Anarchism* (New York: Mother Earth Publishing Association, 1908), pp. 9–10.

31 Proudhon, p. 23.

32 Proudhon, *System of Economic Contradictions, or the Philosophy of Misery*, Benjamin R. Tucker, Trans., *Works of P. J. Proudhon* (Boston: Benjamin R. Tucker, 1888), Vol. I, p. 452.

33 *Ibid.*, p. 433.

34 Bakunin, *The Political Philosophy*, p. 106.

35 *Ibid.*, p. 115.

36 *Ibid.*, p. 111.

37 *Ibid.*, p. 116.

38 *Ibid.*, p. 62.

39 *Ibid.*, p. 207.

40 See Georges Sorel, *Reflections on Violence*, T. E. Hulme and J. Roth, Trans. (Glencoe, Illinois: The Free Press, 1950), pp. 233–234.

41 Max Stirner, *The Ego and His Own*, Steven T. Byington, Trans. (New York: Boni and Liveright, Inc., no date), pp. 50–51.

42 *Ibid.*, p. 48.

43 *Ibid.*, p. 49.

44 *Ibid.*, p. 5.

45 Godwin, *An Enquiry* . . . , Vol. I, p. 86.

46 Bakunin, *The Political Philosophy*, p. 62.

47 Tucker, p. 442.

48 On this issue, see Ammon Hennacy, *Autobiography of a Catholic Anarchist* (New York: Catholic Worker Books, 1954), especially pp. 128ff.

49 "We are not connected with one or two percipient beings, but with a society, a nation, and in some sense with the whole family of mankind." Godwin, *An Enquiry* . . . , Vol. I, p. 127.

50 *Ibid.*, p. 125.

51 Proudhon, *What is Property?* pp. 26–27. The other major work is *De la Justice dans la Révolution et dans l'Eglise* (1858).

52 Tucker believed that he was quite in accord with Proudhon in calling for the end of four important monopolies: the money monopoly, the land monopoly, the tariff monopoly, and the patent monopoly. In doing so, he also found himself in accord with certain principles of the Manchester school of *laissez-faire.* See *Instead of a Book* . . . , pp. 10–13.

53 See Joll, p. 64.

54 Bakunin, *The Political Philosophy*, p. 157.

55 Leo Tolstoy, *What Then Must We Do?*, Aylmer Maud, Trans. (London: Oxford University Press, 1960), p. 342.

56 Godwin, *An Enquiry* . . . , Vol. I, p. 135.

57 See *ibid.*, p. 137.

58 *Ibid.*, p. 147.

59 *Ibid.*

60 "We speak of that justice which is based solely upon human conscience, the justice to be found in the consciousness of every man—even in that of children— and which can be expressed in a single word: *equity.*" Bakunin, *The Political Philosophy*, p. 295.

61 *Ibid.*, p. 156.

62 Kropotkin, *Modern Science and Anarchism*, pp. 65–66.

63 Proudhon, *What Is Property?*, p. 241.

64 Bakunin, *The Political Philosophy*, p. 130.

65 "True, real love, the expression of a mutually felt need, can exist only among equals." *Ibid.*

66 Leo Tolstoy, *The Law of Love and the Law of Violence*, Mary Koutouzow Tolstoy, Trans. (New York: Rudolph Field, 1948), pp. 35, 38, 111, 130.

67 *Ibid.*, pp. 90, 91.

68 Kropotkin, *Ethics: Origin and Development*, p. 3.

69 *Ibid.*, p. 9.

70 Such passages in Chapters IV and V of *The Descent of Man* as the following made a strong impression on Kropotkin: "Animals of many kinds are social; we find even distinct species living together; for example, some American monkeys; and united flocks of rooks, jackdaws, and starlings. . . . Animals also render more important services to one another: thus wolves and some other beasts of prey hunt in packs, and aid one another in attacking their victims. Pelicans fish in concert. The Hamadryas baboons turn over stones to find insects, etc. and

when they come to a large one, as many as can stand round, turn it over to-gether and share the booty. . . . Mr. Blyth, as he informs me, saw Indian crows feeding two or three of their companions which were blind; and I have heard of an analogous case with the domestic cock. . . . In however complex a manner this feeling may have originated, as it is one of high importance to all those animals which aid and defend one another, it will have been increased through natural selection; for those communities, which included the greatest number of the most sympathetic members, would flourish best, and rear the greatest num-ber of offspring. . . . Although man, as he now exists, has few special instincts, having lost any which his early progenitors may have possessed, this is no reason why he should not have retained from an extremely remote period some degree of instinctive love and sympathy for his fellows. . . . Now with those animals which live permanently in a body, the social instincts are ever present and per-sistent. Such animals are always ready to utter the danger-signal, to defend the community, and to give aid to their fellows in accordance with their habits; they feel at all times, without the stimulus of any special passion or desire, some degree of love and sympathy for them; they are unhappy if long separated from them, and always happy to be again in their company. So it is with ourselves. . . . Prudence, on the other hand, which does not concern the welfare of others, though a very useful virtue, has never been highly esteemed. As no man can practise the virtues necessary for the welfare of his tribe without self-service, self-command, and the power of endurance, these qualities have been at all times highly and most justly valued. . . . As man advances in civilisation, and small tribes are united into larger communities, the simplest reason would tell each individual that he ought to extend his social instincts and sympathies to all the members of the same nation, though personally unknown to him. This point being once reached, there is only an artificial barrier to prevent his sympathies extending to the men of all nations and races. If, indeed, such men are separated from him by great differences in appearance or habits, experience unfortunately shews us how long it is, before we look at them as our fellow-creatures. . . . In order that primeval men, or the ape-like progenitors of man, should become social, they must have acquired the same instinctive feelings, which impel other animals to live in a body; and they no doubt exhibited the same general disposition. They would have felt uneasy when separated from their comrades, for whom they would have felt some degree of love; they would have warned each other of danger, and have given mutual aid in attack or defence. All this implies some degree of sympathy, fidelity, and courage. Such social qualities, the paramount importance of which to the lower animals is disputed by no one, were no doubt acquired by the progenitors of man in a similar man-ner, namely, through natural selection, aided by inherited habit. . . ." (Charles Darwin, *The Origin of Species and The Descent of Man* [New York: Modern Library, n.d.], pp. 473, 474, 475, 479, 480, 483, 488, 491–492, 498.)

71 Indeed, examples are provided of social actions performed at the *expense* of the parental instinct. See Kropotkin, *Ethics: Origin and Development,* p. 38.

72 See *ibid.,* pp. 14–15, 50–60. Many of these points were made earlier in Kropot-kin's *Mutual Aid: A Factor of Evolution.*

73 *Ibid.,* p. 30. See also pp. 74, 76, 234, 268–270, 278, 304.

74 Kropotkin argues, however, that man thought in terms of "we" long before he thought of "I." "The self-assertion of 'personality' came much later on." *Ibid.,* p. 60.

75 See Kropotkin, *Revolutionary Pamphlets,* pp. 107–113.

76 "Hobbes and his followers looked upon morality not as the outcome of human nature but as something prescribed to it by an external force. Only, in place of the Deity and the Church they put the State and the fear of the 'Leviathan'—the implanter of morality in mankind." Kropotkin, *Ethics: Origin and Development*, p. 211.

77 *Ibid.*, p. 43.

78 *Ibid.*, p. 21.

79 *Ibid.*, p. 18.

80 *Ibid.*, p. 77.

81 On the Greeks, see *ibid.*, pp. 84–113.

82 *Ibid.*, p. 119.

83 See *ibid.*, p. 127.

84 *Ibid.*, p. 131.

85 *Ibid.*, p. 148.

86 *Ibid.*, p. 252. See also pp. 76, 112, 145, 280–281.

87 "There is no doubt that 'the greatest happiness of society' advocated as the basis of morality from the earliest period of the life of the human race, and particularly put forward in recent time by the rationalist thinkers, is actually the primary basis of all ethics. But this conception taken by itself, is too abstract, too remote, and would not be able to create moral habits and a moral mode of thought. That is why, from the most remote antiquity, thinkers have always sought a more stable basis of morality." *Ibid.*, p. 335.

88 *Ibid.*, p. 97.

89 *Ibid.*, p. 100.

90 Stirner, p. 196.

91 *Ibid.*, p. 219.

92 "Liberalism as a whole has a great enemy, an invincible opposite, as God has the devil: by the side of man stands always the un-man, the individual, the egoist. State, society, humanity, do not master this devil." *Ibid.*, p. 148.

93 "If the State must count on our humanity, it is the same if one says it must count on our morality." *Ibid.*, p. 186.

94 *Ibid.*, p. 176.

95 Stirner's book, wrote Tucker, "is destined to a resurrection that will perhaps mark an epoch." Tucker, p. 24.

96 *Ibid.*

97 *Ibid.*, p. 25.

98 *Ibid.*, p. 41.

99 *Ibid.*, p. 15.

100 Emma Goldman, *Anarchism and Other Essays* (New York: Mother Earth Publishing Association, 1910), p. 230.

101 *Ibid.*, p. 234.

102 *Ibid.*, p. 237.

103 *Ibid.*, p. 242.

104 *Ibid.*, p. 243.

105 See Joll, p. 232.

4

The Modern State

DOMINATION AND POWER

Government

The most obvious criticism the anarchist can make of modern society is that its laws and their enforcement are utterly unjust. Strikers are fired upon, strikebreakers are protected, arbitrary arrests are made, evidence is forged, juries are rigged—all because of the government's steadfast concern to keep a favored few in a position of privilege while holding the others in a position of miserable subordination. "In the war between the classes, the State was not neutral." [1] Russia had its solitary executions, Spain its torture chambers and the garotte, France its mass arrests and false testimony. The state of Illinois hanged four men who were thought (but not proved) to have thrown a bomb in Haymarket Square; the Commonwealth of Massachusetts executed Sacco and Vanzetti on the most circumstantial of evidence, and so on. The anarchists had boundless examples from their own ranks of the flagrant injustice the state handed down to those of its many enemies who dared to challenge it. Aristippus, the ancient hedonist, was an anarchist when, in answer to Socrates' question, he said he desired to belong neither to the governing nor the governed class.

Proudhon wrote:

> To be governed is to be watched, inspected, spied, directed, law-ridden, regulated, penned up, indoctrinated, preached at, checked, appraised, sized, censured, commanded, by beings who have neither

title nor knowledge nor virtue. To be governed is to have every operation, every transaction, every movement noted, registered, counted, rated, stamped, measured, numbered, assessed, licensed, refused, authorized, indorsed, admonished, prevented, reformed, redressed, corrected. To be governed is, under pretext of public utility and in the name of the general interest, to be laid under contribution, drilled, fleeced, exploited, monopolized, extorted from, exhausted, hoaxed, robbed; then, upon the slightest resistance, at the first word of complaint, to be repressed, fined, vilified, annoyed, hunted down, pulled about, beaten, disarmed, bound, imprisoned, shot, mitrailleused, judged, condemned, banished, sacrificed, sold, betrayed, and to crown all, ridiculed, derided, outraged, dishonored.[2]

According to Stirner, the sole purpose of the state is "to limit, tame, subordinate the individual." [3] He is submerged in "a desolate sea of regulations." All this means that the individual is reduced to the most fundamental and literal kind of pauperism: the state does not let him own himself.

While the state can never be concerned with the individual, it is at its best concerned with humanity. So it standardizes, organizes, and unifies. Millions of people become content to be governed by a handful of politicians. Under a benign government, the people come to believe that authority is necessary in order for men to live at peace and to be happy. Their birth, education, love, and development are regulated. "If this state of things continues, we shall lose all initiative, all habit of thinking for ourselves." [4]

Seeing themselves always in relation to the government, individuals lose their sense of personal responsibility, not only for themselves, but for others as well. Kropotkin lamented that men "live side by side without knowing one another." [5] They do not become personally concerned about a social injustice, a starving child, or an act of violence in the street. The state is the great source of "benefits," the only conceivable solution to anything at all. Men, alienated from one another, depend upon an external force to act. When their alienation from one another is so great that open conflict breaks out, they can only look to the state to prevent "anti-social passions from reaching their highest climax." [6] So the state is justified for solving the problems it creates!

Law and Its Enforcement

In the meantime, of course, laws and more laws are passed. A social evil is "met" by passing a law against it. Groups and individuals demand laws to protect their rights and interests. Men, having lost initiative and resourcefulness, require a law for everything: "A law about fashions, a law about mad dogs, a law about virtue, a law to put a stop to all the vices and all the evils which result from human indolence and cowardice." [7] They ignore Buckle's famous dictum: "The best laws were those which repealed the preceding ones." [8]

Kropotkin classified the millions of laws under three headings, concluding that they are either useless and/or hurtful to the vast majority. (1) Laws for the protection of property. These are made in order to secure for certain people the wealth they have stolen from its producers or from society as a whole. There are, however, no laws to guarantee to workers the full fruit of their labor. "Do you wonder that the capitalist and employer, and all those who profit by this order of things, are strong for 'law and order'?" [9] Litigation in the courts, more often than not, merely decides which of two robbers is to have the booty. (2) Laws for the maintenance of government (constitutional law). These "maintain, patch up, and develop the administrative machine." [10] (3) Laws relating to the protection of the person. Since most crimes are caused by the desire to obtain someone else's wealth, they will virtually disappear when economic injustices are removed. In any case, crimes of violence are not deterred by punishment or by increasing the severity of punishment. The criminal, locked in a prison, is merely brutalized by his surroundings and confirmed in his hostility.[11] If punishment could prevent crime, crime would have stopped a long time ago, for men have been punishing one another for centuries. The most that lawful punishment can do is to make some criminals more circumspect, but "even the most severe punishments do not frighten people away from crime." [12] Does anyone today really *believe* that he is protected from crime by statutes and policemen? Do these things truly provide him with a strong sense of security?

It is an anarchist contention that society makes criminals of us all. The existence of so many laws itself makes complete obedience impossible. But more important, they support a system that is unjust and that a man of principle will wish to oppose. Should a laborer permit management to steal from him? Should a man pay taxes to support a bad war? Should a citizen respect laws that are made by venal legislators? It is precisely because the social system is so unjust that it must devise a vast array of laws to maintain it and must support an army of policemen and judges to enforce them. Kropotkin wrote:

When a mother in search of food and shelter for her children must pass by shops filled with the most refined delicacies of refined gluttony; when gorgeous and insolent luxury is displayed side by side with the most execrable misery; when the dog and horse of a rich man are far better cared for than millions of children whose mothers earn pitiful salary in the pit or the manufactory; when each "modest" evening dress of a lady represents eight months, or one year, of human labor; when enrichment at somebody else's expense is the avowed aim of the "upper classes," and no distinct boundary can be traced between honest and dishonest means of making money—then force is the only means for maintaining such a state of things.[13]

The relatively innocent people are locked up. The real oppressors remain free—to continue their theft of the fruits of labor, their false advertising, their "deals" with politicians, their land-grabs, their market manipulations, etc. It is a common saying in prisons that "the little swindlers are here but the big ones are free and enjoy public respect."[14] The big thieves lock up the little ones. Jails are for the unfortunate, not for the criminal. In his well-known pamphlet, "An Appeal to the Young," Kropotkin discussed some legal problems with prospective lawyers. One was this: A rich landowner demands his rent from a tenant farmer who cannot pay. The former does no work and squanders his money; the latter works hard but has fallen into debt. The law says that the farmer should be thrown out. "Which side will you take? For the law and against justice, or for justice and against the law?"[15]

Alexander Berkman, as a convict, spent many years with criminals. In maintaining that society makes criminals, he wrote: "It is economic slavery, the savage struggle for a crumb, that has converted mankind into wolves and sheep."[16] He met many men born in slums, neglected by their parents, and uneducated and untrained by society, who had been arrested and imprisoned for minor violations, then quickly confirmed in their "criminality" by the heartless and ineffectual penal system.[17] "Don't you see," asked Berkman, "that the conditions of [the offender's] whole life have made him what he is? And don't you see that the *system* which keeps up such conditions is a greater criminal than the petty thief? . . . Who causes more misery: the rich manufacturer reducing the wages of thousands of workers to swell his profits, or the jobless man stealing something to keep from starving?"[18] Lawful wrongs are greater evils than unlawful ones. "Society prepares the crimes while individuals merely carry them out."[19]

Bad as all this is, the state does not impartially enforce the laws it has. Not even this minimal requirement of the principle of justice is met. People are *not* equal before the law. Their politics, social class, and economic condition make a real difference in how they are treated by the police, magistrates, and courts. Anarchists in the United States had many celebrated examples of gross misuse of existing laws and the apparatus for their enforcement: the Haymarket riot in Chicago in 1886 and its aftermath, the trial of Thomas Mooney and Warren Billings in California in 1916, and the treatment of Sacco and Vanzetti in Massachusetts a few years later. When the state goes to such lengths as these, *it* can be accused of employing terrorist tactics.

In an even deeper sense, argue the anarchists, the state is the first and original criminal. Man at one time had no master. The state then *invaded* his natural freedom. It was (and is) a violent force from outside which compels man to obey. Officials of the state claim that they aim to benefit the people; in truth, however, they seek their own advantage or that of the classes whose lackeys they are. Law was originally glorified as the instrument of justice—everyone is equal before the law. Law was supposed to be a product of wisdom. Its defenders parroted the expression "rule by law is better than rule by men." But law is the means by which men rule. It is "the product of their passions, their timidity, their jealousies and their ambitions." [20] And law has penalties attached. So rule by government is rule by men through violence. Which is the greater crime: to enslave the people or to violate the laws that the enslavers promulgate? Clearly the first; the latter is no crime at all.

Seekers of Power

The anarchists of a few generations ago were uniformly contemptuous of people who sought to exercise authority over their fellow men. Bakunin believed that everyone possessed at least the germ of the power instinct and that it grew and manifested itself whenever environmental conditions were favorable. If there is a "devil in history," it is this propensity to dominate others. "No one should be entrusted with power, inasmuch as anyone invested with authority must, through the force of an immutable social law, become an oppressor and exploiter of society." [21] And the whole time he may be under the illusion that he is working for the good of those he dominates, that he is their servant!

Contemporary anarchists, still in the old tradition, have analyzed the concept of power carefully. Paul Goodman, for example, points out that in our society power is valued in itself. One seeks to get into positions of power in politics and corporations; he wants to be a "decision-maker." [22] This attraction for power is for power in the abstract; usually it is quite divorced from any conception of what real advantages the position of power may secure for the individual or for society. Conceivably, leadership may be valuable in emergencies, but power-seekers (unlike Cincinnatus) wish to make a career out of exercising power. Such men are deluded. "They are taking a basic and impractical, and indeed neurotic state of affairs as if it were right and inevitable. . . . If a man is not continually proving his potency, his mastery of others and of himself, he becomes prey to the panic of being defeated and victimized." [23] Nor do power structures generate any value in the community: "Very soon society becomes lifeless. The means of community action, initiative, decision, have become preempted by the powerful. But the slaveholders, exploiters, and governors share in that same society and are themselves vitiated. . . . Inevitably, as people become stupider and more careless, administration increases in size and power; and conversely." [24]

Alexander Comfort, another contemporary anarchist-scholar, writes: "No society based on centralized power has been able to dispense with large groups of people whose make-up is in no way different from that of punishable delinquents. . . ." [25] These psychopaths are found at two levels: (1) that of policy-makers and rulers, (2) that of law enforcement. On the first level, "in the case of would-be politicians, these impulses [for authority and control] may spring from a highly developed political and social sense; they may equally well spring from maladjustment and a deep-seated impulse toward self assertion and dominance." [26] With respect to the second level, since police work is poorly paid and has no great advantage for the poorly educated over other secure and established positions, people often enter the enforcement occupation out of a desire for authority and control over others.

It is no accident that the kind of society that produces widespread "abnormal" behavior at the same time produces many people who are zealous to repress it. We call the first "delinquent," but "obedience in modern societies is more often a hideous vice than a Christian virtue." [27] And the latter class of people must always be suspect: "The closest connection between power and abnormality is in the essentially uncreative and unproductive nature of the impulse to regulate by prohibition. This impulse is almost always the expression of a failing, rather than a successful, adaptation. We try to prohibit those things which inspire guilty, resentful, or jealous feelings: prohibition is a substitute for participation." [28]

In short, it is not the case that "power corrupts." One must already be corrupted in order to seek power.

It is an anarchist commonplace that government is the cause of wars. Without a strong central government, no society could wage an aggressive war against people whom there is no good reason to hate. But government is not merely a necessary condition for war, it is often a sufficient one as well. Since political leaders tend to be psychologically unstable, they are likely to extend their desire for power beyond the borders of their own country (or will act aggressively in order to prop up their own power at home). A contemporary anarchist, Colin Ward, neatly turns the tables on his critics: "It is, after all, governments which prepare for war and wage war, even though you are obliged to fight in them and pay for them; the bombs you are worried about are not the bombs which cartoonists attribute to the anarchists, but the bombs which governments have perfected, at your expense." [29]

Democracy

We noted at the beginning of this study that—according to the anarchists—all governments are undesirable, from autocracy to democracy. If it is wrong for one man to dominate me, it is equally wrong for one million men to do so. Anarchists are not interested in ranking forms of government in some Aristotelian manner from the best to the worst. All governments are bad, and each has its particular evils in addition to the basic one of restricting liberty. "Democracy has been defined as the principle that 'one man is as good as another, if not a little better.' Anarchy may be defined as the principle that one government is as bad as another, if not a little worse." [30]

Democracy is the most dishonest form: it often succeeds in concealing its basic tyranny by implicating many people in its oppression and by insisting on certain myths like consent, social contract, and natural rights. Universal suffrage is no panacea in a country where the masses are impoverished and lack education and leisure. Bakunin called it "the most refined charlatanism of the

State." [31] The occasional radical who does occupy office is quickly tamed. He is vain and likes power. Having joined the enemy, he will begin to take on its attitudes.[32]

But the democratic state will increasingly become as responsive as it has to be to certain unmistakable demands: its leaders will buy off as many people as necessary in order to stay in power. Georges Sorel had the greatest contempt for the democratic rulers, decadent and weak, who from fear and cowardice practiced fraud and compromise. Writing in 1906, he said: "One of the things which appear to me to have most astonished the workers during the last few years has been the timidity of the forces of law and order in the presence of a riot; magistrates who have the right to demand the services of soldiers dare not use their power to the utmost, and officers allow themselves to be abused and struck with a patience hitherto unknown in them." [33] Everything must be endured so long as the issue is not joined and the incumbents swept from power. Revolutionary forces must be defused and changes (or apparent changes) grudgingly made. "The majority cannot persist in pursuing schemes which give rise to popular demonstrations of too serious a kind." [34] The ultimate in democratic cowardice was, of course, the almost complete lack of resistance by the "democratic" and constitutional parties to the fascist movement in Europe in the twenties and thirties.

Democrats become increasingly paternalistic in order to keep the people tame and domesticated. Instead of giving them justice, democratic government gives them charity. "The people," wrote Tucker, "cannot afford to be enslaved for the sake of being insured. If there were no other alternatives, they would do better, on the whole, to take Nature's risks and pay her penalties as best they might." [35] The welfare state is very profitable to those in political and economic power. Employers may be forced to pay higher wages and higher taxes, but this does not cost them any more than would a bribe to politicians. "As for the Government, it becomes the benefactor of the people, and hopes that it will do well in the elections; to the politicians, the electoral advantages which result from a successful conciliation are worth more than a very large bribe." [36] Finally, perhaps, the politicians are ready to accept socialism. Now their opportunities for domination are all but infinite. Loaded with money and privilege, they now have the exquisite pleasure of directing virtually every aspect of citizens' lives. The state is always maintained and supported by a privileged class. When all social and economic classes have been transcended by state socialism, that privileged class is the bureaucracy itself. Thus does government serve the people.

Perhaps the most tragic aspect of statehood is the artificial division it has produced within the human family.

> *The State . . . is the most flagrant negation, the most cynical and complete negation of humanity.* It rends apart the universal solidarity of all men upon earth, and it unites some of them only to destroy, conquer, and enslave all the rest. It takes under its protection only its own citizens, and it recognizes human right, humanity, and civilization only within the confines of its own boundaries. And since it does not recognize any right outside of its own confines, it quite literally arrogates to itself the right to treat with the most ferocious inhumanity all the populations whom it can pillage, exterminate, or subordinate to its will.[37]

The morality of the state is called patriotism, and it transcends all moral principles. Thus it is that the state can perform actions which individuals would scruple to do—unless, of course, they do them as patriotic citizens. "The supreme law of the State is self-preservation at any cost." [38] This is no morality at all, for no principles or standards are recognized. "International justice" is a contradiction in terms. How many horrible crimes have been covered by the innocent expression "raison d'état"?

ECONOMICS

Capitalism

Anarchists are not content simply to criticize the fact of political control. They also believe that the economic systems of all states are bad. Government is condemned, therefore, not simply because it dominates human lives, but also because it protects unjust economic systems. It interferes *and* oppresses. In the thinking of some anarchists, the two subjugating forces, government and economics, are hardly distinguishable in actual practice. Hence Berkman can say, "the basis of all liberty is economic." [39] An individualist could convert the proposition to: the prerequisite for economic justice is elimination of the state.

Apologists for capitalism have emphasized its quality of *laissez-*

faire and have marveled at the beneficial consequences of this quality. The critic will point out that while certain capitalists have been "permitted to do," the same privilege has been denied to other groups and individuals. Governments have punished workers for striking, and even for organizing trade unions. They have imposed taxes that drive peasants into the hands of factory bosses. They have protected in sundry ways certain monopolies. "Freedom to oppose exploitation has so far never and nowhere existed." [40]

At any rate, economic systems are such that they set men against one another. My gain must be at the expense of someone else, for his interest and mine are different. "Every man who gets rich thereby makes his neighbor poor. The better off one is, the worse off the rest are." [41] Since the system itself generates antagonisms, one cannot afford to be kind. Many of the common criticisms of capitalism and the misery it engenders are found in the anarchist literature. Since these are familiar to all and are not in any case distinctive to anarchism, they will not be systematically discussed. These criticisms are especially abundant in the writings of such collectivists as Berkman and Kropotkin.[42] The collectivist will stress the profit-seeking aspect of the system; the individualist and mutualist will emphasize the restrictions the state places on free competition. All anarchists agree that labor is the true source of wealth and that the man who labors is cheated of his just reward. It is important, if men are to live together in peace, without government, in a spirit of respect (if not fraternal love), to change both objective conditions and the feelings such conditions produce. That is, injustice and resentment must both be eliminated.

Proudhon was the most influential economist among the anarchists. His aphorism, "property is theft," has already been discussed.[43] Josiah Warren, the first significant American anarchist, developed similar ideas in apparent ignorance of Proudhon's work. The American mutualists and individualists who followed—John Beverley Robinson, Benjamin R. Tucker, and Stephen Pearl Andrews—built on the work of Warren or Proudhon, or both. The collectivist Alexander Berkman also echoed Proudhon when he wrote: "The wealth the workers have created . . . has indeed been stolen from them. And they are being robbed in the same way every day of their lives, even at this very moment." [44]

Andrews pointed out that modern society is structured by false and artificial relations. We feel compelled to help people victimized in such a society, so we have almshouses and all the other features of what later came to be called the welfare state. These bad relations are often economic in origin: "By refusing equity in the distribution of wealth; by reducing the earnings of women, and youths, and hired men, and slaves below equivalents; by thus grasping power over others, through the medium of an undue absorption of the products of their industry, the members of [the] community are brought into the relation of oppressors and oppressed. . . ."[45] The basic structure is so bad that well-meaning people cannot do well. We either help the unfortunates, which confirms them in their dependence and bondage; or we ignore them, which is brutal. "The oppressed classes do not want charity, but justice."[46] Modern society is plainly stupid and inefficient. It creates needless problems for itself. Then, if it wishes to be humane, it expends great sums of money to solve them. The elaborate apparatus for dealing with crime is expensive and ineffective. The welfare programs are superficial as well as expensive and ineffective. Unfortunate individuals are supported in prisons and slums at taxpayers' expense, while the basic causes are not only never found, but are hardly sought. The only solution is radically to reconstitute society.

Monopoly and Privilege

Tucker maintained that society protects free competition in producing goods and in providing labor, but supports monopoly in the important area of supplying capital. Proudhon is correct that the natural wage of labor is its product. "All who derive income from any other source abstract it directly or indirectly from the natural and just wage of labor; . . . this abstracting process generally takes one of three forms,—interest, rent, and profit; . . . these three constitute the trinity of usury, and are simply different methods of levying tribute for the use of capital. . . ."[47] This one-sidedness of competition is faithfully protected by government: "capital [has] manipulated legislation."[48] This is what prevents labor from receiving its full reward and keeps prices above the labor cost of production. That labor does not receive its full reward is an excellent example of the invasion of the individual, of the violence done to his "sphere of action." The capitalist violates the principle of equal liberty and this violation is legalized by government.

In rejecting the presence of the government in the banking business, Tucker argued that government should not conduct *any* business enterprise; it should not compete with people. He gave three reasons: "First, the government is a tyrant living by theft [taxation], and therefore has no business to engage in any business. Second, the government has none of the characteristics of a successful business man, being wasteful, careless, clumsy, and short-sighted in the extreme. Third, the government is thoroughly irresponsible, having it in its power to effectively repudiate its obligations at any time." [49]

Another exponent of Proudhonian economics was Robinson. He singled out several forms of privilege that are sustained by political states. The first is *landownership*. The owner charges a fee in the form of rent, but gives nothing in exchange except the use of the land (which he is not using anyway). Although he did not himself produce the land, his title to it enables him to charge others for the privilege of living on it or cultivating it. Whether he would use or occupy the land himself is immaterial; how many others need it and would use it is irrelevant. Simply because he has a title, the government uses its force to sustain his position as "lord" of the land.[50] "Directly or indirectly everybody must pay rent to the owners of the soil." [51] The second form of privilege is the *money* privilege. The fee for hiring money is called interest. "Restrictive and prohibitory" laws keep the interest rate unnaturally high. This makes it impossible for most workers to borrow money and become proprietors themselves (thus guaranteeing for themselves the full product of their labor). The people are not permitted to establish banks, to issue banknotes, or to lend currency. Gold is fixed by law as the basis of paper currency—which causes financial crises. All this is at the expense of the many and to the advantage of a few.[52] An anarchist society could quite easily remedy the situation.[53] A third form of privilege is made possible by *taxation*. This money is used to provide salary and emoluments for government officials— and to increase their power over the people's lives. The people are not presented with a bargain that they can accept or reject. Their money is taken as a forcible levy. "It is not possible to vote for a representative who will oppose taxation, for it is from taxation that he gets his bread and butter." [54]

These three forms of privilege take from the worker much of what he produces. Great inequalities of wealth develop, the non-workers getting a greater and greater slice from the social product. The poor die of malnutrition, the rich die from overindulgence. Berkman described a great city: "In the distance, great furnaces vomit pillars of fire, the lurid flashes accentuating a line of frame structures, dilapidated and miserable. They are the homes of the workers who have created the industrial glory of Pittsburgh, reared its millionaires, its Carnegies and Fricks." [55] Economic privilege leads to privilege of other kinds. There is not only gross poverty, but ranks of precedence and loss of equality and fraternity. All this is made possible and defended by the state. But the state is not a club from which one may voluntarily resign. The only recourse is to abolish the state.

It may be thought that trade unions can significantly alter economic injustice. It depends upon what type they are. Sorel, of course, had great hopes for non-political trade unionism. When the movement stayed out of politics, avoided centralized leadership, prepared for violent revolution, and refused to settle for any compromise with the rights of labor, he admired it. But when unions plotted with parliamentary socialists, imposed bureaucratic organization over the rank and file, and were willing to be "bought off" by the middle class, he opposed them.

According to several writers, modern trade unions have done all these things.[56] They would therefore forfeit the support of Sorel and most other anarchists. Union officials today are not subject to their rank and file; they manage the union, make the decisions, levy the dues and tell the members what to do. They enjoy high salaries and perfect a bureaucracy as cumbrous and as frustrating as any known in modern society. More seriously, they often fail to represent the workers' interests. They collaborate with management or the government to secure as much gain as seems necessary for preventing the workers from becoming too restive. Since the officials are "reasonable" men, both management and government prefer to deal with them rather than with the workers themselves. The labor bureaucracy, in league with employers and the state, controls billions of dollars and millions of workers. Union members are powerless, while their leadership sponsors a labor front for an oppressive state.

Bakunin

Bakunin, a materialist in his metaphysical outlook, was a bitter and sarcastic critic of the narrow materialism of bourgeois society: "An honest man, a moral man, is he who knows how to acquire, conserve, and augment property, and . . . a property-owner is the only one worthy of respect." [57] These qualities measure his manhood and determine his social position. A common American locu-

tion is "That man is worth a hundred thousand dollars." Nominally
Christian, the bourgeoisie ignore those teachings in the Gospel that
warn of the difficulty a rich man has in entering the kingdom of
God ("eye of a needle"), that forbid the acquisition of great wealth
("where your treasure is, there will your heart be also"), and that
counsel man to imitate the fowls of the air ("they sow not, neither
do they reap"). The bourgeoisie fashioned a "Protestant ethic" and
sought individual "success." Victory over a rival was moral: it was
the reward for industry and work. Exploitation based on individual
merit and resulting from its application is not bad. Work justifies
all. *But,* wrote Bakunin, "there is work and work." To be busy in
exploiting is not to be laboring productively. Highway robbers cal-
culate and plan; they exert themselves too. If their wealth is ill-
gotten, then so is the wealth of entrepreneurs, capitalists, and
rentiers. "It is evident to anyone who does not want to be blind
that productive work creates wealth and yields to the producer
only poverty, and that it is only non-productive, exploiting labor,
that yields property. But since property is morality it follows that
*morality, as the bourgeois understands it, consists in exploiting
someone else's labor.*" [58]

Much of Bakunin's analysis and criticism of capitalism is derived
from Marx.[59] The material collected by Maximoff under the chapter title "The Present Economic Regime" is pure Marx, as these
topic headings would indicate: General Tendencies of Capitalism,
Growing Concentration of Wealth, Proletarianization of the Peasantry, Exploitation Is the Essence of Capitalism, Workers Forced
To Sell Their Labor, Selling of Labor Power Is Not a Free Transaction, Growth of the Proletariat Outstrips the Productive Capacity
of Capitalism, Growing Competition for Jobs Forces Down Wage
Levels, Intensified Exploitation and Its Consequences, The Iron
Law of Wages, etc.[60] Other chapters, equally Marxian, are "Class
Struggle in Society Inevitable," [61] "Checkered History of the Bourgeoisie," [62] and "Proletariat Long Enslaved." [63] Bakunin's frequent
lamentation on the brutalizing effect of industrial work is also
Marxian.

One bourgeois practice that Bakunin opposed and took much
more seriously than Marx was that of inheritance of property. This
right "begets all the economic, political, and social privileges." [64]
It fixes the inequalities of one generation on the next; it imposes
injustice from age to age. In the good society no one will need the
advantages of inheritance and no one will suffer from having had

the wrong ancestor. In the meantime, Bakunin hoped (wistfully, it seemed) that the gradual abolition of the right of inheritance in certain "fortunate countries" might be a prelude to the social revolution. If governments did not abolish inheritance, abolition would take place "on the first day of the Revolution." [65]

Tolstoy

The most eloquent anarchist critic of contemporary conditions was Leo Tolstoy. He was shocked to the core by the urban poverty he examined in Moscow. Some of the people he talked with had low-paying jobs; most had no job at all. All were hungry and cold. Prison seemed a benefit to many, while others begged to be put into an almshouse. Tolstoy suggested that the reason some do not work is that they have not learned to work; they may know nothing even of the discipline for *getting* to work. They may, however, be well schooled in the arts of begging, stealing, and "hustling." [66] "The present appeared to them [the destitute people of Rzhanov House] unnatural, abhorrent, and unworthy of attention. None of them had a present." [67] Tolstoy described the tenements: "Everywhere the same stench, the same stifling atmosphere, the same overcrowding, the same mingling of the sexes, the same spectacle of men and women drunk to stupefaction, and the same fear, submissiveness, and culpability on all faces. . . ." [68]

The condition of industrial workers is not much better. They work under "hard, unnatural conditions of monotonous, stupefying, slavish toil." [69] Tolstoy was as indignant about the "division of labor" in industry as he was about the low wages and unhealthy surroundings: a worker agrees to make one one-hundredth part of an article all his life—many workers do not even know *what* they are making! Some divisions of labor unite men—such as that which occurs in harvesting a crop. But factory work nearly always divides them in spirit as well as function.

Urban poverty, Tolstoy believed, is more cruel and depraving than rural poverty. Yet the poor peasants, unable to feed themselves in the villages, congregate in the cities. Tolstoy stressed the irony of this. It is the same throughout the world: "the passing of wealth from the producers into the hands of the non-producers and its accumulation in towns." [70] In the cities, at any rate, the poor can be *near* the rich; they can pick up some of the crumbs. The luxury and temptations of the city are also factors in the migration—just as they are for the rich. The poor peasants follow the rich to cities "in order to get back somehow or other what was taken from them in the villages." [71] The men in power are quite content. They wish to keep up the level of production and a supply of factory laborers. A cheap labor supply will contribute to "an abundant production of various articles, necessary for their comfort and pleasure." [72]

Why is there poverty in the villages? Many peasants have insufficient land and tools. "The conception of a labourer *includes* the conception of the land on which he lives and of the tools he works with." [73] If the peasant lacks these things, it is because they have been taken away from him.[74] Yet even the smallholder must pay taxes in order to keep what he owns. "Nine-tenths of the Russian people hire themselves out when taxes are being collected, and on account of those taxes." [75] Some survive; some do not. The peasant pays money in order to avoid violence; he works for others in order to avoid starving. "The slaves yield up their labor and at the same time believe that they give it up not because their masters wish it, but because, for their own freedom and welfare, service and bloody sacrifice offered to a divinity called 'the State' are essential, and that while paying service to this divinity they remain free." [76]

The "chief public evil," then, turns out to be the government. Governments, enslaving by violence, have no moral feelings. They are usually in extreme want, for their supporters must be paid and wars must be fought. Statesmen cynically remark, "one must shear the peasant and not let him get overgrown." [77]

Other public evils are the church, universities, science, and art. Their principals "produce nothing palpable or useful to the people, and [their] goods find no demand, but yet (pleading the division of labour) [they] boldly demand to be well fed and well dressed." [78] The church serves only to justify people in their bad lives. Art has lost its purpose; hiding behind "art for art's sake," it purveys idle and pernicious amusements. "We priests of science and art are the most worthless frauds, with far less right to our position than the most cunning and depraved church priests." [79] The "establishment" does nothing practical on behalf of the people. "We do not even know what the working folk need, we have forgotten their manner of life, their view of things, and their way of speaking. . . ." [80]

In describing the conditions of life of the majority of the people, Tolstoy often reported his feeling of shame. He collected money for them in Moscow, contributing much of his own. He was still ashamed of his wealth and privileges and spoke of "chucking away farthings with one hand to those whom it pleased me to select, while gathering thousands from the poor with the other!" [81] His charitable impulses came to nothing. He soon realized that the misfortunes of the poor "could not be repaired by external means and that unless their views of life were changed they could not be happy in any position." [82] One can set some of them on their feet for a time, but it does not last long. Thus Tolstoy's "fruitless attempt to aid the unfortunates" of Moscow.

He finally resolved to remove himself completely from society. "It is really so simple. If I want to aid the poor, that is, to help the poor not to be poor, I ought not to make them poor." [83] So he devised "colonies" where men could live and work together in just, practical, and loving ways, in simple rural settings. Why shouldn't a learned man or an artist "plough or cart manure?" [84]

NOTES

1 Barbara W. Tuchman, *The Proud Tower* (New York: Bantam Books, 1967), p. 77.

2 Proudhon, quoted in Tucker, p. 26.

3 Stirner, p. 237.

4 Kropotkin, *Revolutionary Pamphlets*, p. 197.

5 *Ibid.*, p. 140.

6 *Ibid.*

7 *Ibid.*, pp. 196–197.

8 See *ibid.*, p. 206.

9 Berkman, p. 15.

10 Kropotkin, *Revolutionary Pamphlets*, p. 214.

11 "Only go into the jails and study what man becomes when he is deprived of freedom and shut up with other depraved beings, steeped in the vice and corruption which oozes from the very walk of our existing prisons." *Ibid.*, p. 217. The classic anarchist account of what prison does to man is Alexander Berkman, *Prison Memoirs of an Anarchist* (New York: Mother Earth Publishing Association, 1912). Oscar Wilde's "The Ballad of Reading Gaol" is an excellent poetic source. For example: "The vilest deeds like prison weeds,/ Bloom well in prison air;/ It is only what is good in Man/ That wastes and withers there:/ Pale Anguish keeps the heavy gate,/ And the Warder is Despair."

12 Berkman, *Now and After*, p. 79.

13 Kropotkin, *Revolutionary Pamphlets*, p. 72.

14 See *ibid.*, p. 222.

15 *Ibid.*, p. 268.

16 Berkman, *Prison Memoirs of an Anarchist*, p. 225.

17 See *ibid.*, pp. 224, 432–433, 451, etc.

18 Berkman, *Now and After*, p. 27.

19 Bakunin, *The Political Philosophy*, p. 101. Attributed to Quetelet.

[20] Kropotkin, *Revolutionary Pamphlets,* p. 289.

[21] Bakunin, *The Political Philosophy,* p. 249.

[22] Most of what he says also applies to universities.

[23] Paul Goodman, *People or Personnel* (New York: Random House, 1963), pp. 180, 184.

[24] *Ibid.,* p. 183.

[25] Alexander Comfort, *Authority and Delinquency in the Modern State* (London: Routledge and Kegan Paul, Ltd., 1950), p. xi.

[26] *Ibid.,* p. 16.

[27] *Ibid.,* p. 83.

[28] *Ibid.,* p. 84.

[29] Colin Ward, quoted in Krimerman and Perry, p. 386.

[30] Tucker, p. 159.

[31] Bakunin, *The Political Philosophy,* p. 217.

[32] "Men who were democrats and rebels of the reddest variety when they were a part of the mass of governed people, became exceedingly moderate when they rose to power." *Ibid.,* p. 218.

[33] Sorel, *Reflections on Violence,* p. 89.

[34] *Ibid.,* p. 173.

[35] Tucker, p. 158.

[36] Sorel, p. 228.

[37] Bakunin, *The Political Philosophy,* p. 138.

[38] *Ibid.,* p. 139. Bakunin had much to say about patriotism. See *ibid.,* pp. 139–142, 225–236, 324–326. Patriotism, he argued, had a "bestial origin" and has not improved much.

[39] Berkman, *Now and After,* p. 128.

[40] Kropotkin, *Revolutionary Pamphlets,* p. 183.

[41] Tucker, *Instead of a Book,* p. 361.

[42] Some examples: insecurity in the workers' livelihood, the difference between what is produced by the profit system and what could be produced with modern technology, men becoming appendages to machines, the ironical effect that labor-saving devices have on workers' lives, periodic depressions ("What economists call over-production is but a production that is above the purchasing power of the worker, who is reduced to poverty by capital and State." Kropotkin, *Revolutionary Pamphlets,* p. 127), the necessity of the worker to sell his labor (power) for wages, in an amount far less than the value which that labor-power will produce, the concern of capitalists to acquire markets abroad and the resulting imperialism and warfare.

[43] See Chapter 3.

[44] Berkman, *Now and After,* p. 7.

[45] Stephen Pearl Andrews, "Cost the Limit of Price," in *The Science of Society* (Second Edition) (New York: Fowlers and Wells, 1852), p. 43.

[46] "The True Constitution of Government," in *ibid.,* p. 65.

[47] Tucker, p. 6.

[48] *Ibid.,* p. 9.

[49] *Ibid.,* p. 265.

50 "Ground-rent exists only because the State stands by to collect it and to protect land-titles rooted in force or fraud. Otherwise the land would be free to all, and no one could control more than he used." *Ibid.*, p. 178.

51 John Beverley Robinson, *The Economics of Liberty* (Minneapolis: Herman Kuehn, 1916), p. 70.

52 "The fraud in regard to money consists . . . in limiting by law the security for these promises to pay to a special kind of property, gold, silver, limited in quantity and easily monopolizable. . . . As a matter of fact, the holders of good redeemable money seldom ask for any other redemption than its acceptance in the market and its final cancellation by the issuer's restoration of the securities on which it was issued." Benjamin R. Tucker, *op. cit.*, pp. 271–272.

53 See Chapter 6.

54 Robinson, p. 91.

55 Berkman, *Prison Memoirs of an Anarchist*, p. 22.

56 See, for example, Frank Lanham, "Two Kinds of Unionism: Some Basic Ideas," *Why?*, 5:2 (April 1947); Sam Weiner, *Ethics and American Unionism* (New York: The Libertarian League, 1958). Excerpts from these are printed in Krimerman and Perry.

57 Bakunin, *The Political Philosophy*, p. 133.

58 *Ibid.*, p. 135.

59 At one point Bakunin called him "the illustrious leader of German Communism" and referred to "his magnificent work *Das Kapital.*" *Ibid.*, p. 187.

60 See *ibid.*, pp. 182–188.

61 See *ibid.*, pp. 188–193.

62 See *ibid.*, pp. 193–199.

63 See *ibid.*, pp. 199–203.

64 *Ibid.*, p. 243.

65 *Ibid.*, p. 247.

66 Tolstoy pointed out interesting parallels to the leisure class with respect to ability, motivation, and discipline for work. For both the rich and the destitute, "the ideal of an industrious life has been replaced by the ideal of a magic purse." *What Then Must We Do?*, p. 99.

67 *Ibid.*, pp. 39–40.

68 *Ibid.*, p. 60.

69 Leo Tolstoy, *The Slavery of Our Times*, Aylmer Maude, Trans. (Maldon, Essex: The Free Age Press, 1900), p. 40.

70 Tolstoy, *What Then Must We Do?*, p. 73.

71 *Ibid.*, p. 80.

72 Tolstoy, *The Slavery of Our Times*, p. 49.

73 Tolstoy, *What Then Must We Do?*, p. 108 (emphasis added).

74 "The produce of man's toil passes more and more from the labouring people to those who do no labour." *Ibid.*, p. 98.

75 *Ibid.*, p. 153.

76 *Ibid.*, p. 160.

77 See *ibid.*, p. 127.

78 *Ibid.*, p. 255.

[79] *Ibid.,* p. 303.

[80] *Ibid.,* p. 264.

[81] *Ibid.,* p. 95.

[82] *Ibid.,* p. 40.

[83] *Ibid.,* p. 100.

[84] *Ibid.,* p. 268.

5

Revolution

GENERAL CONSIDERATIONS

In this book the term "revolution" means the more or less rapid and drastic alteration in the political form of a state, promptly resulting in basic economic and other social changes throughout society. In this sense all anarchists—of whatever sort—are revolutionists. To eliminate government entirely is indeed a drastic alteration in political form. The anarchists, furthermore, seek other deep-reaching social changes. The world has already seen many *political* revolutions in which regimes have been replaced with only a slight or moderate alteration of the fabric of society itself. The anarchists demand a radical and fundamental change within society. This is more likely to take place through the *elimination* of government than through *replacing* one form with another. Thus the *people,* rather than government officials, transform society.[1] To use terms like "rapid" and "prompt" in the definition is to infect it with vagueness. But this is appropriate, for it would be arbitrary to specify precisely the time limit for completing the revolutionary process. At any rate all anarchists wish for the changes to come as quickly as possible; they do not see the new society as an ideal dimly beckoning in the future.

There is, however, much disagreement among the anarchists on the forms the revolution will take. Is it to be peaceful, violent, or a combination of both? Is it to be an individual matter or a group effort? How well organized is it to be? These differences will become apparent in succeeding sections. Here the aim is to state some of the anarchists' general ideas on the tactics and strategy of bringing in the new society.

Rejection of Politics

The first thing to note is the rejection of political means. Bakunin criticized the German socialists for trying to reform the state as a prerequisite for social changes under the aegis of a popular government. The workers, he warned, are thus made allies of the bourgeoisie and become patriotic—against their real interests and those of their comrades in other countries.[2] Against this strategy he quotes the program of the International: "The emancipation of the toilers can be the work only of the toilers themselves." Emma Goldman often commented on "the corruption and confusion created among the proletariat . . . by 'democratic' liberty and self-government."[3] Berkman, with typical passion, wrote: "The very essence of politics is corruption, sail-trimming, the sacrifice of your ideals and integrity for success. Bitter are the fruits of that 'success' for the masses and for every decent man and woman the world over."[4] Sorel had the greatest contempt for all politicians and for the career of politics. His infatuation for the syndicates was based upon their refusal to play politics; he hated the "parliamentary socialists" because they did. Anarchists, wrote Kropotkin, "do not seek to constitute, and invite the workingmen not to constitute, political parties in the parliaments."[5] Anarchists should not participate in parliamentary intrigue. Why risk corruption for the sake of piecemeal improvement which is no improvement at all? "When the reformer is honest he is a fool; when he is a politician he is a knave."[6]

The anarchists did not value the right to vote. Most of them abstained from participating in elections as a matter of principle. They spurned it as a tactic (such a means is incompatible with the end) and opposed recognizing the legitimacy of government and giving it even a fraction of a mandate. In more cynical terms Tucker wrote: "Now, what is the ballot? It is neither more nor less than a paper representative of the bayonet, the billy, and the bullet. It is a labor-saving device for ascertaining on which side force lies and bowing to the inevitable."[7] Should we try to purify or reform the government? asked Adin Ballou. No, he answered, because there is nothing good in it to purify. "We have nothing to do with nations, states, and bodies politic, merely *as such;* for they have neither souls nor consciences."[8]

There is one other important aspect to this principle of non-politics. Bakunin stated it innumerable times. The revolution is not to be simply a *political* revolution. There have been enough of these in the past. One regime succeeds another regime; one dominant class is replaced by another dominant class. The masses who do the fighting never benefit. But even if they did, the revolution would still fail to be an *anarchist* revolution. The anarchist revolution must be a *social* one—that is, society itself (especially its economic institutions) must be transformed *along with* the destruction of the state. This must not be permitted to depend on political changes that, one is told, must precede it. "Bourgeois" socialists all over the world would violate this injunction. Marxists are especially suspect. "They are the enemies of the existing powers-that-be only because they cannot take their places." [9] All anarchists are clear that their revolution aims not at transferring power from one set of rulers to another, but at abolishing both the institution of authority and the social system upon which it rests.

Other Principles

The second principle (and agreement on this is not as widespread as on the first) is to recognize the consistency of means and end. This is the general principle under which some anarchists subsume their decision to stay out of politics. Why use the state as a means for eliminating the state? The accommodating means chosen by unionism and socialism, for example, have corrupted their grand aims: they are no longer revolutionary. Emma Goldman distinguished the outlook of the anarchists sharply from that of the Jesuits and Bolsheviks, who hold that the end justifies any means. Actually, she says, methods cannot be separated from the ultimate aim.

> The means employed become, through individual habit and social practice, part and parcel of the final purpose; they influence it, modify it, and presently the aims and means become identical. . . . The whole history of man is continuous proof of the maxim that to divest one's methods of ethical concepts means to sink into the depths of utter demoralization. . . . No revolution can ever succeed as a factor of liberation unless the MEANS used to further it be identical in spirit and tendency with the purposes to be achieved.[10]

We see this principle preached in the same way both by Tolstoy, who advocated methods of love for creating a society bound together by love, and by others who would use the methods of peaceful disobedience against violent, dominating states.

The second principle is also behind the familiar anarchist view that revolutionary bodies be organized in ways similar to the associations that will exist in the good society. There is to be a great deal of autonomy for them, with no centralized authority at the top. Even Bakunin, who loved secrecy and conspiracy, was very lax in organizational discipline. The individualists, of course, advocated individualistic revolutionary action. And finally, in the case of syndicalism, the groups that are to constitute the new society are to be the very groups that will overturn the old one.

Third, there is an inclusiveness about anarchists: bring as many people as possible into the movement—not just the manual workers, but the intelligentsia (engineers, industrial experts, doctors, scientists, artists, etc.) and peasantry as well. Emma Goldman stressed this,[11] and Leo Tolstoy thought it just as necessary for the salvation of the intelligentsia as for the workers among whom they would labor. Much of the anarchists' propaganda was directed to the peasants. Bakunin had great concern for their future and great interest in their revolutionary potential. The proletarians, natural leaders in a revolution, should not scorn them. Ignorant and conservative though they may be, they are physically strong, know how to work, and resent parasites. Organize them, burn their mortgages, abolish their debts. In most countries they will, when aroused, constitute an invincible army. Bakunin also appealed to those who were outside (or below) classes. His favorite term for revolutionary recruits to anarchism is "drudge-people"—"the perpetual victims of civilization, the martyrs of history," the people who had "nothing to renounce and nothing to break away from." [12]

Fourth, there is concern for education. Schools should be reformed. Progressive schools should be established in which children can experience the blessings of self-direction and independence. A proper course of study will explode all the clichés about the necessity of government and authority. Science especially must cease to be the exclusive possession of the privileged few. Both natural and social science are effective avenues to power—for understanding the world and for changing it.

Taking the term "education" in a somewhat broader sense, we note that the anarchists were tireless writers of books and articles; they had their own presses and periodicals. It was important to them to expound their doctrines and to win converts. Also in this broader sense we can take note of the training in libertarian living and revolutionary or social solidarity (if these are not contradictory) that the anarchists expected their voluntary associations—from experimental communities to industrial syndicates—to supply.

INDIVIDUAL PROTEST

All the ways of revolution—the peaceful means of moral resistance, the direct action of syndicates, and the insurrection of organized groups—require the dedicated action of the individual. But the way of individual protest is supposed to achieve a moral realization of satisfaction for its adherents far out of proportion to the changes it actually brings about in society. The individual protestor may indeed favor a successful movement by an organized group with the concrete social changes that involves, but in the meantime he can accomplish his own revolution in his own mind. Finally it may be noted that the method of individual protest can be peaceful or violent; it thus overlaps with material discussed in the next section.[13]

The style of individual protest is well exemplified by Max Stirner. His form of resistance is based on utter defiance of all powers that would limit his freedom or contain his egoism. The demands of God, moral law, family, country, or humanity are not to be simply rejected, but ridiculed as well. The individual bows only to force, and then only when he has to—and provisionally. "I get around a rock that stands in my way, till I have powder enough to blast it; I get around the laws of a people, till I have gathered strength to overthrow them. . . ."[14] Stirner declared himself an enemy of the state, "the established system," against establishment itself.

How is the state to be destroyed? Stirner offered no practical program, no tactics or strategy. Resistance may be physical or mental, but at all times it is to be *spiritual*—that of the thoroughly rebellious ego. Despite his insistence and rhetoric, Stirner's work apparently was only a literary gesture, a philosophical pose, for he did nothing to weaken the establishment. Perhaps he had hopes for the younger generation: "The impudent lads will no longer let anything be whined and chattered into them by you, and will have no sympathy for all the follies for which you have been raving and driveling since the memory of man began; they will not be willing to inherit your stupidities as you have inherited them from your fathers. . . ." [15]

Propaganda by the Deed

The most famous (or infamous) form of individual protest is that known as "propaganda by the deed." These deeds were to be violent (assassination preferred) and calculated to produce widespread publicity. A great many such deeds occurred in the two decades or so at the end of the nineteenth century. An anarchist newspaper in the United States (to which Most had emigrated) published this exhortation: "Dynamite! Of all the good stuff, that is the stuff. Stuff several pounds of this sublime stuff into an inch of pipe . . . plug up both ends, insert a cap with a fuse attached, place this in the vicinity of a lot of rich loafers who live by the sweat of other people's brows, and light the fuse. A most cheerful and gratifying result will follow. . . . A pound of this good stuff beats a bushel of ballots hollow—and don't you forget it!" [16]

In 1878 the Italian King and Prime Minister were attacked and wounded by a man carrying a knife on which was inscribed, "Long live the international republic!" Soon after bombs were thrown into crowds of people in Italy celebrating royal events. In 1879 unsuccessful attempts were made to murder the German Kaiser and the King of Spain. No anarchist connection was ever proved, but anarchists praised the deeds. In 1881 Czar Alexander II was assassinated by agents of the People's Will. In 1886 a bomb was thrown (allegedly by anarchists) into a throng of policemen trying to break up an assembly of strikers in Haymarket Square, Chicago. In 1892 an anarchist in Spain threw a bomb at a general who had executed four anarchists the year before. Another anarchist then threw a bomb into a theater in Barcelona, killing twenty people. Shortly afterward the Spanish Prime Minister was murdered by an anarchist. A bomb was thrown into a music hall in France. In 1893 an anarchist named Vaillant threw a bomb into the French Chamber of Deputies. A year later an Italian anarchist stabbed to death the French President, Sadi Carnot. A bomb-thrower named Ravachol obtained notoriety for his violent deeds, actual and suspected. Another famous self-styled anarchist was Emile Henry, who killed five policemen with a bomb planted in the offices of a mining company. In 1900, two years after the assassination of the Empress of Austria, the King of Italy was assassinated by anarchists. In 1892 Alexander

Berkman tried to assassinate Henry Clay Frick, Chairman of the Board of the Carnegie Corporation. President William McKinley was assassinated in 1901 by a young Pole, believed by the authorities to be an anarchist. In 1912 a second Spanish premier was assassinated. These are some of the more publicized acts of anarchist violence.

On what theoretical ground were they justified? What was their purpose? There were several: (1) To demonstrate to workers and their leaders the power of anarchism and its ruthless determination. Some anarchists in this period were willing to "take credit" for violent actions in which anarchists were not involved. (2) To incite terror in the hearts of the establishment. Many governments did indeed believe that they were threatened by a vast worldwide revolutionary conspiracy. (3) To physically weaken the power of the establishment. (4) To get revenege for specific acts of injustice or for the system of repression in general. (5) To demonstrate contempt for the establishment. This contempt was not limited, of course, to the political establishment. It extended to commercial and recreational aspects of bourgeois society. There was one fanatic who even wanted to bomb a school in order to destroy the next bourgeois generation. (6) To awaken the interest of the people in the anarchist cause and to bring about understanding. Berkman wrote of his own deed: "This is the first terrorist act in America. The People may fail to comprehend it thoroughly. Yet they will know that an anarchist committed the deed. I will talk to them from the courtroom. And my comrades at liberty will use the opportunity to the utmost to shed light on the questions involved. Such a deed must draw the attention of the world. This first act of voluntary anarchist sacrifice will make the workingman think deeply." [17] (7) To achieve moral salvation for the assassin himself, who offers his own life for the cause. Commenting on the Haymarket riots, Berkman wrote: "The tragedy of 1887 lacked the element of voluntary self-sacrifice in the interests of the People. In that distinctive quality my act is initial." [18] An anarchist newspaper in Switzerland praised the would-be assassin of the Kaiser: "Humanity will preserve the memory of the tinsmith Hoedel, who was prepared to sacrifice his life to make a superb act of defiance against society, and, as his blood spurted beneath the executioner's axe, was able to inscribe his name on the long list of martyrs who have shown the people the way to a better future, towards the abolition of all economic and political slavery." [19]

Rarely was the act expected to touch off a real revolution. The unlikelihood of this was one factor that finally led anarchist leaders to deplore "propaganda by the deed." [20] Too often innocent people perished with the rest.[21] "What matter the victims," wrote an anarchist poet, "provided the gesture is beautiful?" "What matters the death of vague human beings, if thereby the individual affirms himself?" [22] It did matter, however, to humane leaders like Kropotkin. Indeed, we find no front-rank theoreticians of anarchism supporting "propaganda by the deed." Bakunin came the closest to it, but he was dead by 1876. The Italian leaders, Errico Malatesta and Carlo Cafiero, expounded the idea. Another problem was the difficulty in drawing the line between "direct action" against illegitimate authority and ordinary criminality. One anarchist, Clément Duval, was arrested for burglary. In his defense he said: "The policeman arrested me in the name of the law; I hit him in the name of liberty." [23] Anyone who flouted laws could claim that morally he was innocent because he did not acknowledge an obligation to obey that which is the "arch-crime of the centuries," the law.[24] Does this mean that he was an anarchist, devoted to freeing his beloved fellow human beings from subjection? He could be merely a psychopathic marauder, hostile to everything and everyone.[25] Some anarchists, however, Johann Most and Elisée Reclus, for example, tended to view criminality as itself anarchistic: the criminal, whether a conscious anarchist or not, is simply striking back at the society that has treated him so badly.

Ironically, at about the same time that "propaganda by the deed" was enjoying its only real vogue, responsible thinkers like Kropotkin and Tucker were trying to express anarchism as a reasonable and even respectable political theory!

THE WAY OF PEACE

Proudhon, Ballou, Tolstoy, and Robinson

If Bakunin was the inspiration of violent protest, Proudhon, that other great founder of modern anarchistic thought, was the forerunner of the peaceful way. As a revolutionist he was prepared to defend the actions of violent rebels. But he himself was a man of peace. Rather than *overthrow* the state, he would establish voluntary associations *within* the state. These associations, not having governments in any usual sense of the word, would not interfere with personal liberty. The economic life of each association would be such as to require no rigid authority, for there would be no exploitation to enforce, no privileges to protect, and no special interests to serve. Associations could choose to combine or federate, if they thought it would serve their mutual benefit. The state, Proudhon believed, would be shown obviously to be superfluous; finally, as the associations spread throughout the nation, the state would dissolve. The state is destroyed, not through force, but through "dissolution in the economic organism." [26]

A predecessor to Tolstoy in the ranks of Christian anarchists was the New Englander Adin Ballou.[27] Holding the familiar Christian principle that one "ought to obey God rather than men," [28] Ballou went on to argue that human government has "no intrinsic authority—no moral supremacy—no rightful claim to the allegiance of man." [29] Governments should be superseded by "the spiritual regeneration of their individual subjects—by implanting in their minds higher principles of feeling and action—by giving them *heavenly* instead of *earthly* motives." [30] Rather than provoking or antagonizing governments, the Christian is to adopt the attitude of non-resistance. Non-resistance is to characterize all his relations with others—thieves and murderers as well as magistrates and policemen. Love is "morally irresistible" and will prevail over the hearts of men more surely than violence. Power, on the other hand, "oftener corrupts its possessor than benefits the powerless." [31]

Such an individual reaction to government makes irrelevant the questions of where and when the revolution is to begin. The new society, like the kingdom of God, begins in the hearts of man. One can begin to act freely now, whatever the consequences. He can act now as he would act in the anarchist society. Such anarchists believe that "any man can free himself from the bonds of social causality. All behavior can be self-governing and individualized." [32]

The most famous proponent of the way of peace was Leo Tolstoy. Like Ballou, he accepted non-violence as a principle. Like Proudhon, he would create good societies in the midst of the bad society. Refusing to use his wealth for the exploitation of the labor and souls of others, he retired to a peasant's house in order to work with his hands in association with those of kindred spirit from all ranks. Tolstoy resolved "to reject the belief in [his] own righteousness and in privileges and peculiarities distinguishing [him] from others, and to acknowledge [himself] as being to blame." [33] All rich, educated, and privileged people should make the same resolution.

Tolstoy adhered to a "pure Christianity" and depended on it to bring men together in loving accord. His Christianity was not based on any church or institution. It was based on neither the sovereignty of God nor the divinity of Christ. It was based on Jesus' teaching of brotherhood and sacrifice. Violence, he taught, only leads to more violence; at best it produces an armed truce. Only love can break the circle. Men are never won over by force; they are won over by love. In suffering more pain than one inflicts, one never gives others any reason to hate. Love does not, however, *have* to win; it suffices, and therefore never loses.

Robinson took an interesting position. As a self-styled egoist, he eschewed moral declamations. But his feelings were much like Tolstoy's. He abhorred violence in all its forms. The good society would not have it (not even for criminals), and it should not be the means for bringing the new society into existence. He called himself a "non-resistant" and refused to retaliate in kind to the violence perpetrated by the state or individual. Men get out of a state of warfare by refusing to fight. When men contend, who can say who is right and who is wrong? "To compel by violence is to govern, and . . . Anarchists who protest against government, should begin by saying: We will govern nobody. We will do no violence." [34] Sociality requires that men bring kindness and understanding to their fellows; retaliation brings pain—it is aggression, a "reversion to an ancestral type." "Anarchism halts as a system of philosophy as long as it uses violence at all." [35]

Tucker

Despite the fierceness of his polemics against his many enemies, anarchists and "archists" alike, Benjamin R. Tucker was a man of peace.[36] His choice of peaceful methods was dictated not by moral or religious principles but by expedience. It was not practical to shoot politicians, dynamite gangs of policemen, or organize armies of insurrection. The force that the state had at its disposal was simply too great for any expectation of success.

There was no more consistent and vehement critic of Johann Most, August Spies, Albert Parsons, and Alexander Berkman than their fellow anarchist Tucker. He did not criticize the terrorists on moral grounds (an invaded individual may choose any method he likes), but on grounds of inexpedience. Bloodshed is of no avail; it merely strengthens the will of the establishment, which has most of the weapons anyhow. The state is the master in the use of violence. Why challenge them on that ground? "I am more desirous of being saved from friends like Berkman, to whom my heart goes out, than from enemies like Frick, from whom my heart withdraws. The worst enemy of the human race is folly, and men like Berkman are its incarnation. It would be comparatively easy to dispose of the Fricks if it were not for the Berkmans. The latter are the hope of the former. The strength of the Fricks rests on violence; now it is to violence that the Berkmans appeal. The peril of the Fricks lies in the spreading of the light; violence is the power of darkness. If the revolution comes by violence and in advance of light, the old struggle will have to begin anew. The hope of humanity lies in the avoidance of that revolution by force which the Berkmans are trying to precipitate." [37]

Tucker also rejected the other extreme: that of retreating from ordinary society to establish ideal anarchist communities. What would occasional success here prove? How many people would be freed? "I care nothing for any reform that cannot be effected right here in Boston among the every-day people whom I meet upon the streets." [38]

Instead of fighting or retreating, Tucker would write and argue. He would "sell" the virtues of anarchism to as many people as he could, while pointing out the idiocies and injustice of existing governments and of government *per se*. People would come to realize that the state, far from being a "necessary evil," was an unnecessary evil. A cogent reasoner, a clever and forceful polemicist, a master of clear expression, Tucker was a superb propagandist for anarchism.

When the way had been prepared, then the method of passive resistance could be employed. Conducted by isolated individuals, it is propaganda: the individual goes to jail, exposing the invasive character of the state. Others may follow his example. Every step is to be publicized in anarchist and non-anarchist journals. But passive resistance is more effective when it is well organized and conducted on a large scale. The "Pay No Rent" policy of the Land League movement in Ireland is an example of successful mass resistance. [39]

In the United States passive resistance could most appropriately and effectively be employed against that "life principle of all the monopolies": compulsory taxation. It is in levying taxes that the *invasive* aspect of government is most nakedly in view. Money is seized by force and used by the state to enforce anything else it wants—including the economic monopolies by which workers are robbed of their just reward. No individual or group of individuals should accept this aggression if any defense can successfully be mounted against it.[40] Without money the state cannot survive; with a decrease in tax receipts it is crippled. "If one-fifth of the people were to resist taxation, it would cost more to collect their taxes, or try to collect them, than the other four-fifths would consent to pay into the treasury. The force needed for this bloodless fight *Liberty* is slowly but surely recruiting, and sooner or later it will organize for action. Then, Tyranny and Monopoly, down goes your house!" [41]

Resistance to paying rent and taxes, together with the creation of mutualist banks, would indeed cause the state to dissolve in the economy. The means used would be consistent with the aim, for they negate the government while at the same time gradually building a new society. "The idea that Anarchy can be inaugurated by force is as fallacious as the idea that it can be sustained by force." [42] The abolition of government could take place in stages, then, beginning with mutualist banks, proceeding to refusal to pay taxes, and finally, perhaps, land reform. At the same time the power of government outside the realm of economics will be waning while that of individualism and voluntary associations wax.[43]

SYNDICALISM:
DIRECT ACTION

The Power of the Proletariat

Although both Proudhon and Bakunin were particularly interested in the condition of the peasants, they did suggest that factory workers could also combine for anarchistic purposes. The watchmakers of the Jura had done so. Industrial anarchism was most conspicuous in France, where the distinction between socialistic politics and trade unionism was always clear. In the 1880s workers formed *syndicats* or unions in individual factories or industries. Soon *Bourses du Travail* were developed on a local geographic basis, and in 1892 these were combined into a national *Fédération des Bourses du Travail.* The Syndicates formed their own combination in 1895: the *Confédération Générale du Travail.* The two union movements united in 1902, retaining the name of the latter. The CGT was now composed of both *syndicats* and *bourses.* Each *syndicat* was expected to belong to a *bourse.* Syndicalism later proved more effective in Spain than in France. The *Confederación Nacional de Trabajo* (CNT) was founded in 1911 and modeled after the CGT. Syndicalism also had its expression in other countries, although not so clearly. It is usually found as a rival to working-class movements stressing political action.

Syndicates differ from ordinary trade unions in two important ways: organization and function. They are not organized bureaucratically with power coming down from centralized authority. Each syndicate preserves its authority and can conduct *ad hoc* action whenever its membership wishes. Combined in great industrial alliances, they present a united but flexible front. The larger syndicates or federations should "weld the workers together as a class and prevent the rise of any narrow-minded factional spirit. In times of local labour trouble they arrange for the solidaric co-operation of the whole body of organized labour in the use of every agency available under the circumstances." [44]

The function of the syndicates is to achieve revolutionary goals through direct action. The converse of this is to "reject any participation in the work of bourgeois parliaments . . . ; they are firmly convinced that parliamentary activity is for the workers the very weakest and most helpless form of political struggle." [45] This is so because the economic system, which is the source of their exploitation, is and always will be protected by the state: it sets the stamp of legality to all the social injustice. It is a common anarchist view, not limited to the syndicalists, that the interests of workers and capitalists are forever separate.[46] There is, therefore, no satisfactory or permanent solution for their conflict within the present system. The syndicates may, however, without losing their revolutionary integrity, bargain with employers for better working conditions. And they are continuously to serve "as the school for the intellectual training of the workers to make them acquainted with the technical management of production and economic life in general so that when a revolutionary situation arises they will be capable of taking the social-economic organism into their own hands. . . ." [47]

What forms is direct action to take? The ordinary strike, which forces an industry to give in to demands, is one. The social strike is another; here the workers, in a spirit of social responsibility, refuse to use inferior or spoiled materials in building, manufacturing clothing, preparing foods, etc. Sabotage is an effective tactic; it is expressed in the slogan "for bad wages, bad work." The workers must realize what power they have. They literally have the means of production (upon which modern society depends) in their own hands. The best form of direct action is the general strike. "At one blow it brings the whole economic system to a standstill and shakes it to its foundations." [48] And this could be the beginning of the final revolution that will demolish government and privilege once and for all.

Sublimity

The above sounds too reasonable, too utilitarian. For Sorel consequences seem almost irrelevant. He was impressed by the moral dimensions of direct action, and for morality heroism is more important than utility. Hating the cunning and corruption of the business community and all politicians, he called for the working class with all its instinctive decency and ferocity to achieve its own violent salvation, a salvation to be signalized in a final catastrophic upheaval. Calculation and prudence finally give way to sublimity.

Proletarian violence differs from trade union negotiation and compromise in the same way that war differs from politics. Violence has a glorious history, from lynch law in the United States to the French Revolution. The workers must not be allowed to suffer the fate of the German barbarians—who conquered, then were tamed by, the Roman Empire. "It may be questioned whether there is not a little stupidity in the admiration of our contemporaries for gentle methods." [49] There is a great ideal to be won (like the Christian apocalypse), a vicious contemptible system to be destroyed. "War, carried on in broad daylight, without hypocritical attenuation, for the purpose of ruining an irreconcilable enemy, excludes all the abominations which dishonoured the middle-class revolution of the eighteenth century. The apology for violence in this case is particularly easy." [50]

Sorel's preference for a higher road to truth than reason is exemplified in his theory of the myth. Myths have produced the great movements of history—which philosophy cannot understand. Utopias are intellectual products and can be disputed; but those who are possessed by a myth, a vision, cannot be refuted. Early Christians achieved great things while under the spell of the myth of the Church militant. Napoleon's soldiers were irresistible simply because they were committed to the myth of bringing the Revolution to all of Europe. "All that is best in the modern mind is derived from this 'torment of the infinite.'"[51] Anyone can find rational objections to myths—if he is "anxious to find a pretext for abandoning any active role, for remaining revolutionary in words only."[52]

Myth is extremely important to the cause of the working class. The greatest myth of the working class is the myth of the general strike. This is the myth "in which Socialism is wholly comprised, *i.e.* a body of images capable of evoking instinctively all the sentiments which correspond to the different manifestations of the war undertaken by Socialism against modern society."[53] Sorel disdained to give details about the way the general strike will work. The influence of the French philosopher Henri Bergson (whom he often cited) is evident when he insists that the general strike must be seen as an undivided whole. "We thus obtain that intuition of Socialism which language cannot give us with perfect clearness—and we obtain it as a whole, perceived instantaneously."[54]

Three final quotations from Sorel: On the ethics of the movement: "This striving toward perfection which manifests itself, in spite of the absence of any personal, immediate, and proportional reward, constitutes the *secret virtue* which assures the continued progress of the world."[55] On the means and end of the movement: "It is to violence that Socialism owes those high ethical values by means of which it brings *salvation* to the modern world."[56] Renan's question: "Religious people live on a shadow. We live on the shadow of a shadow. On what will those who come after us live?"[57] Answer: the myth of the general strike.

It is not only the syndicalist who sees the general strike as the best means of making a revolution. Other collectivists, including communist anarchists, have recommended it. In modern times an armed insurrection could not be expected to prevail over machine guns, tanks, and aircraft. But the workers could effectively harm the state by refusing, all of them, to work. The whole society could be brought to its knees by refusal on the part of the workers in just one important industry (on a national scale would be better; international best of all) to perform their tasks. The natural way to do this is for them to leave their places of work while preventing others from entering. Another way is for the workers to remain at their places while expelling foremen, managers, and strikebreakers.

ORGANIZED INSURRECTION

Bakunin

Although Bakunin is sometimes claimed as the source of the practice of "propaganda by the deed," [58] his actual preference in revolutionary strategy lay on the side of organized insurrection by secret bodies of dedicated anarchists. He was tireless in fomenting revolutions throughout Europe and in taking part in the fights. He sought the support of peasants as well as proletarians, making a special plea for the *"Lumpenproletariat"* despised by Marx. The backward countries, where ignorance and wretchedness were most widespread, would, he thought, supply many recruits. "We must not teach the people," Bakunin wrote, "but lead them to revolt." [59] Bakunin, active in Italy and Spain, thought the great revolution was soon to erupt in southern Europe. During the Franco-Prussian War he urged a great anarchist revolution in France and drafted many plans for utilizing the strength of the patriotic French peasants for driving out the Prussian Army and destroying the French regime. Organizations should grow, collect arms, and take cities or provinces when they could, hoping to bring in the masses for a full-fledged revolution that would topple the government of a nation. A handful of dedicated men could release the dormant revolutionism of thousands. "Whenever a few dozen persons combine to achieve a common objective, this gives birth to a new force which far exceeds the simple arithmetical sum of their isolated individual efforts." [60]

Bakunin's writings on revolution, however, are consistent neither with themselves nor with his actions. In the first place, he denied the efficacy of conspiracies of devoted revolutionists. Participation, or at least cooperation, of the millions is required. Proletarian workers must be recruited. They must be organized and regimented. The approach must be directed to their immediate economic problems, "Their particular, daily, altogether private misfortunes." [61] Trade union work is essential. Strikes must be conducted and won.

Confident militancy must be engendered. There is no significant word more used by Bakunin in his discussion of preparing for revolution than *solidarity*. All programs and all actions are devised for the purpose of engendering a sense of solidarity among the masses. Solidarity is the opposite of "mutual alienation," which fragments the strength of the masses and makes them easy prey for their oppressors. Nothing must be clearer to the worker than the truth that by himself he is nothing, but in union with loyal comrades he can prevail over everything. All trades must be linked, and solidarity even on an international scale must be sought. Both short-range and long-range success require solidarity. In another context Bakunin called solidarity the "first human law." Freedom is the second! [62]

Always concerned for the help and welfare of the peasantry, Bakunin regarded the peasants as a special problem requiring special tactics. Collectivism should not be preached to them, proletarian workers should not dictate to them, educated cityfolk should not humiliate them. And their religion and patriotism should not be insulted. Above all, the organization and regimentation emphasized elsewhere is out of place. Revolutionary authorities "must not try to impose upon the masses any organization whatever, but rather should induce the people to set up autonomous organizations." [63] Leadership should be developed within their own ranks. With proper handling, the peasants *can* be provoked to action, for there are plenty of grievances in the countryside and in the villages.

The urban and rural masses, gaining confidence in smaller skirmishes, reassured by the very number of their comrades, and secure in their solidarity, may finally become educable to the proposition that the economic and social gains they are making will eventually lead to a fundamental social revolution in which their masters will be totally defeated. They will be willing and able to smash all political and religious institutions at the same time they destroy the economic institutions which have oppressed them.

And a great deal of education will indeed be necessary. The workers and peasants are prejudiced and ignorant. They do not know their true interests nearly as well as the bourgeoisie know theirs. They do not know how to organize themselves. While still in the International, Bakunin advised "biding our time" while organizational and educational work was conducted. Discontent, despair, and misery are not enough. Nature has endowed mankind with too much patience.

Will the revolution, when it comes, be a violent one? When he was optimistic over the prospects of the International and its growth throughout Europe and America, Bakunin admitted the possibility of avoiding violence. "Should there be broken heads, it will be only because the bourgeoisie want it." [64] Later he lamented that revolution means war and that "every forward step in history has been achieved only after it has been baptized in blood." [65] Finally he was reconciled to "a terrible and bloody struggle." [66] Privileged classes will not give up their privileges unless they are forced to do so. "Philosophers have not understood that against political forces there can be no other guarantees but complete destruction." [67]

But with all the organization, education, solidarity, resoluteness, and dedicated leadership, one thing more is necessary for a successful revolution. This is an elusive, almost mystical element. Bakunin's clearest statement is this: "Revolutions are not improvised. They are not made arbitrarily by individuals nor even by the most powerful associations. They come independently of all will and all conspiracies, and are always brought on by the natural forces of circumstances." [68] The masses seem to move spontaneously. The people seem to be "stirred by a universal ideal evolving historically from the depths of the folk-instinct." [69] Dominant leaders, so necessary in the conduct of a merely political revolution, are almost superfluous. One can never, apparently, ever be sure precisely when the circumstances are right. This uncertainty, together with Bakunin's own passionate determination not to miss out on the great event, would explain his premature and always hopeful revolutionary activity.

Near the end of his life Bakunin seemed to have abandoned revolutionary theory entirely. In a remarkable passage entitled "In Time of Revolution Deeds Count More Than Theories," [70] he said that the time for developing theoretical principles *and applying them* had passed. Stating that it was now the time of revolution, while admitting that recruitment and organization of a large number of revolutionists in full knowledge of what they were about had not taken place, Bakunin was yet ready to embark. It was almost as if the prerequisites for revolution he had talked about before could now be created by the revolutionary actions themselves! "Now all of us have to embark upon the revolutionary high seas, and henceforth we shall have to spread our principles not through words, but *through actions, for that is the most popular, the most potent, and the most irresistible form of propaganda.*" [71]

Kropotkin

Usually removed from the actual struggle, Kropotkin was the most thoughtful of the revolutionists. His theory, as we have seen, purports to be based on biological and social evolution. Society is "an aggregation of organisms trying to find out the best ways of combining the wants of the individual with those of cooperation for the welfare of the species." [72] One tendency of evolution is thus to realize the fullest freedom of the individual in a way beneficial both to himself and to society. Another is to achieve this end by "integrating labor for the production of all riches in common," making it impossible to discern the fraction contributed by any individual.[73] The future, then, becomes a scientific or empirical question: What is the next stage of evolutionary progress?

In the past the system of serfdom supported the political form of monarchy; today the system of capitalism supports the form of representative government. Only when capitalism disappears, argued Kropotkin, can government disappear. Only when workers freely associate for cooperative production can they dispense with political (class) rule. The "fittest" finally turn out to be not merely those most knowledgable intellectually and productively, but those most attuned to the welfare and survival of their species.

That progress has indeed been made is indicated by the steps society has already taken toward communism. Kropotkin pointed out that we already have public museums, libraries, schools, parks, roads, etc., that are free to all without regard to how much each person uses them or how much he has contributed for them. Numerous free associations outside government have been formed which offer valuable help to its members and to others. "We already foresee a state of society where the liberty of the individual will be limited by no laws, no bond—by nothing else but his own social habits and the necessity, which everyone feels, of finding cooperation, support, sympathy among his neighbors." [74]

So history is on the anarchist's side. What should he be doing in the meantime? Kropotkin is irresolute. A kindly and peaceful man, he disliked terrorism and would prefer to see anarchism come nonviolently. But he was realistic enough to see the unlikelihood of such a means. He perceived "the necessity of a revolutionary whirlwind which will sweep away all this rottenness, revive sluggish hearts with its breath, and bring to mankind that spirit of devotion, self-denial, and heroism, without which society sinks through degradation and violence into complete disintegration." [75] He not only gave verbal support to organizations fomenting insurrection, but refused to condemn vengeance as a motive. [76] At the same time, however, he was realistic enough to see the unlikelihood for success of the premature forays against the state made by the Bakuninists in Italy. So, until the time became more propitious, Kropotkin was content to write in defense of the reasonableness and scientific inevitability of communistic anarchism. "A clandestine pamphlet was worth more than the terrorist's bomb or the assassin's dagger." [77] "It is not secret societies nor even revolutionary organizations that can give the finishing blow to governments. Their function, their historic mission is to prepare men's minds for the revolution, and then when men's minds are prepared and external circumstances are favorable, the final rush is made, not by the groups that initiated the movement, but by the mass of the people altogether outside of the society." [78]

In 1880, however, Kropotkin wrote of the importance of *action* on the part of individuals and minorities, courageous, daring, and (often) tragic actions "to keep the spirit alive, to propagate and find expression for dissatisfaction, to excite hatred against exploiters, to ridicule the government and expose its weakness, and above all and always, by actual example, to awaken courage and fan the spirit of revolt." [79] These "lonely sentinels" enter the battle early, and inspire others to follow. Theoreticians criticize them, label them as madmen, but "by actions which compel general attention, the new idea seeps into people's minds and wins converts. One such act may, in a few days, make more propaganda than thousands of pamphlets." [80] Rebellious actions not only rouse others to support the cause, but under propitious circumstances destroy the unity of the rulers. Some rulers will favor severe repression, others will favor token concession, while others will be willing to make significant concessions. None of these will work. Repression will stiffen the resistance; concession will encourage it. The masses, seeing how the enemy is wavering, will press forward for more concessions—and final victory. There is a time, then, when "premature" action will help create the conditions for, and will lead to, a true revolution.

In 1903 he again wrote of the preparatory stages of revolution. He referred to "incubation," the growth of hope, and increasingly bold action. Many individuals perish—not uselessly, as the "armchair critic" would say. But more and more people take a stand as the revolutionary spirit grows in strength and scope. Many revolts might occur before the successful revolution: "To wait therefore for a *social* revolution to come as a birthday present, without a whole series of protests on the part of the individual conscience, and without hundreds of preliminary revolts by which the very nature of the revolution is determined, is to say the least, absurd." [81] It was Kropotkin, not Bakunin, who spoke of "the grand work of destruction." [82]

Spooner

In the United States a man named Lysander Spooner had defended the right of armed insurrection in 1867. Man has more right to resist government than government has to restrain man. Man had been endowed by nature with the gift of individual freedom to seek his own happiness, without accepting any one as his master. How comes he, then, to be subject to government? The question is Rousseau's, but the answer is Spooner's. Subjection does not come about by consent, for no one *asks* him for consent. The fact that people obey the government, pay their taxes, and use the ballot is not equivalent to universal consent. They simply choose the lesser of bad alternatives. If government is not based on consent, no one is being disloyal or treasonable in resisting it—he gave no promises, pledged no vows. Moreover, since government is not based on consent, it must, for those who do *not* consent, be based on fraud and force. One is always justified in resisting a power so based. We honor the men of 1776, individuals unwilling to consent to the government of Great Britain, who revolted against that government. Those men then formed a *new* government, but they did not, Spooner reminds us, contract for anyone but themselves.

Spooner argued that the situation of men today is the same as it was in 1776, and ever will be. Individuals at any time can resist government without opprobrium. A person's citizenship is as voluntary and provisional as his church membership. This dilemma exemplifies Spooner's position: taxation without consent is either robbery or not robbery. If it is *not* robbery, then any group of people can legitimately demand money from anyone. If it *is* robbery, then every man "has the same natural right to defend his property against a tax-gatherer, that he has to defend it against a highwayman." [83]

Conclusion

Most anarchists are not enamoured of violence. The people may refuse to obey the government or to recognize its officials. They may refuse to work or to serve in the army. They seek to withdraw that support upon which the existence of government depends. They may take the land and begin cultivating it. They may take control of factories. They may, in short, begin to build the good society. The state may then take reprisals—that is, resort to violence. History has seldom recorded otherwise. The revolutionists, then, if properly organized and prepared, may (or may not) choose to meet violence with violence. They will resist the state's ultimate weapon for continued mastery over their lives. Who is to say where the blame lies for resorting to violence? The anarchists did not want bloodshed. They wanted change, and would pay the price.

NOTES

1 The latter was the case in Bolshevik Russia, to the disgust of most anarchists. The Russian people had done very well in overthrowing the czar and the provisional government, in destroying capitalism, and in occupying the landed estates. But when the *political party* took over, the social revolution was doomed.

2 "Working-class candidates, transferred to bourgeois conditions of life, and into an atmosphere of completely bourgeois political ideas, ceasing to be workers in order to become statesmen, will become bourgeois, and possibly even more bourgeois than the bourgeois themselves. For it is not the men who make positions, but, on the contrary, positions which make the men." Bakunin, quoted in George Plekhanoff, *Anarchism and Socialism,* Eleanor Marx Aveling, Trans. (Chicago: Charles H. Kerr & Company, no date), p. 98.

3 Emma Goldman, *My Further Disillusionment in Russia* (Garden City, N. Y.: Doubleday, Page & Company, 1924), p. 147.

4 Berkman, *Now and After,* p. 125.

5 Kropotkin, *Revolutionary Pamphlets,* p. 287.

6 Berkman, *Now and After,* p. 78.

7 Tucker, quoted in Krimerman and Perry, p. 125.

8 Adin Ballou, *Remarks* at the First Annual Meeting of the Nonresistance Society, Boston, September 25, 1839. See Krimerman and Perry, p. 144.

9 Bakunin, *The Political Philosophy,* p. 284.

10 Goldman, *My Further Disillusionment in Russia,* pp. 174–175.

11 See *ibid.,* pp. 167–168.

12 Bakunin, *The Political Philosophy,* p. 359.

13 It is obvious that the classification of methods into individual protest, the way of peace, syndicalism, and organized insurrection—is not a logical one. Two differentia appear to be at work: size of unit and style of action. So be it. The

four categories adopted are quite distinctive and are convenient pegs for an-archist views.

14 Stirner, p. 174.

15 *Ibid.*, p. 86.

16 The newspaper was *Alarm*, edited in Chicago by Albert Parsons. The time was 1886. See Henry David, *The History of the Haymarket Affair*, pp. 112–113. Most had resumed publication of *Die Freiheit* in New York, and August Spies was editing *Die Arbeiter Zeitung* in Chicago. The influence of Most on these American papers is unmistakable.

17 Berkman, *Prison Memoirs of an Anarchist*, p. 59.

18 *Ibid.*

19 Quoted in Joll, p. 125.

20 Andrea Costa early recognized the foolishness of combining assassination and social revolution. The one required conspiratorial secrecy; the other required recruitment and wide publicity.

21 In the courtroom Emile Henry was permitted to defend his position. In his speech he said, among other things: Anarchists "do not spare bourgeois women and children, because the wives and children of those they love are not spared either. Are not those children innocent victims who, in the slums, die slowly of anaemia because bread is scarce at home; or those women who grow pale in your workshops and wear themselves out to earn forty sous a day, and yet are lucky when poverty does not turn them into prostitutes; those old people whom you have turned into machines for production all their lives, and whom you cast on to the garbage dump and the workhouse when their strength is ex-hausted? At least have the courage of your crimes, gentlemen of the bourgeoisie, and agree that our reprisals are fully legitimate!" Quoted in Joll, pp. 137–138.

22 Laurent Tailhade, quoted in Plekhanoff, pp. 140–141.

23 See Joll, p. 133.

24 *Cf.* Berkman, *Prison Memoirs of an Anarchist*, p. 71.

25 Sometimes, of course, the situation was reversed: the criminals were too prin-cipled to work with the anarchists. "In 1873 Malatesta went to Sicily in the hope of recruiting the brigands to the anarchist cause, only to be told that 'the brigands were too religious and honest to take part in a rising in which the ex-ample of the Commune might be followed, where they shot the archbishop.' " Joll, pp. 118–119.

26 *Cf.* Tucker, pp. 104, 208.

27 Neither Tolstoy nor Ballou called himself an anarchist.

28 Acts v:29.

29 See Krimerman and Perry, p. 143.

30 *Ibid.*, p. 144.

31 *Ibid.*, p. 148.

32 *Ibid.*, p. 559.

33 Tolstoy, *What Then Must We Do?*, p. 329.

34 John Beverley Robinson, in a letter printed in Tucker, p. 69.

35 *Ibid.*, p. 79.

36 Tucker did reserve the right to use violence in certain emergencies. But the situation would have to be very serious—such as the absolute suppression of the freedom of expression.

37 Tucker, p. 456.

38 *Ibid.*, p. 424.

39 Tucker suggested that a similar campaign be conducted against the land monopoly in the United States. Occupants would simply refuse to pay rent. If done persistently and on a large scale, the state would have to repeal all land titles.

40 That taxes may, in theory, have been imposed democratically by the majority on itself is no mitigation, as we have seen. For are the scoundrels who desire the taxes excused by the fact that they have managed to dupe a majority of their fellow citizens?

41 Tucker, p. 413.

42 *Ibid.*, p. 427.

43 "When a determined body of people, sufficiently strong in numbers and force of character to command respect and make it unsafe to imprison them, shall agree to quietly close their doors in the faces of the tax-collector and the rent-collector, and shall, by issuing their own money in defiance of legal prohibition, at the same time cease paying tribute to the money-lord, government, with all the privileges which it grants and the monopolies which it sustains, will go by the board." *Ibid.*, pp. 415–416.

44 Rudolf Rocker, *Anarcho-Syndicalism: Theory and Practice* (Indore, India: Modern Publishers, n.d.), p. 107.

45 *Ibid.*, p. 132.

46 See, for example, Berkman, *Now and After*, pp. 89–101. "Have you ever seen a single labor leader, of the American Federation of Labor, for instance, stand up and declare that the whole wage system is pure robbery and swindle, and demand for the workers the full product of their toil?" (p. 94)

47 *Ibid.*, p. 98.

48 *Ibid.*, p. 143.

49 Sorel, *Reflections on Violence*, p. 203.

50 *Ibid.*, p. 302.

51 *Ibid.*, p. 52.

52 *Ibid.*

53 *Ibid.*, p. 145.

54 *Ibid.*

55 *Ibid.*, p. 275.

56 *Ibid.*, p. 228.

57 *Ibid.*, p. 255.

58 This contention is based upon Bakunin's consistent fervor to destroy—smash —authority whenever, wherever, and however he could, and by his conspiratorial and fearless manner. It is also based upon his brief (1869–1872) association with a fanatical terrorist named Sergei Gennadevich Nechaev. Nechaev extolled brigandage, extermination, and merciless destruction.

59 Bakunin, quoted in Joll, p. 93.

60 Bakunin, *The Political Philosophy*, p. 351; see also p. 320.

61 *Ibid.*, p. 304.

62 *Ibid.*, p. 339.

63 *Ibid.,* p. 398.

64 *Ibid.,* p. 322.

65 *Ibid.,* p. 372.

66 *Ibid.,* p. 374.

67 *Ibid.,* p. 376.

68 *Ibid.,* p. 323.

69 *Ibid.,* p. 370.

70 See *ibid.,* pp. 396–397.

71 *Ibid.,* p. 397.

72 Kropotkin, *Revolutionary Pamphlets,* p. 47.

73 *Ibid.*

74 *Ibid.,* p. 63.

75 *Ibid.,* p. 36.

76 "We may say that revenge is no aim in itself. Surely, it is not. But it is *human* and all revolts have borne and for a long time will bear the character. In fact, *we* who, in our houses, seclude ourselves from the cry and sight of human sufferings, we are no judges of those who live in the midst of all this hell of suffering. . . . Personally, I hate these explosions, but I cannot stand as a judge to condemn those who are driven to despair. . . . One single thing—that revenge must be erected into a *theory.* That no one has the right to incite others to it, but that if he keenly feels all that hell and does a desperate act, let him be judged by those who are his peers, his equals in bearing those pariah's sufferings." Quoted in Joll, p. 153.

77 See *ibid.,* p. 150.

78 Kropotkin, *Revolutionary Pamphlets,* p. 247.

79 *Ibid.,* p. 39.

80 *Ibid.,* p. 40.

81 *Ibid.,* p. 191.

82 *Ibid.,* p. 222.

83 Lysander Spooner, *No Treason* (Boston: Lysander Spooner, 1867), No. 2, p. 13.

6

The Good Society

LAW AND ORDER

The common charge that anarchism is disorderly and chaotic is disproved by the many descriptions of the good anarchist society. These descriptions are not always vague and impractical; often they are specific and realistic.[1] It is true that the individualistic Max Stirner avoids being pinned down: "As to what is now to happen further after I have become free, freedom is silent. . . ."[2] The typical anarchist position, however, is to indicate the general structure of the new society while avoiding detailed elaboration. Further development and improvement must not be cut off. "Anarchists do not make any plans for the free society in its maturity, as they believe in the free and continual growth of social institutions, and recognize that any hard-and-fast plan of development will create only a sterile society."[3]

We have noted the difficulty which revolutionary anarchism has in squaring organizational discipline with its basic libertarianism. Anarchism also has difficulty in squaring definite ideas of what the new society should be like with its conviction that people ought to make whatever kind of society they want. In the first case, all anarchists agree that there should be a revolution, but disagree on the form it should take; in the second case, the anarchists agree that the new society will differ fundamentally from the old, but disagree on the basic structure it will have.

Elimination of Government and Law

It is safe to say that the new society will not carry over the authoritarianism of the old. Emma Goldman made the point with her customary fervor:

> All political tenets and parties notwithstanding, no revolution can be truly and permanently successful unless it puts its emphatic veto upon all tyranny and centralization, and determinedly strives to make the revolution a real revolution of all economic and social values. Not mere substitution of one political party for another in the control of the Government, not the masking of autocracy by proletarian slogans, not the dictatorship of a new class over an old one, not political scene shifting of any kind, but the complete reversal of all these authoritarian principles will alone serve the revolution.[4]

There will be no political parties, no politics, and no politicians.

Few people claimed to respect science—natural and social—as often as did Bakunin. Asserting that the scientists knew better than anyone else the nature of genuine law, Bakunin nevertheless denied that they should govern in the good society. Scientists had no better claim to authority than the discredited priests, kings, and politicians. Some of Bakunin's reasons were these: (1) Science is more concerned with general principles than with individual facts; scientists, therefore, would tend to ignore the existence and fate of individual people. Life has too much variety for mankind to be martyred on a Procrustean bed. (2) A society ruled by science would, by definition, fail to understand the rationale of this rule; people would, therefore, be little better than domesticated brutes. (3) Scientists, no matter how illustrious and well intentioned, would eventually become corrupted by their power.[5] Bakunin's basic concern seems to be the deeper one of rejecting government by experts. Proficiency in managing people and societies does not justify such management. *No one* should "manage"—not even the most competent. In the nineteenth century the epitome of competence was science.

Science is, however, to be very important in the good society: "Science, as a moral entity existing outside of the universal social life and represented by a corporation of licensed savants, should be liquidated and widely diffused among the masses. Called upon to represent henceforth the collective consciousness of society, science must in a real sense become everybody's property."[6]

Since the good society will not have government, not even "scientific" government, it will also have no laws in the usual sense of the word. William Godwin early questioned the need for laws. Man has a better chance of doing well by looking to his own rational sense of propriety than to "some foreign guidance for the direction of his conduct." [7] What credit can man take for acting well when such action has been ordered by the state? Where is his morality and dignity? People have supposed that when law is vigorously enforced, it produces order; but lawful societies have never in fact produced order. "Individuality cannot be conquered; it cannot be infringed without engendering infinite confusion." [8]

There being no laws in the new society, there will also be no formal punishments, no carrying out of retributive "justice." The practice of governmental punishment is poorly motivated and notoriously ineffective. Punishment cannot be justified on the principle of giving every man his "just deserts," for no one knows what this is. Godwin admitted that punishment may be justified when it produces an "overbalance of good," but warned against facile "justifications" for this "constructive purpose." [9] It touches neither the mind nor the sensibilities of the recipient. He learns only that he has to submit to force, and he may in the future act from a sense of fear. A theory of law and punishment is worthy of attention only if it concerns itself with the internal feelings and motives of the particular persons involved. But since these data are difficult to get at and since each "crime" is unique, the making and enforcing of law present insurmountable problems. Who can ever accurately ascertain precisely what was in the mind of the offender, what moved him, and whether he or anyone else will be similarly moved again?

How Men Can Live Together

In the absence of law and formal punishment, how are men to live together? Godwin suggested that when quarrels arise between men and the parties cannot themselves settle them, informal juries may invite the parties to accept certain recommendations. Everything would be conducted very rationally. Throughout society "if force [is] gradually withdrawn, and reason trusted alone, shall we not one day find that juries themselves, and every other species of public institution, may be laid aside as unnecessary?" [10]

Andrews emphasized individuality: "This indestructible and all-pervading Individuality furnishes, itself, the law and the only true law, of order and harmony." [11] Unlike Stirner, he opposed the despotic use of other individuals. But he did intend that men would live in societies. Andrews spoke, therefore, of the "concurrent sovereignty" of all men. Each man is sovereign "only within his own dominions"; he cannot interfere with the prerogatives of others. He may bring by his actions agreeable consequences to others or disagreeable ones to himself, but he can never inflict the "cost" of his actions on others without their permission. Where people live in conditions of dependence and "close connection," concessions and compromises are continually required. This is not good. It is to be endured only when the connections are "natural"—for example, that between a parent and a child. Most social connections, however, are artificial or forced. When such is the case, it is much better, when conflicts arise, to "dis-connect" than to seek concessions or to surrender selfhood. These two alternatives, compromise or disconnection, represent two stages of ethics—or, in Andrews' terms, the graduation of the individual "out of the sphere of Ethics into that of Personality. . . ." [12] It is good to help people in a society held together by unnecessary social relations; it is better to have a good society in which people can help themselves.

But what about individuals who seek to harm others in an anarchical society? It is the expectation of many anarchists that informal resistance will spontaneously develop against a harmful neighbor, thereby "containing" him. Sorel had some words of praise for the vigilantes of the American West.

Tucker was somewhat more formal. He recommended "defensive associations." These would be voluntary and would restrain aggression by whatever means are necessary. What to do with the offender? This is strictly a matter of expediency. "If it can find no better instrument of resistance, anarchism will use prisons." [13] It is foolish to endure "the invasions of the incorrigible. In restraining him, we are simply exercising "our liberty to keep others from compelling us." [14] Although membership or participation in a defensive association is not required, the individual who chooses to stay outside is deprived of its protection should he be invaded. Tucker also suggested that one could, if he wished, *buy* protection as he would any other service.

Anti-social behavior will, according to the anarchists, decrease sharply when an unjust and oppressive state is replaced by one that is just and free. Just as bad conditions bred bad actions in the past, good conditions will breed good actions in the future. "To make men moral it is necessary to make their social environments moral." [15] Creation of conditions of justice, equality, fraternity, and freedom marks a radical change; conduct will necessarily radically change.

Not even the anarchist can free men from subjection to natural and social laws. Bakunin and others believed that the planner for the future would be wise to take them into account and use them for the production of a happier and more complete life. A fundamentally revised system of education is also expected to help. The new education will assist in the unfolding of the student's human and natural capacities and will provide early experience in independent action and free association. He will not habitually have to look for authorities to guide his thoughts and actions.

In the economic sphere there will be no privileged classes enriching themselves at the expense of the poor, no unemployment created by the vagaries of the profit system, and no stigma attached to manual work. Everyone will be educated for a job and will find easy entry into a productive and rewarding life. From all this will come a sense of confidence and well-being—a healthiness of spirit— from which will naturally issue, if not warm regard for others, no drives to harm them.

It was with supreme confidence that Kropotkin called on mankind to make a huge bonfire of all its laws, to free itself of its crime-and-punishment mentality.[16] If this were done (and the anarchical society requires it), society would deal with its violent and anti-social elements in a different way. It would not flog them, chain them up, or kill them. Realizing that the "criminal" is simply unfortunate, society would seek to help him "by the most brotherly care." Practical human sympathy is the only way. "Burn the guillotines," cried Kropotkin, "demolish the prisons, drive away the judges, policemen and informers . . . ; treat as a brother the man who has been led by passion to do ill to his fellow; above all, take from the ignoble products of middle-class idleness the possibility of displaying their vices in attractive colors; and be sure that but few crimes will mar our society." [17]

With the end of governments, hostility between states will also decrease. Indeed there will be no "states" in the ordinary sense. The fiction of an individual sovereign nation, subject to no considerations but its own greatness and destiny, will at last be laid to rest. Power, no longer so important *within* geographic boundaries, will be similarly rejected for use *across* geographic boundaries. Not only will "states" no longer be able to marshal all their resources for murderous attacks against others, they will not want to. The end of oppression will be accompanied by the demise of "grandeur" and bellicosity.

In a sense the anarchists have turned the tables on their critics. Violence, which has hitherto characterized the state's control over its citizens and its relations with other states, is to be replaced by tolerance, understanding, and peace. Violence, regarded as almost synonymous with anarchism, turns out to be more applicable to the outlook of its adversaries! Even Tucker, who would resort to violence against invasion whenever expedient, saw many alternatives to force in the inculcation of virtue: education, example, public opinion, social ostracism, freedom, competition, increase of material welfare, decrease of temptation, health, etc. He ridiculed the view that "the only forces on earth that tend to develop the undeveloped and to make the vicious virtuous are our judges, our jails, and our gibbets." This is as bad as a religion which holds that hell is the only safeguard.[18]

Similarly, Bakunin, in rejecting the state, was not rejecting the influences that individuals may have on the masses or that the masses may have on the individuals; he was rejecting only those "fictitious, privileged, legal, and official influences." [19]

Man is to be free, but he does not and cannot possess divine, transcendental freedom that makes him absolutely independent of all natural and social forces. He can, however, achieve a positive, a rational, freedom through a wider knowledge of science. By utilizing the laws of science he can make his effort and work more productive of the ends he desires. Positive freedom is the domination over external things through knowledge and observances of the laws of nature. When this knowledge is widely diffused, instead of being restricted to the fortunate few who have had an education, then society as a whole, through its several members, will be free.

What is the relation of my freedom to that of another? I may influence him, and he may influence me—without, of course, exercising that influence through political institutions. He and I can work together—organize and cooperate—freeing ourselves from subordination to physical nature. "Collective and social labor . . . is capable of transforming the surface of the earth into an abode favorable to the development of humanity." [20] Each is to respect the humanity and liberty of everyone else. "Liberty then," wrote Bakunin in attempting to elucidate a difficult idea, "is not a fact springing from isolation but from reciprocal action, a fact not of exclusion, but, on the contrary, of social interaction—for the freedom of every individual is simply the reflection of his humanity or his human right in the consciousness of all free men, his brothers, his equals." [21]

The relative importance of the political and economic changes promoting the anarchist ideal is an interesting issue. Obviously, it is possible to have communism while retaining government, just as it is possible to have economic individualism and anarchy. Which is more significant for the good life, no government or a new economy? The anarchist's answer is that the type of government (or non-government) and the type of economy go together, that the one implies the other. Some anarchists, however, seem to emphasize one or the other. The collectivists seem to be more concerned with remedying economic injustice and misery,[22] and from *this* go to anarchy. Kropotkin, for example, often said that every economic system implies its own particular political system. Feudalism and serfdom gave us monarchy, capitalism produced representative government, and communism has its appropriate politics, namely, anarchism. The individualists seem to be more concerned with freedom from governmental interference, and from *this* go to mutualism or the "cost principle." In any case, we find that some economic systems (*e.g.,* capitalism, communism) are compatible with both anarchism and "archism," and that the particular "political" system under discussion (anarchism) is compatible with various economic systems. In the sections to follow, we will encounter several anarchistic versions of the good society exhibiting striking differences in economics.

MUTUALISM

Proudhon

Proudhon, whom we have classified as somewhere between the individualists on the right and the collectivists on the left, described the future society as a fusion of the private and the social: mutualism. Individuals can associate while preserving their liberty; they can make contracts and agreements for their mutual benefit. Society will always have its conflicts and tensions, but it is better for individuals to make their own way (and their own contracts and agreements) than for the state to impose a spurious kind of unity at the expense of nearly everyone. The latter is not justice. Justice can exist only when individuals, meeting as equals, forge reciprocal relations.

Private property will continue to exist in the new society, but in a different form. Property will not be owned in that absolute sense which permits (through the connivance of the state) an "owner" of land or capital to exploit the non-owners.

Landownership will be viewed in terms of "possession" rather than "proprietorship." A disciple of Proudhon expressed it this way: The owner "is secure in the tenure of land which he uses and occupies, but has no claim upon it at all if he ceases to use it. He cannot hold it out of use and prevent others from using it." [23] Another disciple wrote: "The Anarchists say to the individual: 'Occupancy and use is the only title to land in which we will protect you; if you attempt to use land which another is occupying and using, we will protect him against you; if another attempts to use land to which you lay claim, but which you are not occupying and using, we will not interfere with him; but of such land as you occupy and use you are the sole master, and we will not ourselves take from you, or allow any one else to take from you, whatever you may get out of such land.'" [24] A "free association" would defend this kind of ownership, ignore claims to proprietorship, and oppose wage labor in farming. Tucker speculated on how an anarchist society could carry out these principles. Voluntary associations will formulate something like this:

> Continuing with our suppositions, we will say that they decide to protect no one in possession of more than ten acres. In execution of this decision, they, on October 1, notify all holders of more than ten acres within their limits that, on and after the following January 1, they will cease to protect them in the possession of more than ten acres, and that, as a condition of receiving even that protection, each must make formal declaration on or before December 1 of the specific ten-acre plot within his present holding which he proposes to personally occupy and use after January 1. These declarations having been made, the municipalities publish them and at the same time notify landless persons that out of the lands thus set free each may secure possession of any amount up to ten acres after January 1 by appearing on December 15, at a certain hour, and making declaration of his choice and intentions of occupancy.[25]

Of course there will be a scramble and some inequality will remain. But a great improvement will have been effected. The possibility of carrying out such a program will depend upon the amount of education in anarchist economics and social science the people have had. It will also depend upon the degree to which the previous state-controlled economy has been weakened. Finally, it should be added, Tucker was seeking through this land reform to achieve not equality of material well-being (which is "meddlesome, invasive, and offensive"), but equality of liberty (which is "simply protective and defensive").

The mutualists believe that labor, and only labor, is productive; it should be the source and measure of (exchange) value. Labor is the proud possession of each individual; the theft of its products by monopolists of capital (rural and urban) is one of the greatest crimes committed in the old society. Capital is nothing but "the remains of past labor." It therefore is something to be *used* by *laborers,* not something to be utilized by industrial owners, bankers, and landlords for extorting the fruits of a worker's labor. Workers must control capital in order to be free from its domination.

One famous and very concrete economic institution which was important in Proudhon's positive thought is a mutualist bank ("Bank of Exchange" or "Bank of the People"). Just as men should freely exchange equivalents in labor (and no one form of labor—say, medical care—is superior to, or more valuable than any other form—say, shoemaking),[26] so too can they pledge to pay equitably for capital, the stored labor of others. Workers *with* capital can produce more than workers *without* capital. Proudhon's bank is an institution for preserving capital without capitalism.

Proudhon's bank could be established with little or no initial capital. It would issue notes based upon the labor of the members who compose it; the currency would thus be fully secured. The money could be exchanged within the community of productive people for the products of their labor. The bank would offer loans at cost: the only "interest" would be that small sum of money to cover the actual transaction of business. If loans were thus easy to get, workers would no longer have to hire themselves out to industrial capitalists. Needing machinery or raw materials, a worker or a group of workers could acquire capital on the promise to pay off the debt through their own increased productivity. Another beneficial consequence of the mutualist bank would be to reduce the need for individuals to pay rent for houses or land. They would buy these things, not through high-interest loans, but through loans obtained from the Bank of the People. The bank frees people at last from the usurer. Moreover, if it succeeded on a wide scale, people would no longer be subject to financial speculations, manipulations in international trade, or the wild speculations of the specie market.

Is this really a practical scheme? Proudhon thought so. The bank could be established in either one of two ways: (1) The existing French government transforms the Bank of France into a mutualist bank ("Bank of Exchange"). The old stockholders would be paid off, and labor, the real basis of wealth, would begin to replace the precious metals as security. If government were to continue, its expenses could be met by charging a small additional interest on loans, thus eliminating the need for tax-assessing and tax-gathering. (2) Individuals associate and start mutualist banks ("Bank of the People"), continually increasing their scope and services. Eventually, normal sources of credit would go out of business, for their interest rates would be too high; they would be ruined by competition. The government, of course, if still in existence, would have to *permit* mutual banking! In either case, individuals would get their loans by putting up collateral of their own or, having none, would get endorsements from solvent persons acquainted with their industry and honesty.

Tucker: Free Capital

Many followers of Proudhon, especially those in the United States, adopted the idea of a people's bank with great enthusiasm, elaborating and refining it. Tucker saw the plan through individualistic eyes: conditions for free competition in supplying capital should be created. To replace the unjust monopoly in interest, rent, and profit, he demanded—in the spirit of Proudhon and in the terminology of Warren [27]—the development of free institutions by which capital could be made available to workers and businessmen *at cost*. He did not, as sometimes charged, ignore the element of security: "Free money advocates hold that security is one (*only* one) essential of good money, and that competition is sure to provide this essential, competition being simply natural selection or the survival of the fittest, and the fittest necessarily possessing the quality of security." [28] John Beverley Robinson in his book *The Economics of Liberty* also called for the establishment of "people's banks": banks depending upon government restrictions on behalf of the "money monopoly" would disappear; in their place would be the people's banks brought into existence by voluntary associations. All the mutualists rejected the Marxist solution. Instead of socializing the ownership of capital, they would socialize its effects by making it easily available to all on an individual basis.

Tucker saw many benefits in (virtually) free capital. Individuals would be able to start their own enterprises and be free of the capitalists who hitherto had stolen from the fruit of their labor. This trend would reduce the labor force, thus enabling those still involved in the wage system to bargain for better wages, wages that would approach the just value of their labor. Prices would come down, because neither merchants nor manufacturers would have to replace an expenditure for high interest payment. The elimination of the tariff and patent monopolies would also, according to Tucker, help bring down prices. House rent would also come down, for with free money many people would be able to build their own houses. But use of occupied land for housing or crops is itself dependent upon available money. Without money, one can neither build nor farm.[29] This is Tucker's version of "consistent Manchesterism," the only version that will actually secure the benefits claimed for it. "Competition everywhere and always." Herbert Spencer and William Graham Sumner were simply not radical enough in their *laissez-faire* philosophy.[30]

Andrews: Cost Principle

One of the clearest expressions of the "cost principle" is found in the mid-nineteenth-century writings of Stephen Pearl Andrews. He inherited the principle from Josiah Warren, extending and elaborating it. It is, according to Andrews, the foundation of the good society.

It is the cost principle that makes intelligible the concept of *equity:* "Every individual should sustain just as much of the common burden of life as has to be sustained *by anybody* on his account." [31] Anyone receiving something from society which cost someone else something would have to transfer an equal amount of something to society for that effort of the other. Cost is effort—or labor. The principle, if we shift to the first person, may thus be stated in this way: the amount of labor that comes to me directly or indirectly from others must be returned to them by my own efforts.

To measure labor solely in *time* is too simple, for some activities are pleasant and some are unpleasant. Only when activities are similar with respect to pleasantness will the time factor be an accurate measure; otherwise a coefficient of some kind is called for.[32]

Who is to judge the degree of unpleasantness? *"Each individual must make his or her estimate of the repugnance to him or her of the labor he or she performs."* [33] Since the cost is the *burden borne* by the active individual the product of whose work I enjoy, it must be repaid by equal burden on my part.

The cost principle "places all in a condition of independence. It dissolves the relation of protectors and protected by rendering protecting unnecessary." [34] Since the principle is one of cost rather than value, it will limit the relative power of the strong and intelligent over the weak and stupid. Moreover, it makes illegitimate the placing of prices on any natural resource that was claimed without effort. There is no reason a thing should bring what it is *worth;* a thing should bring to the individual what it *cost* that individual. If the principle were put into effect, the odious aspects of rent would be eliminated. For no rent could be charged except as it represented the cost of the person's effort who may have improved the land or building rented (or the cost of restoring the land or building that has been allowed by a previous tenant to deteriorate). Speculation is also eliminated, for no one can sell land for anything more than the cost of the efforts made at improving the land. And finally, monopoly is eliminated, for no one can claim anything for land that has not cost him something in effort.

In a society founded on the cost principle, people will freely choose their occupation and compete in carrying it out. Since the person who does a job best will not only produce more but will (probably) enjoy it, he will produce at less cost per unit. He will be encouraged, therefore, to remain in the occupation and continue to produce. This benefits him and everyone else. This kind of competition, then, is "cooperative" rather than ruthless.

Since it is natural for some to plan and direct while others execute, the wage system will not be abolished. But the entrepreneur (perhaps for the first time in history) will be justly recompensed— that is, in accordance with the amount his labor has cost him in time and discomfort. "In the large establishment . . . the proprietor will realize no more in the form of pecuniary results from the undertaking than the humblest laborer employed by him, unless he works harder, *and not so much if he does not work so hard*— taking into account all the elements of labor or repugnance, both physical and mental." [35]

It may well be questioned whether a discussion of individualists like Robinson, Andrews, and Tucker belongs in a section on mutualism. Inclusion of their ideas is justified by the great compatibility they have with those of Proudhon himself. The distinction made in "varieties of anarchism" above is not an absolutely exclusive one. Many bona fide individualists are mutualists about economics. Stirner and Godwin are exceptions, but the Americans surely fall into the Proudhon mold.[36] It is perhaps impossible for an individualist, if he wants to talk about a good society, to avoid taking into account *some* degree of mutual beliefs among its members.

SYNDICALISM

Syndicalism offers the best example of the unity of means and ends, of the similarity of the anarchist movement in its revolutionary period to the organization of the new society.

The syndicates in the new society will be composed of free associations of workers at their places of work. These associations will choose their own leaders and manage their own affairs. Associations in the same industry or trade may freely combine into a syndicate, but the local unit retains full autonomy. "Each working unit, a factory or a railroad yard, will be run by the workers who actually operate it. There will be no authority, no management, and each worker will be jointly and equally responsible with the rest for the proper functioning of the industrial unit in which he works."[37] Syndicates may themselves be federated into larger syndicates. Perhaps an industrial syndicate for the whole society will emerge. Syndicalism, always opposing centralization, "is based on the principles of Federalism, on free combination from below upward, putting the right of self-determination of every member above everything else and recognizing only the organic agreement of all on the basis of like interests and common convictions."[38] Any individual or unit may secede at will.

The productive aspect of the life of a society is not a simple matter. In order to avoid chaos and disorder, production must be organized. But in syndicalism, agreements, promises, and contracts among workers will replace the old system of private ownership and private profit. Workers will have their delegates (to administer, to consult with other units, etc.), but these delegates are not to be thought of as *superiors*. Pay will be virtually equal: one will receive not according to his *worth* (for this cannot be calculated), but according to his *need* (to the extent that production permits it). "Men will decide the standard of life they desire and will work to get it. . . ." [39]

The German syndicalist Rocker did not hesitate to use the word "organization" in summarizing his description of the new society: "1. Organization of the plants by the producers themselves and direction of the work by labour councils elected by them. 2. Organization of the total production of the country by the industrial and agricultural alliances. 3. Organization of consumption by the Labour Cartels." [40]

Is all this feasible? Two testimonials: "The workers, left to themselves, will find the means to operate industry a good deal more efficiently than has been the case under capitalism. . . ." [41] The syndicates in Catalonia proved "that the workers, even without the capitalist, are able to carry on production and to do it better than a lot of profit-hungry entrepreneurs." [42]

COMMUNISM

Socialized Production

The communists begin by criticizing the individualists in the anarchist ranks—in a way not too dissimilar to Marx's denunciation of Proudhon's petty-bourgeois views.[43] There once was a time, perhaps, when a family, more or less self-sufficient on its plot of land, could regard its food, clothing, and shelter as the result of its own (and no one else's) labor. Even then, however, forests were cleared and roads built by cooperative effort. "But now, in the extremely interwoven state of industry in which each branch supports all others, such an individualistic view can be held no more. If the iron trade and the cotton industry of this country [Britain] have reached so high a degree of development, they have done so owing to the parallel growth of thousands of other industries, great and small; to the extension of the railway system; to an increase of knowledge among both the skilled engineers and the mass of the workmen; to a certain training in organization slowly developed among producers; and, above all, to the world-trade which has itself grown up, thanks to works executed thousands of miles away." [44] The worker and his work are so related, so integrated with other workers and work in the same workshop, in the same industry, in other industries, in other countries, in the past, present and future, that the *sociability* of production is an unmistakable fact of life. To abandon all this for a closer approach to individualistic, small-scale production is reactionary and against the progress of civilization. Material wealth —and eventual abundance—requires the continuation of undertakings social in nature.

But Kropotkin would have it both ways: socialized production *and* human freedom. A communist society should be based on free institutions that have their roots in the actual lives and feelings of the individuals. It should be a natural outgrowth, the "product of the constructive genius of the great mass." [45] It will consist of voluntary associations throughout the nation. Genuine communism is thus more than public ownership. The communist spirit extends into personal relations between individuals and agreements between associations. Communism implies feelings of fraternity, cooperation, mutual respect, and solidarity. For these reasons it cannot be imposed from above, it cannot be constructed by legislative decrees. Genuine communism is neither individualism nor statism, although it affords the best means for individual development and social solidarity. Communism is anarchic; anarchism is communistic. The two complement each other.

Only after man's basic needs for food and shelter have been met by cooperative endeavor can those individual human talents, so prized by anarchism, be expressed and freely developed: "his intelligence, his artistic taste, his inventive spirit, his genius." [46] The communist perceives his problem as this: "To *organize* society in such a manner that every individual, man or woman, should, at birth, *find* almost equal *means* for the development of his or her various faculties and the full utilization of his or her work." [47] Communist anarchism is thus a great synthesis of economic freedom and political freedom, a synthesis opening up all the human freedoms to which any individual who lives in such a society can aspire.

The importance of education in such a society is obvious—not just in the trades and the Three Rs, but *"a full integral education, as complete as the present state of the intellectual development of society will permit."* [48] "Everyone shall work and everyone shall be educated." [49] The aim of education is the production of free human beings who respect the freedom of others. Bakunin warned against a "lax" system. The will must be trained. Cravings must be repressed, instinctive drives checked. Only a person who has attained self-control in his youth is capable of enjoying freedom in the positive sense.

Berkman praised communism as a way of life based on absolute equality and wholehearted sociality. The means of production are owned collectively, not by stockholders, but by the whole community. Wealth is produced socially, and all products belong to the community in general. Coal miners will operate the coal mines, railroad workers will run the railroads. "Collective possession, cooperatively managed in the interests of the community, will take the place of personal ownership privately conducted for profit." [50] Bakunin wrote: "The land belongs only to those who cultivate it with their own hands: to the agricultural communes. The capital and all tools of production belong to the workers: to the workers' associations. The future political organization should be a free federation of workers, a federation of producers' associations of agricultural and factory workers." [51]

In the communist society there are no prices and there are no wages, for everyone is encouraged to do what he can and to take what he needs. The slogan "to each according to the value of his work" is transcended, for no one can (or should try to) establish scales of relative value for forms of work or for products. In view of the great interrelatedness of all production, we cannot "pretend to estimate the exact part [each worker has contributed to] the riches accumulated around us." [52] Nor should we try. "Shall we punish the man whom nature has not endowed as generously as his stronger or more talented neighbor? Shall we add injustice to the handicap nature has put upon him? All we can reasonably expect from any man is that he do his best—can any one do more?" [53] In such a society money invented for the purpose of making profitable transactions will disappear.

Distribution

There will, of course, be distribution, but it will not be based upon exchange. Products will be possessions, not property, and actual use will be the only criterion for possessions—whether possession is by a group (miners and machinery) or by an individual (a watch or a pair of shoes). One takes from the social output whatever he needs—subject only to the amount or supply at hand. If there is to be rationing, it should proceed, said Berkman, on the principle of equality. Kropotkin argued that "common possession of the necessaries for production *implies* the common enjoyment of the fruits of the common production; and we consider that an equitable organization of society can only arise when *every* wage-system is abandoned, and when everybody, contributing for the common well-being to the full extent of his capacities, shall enjoy also from the common stock of society to the fullest possible extent of his needs." [54]

It is true that some individuals might shirk their duties, getting, therefore, more from society than they contribute. This is a minor problem. The Bolsheviks made a major problem of it when they tried to put into practice the principle "whoever doesn't work, doesn't eat." The result was an "army of officials" keeping elaborate records of who did what and when. There were endless disputes about the amount and quality of work done. There were finally more people watching (and thus not themselves engaged in actual production) than there would have been shirkers! "The revolutionary community will depend more on awakening the social consciousness and solidarity of its delinquents than on punishment. It will rely on the example set by its working members. . . . For the natural attitude of the industrious men to the shirker is such that the latter will find the social atmosphere so unpleasant that he will prefer to work and enjoy the respect and good will of his fellows rather than to be despised in idleness." [55]

In any case, these matters should not be approached in the spirit of an economics of scarcity. The resources of the earth are vast, and man's technology is great and will be greater. Individualism, in both its liberal and anarchist versions, assumes that what Peter gets, Paul cannot, that the fruits of the earth are limited and must be divided on some principle or another. Communism is not preoccupied with a plan of dividing fixed and meager fruits, but seeks to bring into existence for all the abundance that the material conditions of production make possible.

It was obviously true for Bakunin, Kropotkin, and Berkman (as for most opponents of free-enterprise capitalism) that production will be much higher in a collectivistic system in which it is generated not by the profit motive but by actual need and available resources. A significant factor will be the increased labor force. At present only a minority actually work; in the future all able-bodied adults will work. Not only will parasites be eliminated, but non-productive workers as well.[56] Indeed, the length of the working day will shrink. Man's future will be a time of no depressions, no unemployment, no artificial throttling of technical advancement—all man's productive energies at last liberated from the restrictive network of capitalistic procedures, currencies, markets, duplications—from a system in which more energy is expended in extolling and in selling than in actual production.

Decentralization

It may be noted here that the notion of decentralization, so dear to the hearts of individualists, mutualists, and syndicalists, is espoused by the communists as well. This decentralization follows from the nature of the revolution itself:

> We understand the revolution as a widespread popular movement, during which in every town and village within the region of revolt, the masses will have to take upon themselves the task of rebuilding society—will have to take up themselves the work of construction on communistic bases, without awaiting any orders and directions from above. That is, first of all they will have to organize, one way or another, the means of supplying food to everyone and of providing dwellings for all, and then produce whatever will be found necessary for feeding, clothing, and sheltering everybody.[57]

Organizations should not be on a national scale, production should be diversified and take place in local units, self-sufficiency should be striven for within each region, and small home industries should be cherished and preserved. Kropotkin outlined a plan in *Fields, Factories, and Workshops* whereby large cities could meet their own agricultural needs in their own environs. Berkman challenged the Marxist dictum that centralization alone is progressive and efficient.

Bakunin, on the other hand, rejected the Proudhonian concept of petty handcraft production: "Only associated labor, that is, labor organized upon the principles of reciprocity and co-operation, is adequate to the task of maintaining the existence of a large and somewhat civilized society. Whatever stands for civilization could be created only by labor organized and associated in this manner."[58] Presumably, then, the communists wanted something between Proudhon and Marx: large-scale but decentralized production.

Human Nature

Communism does not run counter to human nature. "The communist tendency is continually re-asserting itself and trying to make its way into public life."[59] Kropotkin cited the development, even in an "individualistic" age, of public bridges, free roads, free museums, libraries, and schools, parks and lighted streets—"tokens showing in what direction further progress is to be expected." [60] These things came into being because they were thought to be valuable to society as a whole, that is, to all of its members. The individual who uses a library is not asked how much he has *given* to society for this privilege and then served proportionately. Society accords this privilege equally to all of its members.

Tolstoy

It is difficult to ascertain the proper location for the views of Leo Tolstoy. He enjoined us not to participate in the people's slavery, not to use their labor. We are not to own land or to spend money. One cannot call himself a Christian if "he devours the labor of those who . . . struggle [for life] and increases by his demands the burden of the struggles and the number of those who perish in that struggle." [61]

No one, not even the educated or the cultivated gentleman, is immune from the duty to work. This work, furthermore, should be humble, basic, physical work. Every person should always be conscious of his duty to work, and should find joy in the struggle with nature. "Service of the people by the sciences and arts will only exist when men live with the people as the people live, and without presenting any claims will offer their scientific services, which the people will be free to accept or decline as they please." [62] Whatever the man of genius produces "should be intelligible to all men whose welfare he has in view." [63] Whatever else they do, educated people must work with their hands. With respect to work, all men are equal; no one is privileged. [64]

Tolstoy was against private property: "Property to-day is the root of all evils: of the sufferings of those who possess it or are deprived of it, the reproaches of conscience of those who misuse it, and the danger of collision between those who have a superfluity and those who are in need. Property is the root of all evil, and at the same time is the very thing to gain which all the activity of our society to-day is directed. It guides the activity of our whole world." [65] The title of Tolstoy's book (*What Then Must We Do?*) is taken from Luke III:10. In answer to the question, the Bible answers: "He who has two coats, let him share with him who has none; and he who has gold, let him do likewise." [66]

Tolstoy himself established no colonies, but he did experiment in communal and ascetic living.[67] The Tolstoyan community would be one in which there was no private property, no escape from work, and no privilege in possession. Equality would be only the minimal principle of association. The teachings of Jesus would inspire a love for others which would go far beyond the requirements of justice. Distribution would thus be a simple matter: no one would want much and everyone would do what he could to meet the needs of others.

The real kingdom of God is not based on a superstitious thirst for a world beyond nature. It begins in the hearts of man and flourishes best in a simple, agricultural community.

While we may call Tolstoy's good society communistic, it is far different from the "scientific" socialism of Marx, the industrial community of Kropotkin and Berkman, or any other theory concerned with high production. Production and distribution are rather unimportant aspects of a society where needs are modest, nature is enjoyed, and love characterizes all relations. Tolstoy's communism, then, is incidental to his vision of a society of love.

INDIVIDUALISM

In the strict sense of the term "society" no individualist can have a theory of the good society, for he opposes social relations in general. While we have had occasion to refer to "defensive associations," "connections," and "unions of egoists," it is nevertheless the case that the individualist is less concerned with society or community *qua* community than are the anarchists of the left. The individualists' theory of society has as its fundamental principle the weakening of those relations that tie people together and produce, at the expense of its members, a society over and above them. In this final section we will briefly indicate the "plans" for the new society set forth by four selected individualists: William Godwin, Max Stirner, Josiah Warren, and Benjamin R. Tucker.

Godwin, Stirner, and Warren

Godwin yearned for a society in which all men are rational and (therefore) virtuous and happy. Property, which is today the cause of so much oppression and crime, will not be very important in the future. People will realize that not much is required for a virtuous life; they will not be given to ostentation and luxury. Godwin counted very heavily on a system of education to make these truths apparent to people.

While methods of production will naturally improve, people will have more important things to do than to work and pile up possessions. These will not, however, be communal or associative. Presumably there will be property belonging to the community in general, but it will not be exploited in common; rather, it will be "available for whoever needs it." [68] As a real individualist Godwin distrusted not only collective ownership but all projects that induce men to depend upon one another. "Vicious cooperation" is one of his terms. The individual is not to get himself entangled. He does what serves his own inclinations and reason. Promises and commitments are to be avoided. One section of Godwin's book is entitled "Of the Mode of Excluding Visitors."

The institution of the family is a conspicuous instance of the loss of freedom. Marriage, for Godwin, is unnecessary: let individuals of opposite sex enjoy each other's company for whatever rational purposes they have, with no surrender of liberty by either party. The American individualists (*e.g.,* Tucker) clearly were more influenced by Godwin on this topic than by Proudhon. With Olympian rationality Godwin wrote: "I shall assiduously cultivate the intercourse of that woman, whose moral and intellectual accomplishments strike me in the most powerful manner. But 'it may happen that other men will feel for her the same preference that I do.' This will create no difficulty. We may all enjoy her conversation; and, her choice being declared, we shall all be wise enough to consider the sexual commerce as unessential to our regard." [69]

Max Stirner had far less concern than Godwin for the welfare of human society. Interferences by, and responsibilities to, *society* are not one whit more acceptable to Stirner than they would be with respect to the *state*. Suppose, then, that the state were annihilated and many Stirnerites inhabited the land. Is a society of radical individualists possible?

It will be recalled that the true egoist does not burden himself with excessive possessions. He may, of course, when it suits his purposes, decide to overpower or dominate another person, but he does not need continued mastery over others. This would be a sign of weakness, of dependence. Indeed, if one *is* unique, he will have little in common with others and little to do with them. People tend to quarrel when they live intimately together (as, for example, members of a family). Opposition between persons "vanishes in complete severance or singleness." Individuals may freely unite for a brief time and freely separate. Stirner prefers to speak of a "Union of Egoists" rather than a society of individuals.

> Community, as the "goal" of history . . . is impossible. Let us rather renounce every hypocrisy of community. . . . Let us therefore not aspire to community, but to *one*sidedness. . . . As we do not see our equals in the tree, the beast, so the presupposition that others are *our equals* springs from a hypocrisy. No one is *my* equal. . . . Only in the union can you assert yourself as unique, because the union does not possess you, but you possess it or make it of use to you. . . . You bring into a union your whole power, your competence, and *make yourself count;* in a society you are *employed,* with your working power; in the former you live egoistically, in the latter humanly, i.e. religiously, as a "member in the body of this Lord": to a society you owe what you have, and are in duty bound to it, are—possessed by "social duties"; a union you utilize, and give it up undutifully and unfaithfully when you see no way to use it further. If a society is more than you, then it is more to you than yourself; a union is only your instrument, or the sword with which you sharpen and increase your natural force; the union exists for you, the society conversely lays claim to you for itself and exists even without you; in short, the society is *sacred,* the union your *own;* the society consumes *you, you* consume the union.[70]

At about the same time as Proudhon was developing his ideas in France and Stirner his in Germany, Josiah Warren was independently developing his anarchist theory in the United States. It had striking similarities to both his contemporaries' (especially Proudhon). Proudhon was critical of Fourier, while Warren attacked the utopian Robert Owen.

Warren's economic ideas have already been dealt with indirectly, in the discussion of mutualism. He held the principle of "labor for labor," and after leaving Owen's settlement at New Harmony, Indiana, established a "Time Store" in Cincinnati. Here goods were sold at cost and labor; notes were the medium of exchange. He then founded genuinely anarchist societies in Ohio (Village of Equity) and Long Island (Modern Times), which were structured on mutualist principles. They were moderate successes.

But it is Warren's individualism we want to note here. Warren believed that New Harmony failed because individualism was always getting in the way of cooperation. Individualism *should* get in the way of cooperation. The good society is one in which cooperation is not permitted to get in the way of individualism. Genuine fellowship is possible only among free persons. Society must be made to conform to the individual. From the fact that all interests, ownerships, and actions are individual, a higher harmony will result. Complicated agreements, artificial organizations, and united interests are to be avoided, for these entail performances by others of more or less definiteness. The terms, qualifications, meanings, and intentions of the agreement come to be misunderstood and confusion results. The only remedy, according to Warren, is *"definiteness* in our obligations. Let every transaction be an individual one, resting on its own merits, and not mixed up or *united* with another." [71]

The typical "equity village" has no government and passes no legislation. Its rules are very simple. An individual may join the village after ascertaining that there is a need for his labor there and agreeing to abide by the rules (which are made very clear to him). He freely joins, freely remains, and freely leaves.

Tucker

Benjamin Tucker's individualism has already been suggested in references to his ethics, economics, and "social convention." It is in that which this convention is to establish, equality of liberty, that one sees his individualism most clearly. Tucker favored a net increase of liberty, but not at the expense of equality of liberty. His position is thus to demand the "greatest amount of liberty compatible with the equality of liberty." [72] This *is* a demand—he would (if he could) *compel* individuals to recognize this principle. It would be better, of course, if everyone accepted the principle, but public acceptance will require time. He was hopeful that people would eventually establish the principle of equal liberty by social convention.[73]

Tucker was not calling simply for a *different* social convention to *replace* those the political philosophers had talked about and that modern states assume as their origin; he was insisting on that social convention which would in itself *exclude* government. The principle of the equality of liberty is the essence of anarchism, for it states that no one may exercise authority over anyone else. It is itself the principle of non-invasion. Whether people are wise enough to recognize it or strong enough to enforce it, Tucker was committed to it for the same reason that he was committed to anarchism.

Individualism does not require anyone to join a defensive association, to borrow money from a mutualist bank, or to give away land he does not occupy—although, in certain circumstances, these actions may be expedient. Strictly speaking, individualism does not even require that the individual recognize and respect the liberty of anyone but himself. But he may finally see that adherence to the principle of the equality of liberty is the *most* expedient thing he can do. He thus becomes a principled anarchist.

With all his individualism, Tucker did not hesitate to call himself a socialist. He (like most anarchists) is a socialist by virtue of refusing to accept the idea that a capitalist can rightfully appropriate any part of the fruits of another's labor. In owning money, the capitalist has already received payment for his own labor; if he uses the money to extract value from someone else, he is again receiving payment. No scheme of "profit-sharing," in which labor gets, say, 70 percent while capital gets 30 percent, would impress him. The non-socialist wishes to preserve a system in which capital can be "farmed out" for a fee, returned intact, and farmed out again—and again and again. This is what Proudhon called "the fiction of the productivity of capital." And it takes place in land rent, bank loans, and hiring of workers. Tucker will not *forbid* any of these activities, but equality of freedom will either reduce them drastically or curb their noxiousness. "Those who would have the usurer rewarded for rendering a service always find it convenient to forget that the usurer's victims would not need his service were it not that the laws made at his bidding prevent them from serving themselves." [74]

But Tucker was strongly opposed to socialism in another sense. State socialism, in which all monopolies are replaced by one great Monopoly, is wholesale invasion. Communist or socialistic anarchism is a contradiction in terms, no matter what the controlling authority is called or how it is disguised. How can a system that denies liberty in production and exchange ("the most important of all liberties") be called *anarchism*? Tucker, with Proudhon and the socialists and the communists, opposes "private property" when the term means "the sum total of legal privileges bestowed upon the holders of wealth." But when the term means "the laborer's individual possession of his product or of his proportional share of the

joint product of himself and others," Tucker and Proudhon, part-
ing company with the collectivists, defend it. The first sense is
theft, the second sense is liberty. Tucker called compulsory communism "the most revolting of Archies." [75]

Conclusion

As a final paragraph, applicable to all the anarchists, not merely
the individualists, we will point out the basic humanism of their
outlook. The great advantage of the new society is to be found in
the vital lives of its members. The economic and political changes
are only means for a higher development of man's natural capacities. Life is to be joyous and complete. Each individual, unique in
himself, will follow lines of growth suited to his interests—sport,
art, science, invention, or whatever. "Imperatives and taboos will
disappear, and man will begin to be himself, to develop and express
his individual tendencies and uniqueness. Instead of 'thou shalt
not,' the public conscience will say 'thou mayest, taking full responsibility.' That will be a training in human dignity and self-
reliance, beginning at home and in school, which will produce a
new race with a new attitude to life." [76] And finally, a vision from
the individualist: every man "adding to his riches makes every other
man richer; . . . increase and concentration of wealth through
labor tend to increase, cheapen, and vary production; . . . every
increase of capital in the hands of the laborer tends, in the absence
of legal monopoly, to put more products, better products, cheaper
products, and a greater variety of products within the reach of
every man who works; and . . . this fact means the physical,
mental, and moral perfecting of mankind, and the realization of
human fraternity. Is not that glorious?" [77]

NOTES

[1] For an interesting discussion of the charge that anarchism is a form of
utopianism, see Horowitz, pp. 585–587.

[2] Stirner, p. 171.

[3] George Woodcock, *Railroads and Society* (London: Freedom Press, 1943), p. 26.

[4] Goldman, *My Further Disillusionment in Russia,* p. 161.

[5] See Bakunin, *The Political Philosophy,* pp. 77–80.

[6] *Ibid.,* p. 80.

[7] William Godwin, *An Enquiry* . . . , Vol. II, p. 409.

[8] Andrews, "The True Constitution of Government," p. 23.

9 When punishment is inflicted for the purpose of *restraint*, it is based solely on suspicion and is arbitrary. When it seems to be inflicted for the purpose of *reformation*, one should recognize that "coercion cannot convince, cannot conciliate, but on the contrary alienates the mind of him against whom it is employed." When punishment is inflicted for the purpose of *example*, it is most barbaric of all. Moreover, the excessive suffering of the victim seldom is salutary to its witnesses. "It may terrify; but it cannot produce in us candour and docility." Godwin, *An Enquiry* . . . , Vol. II, pp. 340–341, 345.

10 *Ibid.*, p. 211.

11 Andrews, "The True Constitution of Government," *loc. cit.*, p. 21.

12 Andrews, "Cost of the Limit of Price," *loc. cit.*, p. 15. The quotation concludes: "out of the sphere of duty or submission to the wants of others into the sphere of integral development and freedom."

13 Tucker, p. 56.

14 *Ibid.*, p. 71.

15 Bakunin, *The Political Philosophy*, p. 155.

16 "There is only one answer to the question: 'What can be done to better this penal system?' Nothing. A prison cannot be improved." Kropotkin, *Revolutionary Pamphlets*, p. 222.

17 *Ibid.*, p. 217.

18 Tucker, pp. 57–58.

19 Bakunin, *The Political Philosophy*, p. 264.

20 *Ibid.*, p. 266.

21 *Ibid.*

22 "Speak not of liberty—poverty is slavery!" Kropotkin, *Revolutionary Pamphlets*, p. 124.

23 Robinson, pp. 70–71.

24 Tucker, p. 351.

25 *Ibid.*, pp. 311–312.

26 This is Proudhon's principle of "Equality of Functions."

27 It should be noted again that Warren, the first important American anarchist, developed his very similar ideas in apparent ignorance of Proudhon. It was only later that Proudhon became significant in the American anarchist tradition.

28 Tucker, p. 249.

29 "A true money reform . . . would abolish almost entirely and directly every one of those forms of usury except ground-rent, while a true land reform would directly abolish only ground-rent." *Ibid.*

30 *Cf. ibid.*, pp. 370–374.

31 Andrews, "Cost the Limit of Price," *loc. cit.*, p. 54.

32 "Of course," exclaimed Andrews' mentor, "the washerwoman must have more per hour than the vender of house-lots or the inventor of pills!" Josiah Warren, *Equitable Commerce* (New York: Fowlers and Wells, 1852), pp. 82–83.

33 Andrews, "Cost the Limit of Price," *loc. cit.*, p. 57.

34 *Ibid.*, p. 44.

35 *Ibid.*, p. 211.

36 The justification for calling Tucker an individualist should be clear in the

last section of this chapter. Tucker should thus be regarded as both mutualist and individualist—a Proudhonian and a Stirnerite.

37 Woodcock, *Railroads and Society*, p. 26.

38 Rocker, p. 104.

39 Woodcock, *Railroads and Society*, p. 27.

40 Rocker, p. 109.

41 Woodcock, *Railroads and Society*, p. 27.

42 Rocker, p. 121.

43 See Chapter 7.

44 Kropotkin, *Revolutionary Pamphlets*, p. 57.

45 *Ibid.*, p. 140.

46 *Ibid.*, p. 141.

47 Bakunin, *The Political Philosophy*, p. 156. Emphasis added in order to point up the great difference between communistic and individualistic anarchism on the implementation of the principle of equality of opportunity.

48 *Ibid.*, p. 328.

49 *Ibid.*

50 Berkman, *Now and After*, p. 272.

51 Bakunin, *The Political Philosophy*, p. 247.

52 Kropotkin, *Revolutionary Pamphlets*, p. 57.

53 Berkman, *Now and After*, pp. 197–198.

54 Kropotkin, *Revolutionary Pamphlets*, p. 59 (emphasis added). Kropotkin, in arguing against the view of certain "collectivists" that distribution be made proportionate to the hours of actual labor expended, had said that this "mitigated individualism" would require a very strong government to impose it—which would rule out anarchism.

55 Berkman, *Now and After*, p. 276.

56 Berkman's examples of the latter: clerks, agents, salesmen, judges, bailiffs, lawyers, policemen, soldiers, sailors, wardens, advertizers, etc., etc.

57 Kropotkin, *Revolutionary Pamphlets*, p. 188.

58 Bakunin, *The Political Philosophy*, p. 341.

59 Kropotkin, *Revolutionary Pamphlets*, p. 60.

60 *Ibid.*

61 Tolstoy, *What Then Must We Do?*, p. 206.

62 *Ibid.*, p. 282.

63 *Ibid.*, p. 301.

64 Bakunin had expressed similar ideas: "In a living and integral man each of these activities—muscular and nervous—should be equally developed . . . far from harming each other, those two activities are bound to support, enlarge, and reinforce each other. Thus the knowledge of the savant will become more fruitful, useful, and broader in scope when he is no stranger to physical work, and the labor of the educated worker will be more productive than that of an ignorant one. Hence it follows that it is to the interest of both labor and science that there be no more workers or scientists but only men." Men of intellectual superiority "will necessarily place their discoveries and applications at the dis-

posal of society, for the benefit of everyone. . . ." *The Political Philosophy,* p. 329.

65 Tolstoy, *What Then Must We Do?,* p. 337.

66 Luke III:11 (RSV).

67 All the Tolstoyan colonies "I have been able to trace failed in a relatively short period, either from the personal incompatibility of the participants or from lack of practical agricultural experience." Woodcock, *Anarchism,* p. 234.

68 See Joll, p. 34.

69 Godwin, *An Enquiry* . . . , Vol II, p. 511.

70 Stirner, pp. 327–329.

71 Warren, p. 90.

72 Tucker, p. 42.

73 "An increasing familiarity with sociology will convince both society and the individual that *practical* individual sovereignty . . . is the law of social life, the only condition upon which human beings can live in harmony." When this truth is accepted, we will have "individual sovereignty" in reality,—not as a sacred right vindicated, but as a social expedient agreed upon. . . . *Ibid.,* p. 132.

74 *Ibid.,* p. 292.

75 *Ibid.,* p. 445.

76 Berkman, *Now and After,* p. 209.

77 Tucker, p. 362.

7

Evaluation of Anarchism

FAILURE AS A HISTORICAL MOVEMENT

Success and Failure

From one point of view, anarchism has had a successful history. It has always had strong appeal to thoughtful and virtuous men. In the hundred years before World War I, especially, it won many adherents; this was its "golden age." And even at the present time intelligent and articulate individuals espouse its principles. As a theory of man and society anarchism has retained its vitality over a long period of time. Unlike, say, Descartes' theory of the vortex, it has not been an idea that had a momentary appeal only to be discarded as history moved forward and men became more informed. The history of political theory also contains ideas that were once compelling but have perished. Theories of monarchy and divine-right rule, for example, are today as dead and irrelevant as Cartesian science. But the theory of anarchy, now as for centuries, remains, on its positive side, a live option for many thinkers and, on its negative side, a penetrating and relevant criticism of modern conditions for a great many more. In this sense, then, anarchism is not a failure as a historical movement.

However, when we seek to examine the states and societies actually affected by anarchism, we are inclined to be impressed with its failure as a historical movement. How many states has the movement destroyed? How long did they remain "destroyed"? How many anarchist societies have been established and how long have they endured? Has the impact of anarchism been such that authoritarian control over people's lives has diminished over the years? Is anarchism in any of its forms a potent force in the world today? [1] The answers to these questions are obvious. The thoughts of the thinkers, the leadership of the leaders, the work of the workers, and the suffering of the martyrs seem, all of them, to have made very little difference in the way the world has gone. The state has grown strong, and anarchism has been reduced, at best, to verbal protest. "Anarchism is in this day and age," writes Horowitz, "more of a literature than a movement." [2]

The concrete failures of anarchism are expressed in such events as the disappointments of 1848–1849, the suppression of uprisings in various Italian, French, and Spanish cities in the sixties and seventies, the execution of rebellious and peaceful anarchists in Russia by the Bolsheviks, the victory of Franco in Spain, the loss of control of the CGT in France to reformists and Maxists, the demise of Warren's communities in America, the quarrels in Tolstoyan colonies in Russia, and the pathetic life of Stirner in Germany.

Reasons for Failure

Why did the movement fail? The first and most obvious answer is that it did not appeal to enough people. Its description of the new society was often too vague to arouse support or too preposterous to be credible.[3] In the meantime, of course, great sacrifices were to be made in the present with utter contempt for any gains less than complete. Great hosts of people, forsaken by their governments, oppressed, angry, and resentful, were available to the anarchist cause. But most of these people turned to other movements that could promise them more definite goals while giving them immediate gains. The anarchists were not the only people who could criticize the present, nor the most effective. Trade unions could improve working conditions, social democrats could widen the franchise and sponsor reform movements, and Marxists could talk about a perfect society while improving the present one. The great and unique anarchist principle, individual autonomy, was too philosophical for the masses, who viewed their suffering in more physical terms.

A second reason (for no one reason is adequate) lies in the organizational aspect of the movement itself and its failure to devise effective tactics and strategy. Now it is surely the case that no revolutionary movement can plan a master strategy and expect to carry it out in detail. But it must *have* a strategy and adjust its tactics to it. It must be able to see opportunities and to exploit them. This requires organization, direction, and coordination among the individuals and groups of the movement. Spontaneity is a fine thing, and the zeal manifested in a genuinely passionate uprising can overcome a battalion of bayonets. But gains have to be consolidated and to lead to other gains.

Anarchism has never, in the nature of the case, valued organization and leadership.[4] This applies not only to Bakunin-style insurrection but to the experimental communities as well. An anarchist leader cannot expect the rank and file to follow him in ignorance of what he is about, and seldom even when it knows. Where individual freedom is stressed, disciplined commitment to the cause of the group must suffer. A brilliant and concerned collectivist like Kropotkin encouraged everyone but directed no one. How can a movement succeed when it makes a virtue of the vagueness of its ends, scorns short-term gains, resists organizational discipline, and distrusts leadership itself?

A third reason for the failure of anarchism is found in the widespread disagreement among the anarchists on fundamental issues. If there had been a natural harmony (if not identity in attitude) among them the first two factors working against success might have been mitigated. A general agreement on the goal (vague though it may have been) and a basic agreement on the means (unspecified in detail as it may have been) could have made possible concerted action when conditions were ripe under *ad hoc* leadership. The required discipline could have reached an effective level in a natural way as individuals, fired by a common vision, did those things that all recognized as an effective means of destroying or replacing a common enemy. Christianity and Marxism early realized the importance of orthodoxy. The faithful must remain united on key principles, and the name itself must stand for definite convictions shared by all. The differences between Christians and heretics, between Marxists and revisionists seem positively picayune when compared, say, with the differences between Stirner and Kropotkin.

A fourth reason for the failure of anarchism is related to the social realities of modern Europe and America. It is surely the case, as many writers have pointed out, that anarchism, with all its anti-centralization and anti-organizationalism, was (and still is) running counter to a strong historical trend. Anarchism failed, then, because it simply could not do otherwise. How could any minority group, no matter how well organized, reverse the trend to large, complex, efficient, and centralized social organization—when that trend was supported by most of the wealth, science, intelligence, technology, and communications of the day? What is beyond dispute is the *difficulty,* at least, of achieving anarchist goals in modern society. How can government—which in every nation has brought thousands (sometimes millions) of people onto its payroll and into its network, which controls vast material resources, which commands masses of armed and trained soldiers, and upon which all its citizens are dependent for roads, schools, and welfare—be destroyed by a hand-ful of earnest individualists? How can a manufacturing concern with plants in several cities employing thousands of men performing hundreds of integrated and technical functions possibly give way to workshops "directed" by workers' representatives? How can vast agricultural enterprises, responsive to giant domestic and foreign buyers, operating irrigated and fertilized fields with expensive me-chanical contraptions, give way to independent peasant proprietors? And how can a society with social security, unemployment insur-ance, mutual insurance companies, and credit cards give way to the kind of person-to-person mutual aid the anarchists talk about? And how is a society burdened with millions of laws and bureaucratic regulations and procedures, a society in which individuals require lawyers and ombudsmen even to survive, to be replaced by one that has no laws at all? Anarchism has indeed failed—but consider the task it set for itself! [5]

It is difficult to see how anarchism could succeed even in its more limited aims. Can successful anarchist communities be set up in the context of modern society? Is there a mountain region in this country or any other so remote from the enforceable requirements of society and government that free individuals can fashion lives of their own based on their own autonomy and personal relations with others? Perhaps Stirner after all was correct. Anarchism can succeed *only* in the mind of the lonely individual, the man who bends his body when he must but preserves at all times his aggres-sive spirit against all those impersonal forces around him which would annihilate him.

FAILURE AS A
SYSTEM OF THOUGHT

Competing Freedoms

Anarchism has been criticized above for its vague and unrealistic descriptions of what the good society is to be. It was this characteristic, among others, that prevented anarchism from succeeding in history. The fact, however, that anarchism goes as far as it does in prescribing the new society (and some anarchists go quite far) suggests a theoretical difficulty that is just the reverse of the practical one. To describe the good society is to structure it. And to structure it is to limit its members' liberty. A member of an anarchist collective will be required to do certain tasks and in a certain way. A member of a syndicate has pledged his skills and loyalty. A member of a voluntary association, in the Proudhon or Warren style, will find himself involved with banks and labor notes. A member of a Tolstoyan community will have to meet the demands of love.

It may be true that an individual need not join any of these and, if he does, may withdraw at will. This, however, would indicate only that he finds this society or that destructive of freedoms he wishes to preserve. An individual who joins and remains, on the other hand, is indicating that he is willing to surrender some freedoms in order to gain others. All this means that freedom *qua* freedom is usually not the goal of anarchism, but that some freedoms (*e.g.,* from the state) are more desirable than others and that there is a great deal of disagreement among the anarchists on the relative importance of the other (positive and negative) freedoms.

It would appear that the individualists would be immune to this criticism. It is for this reason, perhaps, that they maintain that only they are *true* anarchists.[6] But the fact is that all of them (with the possible exception of Stirner) sponsor structures also. The best that can be said for the individualists is that by emphasizing the looseness of the relations among individuals, they tend to espouse a greater *amount* of freedom. But even this is debatable. As any state socialist could argue, freedom consists, positively, of being able to do what you want to do and, negatively, of not being prevented from doing what you want to do. It is thus the case that close support from others may, on occasion, help you do what you want to do (*e.g.,* check a book out of the library); on other occasions such support may eliminate a force (*e.g.*, a thief) that seeks to prevent you from doing what you want to do. What the individualists must prove, then, is that one has a greater amount of the kind of freedom that he prefers in societies characterized by loose relations.

In any case, then, for both collectivist and individualist, the desirability of one or the other anarchist versions of the good society must finally derive not from the importance of freedom itself, but from the valuation he makes of the freedoms promoted and those surrendered. The point of agreement among the anarchists is simply that government is bad, that it is in fact the worst offender against desirable positive and negative freedoms.[7]

Competing Desires

Such a way of talking about freedom gets very close to making *freedom* and *desire* synonymous. That which a person regards as most desirable is elevated by that person to the status of an essential freedom. Robinson was very honest in rejecting all formulas for justice. He said that "all desires stand upon a par, morally, and . . . it is for us to find the most convenient way of gratifying as much of everybody's desires as possible." [8] Perhaps this is what anarchism is all about: satisfy as many desires of as many people as is possible. But with *this* principle, a state socialist could heartily agree.

A critic might think that he had discerned a rather childish attitude in anarchism: conditions are bad—they are not desirable; the government supports the *status quo;* therefore, if only the state were abolished our troubles would be over and people would live together (or apart) harmoniously. Is it not simple-minded to find a scapegoat (government) for everything bad and to believe that if only the scapegoat were dispatched everything would naturally fall into proper place? Such a criticism is *ad hominem* and thus not allowable. But the fact is that a great many anarchists expect a great many things to happen when the state disappears. And these results are all quite different. What each anarchist *expects* to happen is what he *wants* to happen.

Indeed, the results have a fundamental importance of their own. Each particular anarchist seems to be saying, "This is what society should be like; therefore abolish the state, which prevents it." The anarchists are *not* saying: "Abolish the state in order that people may freely choose how they wish to live." They *already know* how people ought to wish to live. Bakunin promised that the social revolution would not chain people to a Procrustean bed, but would give "full liberty to the masses, groups, communes, associations, and even individuals." But this simply does not square with his prescription for a communistic society in which everyone is equal.

The issue of property is a good example. The range of various property arrangements in the new society (in which there is no government) virtually parallels those in the old society (in which there is government). Anarchists range from defense of free enterprise to communism. No other aspect of the new society has had more attention and more space in anarchist writings than property. If *anarchism* is the main objective, then the question of property should be left to be dealt with in whatever ways individuals and groups of individuals choose to deal with it. Actually, however, most anarchists are ready with a fairly comprehensive and inclusive program on the property problem! [9]

Indispensability of Law

The anarchists were much more in agreement on the issue of law and order. The most obvious concern of government in the nineteenth century was to define crime and to deal with it, and its ability to do these things was the measure of its success far more than is the case today when governments emphasize more positive social goals. The anarchists were correct in looking for special interests behind the vaunted ideal of maintaining law and order for the advantage of all. And they were sound in asking how and whether institutional punishment reforms offenders and/or dissuades repetition by others. But they are far from reassuring in their account of how crime is to be dealt with in the good society.

Surely the freedom to steal, to commit acts of violence, and to revolt (or counter-revolt) are not freedoms that should be protected for the individual. Bertrand Russell argued that laws should exist in order to prevent such actions. He believed that even if destitution were eliminated in the anarchist society, some men would want more than their fellows and would, individually or in groups, take it. Public opinion would naturally be against them and forceful action might be taken. "In that case," wrote Russell, we would have revived "the evils of criminal law with the added evils of uncertainty, haste and passion, which are inseparable from the practice of lynching." [10] Crimes of violence are not always caused by oppression, economic or otherwise. They can occur anywhere and at any time. Is not law an indispensable part of the way to deal with them? Finally, if anarchists wish to retain an anarchist society, they will have to have laws to prevent non-anarchists from arming themselves and taking over. Would this not be self-contradictory?

It is axiomatic that whatever laws society has should be enforced. The anarchists are correct in questioning the purpose and practicality of enforcement. Retribution clearly does not justify punishment. Utility to the offender and society does. Enforcement should effectually serve one or more of the following purposes: dissuade future offenders, protect society at large, reform the offender. The efficacy of the punishment in achieving the first has doubtless been overestimated, but the likelihood of apprehension and punishment does in fact *often* dissuade *many* potential offenders. The "propagandists of the deed" were not always dissuaded, but they often were. By what means was the anarchist revolution itself prevented if not by the threat of punishment for those who would attempt it? In dissuading future offenders, law enforcement also serves the second purpose. But something else is intended in the protection of society. Thieves and murderers should not be permitted to go free to repeat their acts against members of society. It is reasonable to kill or cage wild beasts which cannot be driven away. If offenders against society should not be executed or exiled, they must at least be restrained. Had Berkman not been jailed, he would have come back to murder Mr. Frick the next day.

Therefore, enforcement does have at least *some* effectiveness in dissuasion and protection. It does serve the values (misguided as some of them may be) that society has set for itself. Even an individualist society like Tucker's, in which equality of liberty is the ideal, must protect itself. Tucker recommended defensive associations and advocated confinement of dangerous criminals. These associations were to be supported by "voluntary taxation" and were expected to deliver better and less expensive service than governments.[11] And would there not have to be principles established (laws) to distinguish real invasion from mere inconvenience?

Indeed, it is difficult to understand how any particular version of an anarchist society could be preserved without some kind of law to promote certain constructive social actions. Would not the collectivist, for example, have to have some laws *in addition* to those against theft, violence, and rebellion in order to carry on as an orderly system? They might be called "resolutions" or "regulations" or "recommendations," but obedience to them would be expected and disobedience would be met with opprobrium. What other inference could be made from such a statement as: "A man, once he has fulfilled his contractual economic functions, can live as he will, provided he does not interfere with the freedom of his fellows"? [12] Mutualists and individualists would have to have rules of procedure when setting up their banks. These would be even more necessary in dealing with the land problem and ascertaining what is actually used and how many acres an individual could plausibly claim to "occupy." It is true that much of this is to be on a voluntary basis, but the individual's decision on whether to play the game or stay out of it will be made on the basis of knowing the rules of the game. If someone is to live with other people in *any* kind of a community, he will have to subject himself to *some kind* of governing authority.[13]

The dilemma is this: laws of some kind are either needed or are not needed. If the anarchist accepts the first thesis, the force of much that he says against the state is vitiated. The great issue of authority simply becomes a matter of degree. If he accepts the second, he is inconsistent with the positive means he states for conserving his own new society.

The State
as a Friend of Freedom

It is the third purpose (reform the offender) on which the anarchists have commented most persuasively. Perhaps the term "punishment" is inappropriate here. The objective of society surely must be to improve the disposition of the offender, not to inflict a selected amount of vindictive pain on his person. The anarchists are correct in saying that in the great majority of cases prisons do not achieve any real reform or rehabilitation of the characters of their charges. Convicts should be treated, as the anarchists tell us, as misguided, damaged, or sick members of society. They, more than anyone else, need understanding, guidance, treatment, and therapy. And they do not get it. Offenders should not be hurt nor should they be ignored; they should be helped.

The question, then, is whether a society organized as a state or one that is anarchic can best provide this help. The latter is not the case. When one thinks of the complexity of the problem, of the medical, psychological, and moral forces that must be marshaled to create even a chance of occasional success, of the coordination required with various economic, occupational, and transportative institutions, he might conclude that the attack on dangerous anti-social behavior is like waging a war. Voluntary associations and well-intentioned individuals can and do contribute to psychological health, but would not a really comprehensive program require a degree of organization, financing, and, to use a bad word, compulsion, that only a government could bring about?

The anarchist would depend heavily on the power of public opinion to reduce and contain "criminal" behavior. If one grants that public opinion can possess considerable power, the question becomes whether it is better for individuals to be restricted in their liberty by explicit laws and professional law-enforcers or to be restricted by the attitudes and actions of the general public and "volunteers" from that public. The latter can become very oppressive—as some anarchists themselves have pointed out in other contexts. Is control of the social environment for the purpose of producing certain kinds of behavior any less restrictive of freedom than promulgating a law code? The critic of anarchism can argue with some point that the existence of definite laws increases one's net freedom. The citizen is subject to certain laws (and this is bad), but by implication is free in all those areas in which laws do not apply (and this is good). In an anarchist society, by contrast, one is subject to the whole force of public opinion of the entire community; this leaves virtually no area in which he is free.[14]

Leonard Hobhouse wrote: "There are other enemies of liberty than the State and it is, in fact by the State that we have fought them." [15] This is true for several reasons. Two have already been alluded to: (1) the state may act as a hedge against the oppression of public opinion; (2) the state may serve as a means of creating those conditions for positive action in definite ways. More specifically, the state has, historically, taken substantial measures against social institutions that have very seriously limited individual freedom. Examples are: action against tyrannical local governments in feudal *and* modern times, destruction of such extralegal "ruling" bodies as robber bands, weakening control over citizens by organized religions, and legislation against oppressive practices against workers by powerful capitalists and landowners. Predatory types welcome anarchism. Dostoyevsky's Shigalev said, "Starting from unlimited freedom, I arrive at unlimited despotism." Anarchists may mock the freedom that statists have claimed individuals have in a governed society: "How do you live? What does your freedom amount to? Are you not subject to your employer? Is your freedom not seriously restricted by the amount of your wages, the laws that others pass on your 'behalf'?" So Berkman finally says: "Freedom really means opportunity to satisfy your needs and wants. If your freedom does not give you that opportunity, then it does you no good. Real freedom means opportunity and well-being. If it does not mean that, it means nothing." [16] Now *this* conception of freedom is the basis for the welfare state—and perhaps every other state that ever existed.

It may perhaps be conceded to the anarchists that the state is the most obvious source of oppression and has indeed operated as a coercive force. But nothing in the nature of state-ness demands that it always do so. Nothing, that is, unless any action that restricts some people somewhere in some way is an action that diminishes liberty. This, however, is fanatical. The net gain or loss of freedom is the issue. A decision *not* to act in certain contexts can decrease freedom as certainly as a positive decision in other contexts.[17] And the fact of the matter is that the state has often acted in such a way as to serve the needs and purposes of the people—that is, on behalf of freedom.[18]

Invasion and Defense

Tucker was very insistent on his "vital" distinction between *invasion* and *defense*. The former, characteristic of government, is never justified, not even when one *individual* invades another's liberty. The latter is always permissible against such invasion. But it was not always clear, even to Tucker, which of the two was at work. His "voluntary associations" could lock up a criminal—this was defense. But when the state branded an action as criminal and locked up the agent—this was invasion. But the "criminal" in the first instance could charge *invasion,* while the "archist" in the second instance could plead *defense.* The difficulty here is the same as is present in John Stuart Mill's famous dictum on the limits of the power of society over the individual.[19] Robinson, whose anarchism often took the form of non-resistance, debated the issue with Tucker. Who is to judge the point at which invasion begins, the line between something simply undesired and real harm? Tucker, in a literal way, answered that the individual himself, or a combination of similarly thinking individuals, is to decide and act accordingly.[20] Then, more seriously, he admitted that there will be a "strip of debatable land," but that the "growing conception that aggression is an evil to be avoided and that liberty is the condition of progress" will tend to narrow it.[21] Tucker would move in Robinson's direction by *enduring* the actions of others, by giving the freedom of the other person the benefit of doubt, but he did not give up the principle.[22] But he never satisfactorily defended its applicability. It sufficed for him that government was always clearly on the side of the line labeled *invasion* and that individuals should be judged by the same criterion.

This controversy is at the very heart of the issue concerning the truth of anarchism. If the principle is so vague that well-meaning people can disagree on its applicability and take violent action against various "invaders," then anarchism *is* sheer individualism, with all the fights and chaos commonly charged to it. Agreement in principle but disagreement in practice is no more orderly than disagreement in principle with agreement in practice. Everyone wants justice but disagrees on where it lies in individual cases! Indeed, people in such a state of anarchy might well begin to think of seeking impartial arbiters and abiding by majority rule. But this is John Locke, and plunges us right back to statism.[23] Robinson's own solution, as we have seen, is remarkably like Tolstoy's, and probably just as impractical.

The anarchists are perfectly correct in challenging the myth of the social contract. They are correct in saying that the decisions of a man's ancestors do not bind him. They are correct in saying that government is not based upon the consent of the governed, for no consent is ever asked. But are they correct that *tacit* consent is not given by the subjects of a state? I think not. If people were asked to vote on whether their own state should continue or whether anarchism should take its place, is there much doubt about the results? In our own day, at least in the United States, not only is the system preferred by the vast majority but there is great difficulty in even *altering* the system. That revolutionary movements everywhere have difficulty in getting recruits indicates that people tend to prefer what they have, however bad it may be. That the anarchists in particular have difficulty indicates that people prefer to live under a state than to try to get along without one.

These, then, are the basic criticisms of the theory of anarchism. The anarchist society is not necessarily one of greater freedom, but is inspired by different conceptions of what freedom consists of. This society could not easily discard a system of law or an equivalent thereto. And finally, government is not necessarily an enemy of freedom and does, as an institution, enjoy the support of most of its citizens. There are other criticisms that can be made, but none so basic.

Other General Criticisms

One effective, but rather poor, argument set forth by many anarchists is based on the truism that peace is better than war. If there were no states, there could be no great wars; therefore the abolition of states would result in the abolition of war. This may be so, but only if all states were, at one stroke, abolished. When a society is surrounded by a ring of hostile, or potentially hostile, states, it would be foolish to dismantle its government. For if a state is a necessary condition for prosecuting a war, it is just as essential for defending against attack. As Tolstoy's translator and biographer says: "The question, 'Is war right or wrong?' evades the fact that the problems of real life are not simple, but complex. The choice is seldom between what is right and what is wrong; it is usually between a number of possible roads—a choice of evils, or of courses made up of good and evil intertwined." [24] Martin Luther, Machiavelli, Edmund Burke, and Reinhold Niebuhr all knew this—but not, apparently, Tolstoy. His position illustrates not only the pacifism of many anarchists but their simplistic approach to difficult problems. They prefer to describe an ideal state of affairs (*e.g.*, societies with no aggressive impulses) than to find practical means that gradually will produce a particular solution to a particular problem.

The "all-or-none" mentality of many anarchists is nowhere better illustrated than in their attitude toward reform in general. But "reform" need not be a dirty word. If laws are bad, for example, they should be altered or replaced. Laws and courts do not exist in order to enable some to prey on others, "but to supply men with the nearest approach we can get to impartial arbitration for the settlement of their disputes." [25] If workers are oppressed by capital and landlords, let us utilize the power of the state to remedy things somewhat. In short, if the state is not responsive to the wishes of the people, *make* it responsive. This may, indeed, have to be by violent revolution.

Plekhanoff was a bitter critic of anarchism. People like Bakunin, he believed, who despise taking part in political action or reform movements, think that they are being very revolutionary in preventing the workers from being tainted with bourgeois ideals. Actually, however, they are being very conservative, and established regimes rejoice at their position. Workers must, said Plekhanoff, free themselves from moral and political enslavement, *then* make their revolution. A purely economic (or "purely" anything else) revolution is impossible. And what good are riots, "isolated risings of workers and peasants"? They are costly and do not bring matters any closer, "even by a single step, to that 'immediate' economic revolution of which he (Bakunin) 'dreamed.' " [26] Kropotkin, too, is wrong in calling for the revolutionary emancipation of the peasants in order that they can overthrow the czar. Plekhanoff believed that the czar had to be weakened *first* in order for the peasants to become emancipated.[27]

Tolstoy, however, was consistent with a familiar anarchist principle that means be consistent with ends. At the other end of the spectrum the "propagandists of the deed" were not, for they had no regret about the death of the individual person, whether guilty or innocent. What about those in between: Goldman, Bakunin, Kropotkin, Berkman, Sorel, and others? Is violent revolution compatible with the end of peaceful, cooperative, and respectful accord among men in a society of equals? Should not such anarchists change their means or give up their principle? The principle, of course, is cherished by people who spurn political means. But I do not see anything paradoxical in using political means for weakening the state or gaining control of it and then gradually or suddenly dismantling it. It may be psychologically difficult for men accustomed to wielding political authority to give it up; it is not, however, illogical.

A general criticism suggested in the first section can be made of the philosophy of revolution. To replace one form of government with another is no easy matter. To eliminate government entirely is even more difficult. The most thorough kind of organization is required. Collectivists of all kinds emphasize the importance of organizing and disciplining the revolutionaries.[28] They would bring into their net factory workers, peasants, and intellectuals. Plans would be made, timetables set up. The question thus becomes whether the libertarianism so central to the nature of anarchism is consistent with the authority required for successful action against the establishment. If the anarchist chooses to emphasize the libertarianism (as he often does), one wonders how he will ever prevail against the organized state. Some anarchists seek to evade both horns of the dilemma by talking about voluntary and libertarian organizations. This will not do. A serious dilemma exists for the anarchist on the issue of organized revolution, just as it does on the issue of an organized new society.

Plekhanoff sees a fundamental contradiction in the anarchist position on the importance of individual liberty. Individual liberty, say the anarchists, is all-important. Not even the *majority* is to infringe it. If this is so, then why do they oppose the people (majority or *minority*) who use the state to support their exploitation of others? They are doing what *they* want to do—and doing it very well! If everything (freely done) is morally acceptable, then no moral indignation can justifiably be mustered against any action, no matter how "unjust." The dilemma is this: if liberty is always good, the exploiters are beyond reproach; if liberty is not always good, then anarchism must be qualified; therefore, the exploiters are beyond reproach or anarchism must be qualified. The Stirnerite could "grasp the first horn" and hold that no one is beyond reproach or "within" reproach, for moral qualities beyond freedom itself are nonsense. The others might choose to avoid the first horn and be impaled upon the second. They might, that is, be willing to qualify anarchism by making a distinction between desirable and undesirable freedoms—as I have argued previously that all people (whatever their ideology) should do. But I know of no anarchist who has explicitly done so.

One more general criticism. I am reluctant to make it, however, for it is a criticism based on the nature of human nature, and neither I nor anyone else knows what human nature is or is not capable of. Some anarchists, especially Godwin, believe that men with sufficient help in being reasonable will properly judge what is desirable or moral. So great efforts in education should be made to eliminate the distorting medium of political ideology and to develop the ability of the young to make rational judgments on the basis of the facts themselves. But of Godwin three questions must be asked: (1) Is there good reason to believe that the moral judgments will always be correct—*i.e.,* in accordance with the principles of utilitarianism? (2) Is it certain that the person will therefore desire, and thus act on behalf of, the desirable? (3) Will not even the good society engender some general (prejudiced) beliefs? [29]

It seems to be the case that anarchism requires men to be better than they now are. This is not an unreasonable requirement. No theory would be worth discussing which did not impose it. At the very least we can expect improvement in human behavior to result from a judicious alteration of those institutions that condition it. But is it not perhaps possible that anarchism requires too much? Shaw, for one, thinks men are good enough for state socialism but not for anarcho-socialism. In a libertarian society too much may be entrusted to the individual's good nature. If man is so good naturally, then "how did the corruption and oppression under which he [presently] groans ever arise?" [30]

Marx vs. Stirner

We will conclude this section with four special criticisms: a Marxist's criticism of individualism, a socialist's criticism of mutualism, an economist's criticism of syndicalism, and my own criticism of Kropotkin.

Karl Marx dealt with Max Stirner in the mid-1840s in a book called *The German Ideology*.[31] With typical rudeness and impatience, Marx made four fundamental criticisms: (1) Stirner bases his whole philosophy on an abstraction. What is the ego but an abstraction from a whole complex of social relations? Can one strip everything away and find at the center of the web an atomic little ego? No. Stirner had rejected other famous abstractions such as "God" and "man," but he swallowed the most monstrous one of all: the "ego." (2) Stirner fails to see the reality of the state. In spite of all the myths with which it surrounds itself, the state exists and possesses real force. "Stirner forgets," wrote Marx, "that he has only destroyed the fantastic and ghostly form which the notion of 'fatherland,' etc., assumes in the skull of 'the adolescent' (*Junglings*) but that he has not even touched upon these ideas insofar as they express real relations." [32] (3) Stirner fails to realize that genuine self-interest is best realized in a group. The individual may have to make initial sacrifices to the group, but when he identifies himself with the group they seem perfectly natural. The group will then pursue his real interests more effectively than he could himself. (4) Stirner is petty-bourgeois. Obsessed with what belongs only to himself, he tries to abstract his own contribution from the collective fruit of social labor. Stirner, wrote Marx, "offers us an additional proof of how the most trivial sentiments of the petty-bourgeois can borrow the wings of a high flown ideology." [33]

Shaw vs. Tucker

George Bernard Shaw criticized Tucker's contention that the fundamental economic principles "are a logical deduction from the principles laid down by Adam Smith in the early chapters of *Wealth of Nations:* namely, that labor "is the true measure of price." Tucker holds that Warren, Proudhon, Marx, and himself then properly deduce "that the natural wage of labor is its product." This, said Shaw, is not so. Even after assuming the abolition of monopolies and equality of effort, the value that labor commands is determined by the *situation in which it is exercised.* Is your shop on a good street or a bad one? Is your field fertile or rocky? Is your mine rich or poor?

And how do you get good locations under anarchism? Occupy them first? According to certain rules? Perhaps by lot? It really does not matter. In any case, the lucky person will be able to sell or exchange his location for an (unearned!) profit.[34]

Suppose, said Shaw, that someone has some very good land. As more (worse) land is brought into cultivation, the price of our man's labor will rise, for his efforts (in his better situation) produce more. "As the agricultural industry is in this respect typical of all industries, it will be seen now that price does not rise because worse land is brought into cultivation, but that worse land is brought into cultivation by the rise of price. Or, to put it another way, the price of the commodity does not rise because more labor has been devoted to its production, but more labor is devoted to its production because the price has risen." [35]

Labor *should,* perhaps, be the measure of price, but in an unregulated economy it can never be. "Under Anarchism that small fraction of the general wealth which was produced under the least favorable circumstances would fetch at least its cost, while all the rest would be nothing but privately appropriated rent with an Anarchist mask on." [36]

Estey vs. Syndicalism

J. A. Estey presented several reasons for his conclusion that syndicalism will not work: (1) Producers' cooperatives in the past have not worked very well. Why? They have lacked capital, equipment, and good management. Workers have little conception of the importance of good administration. "Qualities of managership they constantly underestimate." [37] If they *get* a good manager, they resent his authority. Matters will be even worse under anarchism. They will "distrust directive ability." Living in an atmosphere in which freedom and autonomy are stressed (*e.g.,* the CGT), "they inherit a spirit of insubordination." (2) "There is nothing about trade union organizations which is peculiarly fitted to educate the labourers in handling modern industries. Trade unions may inculcate the principles of solidarity, they may be useful in gaining material reforms from the bourgeoisie, they may succeed in promoting workmen's insurance or technical education; but with all this they do not supply the quality which can make their members capable of carrying on independently the industries in which they are engaged." [38] Conceivably they could succeed in a small shop. But in modern industry the huge large-scale industries pose the real test. These need centralized, professional control. "But with centralisation Syndicalism has nothing in common, and either Syndicalism will break down or progress will cease." [39] (3) Leadership of some kind will have to emerge. Some (a minority) of the workers would begin to function like employers—the ones with the most seniority, or the most skill, or the most power of persuasion. Workers will squabble with one another. Chaos will result and be paralleled at higher levels, for particular syndicates will squabble with one another. Just as they do *now:* "Far from displaying an edifying spirit of solidarity, the workers of France, in the professedly Syndicalist congresses and organizations in general, have revealed dissensions as bitter as those to which the French Socialist parties have been subjected." [40] There is no reason to believe that solidarity would be greater in a syndicalist society. "When the common oppressor has disappeared, when the capitalist system no longer exists, and the labouring classes become a society of free and equal producers, one of the strongest motives toward union is withdrawn." [41]

Criticism of Kropotkin

All the anarchists discussed above showed great confidence that they were correct in their theories. Not for a moment did they waver in their conviction of what is wrong with society and how the wrongs should be remedied. True, the confidence of the theorists of non-politics is matched by that of the theorists of politics, but one would expect somewhat more reserve and tentativeness from a school of thought that calls for so radical and destructive a break with the past. That the anarchists disagree among themselves on important issues gives none of them pause. They do not comply with Cromwell's injunction, "I beseech you, by the bowels of Christ, bethink that you may be mistaken!"

None of them is more assured than Peter Kropotkin. And none of them makes greater claim for philosophical and scientific support. He eschews metaphysics and religion. He is *au courant* with natural evolution. He knows what evolution is "trying" to produce (a society in which individual wants are best combined with social cooperation). He distinguishes between "the real wants and tendencies of human aggregations and the accidents . . . which have prevented these tendencies from being satisfied"; and pronounces the integration of "labor for the production of all riches in common" to be a real tendency.[42] He has "carefully studied" the origin of government and concludes that it is a modern phenomenon and will pass away. "The ideal of the anarchist is thus a mere summing-up of what he considers to be the next phase of evolution." [43] Anarchism is "a constituent part of the new philosophy." [44] "Anarchism has approached the study of the State exactly in the manner the naturalist approaches the study of social life among bees and ants, or among the migratory birds which hatch their young on the shores of sub-arctic lakes." [45] Kropotkin is certain that his theory of anarchism is correct, because it is based on all that's best and true in philosophy and science.

Now philosophy, in some of its expressions, has indeed been dogmatic, but science, almost by definition, must not be. Its method simply does not yield certainty. Confirmation of its theories is the best it can look for; all its "laws" are hypotheses. Science, furthermore, does not possess any logical means of transforming its statements of what *is* the case (or what was or will be the case) to statements about what *ought* to be the case. At best, science can point out the possibilities, uncover means to ends, and predict consequences. And finally, as Kropotkin himself recognizes, the social sciences are far behind the natural sciences in reliability and specificity. And of the former, the science of history is perhaps most backward. If, therefore, one presents the view that history necessarily and certainly is unfolding some glorious future and calls it a scientific proposition, he has misconceived the nature of science in three ways.

Is it indeed true that Kropotkin's study of natural and social history supports the inevitability of the good society as he envisages it? Or does it merely correct a view (long discredited) that everything in man's natural and social history is bad or that man is fundamentally and necessarily combative and egoistic? From his studies he selects instances and anecdotes of behavioral patterns that support his idea. He has at best only proved that utterly different societies from the present ones are *possible*. It is indeed a long jump from possibility to probability to necessity. The aim of anarchism, Kropotkin bravely wrote, "is to construct a synthetic philosophy comprehending in one generalization all the phenomena of nature— and therefore also the life of societies." Manifestly, Kropotkin has not achieved that aim. He has not established that anarchism "is the inevitable result of that natural-scientific, intellectual movement which began at the close of the eighteenth century. . . ." [46]

But even if one granted to him the patterns and drifts that he sees in history, something more would be required to make the transition from what man "naturally is" or is "naturally becoming" to what man morally *ought* to be. Survival, happiness, peace, self-realization—some essentially moral ideal would have to intervene to justify those encouraging tendencies he sees in human nature and to condemn others that are not so encouraging. Equality of treatment and concern for others do not become moral simply because men in all societies have had a natural capacity to practice them.

Kropotkin's scientific ability has not prevented him from running afoul of a logical difficulty inherent in the "golden rule," this "simple, obvious principle" that expresses "a morality comprising all that moralists have taught." [47] Kropotkin's willingness to use force against oppressors has already been noted. He also defends the right to hate liars.[48] One cannot really determine whether these attitudes are consistent with the golden rule until it is clear what the golden rule actually enjoins. Four interpretations are possible: (1) treat the other as you in fact would want to be treated if you were in his place; (2) treat the other as he in fact wishes to be treated; (3) treat the other as an equal to yourself—that is, as equally subject to an impartial moral law; (4) treat the other as he would, in his deepest being, wish to be treated. The first begs the question, for one does not know, morally, how he is to be treated. Or should one imaginatively project some feeling or another? Altruistic or selfish feelings? The second interpretation would not justify Kropotkin's belligerence, for even the thief and oppressor wish to be treated kindly. The third is void of ethical content but calls aloud for some moral law beneath which all men can equally stand. The fourth interpretation is perhaps that of the Gospels and goes far beyond mere equality. It may be Kropotkin's interpretation as well. If so Kropotkin's belligerence is justified only if it is adopted from a feeling of great and sacrificial love. In any case, the golden rule is far from being "simple" and "obvious."

THE STRENGTHS OF ANARCHISM

The strengths of anarchism have already been stated in the preceding chapters; they emerge from the exposition itself. Some will be singled out here for special emphasis.

Moral Independence

The major truth in the theory is the proposition that no individual, as a moral agent, is subject to the will of the state. "Nature has made . . . you and me, and millions of others of us, to long for life and joy. Is it right and just that we should be deprived of it and forever remain the slaves of a handful of men who lord it over us and over life?" [49]

The individual cannot be bound by any "contract" his ancestors may have entered into. When he reaches the age of reason, he must decide according to his own ethical principles whether his duty to himself and/or to others requires his citizenship in the state in which he is living. If he decides that it does not, he should be free to move to another state or to some frontier to which governmental power has not yet penetrated. If this is impossible, he is justified in rebellious or revolutionary action. These are hard choices. If he decides that his duty does require his citizenship, he accepts the state and has a *prima facie* duty to obey its laws. Even here, however, his loyalty to the state should be provisional. He may well reserve the right to disobey if the state commands him to act in a way he cannot reconcile with his conscience. Should such a command be made, he must ask himself whether disobedience to the state might constitute a greater moral evil than performance of the action. If he in fact disobeys, he must decide whether to accept the punishment in good grace, or to seek to avoid the punishment, or to take revolutionary action against the state. Different recourses might be indicated by different circumstances. The point is that all these decisions are ones that the individual must make for himself. They should be based on his own best ethical thought. My decisions might differ from his, but I am bound to respect a moral conclusion conscientiously arrived at. The individual's response to political authority is his own. There is no ethical, religious, or scientific argument to the effect that man, *qua* man, is necessarily a political animal.

What the anarchist literature presses home on us is the realization that man has not always done well in accepting government and that it is quite possible he is making the wrong choice in any situation in which he does decide to accept a particular government. One should not choose order without scrutinizing its nature. The advantages of government have been pointed out by all the great thinkers in the history of political theory. The anarchists balance the scales somewhat. "Look here," they say, "these are the *evils* of life in a state. These are the freedoms you give up and these are the pains you will suffer." Government may on occasion be seen to be a good bargain. But its goodness is not unmixed; it is a goodness *on balance*.

Libertarianism

The anarchists are the great libertarians of modern times. We are all drawn to support liberty. Who can oppose it? It is liberty that makes a man a man, that makes him responsible for his actions, an autonomous source of his own conduct. Without liberty, he is an object pushed and pulled around by the purposes and designs of others. Everyone instinctively senses the paramount importance of liberty. With liberty, man may succeed or fail, find misery or happiness, love or hate, but these things, the good and the bad, are his. He has lived and performed. Without liberty, man is nothing.

Liberty indeed is so important that no one should be without it (unless, by invasion of others, he forfeits it). Tucker and others were on sound moral ground in rejecting any defense of the *status quo* which accords to some people a great amount of liberty at the expense of others. The net increase, presuming that liberty can be measured, does not justify depriving some portion of the population of the basic liberty of going their own way.

But liberty takes many forms. The anarchists are on one extreme, state communists and fascists are on the other. They mark the spectrum from individualism to collectivism. And since liberty must finally attach to the individual, the anarchists are in theory perfectly correct in their rejection of all government. Most of the rest of us are somewhere between the two extremes. We see that certain freedoms must be given up in order to open up certain others. We realize that we enhance our own individual wishes by conceding something to others in society, and especially to the state. We grumble about paying our taxes and observing all the regulations simultaneously issuing from national, state, county, city, and township governments, but we think that we have made a fair exchange. We have paid our gasoline tax and enjoy good roads; we obey the speed limit and enjoy safety; we marry only one woman at a time and enjoy connubial bliss. We have given up a great deal of freedom, but we have done it willingly and deliberately for the sake of a great many benefits. We have retained our autonomy and our manhood. We have made a "good deal," while retaining an area of choice. Anarchism must always exist as a skeptical force to challenge this kind of complacent rationalization. The anarchists must always caution us to consider whether we are giving up too much, whether indeed our support of the government and its myriad plans is justified in terms of the net results, in terms of our status as self-directed individuals. Authority may simply be saying to us: "No one can do as he pleases. Therefore you must do as we please." [50]

I will not attempt to cite here the various ways in which modern states, corporations, and universities—often with the most laudable of motives—organize (program, rather) human actions and eliminate the personal and individual aspects of modern life. Millions of words written since the end of World War II describe and lament the standardization of human tastes and behavior, the impersonality of social relations, the faceless throng in "the lonely crowd," the transformation of the free individual into an "organization man," etc., etc. Yet we seem powerless to reverse the trend. The computer will devour us all and only the neatly punched cards will survive, a sorry substitute for the hearts and spirits and minds that hitherto peopled the globe.

This trend has had in its support both the discoveries of science and technology and the qualities of intelligence and efficiency. It began around the time of the French Revolution—about the same time as modern anarchism began. So anarchism was fighting a rearguard action all the way. What many anarchists feared has come true in our day with a vengeance. Super-organization has won out. The anarchists were right: it should not have been permitted to win out.

Foe of Injustice

Anarchism is not, of course, always this abstract. In its heyday it could point to the most obvious kinds of injustice, the most brutal exploitation and oppression. It wanted to weaken the power structure in order that profound economic changes could take place. At many times and at many places revolution *should* have come about. The government was indeed the *protector* of injustice. The anarchists were not only courageous in opposing such power, they were *right* that it should be destroyed. If it is true that, at least for a moment, a successful revolution creates anarchism, then many of us are, vis-à-vis the nineteenth century, anarchists. Some anarchists supplied descriptions of the kind of society that should succeed the old; others devised ways of living meaningful lives within the confines of the old society. All were fired by a vision of a kind of justice far superior to that which prevailed at the time. Now that the economic injustices of society are not so glaring, and the governments' connivance in them not so apparent, the sense of outrage conveyed and evoked by the old anarchists is not so effective. But it was effective once, and perhaps a close examination of government and economics would make one hope that it could be effective again.

The Dignity of Man

In addition to giving an earlier (and better) account than Mill of the importance of free thought and expression, Godwin [51] gave significant counsel on the improvement of man. He did not, as is commonly believed, think that man would ever be perfected. He had few illusions: "The history of mankind is little else than a record of crimes. . . . Though the evils that arise to us from the structure of the material universe are neither trivial nor few, yet the history of political society sufficiently shows that man is of all beings the most formidable enemy to man." [52] Men could and did act badly—especially in the present environment. But evil has causes; it is not a case of "original sin." On the other hand, while social and political factors that distort man's judgment may be removed or altered, real improvement lies in the proper functioning of man's reason. This is an internal matter, an individual matter. No social arrangement can (or should seek to) condition or program man to act well. The dignity and freedom of man require that his action come from himself, from his own conception of right and wrong. He is to be educated, not trained. If Godwin overestimated the potentialities of man's reason, he placed the responsibility for human action precisely where it belonged—in the unique and most treasured aspect of his being. It seems to me that all of the anarchists had similar intentions—namely, to create nondirective situations in which the individual could find his own way instead of being impelled to it.

Legitimate Criticism of Law

The typically anarchist impatience with laws is very well taken. There is no justification whatever for the staggering bundles of inconsistent laws, layer on temporal layer, geographic unit on geographic unit, with which man torments himself. Long-winded, wretchedly phrased, extending to the most private areas of behavior, they constitute a situation for all citizens more chaotic and disorderly than any anarchist society could be. It is impossible to respect the laws of a modern state or to get very excited about the importance of lawfulness. Few men can get through a year without engaging a lawyer to help them through the maze. And one is fortunate if he needs to consult only one lawyer, for lawyers today must specialize. Outside his area of specialty the lawyer is often almost as helpless as a layman. The apparatus by which the law is enforced is almost whimsical in the "justice" it hands down. Who today can be assured that he will receive a fair and speedy trial? A society that prides itself on having a government of law, not men, may find on closer inspection that it has neither. The present condition of law and justice lends weight to the anarchist position that no laws at all would be better. Certainly, fewer laws, simpler laws, and more prompt and predictable treatment for those who violate them would constitute a better state of affairs than the current one.

There are many contexts in which people get along together much more harmoniously without rules—or rather with informal "rules" that do not even need to be articulated. When rules are imposed and enforced, one tries (it is almost a challenge) to get around them. One tries to beat the system instead of working or playing with others as people. When people are engaged in doing what they really want to do, they will do it better without formal rules, enforcement, and officials standing by. Examples readily come to mind from such disparate areas as neighborhood projects, camping trips, and athletic contests.[53] There is no point in regimenting man if, in the process, he ceases to be human.

Anarchism as an Attitude of Mind

Anarchism indeed must be taken seriously. As Stirner said, "Authors fill whole folios on the State without calling in question the fixed idea of the State itself. . . ." [54] And the present writer pleads guilty to this. *No* state is an alternative, surely, to statism. It was easy to point out earlier the historical failures in the anarchist movement—the inadequacy of its means, the difficulties in its experimental communities. There is only one thing easier than pointing out the failures of anarchism, and that is to point out the historical failures of states. "Evolution is 'leading us up to Anarchism,'" wrote Tucker, "simply because it has led us in nearly every other direction and made a failure of it." [55]

Anarchism may never depose a great state, and if it did, it well could fail in establishing a viable libertarian community. Anarchism may, in the last analysis, be a false ideology. But those who tend to adhere to it can always act fruitfully in whatever state they find themselves by persistently and militantly asking such questions as these: Is that law really required? Is obedience to that demand moral? Is an organization this elaborate actually necessary? Can't we leave that decision to the individual? Why does that person want to occupy a seat of power? What special economic interest is behind this proposed legislation? Am I doing this because I want to or because it is expected of me? Am I treating him as an individual or a cog in a machine? And a thousand more.

NOTES

1 Because this last question is involved throughout Part II of this study, it will be ignored in the present chapter.

2 Horowitz, p. 24. George Woodcock mentions the few anarchist groups, communities, and periodicals left in the world today. "They form only the ghost of the historical anarchist movement, a ghost that inspires neither fear among governments nor hope among peoples nor even interest among newspapermen." *Anarchism*, p. 468.

3 Kropotkin put it well: "No struggle can be successful if it does not render itself a clear and concise account of its aim. No destruction of the existing order is possible, if at the time of the overthrow, or of the struggle leading to the overthrow, the idea of what is to take the place of what is to be destroyed is not

always present in the mind." *Revolutionary Pamphlets,* p. 156. But elsewhere he wrote: "The economic change which will result from the social revolution will be so immense and so profound, it must so change all the relations based today on property and exchange, that it is impossible for one or any individual to elaborate the different social forms which must spring up in the society of the future." *Ibid.,* p. 248.

4 A distinction should be made between what anarchists *do* (which is the issue here) and what they *say* (which is discussed below).

5 "Perhaps the anarchist revolution could only take place after the total disruption of the means of government, communications, production and exchange by, say, a nuclear war; and perhaps, after all, the terrorists were right, and only a bomb on a larger scale than any they have ever envisaged could prepare the way for the true social revolution." Joll, p. 277.

6 Tucker, for instance, wrote that his own social ideal was "utterly inconsistent with that of those Communists who falsely call themselves Anarchists while at the same time advocating a regime of Anarchism fully as despotic as that of the State Socialists themselves." Tucker, pp. 15–16.

7 This contention must itself be examined. See pp. 152–154.

8 John Beverley Robinson, in a letter printed in Tucker, p. 75.

9 In fairness to the anarchists, it must be admitted that they have achieved general agreement on the proposition that the laborer should receive full reward for his labor.

10 Russell, *Roads to Freedom,* p. 131.

11 Tucker did not, incidentally, satisfactorily answer the criticism of one F. W. Read, who wondered how several "law and order" organizations could compete in the same society without creating a great deal of confusion. See Tucker, pp. 31 ff.

12 Woodcock, *Railroads and Society,* p. 241.

13 This comment by Bakunin on natural law may or may not be pertinent: "Nature, notwithstanding the inexhaustible wealth and variety of beings of which it is constituted, does not by any means present *chaos,* but instead a *magnificently organized* world wherein every part is logically correlated to all other parts." *The Political Philosophy of Bakunin,* p. 55 (emphasis added).

14 Descriptions of experimental societies do indeed report pressure of the group on the individual and the resentment it produces in the individual (as well as in the group when public opinion is not heeded).

15 Quoted in Horowitz, p. 582.

16 Berkman, *Now and After,* p. 16.

17 Bakunin himself wisely wrote: "Nature, as well as human society, which is nothing else but that same Nature—everything that lives, does so under the categorical condition of decisively interfering in the life of someone else." *The Political Philosophy,* p. 167.

18 "The state, in spite of what Anarchists urge, seems a necessary institution for certain purposes. Peace and war, tariffs, regulation of sanitary conditions and of the sale of noxious drugs, the preservation of a just system of distribution: those, among others, are functions which could hardly be performed in a community in which there was no central government." Russell, p. 144.

19 "The sole end for which mankind are warranted, individually or collectively, in interfering with the liberty of action of any of their number is self-protection.

That the only purpose for which power can be rightfully exercised over any member of a civilized community, against his will, is to prevent harm to others. . . . The only part of the conduct of any one, for which he is amenable to society is that which concerns others. In the part which merely concerns himself, his independence is, of right, absolute. Over himself, over his own body and mind, the individual is sovereign. . . . A person may cause evil to others not only by his actions but by his inaction, and in either case he is justly accountable to them for the injury." John Stuart Mill, *On Liberty*, I.

20 Tucker, p. 71.

21 *Ibid.*, p. 74.

22 "No use of force, except against the invader; and in those cases where it is difficult to tell whether the alleged offender is an invader or not, still no force except where the necessity of immediate solution is so imperative that we must use it to save ourselves." *Ibid.*, p. 104.

23 "Tucker, like Spencer, after his admirable criticism of the State and a vigorous defense of the rights of the individual, comes to recognize the right of *defense* of its members by the State. But it was precisely by assuming the 'function' of its weaker members that the State in its historical evolution developed all its aggressive functions, which Spencer and Tucker have so brilliantly criticized." Kropotkin, *Revolutionary Pamphlets*, p. 174.

24 Aylmer Maude, "The Life of Tolstoy: Later Years," *The Works of Leo Tolstoy*, Aylmer Maude, Trans. (London: Oxford University Press, 1930), see Vol. II, pp. 318ff.

25 *Ibid.*, p. 222.

26 Plekhanoff, p. 100.

27 Plekhanoff, *a fortiori*, opposed what later came to be called "propaganda by the deed." Acts of anarchist violence "provide the government with the desired pretext for attacking the proletariat." The anarchist "wants the revolution, a 'full, complete, immediate, and immediately economic' revolution. To attain this end he arms himself with a saucepan full of explosive materials, and throws it amongst the public in. a theatre or a café. He declares this is the 'revolution.' For our own part it seems to us nothing but 'immediate' madness." *Ibid.*, pp. 134–135.

28 For example: "Organization is everything, and everything is organization." "It cannot be stressed too much that *only the right organization of the workers* can accomplish what we are striving for." Berkman, *Now and After*, pp. 249, 259.

29 See D. H. Monro's excellent study, *Godwin's Moral Philosophy* (London: Oxford University Press, 1953), especially Chapter 7.

30 George Bernard Shaw, *The Impossibilities of Anarchism* (London: The Fabian Society, 1893), Fabian Tract No. 45, pp. 14–15.

31 Co-authored by Marx and Engels, it was not published during Marx's lifetime. It was first published in full in 1932. The English-language edition (New York: International Publishers, 1947) unfortunately omits the extremely long section on Stirner. The discussion here is indebted to Sidney Hook, *From Hegel to Marx* (Ann Arbor: The University of Michigan Press, 1962).

32 Karl Marx, quoted in Hook, *ibid.*, p. 178.

33 *Ibid.*, p. 184.

34 Tucker anticipated and answered this criticism in several passages. See, for example, pp. 325, 344–347.

[35] Shaw, pp. 9–10.

[36] *Ibid.*, p. 10.

[37] J. A. Estey, *Revolutionary Syndicalism* (London: P. S. King & Son, 1913), pp. 183–184.

[38] *Ibid.*, p. 186.

[39] *Ibid.*, p. 190.

[40] *Ibid.*, p. 193.

[41] *Ibid.*

[42] Kropotkin, *Revolutionary Pamphlets*, p. 47.

[43] *Ibid.*

[44] *Ibid.*, p. 123.

[45] *Ibid.*, p. 180.

[46] *Ibid.*, p. 192.

[47] *Ibid.*, p. 105.

[48] *Ibid.*, p. 106.

[49] Berkman, *Now and After*, p. 23.

[50] Cf. Tucker, p. 250.

[51] Although it was to the American anarchist Benjamin Tucker that Mill expressed his debt.

[52] Godwin, *An Enquiry* . . . , Vol. I, pp. 6–7.

[53] Compare the zest and mutual respect of the players in a basketball game that has *no* official with a game that has. Basketball is one of the most rule-ridden of games. But in the first situation, fouls are avoided by the player—or, if inadvertently committed, called by himself. Out-of-bounds plays are easily and naturally called. Jump-ball situations are obvious. In the second situation, argument and ill will are continuous. Fouls are committed whenever chances of escaping detection are good. Similar contrasts exist in baseball. In the one situation balls and strikes are called by the catcher (!) and appeals are made to players (of either team) who are in good position to see a close play. In the other situation, spitballs flourish and a certain Chicago manager can win national fame by abusing umpires.

[54] Stirner, p. 46.

[55] Tucker, p. 49.

PART
THE NEW ANARCHISM
TWO

8

The Student Left

ANARCHISM AS THE KEY

The student left has been characterized by itself and by others as anarchistic. Mario Savio said: "American radicals are traditionally anarchistic, and that tendency is very strong here." [1] Daniel Cohn-Bendit, the hero of the 1968 uprisings in France, declared himself to be "above all" an anarchist, and pledged himself to fight repression by the state, authoritarianism, and hierarchy.[2] The emphasis of the student left is on liberty and individualism: "Do your own thing." Social order is at best of dubious value and the representatives of law are looked upon with contempt. Governments are regarded as protectors of a way of life that cannot be defended and as unresponsive to the wishes of the people. The established authorities—political, educational, religious, economic—constrain the individual and bar him from the good life. Peaceful and gradual methods of change are no longer possible or appropriate. Radical and direct action is required in order that the individual may be liberated from a system that would dehumanize him.

The views of the student left have found expression in anarchistic journals. Students admire those among the older generation who are self-styled anarchists or who advocate fundamental anarchist principles. They know and respect some of the great nineteenth-century anarchists. The black flag of anarchism flies at all the major confrontations staged by the student left. There is, *prima facie* at least, a case to be made that the anarchist philosophy is the key for understanding the views of today's student left.

In the present section the many beliefs held in common by exponents of the "old" anarchism and those of the student left will be

presented. The term "student left" is used loosely in order that it
may cover all those people of student age (under thirty), whether
or not they are students, as well as a few older people who have
chosen to identify themselves with the student movement. The
sequence of topics and principles discussed will roughly parallel
that of Part I. In the next section we will set forth certain de-
partures in the student left from classical anarchism and will view
its theory as something less and something more than anarchism.
In the last section some unsystematic critical evaluations of the new
movement will be presented.

Human Nature

In the area of human nature, even after allowing for the intra-
mural disagreements, there is a basic agreement between the spokesmen for the old and the new anarchism. Men have, according to
the student left, sufficient social feelings to live together without
external direction. Various experiments in communal living have
confidently been launched. Where rules are to exist at all, those
who live under them, on campuses and in dormitories, in towns and
in villages, may be entrusted to make them. Relations that are
genuinely human are to be cultivated; those that are artificial and
imposed from above are to be avoided.

People who seek to direct others assume that the other is incompetent. But the truth is just the opposite: the other seems
incompetent *because* he is directed. He is manipulated into incompetence. The Port Huron Statement of the Students for a Democratic
Society says: "Men have unrealized potential for self-cultivation,
self-direction, self-understanding, and creativity. It is this potential
that we regard as crucial and to which we appeal—not to the human
potential for violence, unreason, and submission to authority. The
goal of man and society should be human independence." [3]

Certain vital aspects of human nature have been all but eliminated
by conditions of modern society. The "Yippies" conducted a "Festival of Life" during the "Convention of Death" in Chicago in 1968,
featuring folksinging, poetry-reading, swimming, lovemaking, and a
workshop on "how to live free." The French students, after taking
over the Sorbonne, proclaimed "joy without limits." One of their
slogans was "Imagination Is Revolution," and when they had taken
over the Odéon Theater after marching behind a banner reading
"Let's Take the Bastions of Bourgeois Culture," one of them said,

"Imagination has taken power." The underground newspapers and movies of the young often reflect the zeal to be creative in the face of all inherited standards of taste and decency. Spontaneity and vitality are the marks of humanity; they break through the bonds of civilization and humanity reaffirms itself.

But other, less desirable human tendencies have been promoted and enhanced in modern society. Egoism and acquisitiveness are much more important than they should be. In the Middle Ages people did not seek great wealth; they were not expected to. In today's society man's natural tendency to dominate others is awakened and magnified. One of the graffiti on a wall of the Sorbonne in 1969 stated: "A cop sleeps within each of us; he must be killed." Conventional society elevates and rewards men who assert their will to acquire and to dominate.

Some young people "drop out" of modern society in order to lead a more "authentic" existence. The "hippies" will sometimes rationalize their rejection of civilized society as an attempt to recapture the natural. Even their use of drugs is defended as an attempt to find the rich but elusive resources of the natural spirit. With their long hair and beards, their indifference to modern luxuries, their obliviousness to the need for regular employment, they seem to be looking for a state of nature in the purlieus of large cities. They alone are free; the "straights" have been corrupted by artificial society and have lost their innocence. "Release those who are alive within the prison into consciousness, imagination, love." [4]

Ethics

The ethical views of the student left suggest idealism, cynicism, and amoralism. In all these attitudes they parallel the old anarchists. Their idealism expresses itself in demands for full rights for racial minorities and improved conditions of work for workers.[5] Their enthusiasm for these aims is hardly dampened by the frequent rejection of their help by Negroes who prefer their own leadership or by workers who fear their radicalism. White and middle-class themselves (for the most part), they express rage at the plight of the racially and economically oppressed. The greatest and most unanimous zeal is expressed toward ending the war in Vietnam. This feeling is strong not only in the United States, where students may become soldiers, but throughout Europe.[6] War is wrong because it brings death and suffering to soldiers and civilians of both sides.

Many of the student left are partisans of North Vietnam and the Viet Cong—that is, of the Vietnamese people against Western imperialism. Also, like the anarchists of old, the students regard the right of individual choice as a fundamental moral principle. This has two aspects: the individual must be willing to affirm his own liberty by acting in every situation in accordance with his beliefs, no matter what it costs him; and society must reduce or eliminate those forces that constrain the individual to do its will. The student left condemns both "the establishment," which demands obedience, and the "cop-out," who accedes to it. Finally, the student left is committed to continuous social and individual improvement. Bob Dylan sings, "the times they are a-changin'." The institutions of society carry over the evils of the past. The young are not satisfied with their inheritance.

The student left finds no great moral value in earning a living; indeed, successful performance in the economic system, requiring as it does competitive effort, is probably immoral. One "gets ahead" at the expense of others—fellow workers or consumers. If he participates in a rat race, he can only be a rat. Far more important to the young idealist than the economic rewards of selfish endeavor are love and honesty. These latter do not flourish in the corporation or in the marketplace.

There is a certain tension between two strands of the new left ethics. On the one hand, the leftist will say, "do your own thing"—do that which pleases you. Free yourself from all restraints, especially those that tradition or the older generation would impose. On the other hand, society must be transformed—and that means *work*. This tension between the demands of individual morality and those of social ethics might be expressed this way by a student activist: " 'Do your own thing' was valid at one point, but now we see that the system must be destroyed in order for that to be possible." "Make love, not war" is a good slogan, but "Make revolution, not love" may be better still!

This tension is common to many ethical, religious, and social theories. Which has first priority? To lead the "authentic" life or to change society so that others can more easily lead it? The presence of both tendencies among the young suggests that the familiar distinction between the passivists (hippies) and the activists can be a misleading one. The individual may often and rather easily switch his role. The student activist often seems to have greater rapport with the "dropout" than with the "straight" reformer—to the dismay of the traditional liberal.

Cynicism often accompanies idealism. If one is deeply committed to high ideals and sees them violated by society, he becomes cynical toward that society. This is especially the case when respected leaders in the society give lip service to certain ideals but fail to put them into effect promptly. Housman had said, "Let us endure an hour and see injustice done." The student left will not wait. Delay is a sign of bad faith. The older generation says one thing but continues to do another. The great fault in the eyes of the young is hypocrisy, and the old are drenched in it. The liberal talks about reform through orderly processes; in the meantime thousands suffer.[7] The establishment is not devoted to brotherhood, justice, peace, spiritual values, freedom, or change, but to the *status quo:* oppression, profits, war, consumer goods, and authority. The old guard, the relaxed and comfortable officials of schools, government, business, and churches,[8] speak of moral ideals but do not practice them.[9] This is hypocrisy. So their pronouncements are received by the radical left with cynicism. The young claim to know their enemy.

The ethical position of the student left, like that of the old anarchists, seems to their critics to be one of amoralism. But many extreme "amoralists" or "nihilists," such as Benjamin R. Tucker and Mikhail Bakunin, presupposed ethical standards quite as lofty as those cited above. What is the basis for the charge of amoralism?

First, no individual who prizes his own integrity and autonomy will accept uncritically, unthoughtfully, or on faith a system of moral injunctions. He will, as Socrates advised, *examine* the principles that are supposed to rule his life. In this period of examination many traditional norms will be qualified, set aside for a while, suspended, or rejected. Such a process is not amoral, though to a conventional person it might seem so. Second, when the norms are rejected, it appears that morality itself has been rejected. Examples are injunctions against drug use, homosexuality, free love, abortion, obscenity, pornography, and insolence. Many students of the left regard such matters as entirely outside the province of morality, as fairly unimportant or trivial violations of morality, or as positive goods.[10] When a student says, "Make love, not war," he is not abandoning morality so much as reinterpreting it.[11] If the young seem to flaunt their new private "values" in the face of their elders, it is because to the young these values seem to be vital and human. They were discovered independently, but require public recognition and acceptance! And third, the enemies of the young (the "establishment," the school administration, the parents, or whoever) rely on certain moral standards of their own in condemning the actions of the young. If *this* is morality, say the students, then we (like Nietzsche) are immoralists. Conclusion: the student left has a naïve and rudimentary moral stance that rejects many conventional middle-class values, but it is not for the most part amoral.

There is even a religious quality in some of the new student left attitudes. Some observers perceive an analogy in the style of the early Christians—the impatience and intolerance of unkempt pacifists toward the luxurious, urbane, and rational establishment of the Roman Empire.[12] More important, however, is the desire in many circles of the student left for some kind of visionary community where interpersonal relations achieve a genuineness and intimacy not found in ordinary Western society. This is associated with mysticism and the "expansion of consciousness," interest in Eastern religions, and drugs. Science and reason must be transcended in order to discover a higher reality. "The dissenting young have indeed got religion. It is not the brand of religion that Billy Graham or William Buckley would choose for youth's crusade, but nonetheless it is religion. What began with Zen has now rapidly, perhaps too rapidly, proliferated into a phantasmagoria of exotic religiosity." [13]

Critique of Capitalism

The student left is vigorously critical of modern society. Many of its criticisms are similar to those made by the old anarchists.

The economic system is a familiar target. Many students accept the socialist criticism of capitalism: "Private property and the profit motive are anachronisms under conditions of abundance." [14] Capitalism rewards some people too much and others not at all. It encourages people to compete with one another, to win victories at one another's expense. And it measures the value of people by their ability to make money. The ultimate values of capitalism are materialistic. "There is surely more to work," say the students, "than making a living and more to success than wealth." [15] The importance of the profitmaking principle permits capitalism and all who are involved in it to ignore all other considerations—unfair distribution, looting of natural resources, pollution of air and water, production of weapons of military destruction, misrepresentation in advertising and packaging, etc. And with all of this, there is joblessness and poverty.

The younger generation is not grateful to capitalism for the economic opportunity it affords, for the low rate of unemployment, for the enormous gross national product. This generation, never having experienced a major depression or difficulty in finding a job, seems more antagonistic toward capitalism's successes than its failures. Abundance there is—but it is not shared equally. Abundance there is—but it has made us a "consumer society." Abundance there is—so we rejoice in our goods and gadgets and ignore human or spiritual values. Our "rush to well-being" has cost us our soul.

Even more in evidence than the black flag of anarchism at the demonstrations of the student left is the red flag of socialism/communism. But the latter more often symbolizes the historical disgust of the left with free-enterprise capitalism than it does approval of Russian-style communism. For the materialism attacked in Western society is not very different from the materialism celebrated in Russia and some of the satellite countries. The Soviet Union, like any materialistic state, can be imperialistic. Czechoslovakia was *Russia's* Vietnam—"not as brutal or bloody but just as politically obscene." [16] The student left detests materialism whether it is proclaimed by the Chamber of Commerce or councils of commissars. Even the Communist Party (like the labor unions) is infected with materialism; this materialism inspires its efforts for pecuniary gains for the worker rather than for fundamental changes in the role of labor in the productive enterprise.

To be sure, some of the radical left admire the communism of Mao Tse-tung and other leaders of the "third world." Asia, Africa, and Latin America are not industrialized and great struggles for survival are going on. Students who tend to romanticize these struggles glorify the leaders who strive against dictatorship, Western imperialism, and nature itself. Ché Guevara is already a legend. The student left, generally opposed to Soviet communism, stresses the alternative forms that communism can take. It can thus reject one form while admiring another—such as China's.

For the student left, as for anarchism, criticism of capitalism does not imply support and admiration for organized labor unions. Unions are conservative. Too often they have been allies of capitalists in resisting participation (industrial democracy) and fair employment practices. Moreover, they are more concerned with protecting those already employed and unionized than with assisting those who are employed but not unionized and those who are not employed at all.

Critique of Government

A second target of the student leftists is their own government. Government, nominally democratic, is unresponsive to the popular will. The American student leftists were furious at the choice of Hubert Humphrey as the Democratic Presidential nominee in 1968 because that choice was made by political professionals rather than by the rank and file. The French regarded De Gaulle as a dictator surrounded by democratic trappings. Some students believe "that to have apparent but ineffective freedom might be a worse state than to have no freedom at all." [17] Bourgeois democracy exists to preserve the system with all its injustices. Even poverty programs, too little and too late, get watered down and are more profitable (legally and illegally) to those who administer them than to those who are supposed to benefit from them.[18] Liberals defend orderly methods because they fear fundamental changes: their vested interests will not be harmed by gradual and moderate reform. With their reasonableness and kindliness they are the most valuable spokesmen for the establishment. They know all the pitfalls of hasty action and can expose all the oversimplifications: Social change, they say, is very complicated—so much is involved, so much has to be taken into account. Spender describes the students' reaction to this: "If there are reasons so complicated that they cannot be explained to people to justify the politics that the most intelligent and thoughtful of the young find immoral, then politics becomes a mystery which can only be played by the most powerful and astute, and only understood by the most learned. This makes democratic process irrelevant and mischievous. . . ." [19] "Elections," pronounced Daniel Cohn-Bendit, "are treason." [20]

The government is not the people's government, but an instrument by which the military-industrial complex protects and enhances its selfish interests. C. Wright Mills's book *The Power Elite* is often cited by the young rebel. So the government abets not only profit-making at home but imperialism abroad. "We can accelerate the breakdown of confidence in the government and military by stressing that the decisions which led to the Vietnam war were rigged in the same way and by the same people who are rigging the conventions and elections in 1968." [21] That American participation in the Vietnam war is wrong is the most widely shared feeling among the young leftists. This war is the symbol of all the evils of governments and of the societies that tolerate those governments. Nothing is clearer to the young than that war is murder and that the willingness of government to conduct war is an indication of its moral bankruptcy. Here the student left is very close to the old anarchism. Both are categorically pacifistic. If the liberal, with his typical ability to see both sides of a question, suggests that pacifism is an oversimplification, and that there may indeed be good, if not compelling, reasons for giving military support to the government of South Vietnam, the young leftist will retort that war itself is the great oversimplification in "solving" international problems. He does not have to know all the aspects of a complicated problem in order to recognize an evil. Just as he is certain that poverty in an affluent society is wrong, he is certain that war in a foreign country is wrong. On no single issue has government so unmistakably disqualified itself as on its willingness to force its young men to kill others in war.

Disrespect for government easily extends to disrespect for law and law-enforcers. "Can people who see the law protecting slumlords (by fixing ridiculously small fines for violations), protecting Southern whites whose murder victims happen to be Negroes, allowing tax loopholes for the rich, etc., be expected to conclude that law is something superhuman and sacred instead of the expression of the will of those who have influence?" [22] Even if laws are backed by the majority, that does not necessarily make them right. Democracy means more than majority rule. It means respect for the individual and minority groups. The students in France made international capital of the legal but archaic and high-handed methods of making arrests and holding people prisoner incommunicado and without charges. Law obstructs freedom, disrupts beneficial social action, and employs violence. Its aim is to preserve an "order" that is rotten to the core. Laws therefore should be disobeyed whenever they violate moral conscience or whenever their application stands in the way of noble aims. Amnesty for disobedience to bad laws is always right and proper. "An amnesty," stated a French graffito, "is an act with which the sovereigns most often pardon the injustices they have committed." Those mercenaries who seek to enforce bad laws should be treated with the contempt they deserve. The enforcement of law is itself arbitrary and malicious. At Berkeley and Columbia, in Paris and Chicago, in Mississippi and Ohio, the student left has counted on the brutality of the police and has seldom been disappointed.[23]

The fantastic conduct of the "Chicago Eight" in Judge Hoffman's Federal courtroom (1969) was a deliberate expression of contempt for law and legal procedures. It is widely believed today that black revolutionaries cannot "achieve a fair trial anywhere in the United States." [24]

Like the old anarchists, the young rebels are unpatriotic. Draft-card burning and flag desecration come naturally to people who deplore the economic imperialism of a major power. "Through [large] corporations . . . we exploit the natural riches and the cheap labor of helpless under-developed countries, while suppressing their nationalistic aspirations and drive. In short, these poor countries subsidize our high standard of living." [25] The students tend to feel much closer to revolutionaries of another state (Cuba, Vietnam, etc.) than to the authorities of their own. There is among the student left an infatuation with the "third world." Societies in Asia, Africa, and Latin America are, or can be, far superior to those of Western capitalism or Russian-style communism. Ché Guevara, Ho Chi Minh, and Mao Tse-tung are more admirable than General Eisenhower, Joseph Stalin, and Charles De Gaulle.

Critique of the University

The third great institutional foe of the young rebel, and the one most conveniently at hand, is the university. Many observers believe that students experience their first sense of outrage from conditions in society *outside* the university. "The students proceed from protesting about Vietnam, desegregation, the Third World, etc., to finding—or hunting out—things in the university which correspond to their grievances about society." [26] The old anarchists, perhaps feeling that meaningful change of the universities was a hopeless cause, left them alone.

The contemporary anarchists perceive the university as the great ally of the business, military, and political establishments. One SDS member called universities "service stations for military and corporate interests." [27] In his much discussed Godkin Lectures, Clark Kerr, former president of the University of California, stated that the university "has become in America and in other nations as well, a prime instrument of national purpose." [28] The university teaches the courses that will be helpful to future members of the business, military, and political communities, defends their hypocritical ideals, supports their research, and copies their styles of organization. The university, which should be a free institution, a place in which other institutions are freely studied and freely criticized, is instead a dutiful servant to the power complex. One of Clark Kerr's critics wrote: "It is not 'society' that the multiversity must merge with: it is the *leadership groups in society*,' which to the mind of the captain of the bureaucracy, are identical with 'society.' "[29] Three other of his critics wrote: "The principal functions of education are to train the bulk of the population to 'receive instructions, follow instructions, keep the records,' and to train the managers, engineers, and civil servants to operate this system." [30] This is how the universities make men free!

It is in the criticism of the university that we find three frequently used words that were also part of the vocabulary of the old anarchism: *bureaucracy, participation,* and *alienation.* The first is a system, the second is an action, and the third is a state of mind. They apply to all the institutions of modern society. These institutions are organized as *bureaucracies,* deny *participation,* and thus produce in all sensitive individuals a feeling of *alienation.*

The university is a great bureaucracy. Students are subject to a mass of regulations. Where do they come from, how are they changed? No one knows. What is their rationale? Various answers are given, none wholly satisfactory. There is no point in leaving one university and going to another: they are all the same. Whether they are large or small, they treat the students as objects to be processed in a great machine. The machine has a life of its own; students do not. "The 'Managerial Revolution' has come to the campus; now the most important stratum of the university is not the faculty, nor the students, nor any single educational Idea, but rather the manager and the administrator. The 'multiversity' is a 'mechanism held together by administrative rules and powered by money.' To guide this mechanism through its many complex functions, the university president must be guided primarily by the tools and arts of manipulation and mediation." [31] When trouble comes, the mechanism smoothes it out, or adjusts it here and there and *then* smoothes it out.[32] The trouble at Berkeley, for example, "resulted from a temporary failure in administrative technique." [33]

The student's acquaintance with the educational bureaucracy makes him sensitive to the existence of bureaucracies elsewhere in society. As a consumer he receives a number and a credit card. As a prospective employee he faces the likelihood of becoming a little cog in a gigantic business corporation or a mammoth labor union. Or, he will serve as a soldier in an even larger enterprise. Through it all he is subject to a government that makes laws he cannot understand and whose very operations are utterly secret or so complex that he cannot follow them. Nowhere is he treated as a person, nowhere does he find understanding. He is constantly subject to procedures, efficient and encompassing, to which he must make the appropriate responses. He is a pawn in a game the rules of which he does not know—or finds changed as fast as he learns them.

These vast organizations are staffed by human beings like himself, but they too are prisoners of the system. They are helpless to react in any way for which they have not been programmed. They cannot explain or deal with the exceptional case. Their intelligence and humanity are virtually canceled out by standardized methods, "proper channels," and appropriate forms. An essential feature of bureaucracies is that no one seems to be able to make a decision. Student activists learned early that they were wasting their time in talking to anyone but the university president. There are signs today that the president is "passing the buck" to the governing board. Eventually it may turn out that *no one* can intervene in the operations of the bureaucratic machine. This will be its ultimate triumph: it will have achieved a life of its own! [34]

Herbert Marcuse, an elderly German-born professor, has had a curious influence on the American student left. Marcuse regards himself as a Marxist (but not a Stalinist) and a Hegelian (but not a reactionary). Always opposed to totalitarianism, he describes a new form of subjection in *One-Dimensional Man,* published in the fifties. The capabilities of advanced industrial society, he argued, are being misused for repressive functions. In modern American society, the contradictions between the world and the spirit are smoothed over ("contained," "integrated," "incorporated," "absorbed," etc.). The repressions are so streamlined that one hardly knows they are taking place. Men are mesmerized and manipulated by omnicompetent administrations. The "system" is overwhelmingly pleasant and comfortable. It threatens to engulf backward countries as well. In the sixties, however, it became apparent that Marcuse was mistaken: the critical revolutionary spirit was not dead after all. Vietnam resisted. Negroes rioted. Students disrupted. The "Great Refusal" called for in *One-Dimensional Man* was taking place. Why did Marcuse's theses appeal to rebellious youth?

Because he offered them an awareness of absorptive power, by propounding the falsehood that everyone had been or would be absorbed. He proclaimed the old methods of protest ineffective, and was unable to prescribe new ones, but others found roads through the obstacles he helped them see. The extreme spontaneity of contemporary radicalism is an echo of and an answer to his insistence that structured opposition becomes part of the structure. When critics complain that the movement lacks coherence, it adopts definite aims, and falls prey to society's mechanisms of introjection: the establishment invests money in it. It is true that radicals would now like to surpass spontaneity without suffering containment. But eruptive politics were needed in the beginning, and their necessity fits into Marcuse's book. Though the shell was not as hard as he made out, the first task was to break through it. This provides some rationale for the fact that student activists are often inspired by Marcuse. They act in order to negate the reality he described, even if that entails negating his theory at the same time.[35]

It is bad that individuals are subject to external control; it is intolerable that this control is impersonal. The student leftist insists on participation in all areas that govern his life. Not having this participation, the younger generation reports a feeling of alienation from the entire society.

Alienation is not regarded as a feeling unique to the young. Society is such that there is no prospect at *any* age of being involved *in* it without being alienated *from* it. Alienation means one thing to the Marxist and something else to the existentialist. To the student left it is simply the full and sobering recognition that the real aims of modern society make no vital appeal to him, that he is caught in a system that is inimical to his humanity, and that there is no way within that system to change it. The young are always on the lookout for "traps." Traps await them in society, no matter what direction they take. Since society is a complex of traps, they cannot think of it as their society.[36]

Tactics

If society is a complex of traps, it would follow that it must be escaped or transformed. Paralleling the anarchists of old, the young rebels divide themselves into the "passivists" and the "activists." The former, successors to the beatniks of the fifties, retreat from society into settlements of their own. The "hippies" have their own attire, their own ethical code, their own language. Society can go to hell;

they will enjoy their own company and their own consciousness. Occasionally they will emerge for a moment to thumb their noses at society, as the "Yippies" ("hippies turned inside-out") did in Chicago, but they usually are quite content with a passive role. Too proud, too lazy, too pessimistic, or too selfish to rectify the ills of society, they will seek their own salvation apart from it. "Escape from the monster by ignoring it." [37]

The activists are more interesting. Their tactics and strategies are in many ways reminiscent of the old anarchists'. But just as there was great disagreement in methods among the old rebels, so too is there disagreement among the new. As a result of the diversity of views among its members, the Movement (like the old anarchism) "has defied all attempts to bring its members together into disciplined cohesiveness." [38]

One simple response to the system is to disobey laws and regulations. "Regardless of any political effectiveness, civil disobedience as an act of conscientious dissent is an act which will at least leave one's conscience clear." [39] One not only avoids involving himself in society's injustice, but he can also, if he disobeys publicly, "cause other citizens and leaders of the nation to realize their error." [40] A recent graduate of Harvard wrote: "We lawbreakers will accept our punishments to show that we do believe in the principles of our democracy but we DO NOT by any means claim that we have a right to break laws simply because we accept the punishments; we claim that we have the right to break these laws because they are morally wrong and illegal. . . . Man's law and man's sentence is irrelevant compared to justice and morality." [41] Some students refuse to accept punishment, demanding amnesty instead.[42]

What kind of laws or regulations are to be broken? Some are directly connected with a "moral" issue. Draft laws, segregation laws, and dormitory regulations are examples. Others should be broken because they stand in the way of achievement of desired goals. Student leftists will march and demonstrate without a permit, take over buildings, sleep in parks, and publish or display illegal materials. "The government and the establishment would like us to demonstrate and protest—quietly, that is, so as not to make any threatening vibrations. But we are demonstrating and intend to demonstrate, in a way that the government can neither applaud nor fail to notice. We want to cause discomfort among the apathetic because we want to cause change. The biggest struggle is to shock people like Mr. Kennan out of their smugness." [43] "Disruptive tactics obviously impose a high cost upon society and its leaders and eventually, the dissidents argue, the price will become too great." [44] An SDS poster in Chicago enjoined its followers: Don't let "the fucking system work." [45]

The advocate of government breaks laws only with great reluctance, for disobedience weakens the governing authority. He considers obedience itself to have some moral value. But many young leftists do not reserve disobedience for extreme situations. They disobey as a matter of principle, and often their actions have only the remotest connection with an important moral principle. This is truly anarchic, an unmistakable attack on authority *qua* authority. Thoreau's famous act of disobedience did not in itself make him an anarchist—that rebellion was temporary, provisional, and centered on a specific issue.

On this issue of violence we find conflicting points of view in the student left. At some times the Movement has been more inclined to violence than at other times. Certain organizations (*e.g.,* SDS and SNCC) have varied their stand on this point of tactics. And it is impossible, even if one selects a certain point in time, to formulate a position on violence which would apply to an overwhelming percentage of the student left. In this respect, then, the Movement is similar to old anarchism.

We find the peaceful point of view expressed in such statements as these: "It is axiomatic that you cannot draw a man to you by striking him a blow. Neither a left uppercut nor a right cross nor even a haymaker can win a man's love or admiration or cooperation. . . . The nonviolent approach is designed to leave our opponent a facesaving device so that there will be little bitterness when the fight is over." [46] Such new leftists resent the popular conception of the whole Movement as a violent one. The media, always after a story (and willing to provoke one), "play up" the spectacular. "One scene of violence or one hippie gets headlines and the thousands of peaceful protestors and non-violent rallies and square students and elderly men and women are ignored." A recent Harvard graduate insists that "the violent faction of the radical left is less than a minority: it is the shadow of a minority." [47]

Many leftists eschew violence, but find it difficult to draw the line between passive and active physical resistance. They may "go limp" when carried away or they may struggle for a time. They may physically prevent officials from entering a building or they may eject an occupant. They may stop short of gunfire, but resort to weapons in self-defense. They may throw rocks at windows or at policemen as well. They may themselves refrain from rioting but deliberately make speeches that provoke others to riot. There are so many degrees of peaceful and violent action and so many actual instances of action across the whole spectrum that it is impossible to find a viable distinction in the Movement as a whole or in part of the Movement between the violent and the non-violent. The agitators know, just as the police know, that a crowd of peaceful demonstrators, by no means committed to violence, can be transformed under the right circumstances and through skillful incitement into a destructive mob.[48] The distinction between defense (in which, presumably, violence can be used) and attack (in which it cannot) is also difficult to draw. The style is up to the individual.[49] Nor can leaders depend upon the conduct of the followers in a given situation. Unlike Gandhi's movement in India, organizations of the student left do not excel in discipline and self-control. French student leaders often had to implore, "Un peu de discipline!"[50]

For some activists non-violence is only a matter of expedience rather than moral principle. Its practice is thus subject to changing circumstances. Some leftists will postpone violence until the day it will do the most good—when the rebels are stronger or the establishment is weaker—using it now only in a restricted and selective way. But others are willing to attack the establishment violently right now. The extremists of the new left do not draw back from violence of the most militant form. These radical radicals are ready to engage in "urban guerrilla warfare."[51]

If the rebellious action (whatever its degree of violence) is to be effective in arousing public support and bringing the moderates into the movement, it is important that it be done in the glare of the fullest publicity—preferably in direct view of the television cameras. The new rebels thus have a tremendous advantage over the old. "What 'the whole world was watching,' after all, was not a confrontation but the picture of a confrontation, to some extent directed by a generation that had grown up with television and learned to use it."[52] A Princeton graduate student wrote: "After all, as the world gets bigger and fuller, it becomes impossible to be heard. You have to get into the mass media and violence is one sure way to do it."[53] One former SDS president wrote: "For the first time in memory students have found a sympathetic press to publicize their actions."[54] In order to have the media bring the facts to the public most dramatically, student leaders advise "creative disorder."

Hopefully, the action, whether it consists of demonstrating in Grant Park in Chicago or taking over a university building, will provoke the authorities to violent reaction. This lesson was learned early in the Movement: the segregationist officials reacted to the Freedom Riders irrationally and violently. Many activists are now experts in courting overkill. Tom Hayden stated: "We should have people organized who can fight the police, people who are willing to get arrested." [55] A veteran of the march on the Pentagon "suggested that volunteers be urged to disobey any curfew, in order to force the police into a mass arrest situation." [56] Abbie Hoffman, in planning for the Chicago demonstrations in 1968, said: "Urban guerrilla warfare is a psychological attempt to trick the enemy into developing a policy of over-kill." [57] The authorities are "unmasked" by being made to seem worse than the rebels. The behavior of the mob in Chicago was thoroughly despicable in word and deed, but they finally were able to provoke the authorities to such reaction that the sober and searching Walker Report could call the events of those incredible few days a "police riot"!

As the pitch of disobedience becomes more exciting, more violent, and more vicious, all sorts of unsavory elements join forces with the young left. These new "recruits," like the criminals who were attracted to the "propagandists of the deed," are not motivated by ethical concerns. They are sensation-seekers, idlers, and hoodlums who want to be where the action is and/or to vent their chronic hostility against social institutions. Just as the violence of the defenders of the law and order attracts the moderates to the student side, the violence of the students attracts the unprincipled rabble.

Revolution

The most successful leaders of the student left are revolutionaries.[58] To be satisfied with reforms is to brand oneself a conservative. Clark Kerr's excellent record against right-wingers in California did not spare him from brutal attack. The radical leaders do not know exactly what course the revolution is to follow, but it is to be kept alive until fundamental changes are achieved. One SDS poster in Chicago stated: "When you seize a town, a campus, get hold of the power stations, the water, the transportation, forget to negotiate, forget how to negotiate. . . . you are not demonstrating: you are fighting a war, fight to win. . . ." [59] Support may be won on particular issues like the examination system in French universities, "free speech" at Berkeley, nomination procedures at Chicago, or military research at Columbia. But such causes are only the beginning. Since the evils are symptoms of a serious and pervasive illness in society, the Movement cannot stop with their rectification. The demands of the rebels, therefore, escalate with every success, with every concession. As one slogan has it, "Be realistic. Demand the impossible."

The moderates, of course, are often content with partial success. Brought into the Movement by concern over a specific issue, they may be content to fall back when that issue has been won. A young French activist said, "I was disappointed that he [Prime Minister Pompidou] made concessions. It could have killed the movement." [60] The group, whether a student body or a gathering in a park, must be impelled to grander goals. Under the spell of revolutionary euphoria, it must seek ever greater gains. This process is called radicalization. Mark Rudd of Columbia described it: "When we started this, we were talking about changing a few things: the gym, IDA, etc. But then people began to talk about student power and a free university and everything else, and it got completely away from us. . . . And so what we're engaged in, to use a piece of SDS rhetoric, is the process of radicalization; we make no bones about this." [61] When there is widespread unrest and poor leadership among the established powers, a tiny group of militant radicals can capture the support of enough other people (sympathizers) to wreck or disrupt an institution for an indefinite period of time.[62] The movement in France started with demands for modest reforms of the universities and ended with something like this: "The function of the university is to work for the subversion of the society which surrounds it." [63] The Movement, unlike trade union work or political work (but like the anarchist ideas of Bakunin), has a disinterested spontaneity and is to produce an uncontrollable spirit of revolution.

The most anarchistic aspect of the tactics and strategy of the student left is its preference (insistence, in fact) for the methods of direct action.[64] Government is so badly structured and so infested with venal officials that it is hopeless to seek change through ordinary political channels.[65] Why go through channels when they lead nowhere? To work through such channels is indeed a sign of bad faith; it means that one is not really committed to the goals of the Movement. Established political parties and trade unions have too great a stake in society to consider fundamental alterations. Their sympathetic but lethargic support for some of the causes of the left constitutes a trap. The issues get warped and eventually lost. The cutting edge of the demands is dulled, enthusiasm is dissipated, and student power is neutralized. The rebels have already opted for a "politics of consensus." The French students were blessed (before De Gaulle finally prevailed) with a vast and successful general strike —a sound anarchist tactic. The American students have not been so fortunate. The Vietnam Moratorium was an attempt at the next best thing.

According to the new left, direct methods do not require any great moral defense. When there are no institutions for correcting social injustices, or when they will not respond, radical action is necessary. Radical direct methods are at least as moral as such conventional indirect methods as contributing to political campaigns, lobbying, bribery, and political favoritism. When the system is corrupt, it is better to work "outside the system." [66] Revolutionists have long argued that the end justifies the means, even when they seem to be incompatible. The old anarchists have been divided on this (e.g., Tolstoy and Bakunin). The student leftist who can say, "You have to create peace by destroying the people who don't want peace," are siding with Bakunin.[67]

The militant activist suspects even the most radical and revolutionary political parties and organizations. Politics necessarily involves itself with government (whether to attack, defend, or to deal with it), and government is authoritarian and vicious. Politics is an enterprise of the old—or at least the adult. Since it has been established that political endeavor is dirty and hopeless, students are not inclined to show much gratitude for occasional support by political organizations. Bettina Aptheker, Communist, was regarded as a fairly conservative member of the Free Speech Movement steering committee. One observer said, "If there were any orthodox Communists here, they would be a moderating influence." [68]

The leftists manifest the same contempt for the authorities as was displayed by the anarchists—most notably Georges Sorel. Corrupt and comfortable, the authorities lack the courage even of strong principles. University presidents make one concession after another, giving in to demands in order to purchase peace and to retain their position. Officials will sell their very souls if the structure can be preserved. Heads of all "power structures" are soft and weak. Only when the mercenaries are called in is there a sign of strength, and here it is spurious and hysterical. In the universities this contempt is expressed toward the faculty also, many of whom have been sympathetic and helpful. "Even after their victory" at Berkeley in the Free Speech Movement (which was supported by the faculty), "Draper, Savio and Weissman spoke with utter contempt of the faculty as frightened into agreement by the shock tactics of sit-in and strike." [69] The leaders in that movement learned "that extreme tactics could be used without censure from the faculty." [70] "It does make you wonder," said a professor at Berkeley, "when time and time again you advise them against doing something outside the democratic processes we're used to and time and time again they do it and win their point that way." [71] Contempt for the enemy may be as important a factor as conviction of the truth of their cause in making student leaders violent and inflexible in their negotiations. Violence does establish the possibility of the impossible.[72]

The young rebels, while admiring individuals like Ché Guevara, are like the old anarchists in their refusal to develop a personality cult. Leaders are reluctant to "take credit" for victories achieved by groups. Mark Rudd's leadership in the SDS was questioned because he had been glorified so much for his part in the Columbia revolution; he was thought to be a personality created by television. At the Sorbonne different chairmen were chosen for each meeting. "Nous ne voulons pas des personnalités!" was a familiar chant. The selfless sons and daughters of the bourgeoisie wish to present themselves as disinterested revolutionaries, seeking neither gain nor glory.

The Good Society

What *are* they seeking? Like the anarchists, they want a good society, and since the old one is so bad, it must be a *transformed* society. The mere replacement of one political regime by another is not sufficient.

One characteristic that any good society must have is *participation* by its members in all decisions that significantly affect them. The term "participatory democracy" is frequently heard. Jack Newfield defines it to mean: "The idea that social reformation comes from organizing the dispossessed into their own insurgent movements rather than from forming top-down alliances between liberal bureaucratic organizations. The insistence on fraternity and community inside the movement. The passion against manipulation and centralized decision making. The reluctance to make the New Left itself a machine tooled and fueled to win political power in the traditional pit battles." [73] This sounds very much like a familiar anarchist view and, like the latter, preserves the consistency of means and ends. In the new society participation will involve decentralization and communitarianism. The hierarchical form of organization, a relic from the days of kings and chieftains, is improper for modern free men. "The world has become too small, populations too large, and the means of production too vast to be run by élites of frightened men." [74]

In the economic sphere, this seems to imply that the conditions of work, the method of production, the quality and quantity of commodities and services, and the plans for distribution should be prescribed by the workers themselves. In France, these demands were raised by the students, although most of the workers, concerned with more familiar bread-and-butter issues, were less than lukewarm about them. During the general strike the students tried to convince the workers that occupation of a factory was more than simply a strike: it proffered much grander opportunities. The French revolutionaries cited the experiences of the sailors at Kronstadt during the Russian Revolution: they set up their own communes, took over factories, and ran them themselves. This anarchistic effort, like many others in Russia, was finally crushed by the Bolsheviks. The argument against it was the familiar one based on fear of chaos. Communistic anarchism, distinct from the state communism of Marx and Russia, has drawn support from American rebels also, although in this country the preference leans toward the smaller self-sufficient communes similar to the mutualistic groups advocated by Josiah Warren. There is fairly general agreement among the student leftists that capitalism should be replaced by a system in which the means of production pass from private ownership into public.

Students have had experience in governing themselves and their territory as a result of the many takeovers of college buildings. They have shared conditions, made decisions, and administered things and people.[75] The most extensive experience, of course, was the control of the Sorbonne for several weeks in May 1968. The style that emerged was one of "direct democracy"—everyone got to vote on major issues, and decisions were made at the bottom instead of the top. Committees were established and consulted. The problem was to be organized enough to remain in power and to consolidate gains without giving up individual liberty and spontaneity. The organizational forms of the new society must be structured in such a way that citizens can participate in their own localities in those instances in which regulations have to be made. If there is to be a government at all, it will leave most decisions up to the individual; where this is impossible, authority will be decentralized. "The people on the bottom don't need leaders at all. What they need is the confidence in their own worth and identity to make decisions about their own lives." [76] Power will come from below and fan out into the nation. It will never come down *to* the people from above.

All this is very vague and unsatisfactory. But the students, like many of their anarchist predecessors, refuse, as a matter of principle, to spell out the details. "Organized programs can come later," wrote a recent graduate of Rochester. "First people must be convinced of the absolute necessity of a new approach to American society." [77] Calvin Trillin wrote: "Most FSM leaders make no attempt to disguise their deep alienation from American society, but they regard allegiance to any specific alternative as utopian, divisive, and immobilizing, and—perhaps most significant—not their 'style.' " [78] Students can find plenty of specific evils to attack; for the present they prefer to emphasize action rather than ideology. Nor will they be trapped by the rigid dogmas of the old left. The older generation has given us two worlds: the Communist world of Russia and the satellites and the capitalistic world of the United States and western Europe. Both are rotten and must be exposed. The new world will be different, but its outlines must remain hazy for awhile.

The student left is much more definite on the question of the transformation the universities are to undergo, although even here no complete program is offered.[79] Much has been written by the students and about the students and their demands for changes in the university. All that will be discussed here are the general principles that are most anarchistic in nature. They appear to be two: (1) the university should be controlled by all of those, and only those, who are part of it; (2) the university should involve itself in the problems of society.

On the first point, it is clear that the students wish the university to be completely free from the control or influence of governmental bodies and business interests. It should be willing to accept money, but only if no strings are attached. On the positive side, the university is to be controlled by the faculty and students. Governing boards, presently composed of old, rich, conservative businessmen, should be reconstituted. Administrators, if indeed they are necessary, are to serve at the pleasure of faculty and students. The students are to be a "very equal" partner in the enterprise. They will evaluate instructors and teaching methods, examine curricula, establish class sizes, create new courses, deliberate on budgetary allocations, and set up and help administer disciplinary proceedings. Needless to say, *in loco parentis,* and bureaucracy will finally be transformed into a community of persons engaged in learning. Students will actually live; hitherto they were expected to "prepare" to live.

On the second point, the students insist that education be made "relevant." This does not mean that the "ivory tower" will disappear—it will remain for the scholar who wants a traditional academic education. Nor does it mean that emphasis will be placed on vocational training or preparation for a career in business.[80] "Relevance" for most spokesmen of the student left means "useful for the understanding of man and for the solution of concrete social problems." The university will offer courses and programs (not all education need take place in *courses*) that involve the students in the community. Social issues will be debated on the campus and action will be directed out into society. The universities are not only the conscience of the nation; they are also the places where concerned young people begin to *change* society. Like the anarchists of old, many young rebels believe that the sociologist, the scientist, and the artist should all be humanists. That is, they should not engage in their work aloof from the needs of their fellow man.[81]

Since war is an unmixed evil, the social concern of universities will not extend to such things as providing facilities for ROTC programs, space for recruiters for the armed services or war-related industries, sending class rankings to draft boards, or conducting military research for the government. Work in the ghettos is good; work for the Vietnam war is not. Special courses and quarters for Negroes who enter college with educational and psychological problems are acceptable; special courses for those who would take part in military affairs are not. So Kerr was not mistaken in calling the university a part of the "knowledge industry." But one must exercise the proper discrimination. "When students see work being done at a university on the application of science to spreading death and destruction in Vietnam, but little evidence of similar work on eliminating poverty and racial injustice, they are naturally concerned about the decision-making process." [82] This brings us back to "(1)". Proper control implies, and is implied by, proper goals.

ANARCHISM AS AN OVERSIMPLIFICATION

Many of the major principles of old anarchism have been expressed by important spokesmen of the student left. One should be wary, however, of concluding that the position of the student left is primarily anarchistic. In the first place, the fallacy of "undistributed middle term" must be avoided: A believes in X, Y, Z; B believes in X, Y, Z; therefore, B is A. Before the conclusion can be drawn, X, Y, and Z must be shown to be the *defining criteria* of A. There is reason to believe that the principles of anarchism involved in the leftist movement do not quite constitute the defining criteria of anarchism. Second, important spokesmen of the student left can be found who do *not* espouse the major anarchistic principles. The student left is a "mixed bag." It is important, therefore, to avoid stereotyping. It is just as risky to call the student left anarchistic as to call it atheistic, reformist, or communistic. Some groups and individuals have these characteristics; some do not. In the third place, the possibility must be left open that a given spokesman of the student left is not consistent in his own mind. He (and his followers) may hold several conflicting points of view. He *is* an anarchist but frequently will espouse views incompatible with his anarchism (or vice versa). In short, while the ideas of old anarchism are very useful for understanding the ideas of the student left, their importance should not be overestimated. The "archistic" ideas of the student left are also important.

The Revolutionary Tradition

No leader of the student left defines himself as an anarchist in the clear and unmistakable manner of a Proudhon or Kropotkin. Some leftists may emphasize individual freedom, but seldom go on to demand the complete elimination of government. Anarchism represents for them a feeling rather than a concrete objective. That the SDS sold buttons saying, "I am an enemy of the State," was a joke rather than a serious announcement of intended action. One young activist in France commented on Daniel Cohn-Bendit: "He has extraordinary charm and is dynamic. His anarchistic side was amusing." [83] The students are expert at the "put-on." For many of them the pose of anarchism, in the sense that anarchism means destroying all government, is a put-on.

Commentators have referred to the anti-intellectualism of such groups as the SDS.[84] Kennan says that the young rebels have read very little even in the radical tradition.[85] There is no evidence that they have studied the anarchist tradition at all. If their anarchism were serious, they should have a decent acquaintance with the thought and lives of such men as Godwin, Bakunin, and Tucker. The only anarchist who is mentioned with any frequency at all is Thoreau, and his contribution to the anarchist literature is very small. The heroes of the student left are men like Herbert Marcuse, Ché Guevara, and Allen Ginsberg—who are by no means anarchists. The student left has made no attempt to link up their movement with persons and parties of the old anarchism.

Like the anarchists of old, the student leftists are distinctly in the minority. They are a minority of the young, and they are a minority of the university population. They need recruits. They have sought them among the Negroes, with very little success. They have sought them among the workers, with even less success. Like the anarchists, they are educated people from middle-class or upper-middle-class homes, but unlike the anarchists they have seldom worked with the dispossessed among the urban proletariat and peasantry. They have achieved solidarity only among themselves. They write and perform for one another. They are happy to be told by Paul Goodman that they, the middle-class youth, are the major exploited class in the United States. And a Berkeley leader, Larry D. Spence, proclaimed the events at California "the first significant white-collar rebellion in our time." [86] We will have to take the students at their word: they *are* an "unprecedented generation." This separates them from the anarchists, who were fighting a battle as old as civilization itself. The student left becomes, then, not a social movement, but a special-interest group.

There is some reason to suspect that the student left is not quite so revolutionary as its leaflets would indicate. Where is the organization for bringing down the authorities? Where are the troops and the weapons? The student left prefers to insult and shock and threaten (and it is very good at these), than to destroy the power of the state. Johann Most made bombs out of dynamite; the "Yippies" in Chicago drove nails through golf balls. They do not want to take over, because they are not ready to shoulder that responsibility. But they will demand and disrupt for whatever "instant gratification" that may yield. With some few fantastic exceptions, the college radical is careful not to burn his bridges behind him. Denying *in loco parentis,* he yet hopes that the university family will take him back to its bosom, like his natural family at home who pays his bills. The Communists in France, moribund as they may be, nevertheless know something about revolution; and they believed that the students were "playing with revolution." *L'Humanité* called them "pseudo-revolutionaries" pursuing "political adventurism." [87]

Although both the student left and the old anarchism each contains within itself conflicting viewpoints on tactics and strategy, the student left, by and large, does not seem to be as committed to violence as the old anarchism. Fewer student leftists are (at present) violent, and the intensity of the violence they espouse is less. Although these are differences only of degree, they are significant nevertheless. The students are not revolutionists in any classical sense because they are not an oppressed class, nor have they any great stake or influence in any class that is oppressed. And if they did achieve the latter, their own identity would be lost and the Movement would take on an utterly different form.

It is true that one can be a revolutionist in quite a different sense from that implied above. But if "revolution" does not have to mean "violent destruction of the existing political and social order by an oppressed class," it does have to mean "radical transformation." At least that is what the anarchists meant by the term. But the student left is concerned quite as much with *reform* as it is with revolution. The zeal and anger of the students, their willingness to employ the methods of direct action, must not conceal the fact that often what they are after is reform: broaden the base of control in the universities, amend the U.S. Constitution, throw out venal politicians, clean up the air and waterways, get out of Vietnam, reduce the power of the military, feed the poor, accord full civil rights to Negroes, etc. All of these are quite possible without fundamental alteration of the social and political structures. These are all rather specific goals; they are not blueprints for a new society. As one student leader put it: "We are achieving the declared goals of liberalism but we are not doing it in the liberal way."[88]

Law and Politics

Much of the early enthusiasm of the students stemmed from the experience of working for civil rights for Negroes in the South. The students disobeyed local laws, engaged in passive resistance, conducted marches and demonstrations. This was direct action of the anarchistic kind. However, they justified their actions by *legalistic* arguments. The law of the land guaranteed certain rights to the Negroes and to themselves as activists. In disobeying local law, they were only disobeying that which was incompatible with Constitutional law. They often will work through the courts to achieve their aims. An anarchist would not base his case on law—except, perhaps, moral law. But ordinary law is the product of government and is therefore "invasive."

Other examples can be given of the resort to law by student leftists. The trouble at Berkeley began when students asserted a legal right they believed themselves to have, to conduct political (!) activities on the grounds of the university. Their argument against "double jeopardy" (being punished by both civil courts and the university for the same offense) is also legalistic. "Students are entitled to the same rights of free speech on the campus that they have in the community at large. This implies, among other things, that there should be no double punishment in these matters, and that the University should leave to the courts ticklish questions of what is and what is not constitutionally protected speech." [89] Defenders of the "Chicago Eight" [90] argued that their arrest is in violation of rights guaranteed by the First Amendment. They were accused of crossing state lines in order to conspire "to incite, organize, promote, encourage, participate in and carry on a riot." This is in violation of the "anti-riot" provision of the Civil Rights Act of 1968, a rider attached to the main act to deal with "outside agitators" in urban riots. The First Amendment is infringed upon by the attempt to deal with *conspiracy*—a term so vague that it can be used to cover any action of which the state disapproves. Actually, it is argued, a Federal statute is unnecessary, for there are already many state and local laws to deal with specific acts of violence, incitement, and disruption.

Students can become vigorous defenders of individual rights when they are threatened by the popular will. Individuals and minorities should be protected from the will of the majority. But this protection, many students argue, is a Constitutional matter—that is, something to be enforced by government and its courts. Many such students are no more anarchistic than Thomas Jefferson.

In its attitude toward politics, there is a rather strange paradox at the center of the Movement. While proclaiming the purity of

the non-political, students' attitudes and actions are strongly political. They follow the deliberations and actions of politicians and
officials. They are so concerned with political matters that they see,
or fancy that they see, a political dimension to every social problem.
Even private matters of individual taste or decision (sex, music,
clothing) take on political significance. The students seem to possess
an odious facility for turning everything into politics.[91] They insist
that courses be made politically (or socially) relevant. They invest
scientific, philosophic, and artistic areas with political significance.
Participation in the Olympics or a vote for a campus queen becomes
a political act. They try to arouse in others feelings of indignation
for social wrongs and they seek proselytes among their fellows; they
wish to "politicize" the student body and surrounding neighbor-
hoods. They organize themselves into parties, societies, and associations. The whole educational process seems to be simply a course
in political thought, the campus a sanctuary for political activists,
the university nothing more than a forum for political thought and
action. To the degree that students take politics seriously, they are
not anarchists.

Student leftists act very much like politicians in building their
organizations and conferring with friends and foes. Often they are
willing to take part in student government—which, of course, is not
the anarchist way. The Free Speech Movement at Berkeley called
the student senate a "sandbox government," but successfully supported seven candidates in the fall of 1964.[92] They often conduct
themselves like politicians (rude politicians) when negotiating demands. Nathan Glazer, who was on the scene, said that the FSM
leaders "acted as if they were preparing themselves for service on
the UN Security Council or the Korean Truce Commission, when
they might have acted as members of an academic community trying
to work out reasonable rules." [93] As they become more and more
successful, they must become more and more organized. Discipline
becomes more important than participation, positions of power
corrode freedom, and authority is more important than anarchy.
The existence of full-time leaders or campus politicians or national
officers is more important to the Movement than the principle of
voluntary association. Some of the features of bureaucracy begin to
appear. One Vietnam Summer worker reported: "In terms of my
own development, I feel that I've developed administrative skills,
and I can run an office. . . ." [94] As early as the spring of 1965 the
FSM had to borrow the university's hated IBM machine in order

to keep track of all the people involved in its legal affairs.[95] One leader of the Young People's Socialist League lamented: "We lack the organizational base, the financial resources, and the stability of leadership required for the kind of massive assault that alone can demolish the political structure on which the Southern oligarchy is perched. If only we had the resources! If only others had our will!" [96]

The student strikes in the spring of 1970, already planned before the invasion of Cambodia and the deaths at Kent State, had several objectives. These objectives are not especially anarchistic: (1) To *symbolize* student support for "good" causes and opposition to "bad" ones. We will not engage in "education as usual" when Black Panthers are being persecuted and countries are being invaded. The university should take an official stand against these outrages. (2) To afford more time for *engaging* in discussion of burning "relevant" issues and actively to work for social and political causes. (3) To *apply pressure* to normal authorities to do something about war and racism. The demands have been issued, said the students; higher education will cease until they have been met. These objectives do not suggest eliminating governmental authority, but calling it to account. The means are drastic, but not all instances of drastic action are designed to serve anarchistic ends.

One may argue the other side: the students are really concerned with *social* problems. Normal politics has a hand in these problems and so must be examined. But since normal politics has either created, deepened, or failed to solve these problems, certain direct tactics are now in order. The concern, then, is not so much with politics as with social problems. The students do *not* take politics seriously; they merely perform in the political arena in order to show how useless political methods are. There is some truth in this point of view, but one still feels that students are fascinated with the monster they profess to detest.

Keniston speaks of a "cultural" revolution which assumes that "the only lasting changes are those that occur in men's minds and outlooks; meaningful change, therefore, cannot be achieved via 'mere' political manipulations and changes." [97] The methods of the radical left may "politicize" the apathetic, but they are intended to produce a result that transcends normal politics. Very well. But to view political change as a means for improving the quality of life lived in the good society of the future is not to be anarchistic; *most* political theories subordinate politics to more transcendent values. Politics is nearly *always* seen as a means. Nor is the intention of some student leftists to produce a revolution by means *other* than political ones necessarily anarchistic. Clearly, one can dispense with the sanctioned forms of political methods in order to produce a society with a *different* set of sanctioned political methods. Direct action is typical of anarchism, but not definitive. It is not definitive because it is available to the non-anarchist as well as the anarchist. All revolutionists tend, *for the duration of the revolution,* to be anarchists. As history has shown, however, this anarchism is only provisional—until a new regime can be set up. Only if the cultural change that activists seek finally dispenses with politics is it anarchic; if it merely replaces one political system with another, it is not anarchic.

The New Society

If extensive organization is needed to work for social changes, how much more will be needed to *carry out* the changes? "It takes a mighty swarm of mosquitoes to poison a Leviathan; and would not such a swarm be a Leviathan itself?" [98] The realistic members of the student left realize that ambitious programs for the transformation of society can be carried out only by large-scale, positive, socialistic, authoritarian government. Tom Hayden, in *Rebellion in Newark* (1968), wrote:

> These tactics of disorder will be defined by the authorities as criminal anarchy. But it may be that disruption will create possibilities of meaningful change. This depends on whether the leaders of ghetto struggles can be more successful in building a strong organization than they have been so far. Violence can contribute to shattering the status quo but only politics and organization can transform it. In order to build a more decent community while resisting racist power, more than violence is required. People need to create self-government. We are at a point where democracy—the idea and practice of people controlling their own lives—is a revolutionary issue in the United States. [99]

There is much in this quotation: provisional acceptance of the tactic of disruption, need for better organization, dependence on democratic politics. The objective is not the annihilation of government (which is what anarchism is all about), but perfecting its democratic form so that it is responsive to the people and able to take positive action in building a better society. The SDS has long stressed local action, but one of its presidents could write: *"Who else but the federal government* has the power to create jobs, to raise income, and to build the schools and hospitals and other civic centers required for the age of decency?"* [100] The purpose of much of what the leftists do on the *local* scene is to demonstrate the *necessity* for Federal intervention.

Many student leftists have their own conception of what democracy should be. "Participation" has already been discussed. But any government, even when perfected by the principles of participatory democracy, is still government and not anarchism. When, precisely, does participation in selecting and enacting social goals go beyond anarchism and become government?

There is doubtless a division of opinion in the ranks of the student left—both within the movement and within its individual members. The desire for an effective, well-organized, and well-financed national body is opposed by the desire for informal local autonomy. The desire for a quasi-professional and permanent leadership contends with the desire for improvised and shifting leadership. The declared aim of achieving political power is countered by fear of becoming part of the ruling establishment. The demand for "one man, one vote" is accompanied by the feeling that voting itself is irrelevant. These ambivalences exist with respect to the methods of changing the old society and to the nature of the new society that will replace it.[101]

It is the feeling of this writer that the new leftists will accept much more government in principle than would the old anarchists. The former seem more concerned with *perfecting* government than with eliminating it, while the latter are more concerned with showing how people can live without government at all than with transforming the institution itself. The student left opposes unjust government, with emphasis on the word, "unjust"; the cure for democracy is more democracy. One can argue against interpreting the student left as anarchistic by saying that it is not authority *per se* that the activists attack, but the *source* of that authority and the *uses* to which it is put.[102] The movement began with voter registration in the South. Will it end with the election of responsive legislators?

CRITICAL COMMENT

The views of the student left will be discussed here from two points of view: that of democratic liberalism and that of old anarchism.

The Liberal Point of View

The democratic liberal, while looking for general principles and attitudes in the movement, will seek to avoid stereotyping. He perceives the widespread disagreement in the student left as to both means and ends. He will therefore find some groups to praise and some to condemn. He will, moreover, find in the views of a single group (or a single individual) some aspects to praise and some to condemn. He believes that most politically concerned students are not members of extremist organizations, but are liberals like himself. And he fervently hopes that this numerical superiority continues to be the case, and that these concerned liberals will resist being stampeded by the radicals.[103]

The liberal is very sympathetic to the view that democracy should be restructured in a way that will make the individual's vote count more than it currently does. He too is concerned about corruption in government and the disproportionate influence exercised by the industrial and military powers. He agrees that racial minorities have been unjustly treated and urges full equality. He believes that students (and faculty) should be accorded greater say in the life of the universities, that universities are overdue for deep-reaching reform.[104] All this, and much more, is part of the grand struggle that liberalism has conducted for decades against the forces of darkness. The younger generation has learned much of its idealism from its elders—and part of its anger results from impatience with them for not enacting their reforms.

A great many liberals agree with the students in opposing the war in Vietnam and in feeling dissatisfaction with the draft laws. They too have long been distressed with the bureaucracy and impersonality that characterize the large organizations that dominate modern society. Furthermore, the democratic liberal will countenance, up to a point, tactics of direct action. Demonstrations, marches, disobedience, and strikes have long been a part of the American tradition. Americans prize order, but not at any price.

It is at this point, however, that we see the break between the liberals and some of the student left. The liberal prizes the democratic method. He and his forebears have fought for democracy for centuries. With all its faults, he will not give it up—or even see it weakened. Democracy is still the best hope of mankind for living together peaceably, for constituting a society in which free men live under rules of their own making. Social changes must come about, society must constantly renew itself, but democracy must provide the forms for orderly, peaceful, and popular reform. Government should not respond to angry and violent special-interest groups of the left any more than it should respond to those of the right. A democratic government should respond only to the will of the electorate through its popularly elected officials.

The liberal, then, is no anarchist. Government is necessary as the instrument through which citizens establish the rules that enable them to lead satisfying lives. Doubtless, the rules should be changed. The apparatus of democratic government should also be changed. But the system itself, however bad it may be, provides means by which these changes can be made. No minority, no matter how idealistic or certain of the correctness of its own judgments, has the right to short-circuit democratic procedures and impose its vision of truth on the rest.

Disruption and Violence

The fact is that many who speak loudest about "participatory democracy" (e.g., certain SDS leaders) are so domineering that they will not even listen to ideas other than their own. The radical minority will employ whatever coercive means are available: vandalism, silencing of opposing speakers, and threats of violence. Its favorite term is "demands." The liberal soon finds that dialogue is pointless and that compromise is impossible with people who bring to real problems what S. I. Hayakawa has called a "two-valued orientation."

The spring of 1970 was the most active period in the history of the student left. Never before were there so many disruptions. The Urban Research Corporation reported that at least 760 campuses played some role in the national student strike in May. More students and more faculty were involved than ever before. Most of these schools closed for one day, 18 percent closed for a week, and about 10 percent closed for the rest of the year. President Brewster of Yale called the strike an "irrationality which results from the inability to find any other way of shaking the regular political system into its senses." While he shared the students' feelings about the war, he hoped that "we are smart enough to devise a better way to demonstrate our dissent than to curtail education." [105] While violence occurred on less than 5 percent of these campuses in the

first two weeks of May, enormous concessions were won from university administrations in order to avoid violence.

But violence there has been! In addition to a lot of small-scale
"trashing," the University of Wisconsin reports attacks on six buildings and $300,000 in property damage. At Penn State, Washington
University, Kent State, Oregon, and Texas A & M the ROTC buildings were bombed and/or burned. The Bank of America building
near Santa Barbara was burned by students in February 1970, and
several other branches have been attacked since. Demonstrators
at Ohio State, Southern Illinois (Carbondale), and many other
campuses have caused substantial damage.

In addition to all this there have been bombings and arson off
the campus. The extent to which activists of the student left are
responsible for this may never be known.[106] In New York City alone
there were 4015 alarms and 368 bombings in the first four months
of 1970. Bombings occurred in the Manhattan headquarters of the
police department (seven were injured), and the offices of IBM,
Socony Mobil, and General Telephone and Electronics. During one
month—May—stores, theaters, and private homes were bombed.
In other cities draft board and recruiting offices were bombed. The
years 1969 and 1970 have exceeded in violence any two years of the
old anarchist threat.[107]

The liberal cannot condone bombings regardless of the merit of
the results they are intended to produce. Liberals, long the foes of
the radical right, now feel that the radical left constitutes the greater
danger. The threat is against security of life and property. The
actions are no longer political; they are of a nature that no orderly
body politic can endure. Since they constitute a reversion to a state
of nature, the full force of constitutional government must be
turned against them. Liberals must tolerate dissent; they cannot
tolerate lawlessness.

Also disturbing to the liberal is the blacklash such violence inspires. Financial support for education from private, state, and
Federal sources is more difficult to come by. By July 1970 thirty-two
states had passed special laws to deal with campus disorders.[108]
National and local legislation has been debated and passed which
curtails individual rights in important areas. Preventive detention,
surveillance, and conspiracy laws all tend to discourage legitimate
dissent. The "vital center" is losing supporters to the extremes of
the left and the right. The "hardhats" have occasionally taken the
law into their own hands. Vigilante groups have been formed. As

a result of student activism, students have been killed at Kent State, Kansas, and Jackson State, and have been wounded elsewhere. Thus the excesses of the left discredit liberalism while inspiring counter-illegality and violence from the right. As Senator Margaret Chase Smith has pointed out: if the choice has to be made between anarchism and repression, the American people will choose repression.

Some people, otherwise "liberal," are ready to favor suits brought by students against other students and university administrators who have closed schools or suspended classes, thus interfering with the rights of the complainants to receive the education they have contracted for. Some liberals can also sympathize with suits brought against universities, which are tax-exempt institutions, for participating in political campaigns. There is much talk of passing laws that would punish people (students *and* administrators) who interfere with others' freedoms of speech, press, religion, or assembly. The First Amendment Freedoms Act has already been introduced in the Senate.

The University

On the campus the student left will defend minority rights when it is the minority. But where it is a majority it will often override minority rights. The radical faction of the student left, always a minority on a campus, often seeks to impose its will on the majority. The views of other people simply do not count when "truth" and "justice" are at stake. The Vietnam Moratorium and national student strike movement illustrate this. The universities are to be shut down for *all* people: those who are for the war and those who are against it, those who are against the war but oppose the particular method of protesting, those who consider university education important and those who do not, those who want to attend class and those who do not. All complications are transcended, all gradations of feeling are overlooked, and all sensibilities are ignored. The universities, by God, will be closed—by the majority if possible, by the minority if necessary. This is simply arbitrary and intolerable.[109] "Sober academicians, who have long fought threats to academic freedom from the radical right, now genuinely feel that the radical left poses the greatest danger." [110]

Many leftists, even while they are closing it, see the university as a strong force for social change and seek to enlist it for their own points of view. In crucial times like these, they argue, the university cannot afford to be neutral. It must take a stand on behalf of such indubitable values as peace, justice, clean environment, and so on. To be silent when men are being drafted to kill Asians, when Negroes are being denied full rights, when the environment is being made unfit for future generations, is to aid and abet these evil trends. Neutrality, they argue, is either undesirable or impossible.

Many liberals reject this argument. They defend the principle of institutional neutrality as being the only one consistent with the ideal of academic freedom and see the university as an open forum where all points of view can be heard and individuals are free to reach their own conclusions. The university cannot have an official view of anything, for to do so is to venture down the roads of indoctrination (of the weak) and discrimination (against the strong). The university is dedicated to the pursuit of truth. Individuals will differ on where the truth lies—especially in matters ethical, political, and social. Organizations (whether universities or professional associations) cannot by their pronouncements make a point of view a true one. An organization that sponsors an official truth does a profound disservice to those who belong to it. If they are in disagreement, they find themselves in the uncomfortable position of being expected to support an institution whose opinions they cannot assent to. If they are in agreement, they are in the uncomfortable position of seeming to require for their point of view the external support of the institution's prestige and influence—as if the facts and argument of the case at issue were not enough.

The classical anarchists would have been very sensitive to the absurdity of an institution's having an opinion on something. Only individuals can have opinions, and these opinions derive from the individual's own thoughts. Here the anarchists and liberals come together in the tradition of libertarianism that spawned both William Godwin and John Stuart Mill. A university is a place where teachers and students examine evidence, scrutinize arguments, and debate issues. They are engaged in the common task of acquiring knowledge. But what is knowledge for X may not be knowledge for Y. The university must be big enough for both of them. Free dialogue cannot take place in any other context. What radical leaders want when they demand that the university be "opened up" as a center for efforts to end the war in Asia is precisely the opposite: that it be "closed down" to any other view.

Just as conviction is ultimately an individual matter, so too is action. What a student or a teacher does as a concerned citizen is his own affair. He may work with whatever organizations he chooses, and on his own time. A university, *qua* university, is involved in only one kind of action: education in the broad sense. It cannot descend to special interests or preferred positions and remain true to its *raison d'être.* "Men of conviction need not wait to receive a moral imperative from their university in order to work for a better world." [111]

Various rebuttals may be raised from the other side: (1) These are times of crisis. Neutrality may be acceptable in placid times, but society is now on the verge of destruction. Answer: [112] It is *especially* during times of crisis that neutrality should be preserved. A time when there is widespread disagreement on possible courses of action is precisely the time when hearings must be given to all projected courses of action. (2) Neutrality is impossible. If the university does not attack the "establishment," it is really supporting it by making it easier for it to continue. Answer: Individuals may make whatever criticisms they like, but the university must do, within the limits of its charter and the law, whatever best serves its *educational* aims. Institutional neutrality does not mean approval any more than it means disapproval. It means that policy decisions are left to others. (3) No educated person is against peace and for racism. Surely the university can take a stand here. Answer: These terms are vague and ambiguous. To the extent that they are made precise and unequivocal, to that extent do they become involved in factual and moral disagreement—*i.e.,* controversial. Individuals and other institutions may engage in controversy. Universities may not—except in the area of educational policies and aims. (4) Should not the university take the leadership in dispelling racism in its own province? Answer: Laws exist in the Constitution and elsewhere against racial, religious, and sexual discrimination. The university should enthusiastically obey these laws (and all others to which it is subject). (5) Should the university continue to engage in research for the more efficient conduct of the war? Answer: University faculties must allocate physical and human resources in the way they think is most compatible with their twin goal of acquiring basic knowledge and aiding the intellectual development of their members. While they should not directly support research on aggressive and effective ways to kill, they are not responsible for the uses that government makes of their theoretical findings. (6) Isn't it impractical to try to isolate the university from society? It is impossible to separate the university from political, social, and moral questions. Should it not

be the means by which society achieves its highest goals? Answer: Universities *must* isolate themselves from social pressures; they must preserve their detachment and objectivity. They must be especially vigilant in preventing external political, social, and moral pressures from dictating how they will pursue their educational aims. Radical causes and radical students and radical faculty would very quickly disappear from the campuses if the university were simply the agent for prevailing social moods. History teems with instances in which universities, losing all independence and integrity, simply responded to those social and political winds which blew the strongest.[113]
(7) Shouldn't the university seek to identify social evils and prescribe their cures? Answer: The faculty of a university should identify whatever social conditions its members think are evil. On this, disagreement is to be expected. The faculty may prescribe cures. Here also there will be disagreement. But the final decision on what in fact are evils and what are cures rests with the electorate. The university owes society its best thoughts. Society determines the uses (if any) to which these thoughts may be put.

George F. Kennan, in his wide-ranging criticism of the student left, argued against violent and lawless methods. When liberals see an administration is threatened and intimidated "into doing things for which it can itself see neither the rationale nor the electoral mandate," they have no choice but to place themselves on "the other side of the barricades"—no matter how sympathetic they may have been to the cause itself.[114] The students too often "endeavor to shock people in government, not to persuade them." [115] In rejecting normal electoral processes, they assume an absolutist position: the majority is uninformed, Congress is wrong, the President is misguided, and university administrations are evil. The authorities must make an instantaneous capitulation to any viewpoint strongly held and vigorously proclaimed.

The student left, according to Kennan, misconceives the function of the university. The function of a university is to assist the young to learn "about life in its wider and more permanent aspects" and "to tap something of the accumulated wisdom of the ages about the nature of man and his predicament." The activists do not have "respect for intellectual detachment." [116] They are too involved in the present political scene. They are excited about causes, injustice, social problems. We may, Kennan says to them, admire your unselfishness, idealism, and courage. "But what in the hell—if we may be so bold as to ask—are you doing on a university campus?" [117]

Kennan concludes, with some seriousness, that what we perhaps should have is two distinctive kinds of universities for high-school graduates: one, where students involve themselves in the passing scene—"one uninterrupted current events course"; the other, where students learn and prepare for a profession.

Another critical liberal is Sidney Hook, who turned his penetrating vision on the movement at Berkeley. Hook praises social concern, but like Kennan believes that an education can be acquired only by "hard intellectual discipline." "Good works off campus cannot be a substitute for good works on campus." [118] He accepts the principle of civil disobedience, but argues that it is justified only "in extreme situations in behalf of basic principles of freedom." [119] The situation at Berkeley was in no sense comparable to that in Mississippi. "I have no objection to democratic students rioting to protest racial, religious and grave political persecution, *if no other means are available to them.*" [120] Channels exist in the university and in the government for bringing about the changes the students agitate for. They should be used.

Hook very effectively meets the argument that only actions forbidden by law should be forbidden by the university and its corollary that no punishment beyond that meted out by the courts should ever be handed down by the university. "One can easily imagine situations in which student off-campus activity, legal or illegal, might very well have a definite bearing on values and standards regarded as precious to the educational community," [121] and he provides many such examples. Some things are legal, but should be forbidden (and punished) by the university—*e.g.,* plagiarism in term papers and cheating on exams. Some things are illegal, and should be punished by the university after the law has taken its course—*e.g.,* rifling lockers, stealing books from the library, libeling professors in off-campus newspapers. A student may be dealt with on *educational* grounds as well as on legal grounds. What the other side presupposes is "that a faculty has no right to require of students (or for that matter its own members) a standard of conduct in speech or behavior higher than what will enable students to stay out of jail. This is preposterous on its very face. For the university is fundamentally a community of scholars dedicated to the discovery and teaching of the truth. No one is compelled to seek entry to it. It has not only a legal and moral right but an educational obligation to raise its standards *above* that of the community whose law often expresses no more than the lowest common denominator of what is necessary to prevent men from breaking the social peace. It can therefore require of both its students and faculty conformity with a code of manners, speech and conduct, provided it is not unreasonable or unjust, higher than what obtains in the market place." [122]

Letters from Afar

The anarchists of the past would be interested in the "anarchism" of the present. Let us imagine what some of them would perhaps say to the student left of today.

Mes Enfants:

I have been called petty-bourgeois, so I thought I could perhaps understand your problems. But I cannot. In my day and age people had to struggle for a job, then were cruelly exploited when they found one. But you are affluent. You have plenty of money and have no doubt at all that society will provide you with a job when you are finally ready to go to work.

You are quite right to fear the dehumanization that will take place when you join a large corporation. Your organizations are so much larger and efficient than those of my day!

How do you intend to escape the evils of large organizations? Active participation? This might make you even greater captives. You know that some of those books you've been reading about "organization men" point out that the person who has no stake can at least call his soul his own! But anyway, it certainly would not further your wishes for greater individual liberty to be recognized as an infinitesimal part of a business corporation. Your role in setting policy there would be as frustrating as your role in setting policy in a democratic state. If you are really concerned with escaping the tyranny of bigness, may I suggest that you begin to think on a smaller scale? Ask yourself: What can an individual or a small group of individuals do to make their own way in the world? As long as you are employees, you can never be free.

I must say, however, that your capitalistic system seems to be working very well—even though it is based upon private property that has been stolen from the labor of others. But it was only a generation ago that your world was struck by a depression greater than any I had ever known or thought possible. The result was fascism worse than the regime of Louis-Philippe and war more destructive than Napoleon's. Can this happen again? Your economy is propped up by war production, but how long will this last? It is also maintained by deficit government spending—which is a very bad way to run *any household.* My point is that you should spend some time in studying economics. I know that it is an arduous subject and that you are very busy with your political activities. I might mention that I had to do most of *my* studying as an underpaid and overworked printer.

One final word, which I hope you will not think patronizing (I do know how you hate to be patronized). You are on very firm moral grounds in protesting the war in Vietnam. Indeed, I detect a real streak of moral earnestness in many of you. I don't know how to reconcile it with the licentiousness and debauchery you exhibit to the public.

I have a question you could perhaps answer. Why are you so concerned about the poor? They are much fewer in number than the impoverished masses of my day. Can't they rather easily find jobs in your society? They already live better than the landless peasants and urban wretches *I* knew! Shouldn't you be more concerned with the economic system that steals from those who *do* work?

Incidentally, I am very pleased that you have not fallen victim to the ideas of that Prussian Jew who libeled me so often in his writings. Karl was an authoritarian of the worst kind. I know that you quote many of his criticisms of capitalism, but that's all right; he got most of them from me.

Yours in peace,
Pierre-Joseph Proudhon

Comrades:

The war in Vietnam is an excellent issue, but how long can it last? When it is over you will have to have another great social injustice to play up and fan the embers of revolution. The race issue is a good one too, but your bourgeois society has made enough concessions to take the edge off that one. What you lack is a vision of a great society which will inspire the masses to heroic action. In my day it was abundance and equality, but you already have the abundance and most of your comrades have no interest in equality.

You also lack inspiring leaders. One chap wrote a nasty letter to the headmaster of his school. Another tried to seize a microphone at a meeting. Some leadership! How many of you have been beaten, imprisoned, and executed? It is true that you managed to create some artificial martyrs at Chicago and elsewhere, but does any of them possess the charisma that—well, never mind.

Your whole revolution is too narrowly based. You console one another—one bourgeois holding the hand of another bourgeois. Have you taken your message to the slums, to the workers, to the peasants, to the disinherited of this world? Some of you have, I think. But these people do not believe you, do not understand you. You have to work with them, live with them, suffer with them.

Another suggestion on this point. You are too provincial. Don't you know that any great revolution must be international in scope? Do you know how many members we had in the First International before the authoritarians scuttled it? I'd tell you, but such figures are secret. But you Americans do not work with the Frenchmen. The West Germans do not work with the East Germans. And the revolutionary potential of Switzerland is utterly untapped by the student movement.

I have found much to admire in your violent tactics. These violent confrontations can win attention and converts. There were, however, a lot of clowns in Chicago. Were they part of your organization? I knew a young fellow named Nechaev who could have taught them something, but I'll not go into that. But those freaks in Chicago seemed more concerned with putting on a performance than with winning a victory. The issues got awfully blurred.

There is an important criticism I must make. You people don't know anything about science and philosophy. Don't you ever read anything but pamphlets and underground newspapers? Knowledge is power, friends, and you're not getting much. Don't you know that philosophy will free you from superstition, sharpen your thought, and give you a profound basis for criticizing authoritarianism? Surely you must know that the face of the world must be changed and that it can be changed only through the application of the principles of natural science. "Relevance" is a term you often use. If cataclysmic change is your objective, then philosophy and science are relevant!

Yours in revolution,
Mikhail Bakunin

Gentlemen of the Student Left:

I am very pleased that you picked up the banner of social justice and are carrying it forward with such courage. Your elders apparently feel that progress has already reached its zenith, that social development has about run its course.

Your realization that man has evolved to work together in a friendly and amicable way causes me to rejoice. Your rejection of dog-eat-dog competition in the business world and warfare between peoples causes me to rejoice. You have developed in your own communes ways of mutual aid which were completely unknown to my generation. Surely your work and very existence demonstrate that mankind has indeed advanced since my day. Many of us thought we had all the answers. You, happily, proved us wrong. And if you should ever become narrowly doctrinaire, your children will prove you wrong also.

You have built on the achievements of the past. I have not yet, however, seen your acknowledgment of this. I am sure it exists. I am sure you are studying assiduously. Nothing clarifies the present and future so well as a thorough knowledge of the societies, movements, and ideas of the past. Indeed, ethical judgment itself is a product of history.

You young anarchists are very confident in your moral judgments. This must be because you have studied philosophy and natural history and have carefully examined the interplay of social change and man's evolving moral sentiments. I wrote a whole book, you know, to show that there is a scientific basis for the "golden rule"!

I wish I could help you in your patient but persistent efforts to bring peace and brotherhood to all the peoples of the world. You have my moral support in whatever you do.

I am in heaven, you know, the only anarchist here. My countryman who wrote those long novels did not make it. Perhaps my knowledge of geography helped me reach this destination!

Yours in justice,
Peter Kropotkin

Dear Friends:

I saw much in my long life to make me cynical. Looking always for heroism and sublimity, I saw too often self-seeking of the crudest kind. Political corruption still abounds; and the more corrupt one is, the more power is granted to him. Proof of this thesis: Richard Nixon.

Since my death I have learned that a socialist journalist in Italy named Mussolini stole my theories, distorted them, and built a fascist state. Then, a few years later, the noble anarchists in Spain were put down in the cruelest way—by fascists! Bitter irony! The CGT in France, for which I once had great hopes, is now controlled by the debased and moribund Communists who no longer have the zeal and idealism once imparted to the movement by Lenin. Syndicalism, alas, is dead in Europe.

You students in France embarked upon a grand mission. You were absolutely right in calling for the aid of the workers and in supporting the general strike. The times seemed more favorable for success than at any time since 1936. Your mistake, of course, was to expect that the workers would stand firm. They displayed spinelessness of the worst kind and should now be written off as a revolutionary class—in France and elsewhere. They have been completely tamed by their Communist union leaders. They seek only more money and shorter hours. You offered them *participation,* control of their own workshops—realization of the syndicalist ideal. But they do not want to manage their own destiny. They want security and physical comforts. They are nothing more than bourgeoisie with black lunch buckets.

I see only one ray of hope in your overmanaged and overabundant societies. And that ray comes from the West, from the United States. This may surprise you, but the only class which I see with revolutionary potential is the American Negro. He has not fully been tamed by the system. He is developing pride and evincing anger. Tired of fighting his battles in the unions, legislatures, and courts, he has taken to the streets. Martin Luther King taught him the efficacy of direct action, but he has gone beyond his teacher. He is reluctant to take on the middle-class values of white America, knowing instinctively (as Bergson and I did) that life holds more for man than a steady job and a home in the suburbs.

I am pleased that you on the student left so vigorously expose the rottenness of bourgeois society and are working hand in hand with your black brothers. Do not deprive them of roles of leadership. You have more to learn from them than they from you. If they go their separate way, you are all lost. But if you go *with them,* society could be regenerated. I don't know *where* they are going, and neither do they. But it's not important. For they have faith, and they have their myths. Even King said, "I have a dream." Fascism showed how powerful these feelings can be and what havoc they can make. The Negroes have "soul"—they may recreate the Western world. If your movement fails, you will have lost nothing, for there is nothing in established society to respect. If it succeeds, you will enter a new epoch in the life of man.

Apocalyptically yours,
Georges Sorel

My Beloved:

What have your self-appointed leaders permitted to happen in your great cities? I thought Moscow was bad in 1880, but you in America have a thousand cities immeasurably worse. I have been told of your filthy slums, your crowded ghettos. People cannot live this way—they soon cease to be people.

Your waterways have been polluted, the very air you breathe poisoned. Your lovely countryside has succumbed to concrete highways and filling stations. Hills of flowers have been leveled to build "cloverleafs"—ironic term. Horse and carriage served us well in my day. They were cleaner too than the belching rockets you use now and which devour your income, space, and time.

Industrial growth has blackened the face of your entire nation. You do well to oppose this historical development. Somehow, you must turn history around and recover the natural simplicities of a bygone age. Abandon the cities, abandon the suburbs. And above all, destroy the government that servilely carries out the policies of the manufacturers and businessmen whose greed has created a country consisting of urban centers of misery and vice tied together by a network of roads. St. Louis to Chicago, Chicago to St. Louis—six hours! Why go? Why not?

But you already know these things and are working to change the industrial society to which you were born. I commend you and bless you.

I cannot close, however, without chiding you on the means you choose to bring about your splendid goals. Violence, dear friends, accomplishes nothing. You rightly oppose the method of violence when, as national policy, it engages in war to settle the problem in Vietnam. You know that napalm will not make the Vietnamese love you, that supporting a puppet government with tanks and bayonets will not train the people for self-government. You rightly point out that you are no better than the North Vietnamese by imposing your will in the same way that they do. Why, so clear in this, are you so confused on domestic issues?

Do you think that disrupting classes, taking over university buildings, and insulting deans will make university officials love you? Do you think that such actions demonstrate your maturity and qualify you for the responsible roles in policy-making you are demanding? Your means are utterly inconsistent with your ends. They destroy them while they seem to promote them. You get short-term gains and forfeit the opportunity for genuine fellowship. You cannot *demand* understanding. To be understood, you must yourself be understanding. To be respected, you must yourself respect. And to be loved, you must yourself love.

I know that there are important changes that the universities should make. I had much to say about "relevance" in my day. But, again, it is a matter of method. Remember the cardinal principle: one reaches accord with another by suffering more pain than he is willing to inflict. And if you practice Christ's love for all mankind, you will inflict none at all.

I was very distressed by the activities in Chicago. The Walker Report rightly called it a "police riot." But your hands are not clean. You (or your lunatic fringe) provoked it, wanted it, courted it. In Chicago you turned my admonition inside out. You practiced violence in order to provoke greater violence! Yes, in the end, you may have suffered more. But the point is to practice love in order to *reduce* violence! You took advantage of the police. You drove them beyond human endurance. Their uniforms do not make them divinely patient and wondrously understanding. They are, after all, ordinary men—men without the advantages of family and education which you have had. Your aristocratic position, relative to them, imposes the duty on you to elevate them, assist them with your love. You could have awakened their humanity. But instead you brought out their bestiality. You called them pigs until they acted like pigs. Yes, my friends, I wept when I heard about Chicago, I wept for you and I wept for Mayor Daley.

One last word. Don't be so cruel to your parents. They love you and have given you much. Don't be ashamed to return that love. The love that must finally unite the human race in brotherhood is learned and nurtured in the family.

In Jesus' name,
Leo Tolstoy

NOTES

1 See Calvin Trillin, "Letter from Berkeley," in Michael V. Miller and Susan Gilmore, Eds., *Revolution at Berkeley* (New York: Dell Publishing Co., 1965), p. 276.

2 See Allan Priaulx and Sanford J. Ungar, *The Almost Revolution: France–1968* (New York: Dell Publishing Co., 1969), p. 12.

3 See Mitchell Cohen and Dennis Hale, Eds., *The New Student Left* (Boston: Beacon Press, 1967), p. 12.

4 See Stephen Spender, *The Year of the Young Rebels* (New York: Vintage Books, 1968), p. 107.

5 Kenneth Keniston, a sympathetic observer of the student left, perceived in the leaders of Vietnam Summer a strong belief in justice, decency, equality, responsibility, non-violence, and fairness. See his *Young Radicals: Notes on Committed Youth* (New York: Harcourt, Brace & World, 1968), p. 28.

6 The Kabouters, an anarchist group (successors to the Provos) in the Netherlands, will replace the War Ministry in their utopian state with a "Ministry for the Sabotage of Might and Main."

7 "For the past year-and-a-half, I have lived and worked in the Bedford-Stuyvesant Community. . . . I have seen what American society does to those who are black and to those who are poor. . . . Bedford Stuyvesant has turned me into a revolutionary." David Lee, letter to *The New York Times,* in George F. Kennan, *Democracy and the Student Left* (New York: Bantam Books, 1968), p. 35.

8 The student left reminds us very much of the old anarchists in its denunciation of religious establishments. "Students who instinctively 'want to do something' are often repelled by the hypocrisy of churches which engage in segregation while preaching equality. Stress on fund-raising and building programs rather than on feeding the poor and helping the needy is hardly in keeping with the teachings of Jesus or the tradition of the Old Testament prophets." Philip Altbach, in Cohen and Hale, p. 24.

9 "Nearly all the liberal institutions will go along in rhetoric with such demands [political and economic changes of substantial benefit to the Negro and white poor], but few will follow up with a massive action program to make rhetoric reality." Carl Wittman and Tom Hayden, in *ibid.,* p. 185.

10 The programs of the various factions of the SDS profess a rather puritan position on sex; the SDS, however, strongly favors free expression and insolence.

11 One Yippie flyer distributed in Chicago stated: "What's needed is a generation of people who are freaky, crazy, irrational, sexy, angry, irreligious, childish and mad: people who burn draft cards, burn high school and college degrees: people who say: 'To hell with your goals!'; people who break with the status-role-title-consumer game; people who have nothing to lose but their flesh." See Daniel Walker *et al., Rights in Conflict* (New York: Bantam Books, 1968), pp. 86-87.

12 See, for example, Daniel P. Moynihan, "Nirvana Now," *The American Scholar,* Autumn 1967.

13 Theodore Roszak, "Politics of the Nervous System," *The Nation,* April 1, 1968, p. 439. See also, Myron B. Bloy, Jr., "Alienated Youth, Their Counter Culture and the Chaplain," *The Church Review,* November 1968.

14 Larry D. Spence, "Berkeley: What It Demonstrates," in Miller and Gilmore, p. 223.

15 "An American Student Manifesto," in Editors of *Fortune, Youth in Turmoil* (New York: Time-Life Books, 1969), p. 50.

16 Karl Hess, "An Open Letter to Barry Goldwater," *Ramparts* 8:4 (October 1969), p. 30.

17 Spender, p. 104.

18 See Rennie Davis, "The War on Poverty: Notes on Insurgent Response," *Venture,* Winter 1965.

19 Spender, pp. 124–125.

20 See Priaulx and Ungar, p. 135.

21 Rennie Davis and Tom Hayden, in Walker, p. 20.

22 Michael L. Tickton, letter to Mr. Kennan, in Kennan, p. 29.

23 Jerris Leonard, civil rights chief of the U. S. Justice Department, has signed a statement calling the shootings at Kent State (May 4, 1970) by Ohio National Guardsmen "not necessary and not in order." He suggested that six guardsmen be criminally charged under Ohio law. His ten-page memorandum is based on an extensive investigation by a hundred FBI agents. He asserts that the guardsmen had not been injured, were not in danger, and still possessed tear gas. See *Akron Beacon Journal*, July 23, 1970.

24 See Kingman Brewster's famous statement, *Yale Alumni Magazine*, May 1970, p. 70.

25 "An American Student Manifesto," in Editors of *Fortune*, p. 52.

26 Spender, p. 172.

27 Andrew Levine, letter to *The New York Times*, in Kennan, p. 37.

28 See Miller and Gilmore, p. 61.

29 Hal Draper, an older leader of the student left, has written a devastating article on Clark Kerr's bureaucratic ideas. See "The Mind of Clark Kerr," in *ibid.*, pp. 68–69. The interior quotes are from Clark Kerr. As a pamphlet the article was widely circulated among students at the University of California and elsewhere.

30 Bruce Payne, David Walls, and Jerry Berman, in Cohen and Hale, p. 230.

31 Sol Stern, "A Deeper Disenchantment," in Miller and Gilmore, p. 228.

32 See "The Mind of Clark Kerr," in *ibid.*, pp. 62–77.

33 John F. Boler, "Behind the Protests at Berkeley," in *ibid.*, p. 107.

34 There are already signs that top bureaucratic officials no longer perform as persons but as inhuman functions of a machine. Perhaps this is why they are addressed so insolently and mockingly by radical student leaders. Example: Mark Rudd's famous and shocking letter to President Grayson Kirk of Columbia.

35 Jerry Cohen, "Critical Theory: The Philosophy of Marcuse," *New Left Review*, September–October 1969, p. 48.

36 The main difference between this sense of alienation and that of Marx is that for the latter alienation is between *two aspects of the same self*—that is, the self is alienated from itself. The worker, for example, sells his labor power in order to make a living, and from this sale arises a commodity which, though containing his labor, is foreign to him and beyond his understanding or control. In a larger context society also is alienated *from itself* in creating a vast economic system—a monster that destroys it. This is perhaps a more poignant kind of alienation than the one the students are talking about. The student feels overwhelmed by a culture he had no hand in creating. He is condemned to live in a "foreign" culture. For the Marxists one is powerless to control what he has *himself* produced; for the student one is powerless to control what *others* have produced.

37 David C. King, letter to Mr. Kennan, in Kennan, p. 25.

38 Charles Burck, " 'The Movement': Freeform Revolutionaries," in Editors of *Fortune*, p. 134.

39 Curtis M. Dowds, letter to *The New York Times*, in Kennan, p. 59.

40 Robert Hallem, in *ibid.*, p. 60.

41 Nicholas Macdonald, in *ibid.*, p. 80.

42 A statement from the Strike Coordinating Committee at Columbia in 1968:

"We striking students reaffirm our six demands, including amnesty. Amnesty must be a precondition for negotiations; our demand for amnesty implies a specific political point. Our actions are legitimate; it is the laws and the administration's policies, which the laws have been designed to protect, that are illegitimate." Quoted in Archibald Cox *et al.*, *Crisis at Columbia* (New York: Vintage Books, 1968), p. 132.

43 Barbara Bernstein and Susan Brown, in Kennan, p. 83.

44 Walker, p. 18.

45 See *ibid.*, p. 142.

46 Charles McDew, in Cohen and Hale, pp. 55, 57.

47 Nicholas Macdonald, letter to *The New York Times*, in Kennan, pp. 76–77.

48 "The transcendent fact is that violence is virtually certain to occur when, in an emotional environment, one group moved by its conscience undertakes physically to obstruct another group which is, in equally good conscience, performing its civic duty." Cox *et al.*, p. 122.

49 David Dellinger said before the Chicago riots: "We are flexible enough to permit each to act in his own style and we will support all of our associated groups." Later, during the riot in Grant Park, Dellinger himself was heard shouting into a microphone: "Be calm! Don't be violent!" See Walker, pp. 35, 226.

50 Marshals in Chicago were shouted down as authoritarian: "Fuck the marshals! Down with the leaders!" "Daley gives orders; don't [you] give us orders, you fascist." See *ibid.*, p. 148.

51 Many observers believe that the future of the Movement will be increasingly disruptive, violent, and militant. This has certainly been the line of development of the Student Non-violent Coordinating Committee, the Students for a Democratic Society, and the Black Panther Party.

52 Walker, p. 16.

53 Michael L. Tickton, letter to Mr. Kennan, in Kennan, p. 30.

54 The quotation continues: "Perhaps it is a press gloating over the extra-legal, the deviant and the irresponsible, picking up an isolated instance of student rascality, giving it national attention and soon finding it repeated on half a dozen campuses." Robert A. Haber, in Cohen and Hale, p. 35.

55 See Walker, p. 30.

56 See *ibid.*, p. 40.

57 See *ibid.*, p. 87.

58 The ratio between reformists and revolutionaries among the rank and file of the student left is unknown. Certainly most concerned American youth is reformist rather than revolutionist. A poll of 718 representative college youth in the fall of 1968 by *Fortune* divided them into the "practical-minded" (college is for preparing for a lucrative and interesting career and achieving a better position in society) and the "fore-runners" (college provides the opportunity to improve society). Only 5 percent of the former and 19 percent of the latter reported feeling "a sense of solidarity and identification with the new left." See Editors of *Fortune*, p. 38.

59 See Walker, p. 142.

60 See Priaulx and Ungar, p. 67.

61 See Spender, p. 21.

[62] See Cox *et al.*, pp. 58–59.

[63] Spender, p. 23.

[64] *E.g.*, demonstrations, marches, sit-ins, work strikes, rent strikes, boycotts of stores and schools, occupation of buildings, vandalism, disruption of meetings, trials and public business, destruction of buildings symbolic of repression, etc.

[65] The lack of interest among leftist students in such Congressional debates as the Cooper-Church Amendment and the repeal of the Gulf of Tonkin Resolution is obvious. No great celebrations in the leftist camps were observed when Congress passed (and the President signed) the bill to lower the voting age to eighteen.

[66] "The first impulse of most young radicals was to attempt to work within the System; and it was often only after the apparent failure of such efforts, and only with the developing conviction that the System could not be trusted to remedy its injustices, that they turned toward a Movement that stressed the need for new institutions." Keniston, p. 129.

[67] Quotation attributed to Douglas Miranda of the Black Panthers. See *Yale Alumni Magazine*, May 1970, p. 19.

[68] See Paul Jacobs, in Miller and Gilmore, p. 80.

[69] Sidney Hook, "Second Thoughts on Berkeley," in *ibid.*, p. 147.

[70] Nathan Glazer, in *ibid.*, p. 195.

[71] See Calvin Trillin, "Letter from Berkeley," in *ibid.*, pp. 266–267.

[72] An instructive, but not unique example: Kenneth S. Pitzer became president of Stanford University in December 1968. His liberal credentials were impeccable. He was an active opponent of racism and the war in Asia. During his administration, competition with Brigham Young was discontinued, the curriculum was significantly altered, judicial processes were introduced into disciplinary proceedings, student participation in decision-making was broadened, etc. Yet police had to be summoned to the campus at least thirteen times in the spring of 1970 alone. Effective August 1970, Dr. Pitzer resigned.

[73] Jack Newfield, *A Prophetic Minority* (New York: Signet Books, 1967), pp. 23–24.

[74] Larry D. Spence, "Berkeley: What It Demonstrates," Miller and Gilmore, p. 223.

[75] One eyewitness report from Fayerweather Hall (Columbia) after two days of occupancy: "The demonstrators were in good spirits and very highly organized. Food was plentiful, a first aid station was set up, a lost and found office, a communications room, a newsletter was mimeographed. People slept in classroom buildings and hallways. And always meetings and more meetings, lasting long into the night. Participatory democracy. There was a real community spirit; everything belonged to everybody; the building was 'liberated.' Girls—about 40%—were not expected to do the kitchen work alone, for this was a 'liberated' area, and boys had to help. Couples slept together in public view, nobody cared, we were 'liberated': here was a single commune in which adult hypocrisies did not apply any longer, where people shared and shared alike, where democracy decided everything, where people were free of adult values and codes. Fayerweather was tense, 'up tight,' but free and in high spirits." See Cox *et al.*, p. 138.

[76] Bob Parris, in Cohen and Hale, p. 90. Compare with: "Among the uneducated, the poverty-stricken, and the segregated, there is a lack of leadership and

administrative ability and even of an ability to focus on issues and verbalize general dissatisfaction." Wittman and Hayden, in *ibid.*, pp. 196–197.

[77] Alan Finder, letter to *The New York Times*, in Kennan, p. 53.

[78] "Letter from Berkeley," in Miller and Gilmore, p. 274.

[79] " 'Campus Left' " is only a euphemism for a series of *ad hoc* reactions by a myriad of students protesting a myriad of problems at a myriad of different schools and locales. Due to the different nature of the problems on the different campuses, and due to a turnover that would bar any continuity, I feel there can never be a monolithic entity called the 'Campus Left.' After all, we don't expect a program from the 'Adult Right' either." David Gould, letter to *The New York Times*, in Kennan, p. 47.

[80] "The simple fact is that a constantly growing proportion of the best students does not look forward to careers molded along the established lines of professional or business success. . . . Too little of the whole elaborate paraphernalia of academic activities appears to be concerned with the conduct of a man's life." Cox *et al.*, pp. 22–23.

[81] "Whether students stay in college, or leave to work in the movement, they need constant immersion in the content of at least the social sciences and humanities." Wittman and Hayden, in Cohen and Hale, p. 207. The Port Huron Statement stressed the importance of the development of intellectual skills.

[82] Cox *et al.*, p. 21.

[83] See Priaulx and Ungar, p. 67.

[84] Even a friendly observer like Paul Goodman was "appalled" by the low level of intellectual analysis in FSM publications. See Miller and Gilmore, p. 287.

[85] Kennan, p. 124.

[86] "Berkeley: What It Demonstrates," in Miller and Gilmore, p. 217.

[87] See Priaulx and Ungar, p. 32.

[88] Thomas Kahn, in Cohen and Hale, p. 57.

[89] John Searle, "The Faculty Resolution," in Miller and Gilmore, p. 104. Searle is not a student. He is professor of philosophy at the University of California (Berkeley).

[90] David Dellinger, Rennie Davis, Tom Hayden, Abbie Hoffman, Jerry Rubin, Lee Weiner, John Froines, and Bobby Seale.

[91] "The external world seems to threaten actually to disrupt the values of the inner world. To realize and even retain his own values the student has to convert the most personal values of his own being into political counteraction." Spender, p. 118.

[92] The anarchistic Kabouters in the Netherlands were somewhat embarrassed by their victories in the municipal elections of 1970. One of them pronounced: "If a Kabouter really wants to do something, then he must do nothing." Another then said that the Ministry of Education of the future would favor schools that would seek to make students unadaptable. See *The New York Times*, June 19, 1970, p. 2.

[93] See Miller and Gilmore, p. 194.

[94] See Keniston, p. 40.

[95] See Calvin Trillin, "Letter From Berkeley," in Miller and Gilmore, pp. 257–258.

[96] Thomas Kahn, in Cohen and Hale, p. 65.

97 Keniston, p. 185.

98 Christopher N. Reinier, in Cohen and Hale, p. 27.

99 See Spender, p. 6.

100 Todd Gitlin, in Cohen and Hale, p. 130.

101 "The extent to which it is possible to retain an unmanipulative and participatory style, and yet mount an effective program on a national scale, is one of the unresolved questions of the New Left." Keniston, p. 171.

102 Keniston, a psychologist, does not find the source of youthful radicalism in rebelliousness against parents and the older generation. For the radicals he studied the "red diaper" hypothesis is more plausible: their parents were very radical or very liberal themselves, and they emulated them. Actually, Keniston's explanation is neither of these. His explanation is plausible and carefully stated, but cannot be summarized here.

103 One poll conducted at Columbia during the height of the troubles in the spring of 1968 revealed that most of the students opposed amnesty for the students "involved in the demonstrations of the last three days," while favoring the two substantive demands (end gym construction and break University ties with IDA). See Cox *et al.,* p. 137.

104 The fact-finding commission appointed to investigate the 1968 disturbances at Columbia concluded its report: "We are convinced . . . that ways must be found, beginning now, by which students can meaningfully influence the education afforded them and other aspects of the university activities." *Ibid.,* p. 198.

105 See *Yale Alumni Magazine,* June 1970, p. 34.

106 The U. S. Justice Department on July 23, 1970, indicted thirteen leaders of the Weatherman faction of the SDS for plotting to conduct bombings in four cities. Most of the thirteen are in hiding or abroad—including leaders Mark Rudd and Bernardine Dohrn.

107 According to Eugene T. Rossides, Assistant Secretary of the Treasury, a survey conducted by the Alcohol, Tobacco and Firearms division of the IRS reported the national figures for the period January 1969 to April 1970: 35,129 reports of bomb threats, 4330 actual bombings, 43 persons killed, 384 persons injured, and almost $22 million in damage.

108 Typical provisions: no state aid to illegal demonstrators, strict regulations to keep outsiders (including suspended and dismissed students) off the campus, swift and severe punishments for disruptive and destructive acts, dismissal of faculty activists, searches for guns and other weapons.

109 A most insensitive use was made in Washington in November 1969 of the names and memories of American soldiers killed in Vietnam. They were exploited for a particular political position—whatever their views (and that of their survivors) may have been. This is quite parallel to the use made by Robert Welch and his people of the name of Capt. John Birch, a gallant soldier also dead and unable to express his own views.

110 *Newsweek,* June 15, 1970, p. 67.

111 Winton U. Solberg, "On Institutional Neutrality." *A.A.U.P. Bulletin,* March 1970, p. 13. The American Association of University Professors on November 1, 1969, raised the question of institutional neutrality (see *Bulletin,* December 1969, p. 488) and asked for discussion. Two viewpoints were later presented (see *Bulletin,* March 1970, pp. 11ff.). Further comments were printed in the summer (see *Bulletin,* June 1970, pp. 123ff.). The Association has not yet issued an

official point of view. On the issue of neutrality it is not thought wise to be neutral.

[112] None of these answers can be complete. They simply indicate the line of thought this writer would take.

[113] It must be admitted, however, that the university is a part of society and is involved with it. Columbia University President Andrew W. Cordier wisely said that the university cannot long live in the community unless it lives with the community. There are actions the university may take in cooperation with the community which do serve that community. But these should be consonant with its own educational aims, should not reflect a partisan position on controversial social issues, or compromise the integrity of the university as a free forum for all ideas.

[114] Kennan, p. 15.

[115] *Ibid.*, p. 163.

[116] *Ibid.*, p. 131.

[117] *Ibid.*, p. 130.

[118] Sidney Hook, "Academic Freedom and the Rights of Students," in Miller and Gilmore, p. 41.

[119] *Ibid.*, p. 39.

[120] Sidney Hook, "Second Thoughts on Berkeley," in *ibid.*, p. 117.

[121] *Ibid.*, p. 122.

[122] *Ibid.*, p. 126.

9

The Radical Right

OPPOSITION TO ANARCHISM

Boundaries of the Radical Right

The term "radical right," like "student left," stands for a wide spectrum of political and social thought. The student left, while it agrees on the urgent need for fundamental changes that can only be described as revolutionary, ranges from peaceful advocacy of orderly methods to violent destruction of democratic processes. The radical right, while it agrees in opposing the important social trends of the last forty years, ranges from the views set forth by the supporters of Senator Goldwater to those proclaimed by Robert Welch. Since this selected range covers a wide territory, including as it does McCarthyism, the Christian Crusade, and the relatively thoughtful views of the writers of the *National Review,* one must be cautious in generalizing about it. There are real differences between the "moderate" and "extreme" wings of the radical right. However, once differences of methods and emphasis are recognized, there is a harmony of basic ideas.

The radical right is bound on one side by conservatism. It is at this point (if a point could be found) that the moderates of the radical right mingle with those who accept some of the reforms of the past few decades. We may call these moderates "conservatives," but their conservatism is qualitatively different from that of Walter Lippmann, Peter Viereck,[1] Clinton Rossiter,[2] and Dwight Eisenhower.[3] Conservatism will accept the recent past. While concerned to preserve that which is valuable in society's heritage, it will seek to improve that heritage gradually for the benefit of the next generation. It will seek a consensus with the moderate ideas of all responsible areas of public thought. It will never undertake a fundamental change of the edifice of society, even though it recognizes that this edifice is imperfect. The radical right, however, including its moderate wing, is ideological. It has more or less definite principles for the alteration of public policy and these principles are quite at odds with current consensus. "Compromise with the dominant forces of this age is not possible." [4] The radical right is bitterly opposed to the ideas of Lippmann, Viereck, Rossiter, and Eisenhower because they refuse to disrupt the basic patterns of American life. Conservatism says, "Let us consolidate our gains but go slowly in making future changes." The radical right says, "Let us dismantle the programs of the recent past and recover as quickly as we can those permanent principles of Western civilization and American life." The radical right, furthermore, is so bitterly angry against all governments since 1932, duly constituted though they may be, that it may be said to advocate a "psychological insurrection." [5] Its adherents constitute not a "loyal opposition" but a radical dissent.[6] The moderate M. Stanton Evans often speaks of the conservative "revolution." [7] And his fellow moderate, Frank S. Meyer, can say, "The role of radical is temperamentally alien to the conservative, but in the circumstances of Liberal domination under which we live, that role is demanded of him." [8]

The radical right is bound on the other side by the lunacy of anti-Semitism, racism, and popular fascism. It is here that the extremists of the radical right mingle with such people as the followers of Merwin K. Hart's National Economic Council and Gerald L. K. Smith's Christian Nationalist Crusade and descendants of the America First Committee.[9] Racism is not characteristic of the radical right in either its moderate or extreme versions. Spokesmen for even the extreme wing of the radical right (Robert Welch and Kent Courtney are examples) strongly disassociate themselves from anti-Semitic, anti-Catholic, and anti-Negro positions and their implications. Nevertheless, they have had friendly relations with some who do not and many of the racist lunatics are also supporters of the extremists of the radical right and are ready to make common cause against liberalism with their more respectable co-workers.

Nationalism

The first important principle to be noted in the ideology of the radical right is that of nationalism. The rightist, unlike the anarchist, has a strong sense of identification with his country. He views it as a sovereign state to which absolute loyalty (under God) is due. He is proud of its history, zealous for its present security, and ambitious for its future greatness. He opposes any limitation of its sovereignty, any diminution of its autonomy in international relations. The rightist is unabashedly patriotic.

The United Nations is the target of many members of the radical right.[10] "Get the UN out of the US and the US out of the UN" is a favorite slogan. America compromises its sovereignty in such a body and is induced to make concessions to its Communist enemies, while providing a haven for spies in New York. The International Court of Justice, the Arms Control and Disarmament Agency, and Cultural Exchange threaten American interests. Even the United Nations Children's Fund is regarded as communistically conspiratorial by extremists.

The radical right is opposed to most forms of foreign aid, the United States Information Agency, the Voice of America, the Peace Corps, etc. American taxpayers have no obligation to help foreigners —especially when they tend to be hostile to us. The only kind of foreign aid that can be defended is that which provides military assistance to those powers that are pledged to stand with us in any showdown with Communist states. Otherwise, America simply weakens itself to the advantage of the Communists.

The nationalism of the radical right implies constant vigilance over the machinations of its enemies. The greatest enemy of the United States is Communism. Communism is an enemy because it is godless, materialistic, collectivistic, state-centered, and undemocratic. "Communism, in actual and objective fact, does represent an absolute black, and the West as a civilization is *in its essence* as close to an absolute white as is possible in the subdued light which illuminates this imperfect world." [11] Communism is pledged to world domination, and already has come to power in states in Europe, Asia, Africa, and the Western hemisphere. The United States, the last resolute defender of Western civilization, is its ultimate target. The Communist threat at home and abroad must be dealt with by all effective means. When the security of the nation is at stake, a liberal interpretation of such rights as free speech and press, freedom of travel and assembly, and freedom to hold a government job, teach, or conduct research without political tests would be foolish, cowardly, or treasonable.

The radical right proposes an aggressive foreign policy. Break off diplomatic relations with Communist countries. Unleash Chiang Kai-shek. Launch a preventive war against the Soviet Union. Bomb the Chinese beyond the Yalu River. Support revolutions like those in Hungary and Czechoslovakia. Support the Katangese rebels in Africa. Destroy Castroism in Cuba. Win a decisive military victory in Vietnam.[12] For too long we have been following a policy of accommodation. Action, not drift, is the American way—see things through to a successful conclusion. Despite the fact that the United States had an overwhelming military advantage over the Soviet Union and its friends after World War II (the difference is not so great now), we have permitted Communism to take over another third of the world. Eisenhower (and other liberals) say, "War is unthinkable." But it is better to die on your feet than to live on your knees. American and Western civilization can be made secure only by the military defeat of Russia and China. Coexistence is not possible.

The radical right takes a skeptical view of schemes to stop nuclear testing and limit armament.[13] Outnumbered as we are—and "outterritoried" too—it cannot be to our interest to agree to limit our defense. We need strength *vastly superior* to that of the Soviet Union. Russian promises cannot be believed. Russian interest in disarmament is simply a trick to induce America to reduce its defensive power so that Communism can expand again—perhaps into North America itself. The best way to spend the taxpayers' money is for preparedness: massive retaliation.[14]

Frank S. Meyer outlined a plan of nuclear strategy in the *National Review* in 1963 ("Just War in the Nuclear Age"). It is based on the beliefs that Western civilization (under American leadership) is good, that Communism is bad, and that Communism is committed to worldwide domination by any means at hand. Meyer's first step is "peripheral warfare" by conventional weapons. The aim would be to "drive Communist power back to its original borders . . . and then to preside over the dissolution of the Communist regime." [15] In response to such a strong policy the Soviet Union would be inclined to strike back with nuclear weapons. We might be able to deter such a response by possessing massive nuclear bombs that could destroy the Communists' civilian population. But since deterrence might not work and a Russian first-attack would weaken our counter-attack, it is probably better to strike the first nuclear blow ourselves. The United States should thus *initiate* the attack and destroy the Soviet Union's air and missile delivery systems. This would save civilian life on both sides. "In defense of a just cause, uncontaminated by impure intentions, strictly proportional in force employed to the purpose (destruction of the enemy's nuclear power), a first-strike counter-force nuclear blow, minimal in its effects upon the civilian population, meets every moral criterion." [16] A few years later (1966), Meyer was ready to welcome Chinese intervention in Vietnam: It would be "an opportunity to destroy its nuclear potential and set back its development as a serious military power for years." [17]

The domestic side of the same coin is the issue of gun control. To require registration of guns is merely a preliminary to confiscating them. The Constitution protects the right of citizens to bear arms. This right should not be withdrawn. Laws would only prevent "good" people from concealing or possessing weapons; criminals and leftists would not obey. The Minutemen argue that a great deal of firepower must be accumulated to be used in the event of a Communist takeover.

There is widespread disagreement on where international Communism is to be stopped. Is it to be stopped in Korea, Laos, and Vietnam? Or is it to be stopped in Africa, where we still must bear the white man's burden? Or is it to be stopped in Western Europe, where the always valuable Western civilization began and still survives? Or, as the Monroe Doctrine insists, is it to be stopped in the Western hemisphere? Or is it to be stopped in North America itself, the final fortress of the free society? No spokesman of the radical right is really an "Asia Firster"; characteristically, he desires nothing more than American greatness. Disagreement is one of strategy only. Where, *in the interest of the United States of America,* should Communism be stopped? The isolationist antecedents of the radical right still apply. The United States is not charged with the responsibility of saving the world. It must, however, save itself. To do this, intervention in Vietnam may (or may not) be necessary.

Law and Order

The second great contrast between anarchism and the new right is on the issue of law and order. Laws must be upheld, whatever they may be. Punishment should be swift and sure. Technicalities that get in the way of speedy justice should be removed. One of the many failures of the Supreme Court in recent years has been to tilt the scales of justice in favor of the accused. This has made it increasingly difficult to deal with offenders against the nation's peace and security. The innocent thus have insufficient protection from traitors, rioters, thieves, muggers, and murderers. The nation is not safe—either in its traditional freedoms or its city streets. Too many appeals succeed, too many convicts are paroled, too many cases are dismissed. Clarence Manion, of the Manion Forum, wrote in 1961: "The record reveals that the chief, if not the only beneficiary of the Warren Court's Constitutional constructions have been convicted criminals, Communists, atheists and clients of the NAACP." [18]

Most spokesmen of the radical right are impatient with the sociological approach to crime. Young people who break the law are criminals, not "juvenile delinquents" or "misguided youths." The cause of their behavior is to be found in their will, not in the economic conditions of their lives, their home backgrounds, or maladjusted personalities. They are better helped by being made to suffer the consequences of their actions than by social rehabilitation or psychological counseling. Crime has increased because authority is no longer respected. It is no longer respected because it fails to take decisive action against the enemies of law and order.

The radical right would take a strong stand against demonstrations in the streets and in the schools.[19] Even when they are advertised as peaceful, they are intended to arouse violence on the part of the more unrestrained demonstrators or to provoke it from the police. In any case they disrupt and create pressure on officials, legislators, or courts to make immediate redress of "grievances." The normal, Constitutional channels are bypassed. Emotional mob action takes the place of deliberation, and capitulation to demands overrides justice. Behind all the demonstrations, there is, especially among the Negro militants, the unspoken (but not always unspoken!) threat of riot and revolution. Officials do not have to respond to this any more than they have to respond to extortion or blackmail. "No society—least of all a free society—can subsist if the challenge of illegal violence is not met with all the force of legal authority necessary to subdue it." [20] Court injunctions and restraining orders are easily secured. Those who disobey are in contempt of court, and police are always available to make arrests.

In the view of the radical right the "People's Park" riots at Berkeley (spring 1969) occurred because the students had *earlier* been permitted to win victories. The radical left was *established* in Berkeley, and its subculture was accepted there. In the park it found a fine issue ("grass and motherhood") by which to win the support of the students and "street people" against the university administration that had planned to create parking lots and soccer fields. The new left (students and non-students), already securely in possession of *breathing* space in Berkeley, now wanted *living* space. So there was war—the worst yet on an American campus. "The New Leftists and street people, no longer content with unofficial occupation, decided officially to annex a chunk of university territory, and by so doing to legitimize their culture. . . . And it was the legitimacy of its authority, long undermined, which the university decided it must reassert. . . . It finally attempted to check the growth of the alien culture which has put down roots along Telegraph Avenue and on the Berkeley campus. The People's Park episode was the first overt attempt to uproot this culture, to begin to deny it growing space. . . . And so the university administrators, their backs against the final wall, did what they had to do. Their action, inevitably, was ill-timed, the execution execrable and typically blundering. Had they acted steadily and systematically to achieve their ends, the problems would never have arisen." [21]

One hopeful countervailing power to the student left is Young Americans for Freedom. It has been advised to: (1) Circulate petitions against radical demands and methods. (2) Demand student referenda on issues (*e.g.,* should ROTC be permitted?). (3) Set up counter-demonstrations—heckle and picket. (4) Establish lines to protect buildings from takeovers. "Battling people from their own college tends to explode the myth of student solidarity which radicals love to perpetuate. Too, by having to face other students they are denied the opportunity to provoke the police to violence and instead are placed in the position of initiating the violence themselves as evidenced by the incidents at Stanford and Columbia. Thus, even if the conservatives are unable to forestall a radical disruption they can blunt its impact significantly through the use of 'counter-confrontation.' " [22] (5) Photograph any illegal actions by the enemy.

The propensity of our young people today to break the law (as criminals or as demonstrators) may be attributed partly to the poor education they have received in their schools and homes. They have not been educated for good citizenship, in the values of Western civilization, to the respect to which authority is entitled, or to moral principles in general. The younger generation is the result of the corroding influence of the ideas of John Dewey and permissive parenthood. Its attitude is the tragic consequence of the fashionable and dominant intellectualism that questions absolutes and dissolves all convictions in a sea of doubt and relativism. Rejecting objective standards of truth and reality, their tutors have taught the young to be critical, to question everything. When nothing stands, anything goes. The young finally make official their abdication of humanity: they sink into the drug-induced oblivion where truth, value, and reality are utterly irrelevant.

Members of the student left learned much of their militancy from their tutors in academe: sit-ins in the South, for example, were illegal but widely applauded. Professors and chaplains often accompanied protestors in demonstrations and demands for "civil rights." The liberals in the universities now are alarmed. After having encouraged disruption of other institutions for "moral" reasons, they now wring their hands when their own is under fire. Having taught their students not to tolerate law and order without due concern for the *quality* of that order, they must now witness the destruction of academic law and order.

Political Action

The third great difference between anarchism and the radical right lies in the great propensity of the latter for political action. The right may be radical, but it will use political methods and the established apparatus for its special goals. The members of the John Birch Society and other extremists sought to get Chief Justice Warren impeached by "educating" constituents by means of the *Warren Impeachment Packet;* after reading the materials in this package, they were to bring pressure on their Congressmen to institute an impeachment proceeding.[23] The moderates, also relying on political means, seek legislation that would limit the power of the Supreme Court. Mass petitions and letters to Congressmen and others are employed for many rightist goals.[24] There are several guides to Congressional voting, which are distributed to citizens; these provide ratings like those of the liberal Americans for Democratic Action. *Human Events* and the Americans for Constitutional Action publish guides that rate a Congressman's degree of "conservatism." The most rigorous such guide was published by the Conservative Society of America under the Courtneys: *CSA Voting Index.* One issue in 1962 gave HUAC chairman Francis Walter a "100% Liberal-Socialist" grade—very soft on Communism! Certain candidates for local and national office are supported; others are attacked. Robert

Welch has declared that "we would put our weight into the political scales in this country just as fast and far as we could." [25]

The creation of "reading rooms," building up the rightist holdings of public and school libraries, placing reading materials in barber shops and doctors' offices, and radio and television broadcasts—all of these are to be used to politicize citizens. The radical right produces an impressive number of books and periodicals. Important among the latter are *American Opinion, Human Events, National Review, Weekly Crusader, The Dan Smoot Report,* and *John Birch Society Bulletin.*[26] Other techniques of political action are not so honorable. *The Blue Book of the John Birch Society* provides ways of exposing Communists and "Comsymps" in debate and in the lecture room. These techniques depend on the use of loaded questions and a series of "innocent" queries, truthful answers to which would have "devastating implications." "The question technique, when skillfully used in this way, is mean and dirty. But the Communists we are after are meaner and dirtier, and too slippery for you to get your fingers on them in the ordinary way. . . ." [27] Radical rightists are also encouraged to get on the program committees of PTAs and service clubs. Organizations exist to provide lectures, seminars, and anti-Communist courses. The Christian Anti-Communism Crusade, under the leadership of Frederick C. Schwarz, specializes in "schools" of anti-Communism: "You can't fight Communism unless you understand it."

The radical right has tried to capture the Republican Party for a long time, but the liberals succeeded in naming Willkie and Dewey as Presidential candidates in the forties. In the fifties the liberals, still in control, nominated and elected Eisenhower. "The Eisenhower tenure in Washington served to make clear the central fallacy of the liberal Republican formula. Having accepted the Democrats' approach to public problems, the liberal GOP has no ideology; and having no ideology, it can have no major impact on the fundamental direction of the nation's politics." [28] In 1964 the radical right succeeded in nominating Goldwater. His defeat in November can be explained in terms other than repudiation by the voters of the "conservative" point of view.[29]

The rightist often speaks of forming a third party because the programs and Presidential candidates of the two major parties are so often so similar in their liberalism.[30] Many strategists of the radical right believed that the third party idea makes an excellent threat, but that substantial political success must ultimately come about through one of the two major parties. While there are radical conservatives in both parties, the best chance lies with the Republicans, for they have most consistently opposed the social legislation that began with Franklin D. Roosevelt. M. Stanton Evans' *The Future of Conservatism* is an excellent (and optimistic) study of the political potentialities of the "conservative" (radical right) movement. There are more "conservatives" than there are Republicans and, in 1968, almost as many "conservatives" as "liberals." Evans shows where they are to be found and how they can win political victories—hopefully, within the Republican Party. He also explains why they have failed in the past.

An interesting piece of strategy favored by some of the moderate leaders of the radical right is to welcome the presence and activities of the extremists of the right, for such extremists will draw away most of the invective traditionally directed at the right, thus making it easier for the center to project a "moderate" image. Followers of the "Conservative school," wrote John Hilberg in *The Individualist,* "can hardly expect to gain a major electoral victory unless they can emulate their opponents in projecting themselves as some compromise solution to a fantastic aberration of the far Right. It is, therefore, in the interests of all Conservatives to support the illusions of Rightist extremism circulating around such groups as the John Birch Society. . . ." [31] It is quite possible that the extremists sometimes have the same idea in their frequent toleration for the racial lunatics to *their* right.

The dynamics of the relations between moderate and extreme elements of the radical right (and between the extremists and the lunatics) are by no means as simple as implied here. Groups with disparate viewpoints often work together and share the same platforms, but frequently the more moderate leaders are embarrassed by the immoderates. A common stance for the moderate is to denounce the excesses, say, of Robert Welch, but to praise the organization he leads—or to denounce an organization but to praise the many "good Americans" who belong to it. There are, across the whole spectrum, common interests and overlapping concerns. A Robert Welch may hire a Westbrook Pegler to write a column, pleased with his anti-Communism but uneasy with his racism. William F. Buckley, Jr., may disapprove of Senator McCarthy's tactics but will defend the services he rendered the nation. [32] The critic of this should avoid falling victim to the "guilt by association" syndrome. Some socialists have points of accord with Communists without being Communists; some liberals have points of accord with socialists without being socialists; some moderate Republicans have points of accord with liberals; and some reformers of the student left have points of accord with the revolutionaries of the new left. Similarly Welch, Hargis, Bundy, and Manion have cooperated with the lunatics, and Buckley, Evans, and Meyer have cooperated with the Birchers. The radical right is no more homogeneous than the anarchist group or the liberal "establishment." We are concerned here, however, more with the areas of fundamental agreement than with making distinctions.

Despite the tax-exempt status of many organizations of the radical right as "educational," "religious," or "charitable" institutions, the movement is decidedly political. The radical right has a political program consisting of such measures as limiting the Supreme Court, reducing or eliminating the income tax, passing "right to work" laws, and repealing social legislation. It seeks to get "right-minded" candidates elected President, governors, and Congressmen. And it seeks to influence these people once they have been elected. It is thus at the opposite pole from the anarchists, who feel that political action is debasing.

Morals and Religion

Unlike anarchism, which tends to be non-religious, the radical right, in its fashion, strikes a religious tone. Its conservatism is often based on the recognition of absolute moral verities grounded in the Divine. The religion, usually a version of Christianity, does not stress the "social gospel." The "elect" have no social responsibility to the unredeemed and such organizations as the National and World Councils of Churches are often criticized because they assume such responsibility in the eyes of the radical right. Many of the leaders of "social gospel" organizations are misguided liberals in theology and in social theory. A. Charles Poling, an associate of the Christian Crusade, wrote: "Practically all of our National Council leaders" have been "following the Communist line. . . . Personally, I find it impossible to play on the same team that joins forces with Communism." [33]

Several important leaders of the radical right are fundamentalists and ordained Protestant ministers. In addition to Billy James Hargis, who directs the Christian Crusade, there are Carl McIntire and Edgar C. Bundy. McIntire organized the American Council of

Christian Churches as a counter-force to the National Council of Churches. Bundy is the longtime executive secretary of the Church League of America. Myers G. Lowman, a layman who is president of the Circuit Riders, also belongs in this group. Lowman prepares lists of collectivists and Communists who have "infiltrated" religion and education. Since liberalism in religion and politics is essentially the same thing, liberals are traitors to both God and country. "Wherever issues are drawn between opposing sides, there are always those who desire compromise and a middle course. . . . But where one of the sides in the conflict has the eternal truth, as is the case of those of us who embrace the great doctrines of the historic Christian faith, to compromise in the slightest is to dishonor and destroy the faith." [34] Clarence Manion and William F. Buckley, Jr., are Roman Catholics who find absolute social principles in their religion. Buckley leaped into national prominence with the publication in 1951 of *God and Man at Yale,* which "exposed" the atheism of the administration and faculty of Yale University.

Perhaps related to religious convictions is the opposition of the radical right to the "sexual revolution." For anarchists sex is natural and therefore good. For the radical right sexual behavior is often based upon "original sin" and is to be regulated by certain definite rules. The radical right has opposed eroticism in films, plays, and literature. "The cult of erotica," warns Hargis, "has established the 'high places.' The phallic society is almost here." [35] The radical right opposes sexual relations outside marriage, homosexuality, and pornography as well as nudity, "sensitivity training," sex education in the schools, coeducational dormitories, and indecent speech.[36]

Leadership

Another difference between anarchism and the radical right is suggested by the rigidity of some of the radical right organizations. Despite its emphasis on individualism, the radical right values the principle of leadership highly. In many of its organizations authority is at the top. Unlike the anarchists, the rightists often function in structures in which the "rank and file" gives unquestioning loyalty to the leader, receiving its directions in regularly published journals such as the John Birch Society *Bulletin.* Robert Welch clearly stated that his society was not a "debating society" but "a monolithic body" operating "under authoritative control at all levels." [37] The Young Americans for Freedom is controlled by a board, but the membership neither chooses it nor controls that body. Many radical right enterprises are "one-man shows." It would be unthinkable for anyone in the organizations of Carl McIntire, Billy James Hargis, Edgar C. Bundy, Clarence Manion, Frederick C. Schwarz, or George S. Benson to challenge the authority of his leader. The *National Review* is clearly under the control of William F. Buckley, Jr. The principle seems to be: if you like what we're doing, cooperate with the leadership; if you do not like what we're doing, get out.

Racism

As was mentioned earlier, the radical right—except in its lunatic fringe—does not uphold racism, and it would be wrong to fasten guilt on those right-wing extremists (and moderates also) who have occasionally associated with peddlers of racial hate. However, it should be noted that the radical right takes far different positions on the problem of the Negro in America than does the conservative-liberal center. A Christian Crusade pamphlet entitled "The Truth About Segregation" states: "The entire problem that confronts America today was bred in the pits of Communist debauchery and conspiracy. . . . Segregation is one of nature's universal laws. . . . It is my conviction that God ordained segregation." [38] Civil rights legislation is backed by Communists in order to arouse the Negro and split the country. Hargis argued that the religious concept of the brotherhood of man is misused when it is taken as a call to social action. A recent article by Professor Arthur R. Jensen (University of California) in the *Harvard Educational Review* has attracted the attention of the radical right. Jensen "maintained with impressive scholarship that (a) Negroes as a group tested out poorly where abstract reasoning and problem-solving are concerned, and that (b) this aspect of intelligence is mostly inherited, a matter of genes, and therefore beyond the reach of compensatory education and other kinds of environmental amelioration." According to the *National Review,* leftist critics tried to suppress the article, question its conclusions, and discourage the kind of research it represented. Such research does not establish Negro inferiority, but it does question a fundamental liberal assumption—that environment can do it all.[39] There is widespread conviction in the ranks of the radical right that the National Association for the Advancement of

Colored People, the American Civil Liberties Union, the Southern Christian Leadership Conference, and the Congress of Racial Equality are infested (or controlled) by socialists and Communists.[40]

The radical right believes that if race is a problem for government at all, it is one that each state should solve in its own way. The Supreme Court acted unconstitutionally in 1954 in declaring segregation of schoolchildren a violation of the rights of American citizens.

The general opposition of the radical right to Federal aid for education takes the form, in some organizations, of removing schools completely from governmental control. Some spokesmen argue for the right of individuals to be excused from paying school taxes so that they may set up and control private schools of their own. This approach has real relevance for those elements of the radical right that are opposed to integrated schooling; it has become popular with the kind of people who join White Citizens' Councils.

Evans argued that compulsory action by the government, instead of helping the Negro cause, will harm it by stirring up racial antagonisms. "Open housing," "busing," fair employment practices, public housing, etc., attempt to create "artificial economic rights." "Self-help programs, job-training projects, and employment programs" are more hopeful than "compulsions handed down from Washington." [41] White ethnic groups, which are disproportionately members of the radical right, are inclined to expect the Negro to "make it on his own," as the immigrant Irish, Italian, and Eastern Europeans did. Where most anarchists (even the individualists) stressed "mutual aid," the radical right stresses "self-help." One cannot legislate brotherhood.

ANARCHISTIC PRINCIPLES

Individual Liberty and Responsibility

The rightist is genuinely concerned with preserving as wide a sphere as possible in which he can act according to the dictates of his own personal will. His nationalism is predicated on the belief that America is the last hope for human freedom; no sacrifice is too great to preserve the state most committed to freedom. Communism is the greatest enemy of the radical right simply because it is the greatest enemy of the kinds of freedom the radical right cherishes. His "authoritarianism" is predicated on the belief that those who interfere with the person and property of others are destructive of the conditions of freedom. Their incursions into the private lives of others introduce totally unjustified external constraints. Strong law enforcement preserves the peace in which individuals can make their own lives. Strong legislation and enforcement should also prevent domestic Communists from carrying out actions intended to destroy individual freedoms. Liberals who are "soft" on Communism fail to understand that it is not inconsistent to reduce the freedom of individuals who are working for the destruction of the freedom of others.[42] This is the general principle for infringing *any* freedom! And the political activism, apparently so unanarchistic, is really, one could argue, a very practical way of using the channels government provides for the purpose of limiting the power of that government. The radical right rather consistently pushes back the interfering arms of the state. Therefore, the radical right manifests anarchistic concerns on those very issues that tend to separate it from anarchism. Nationalism, "authoritarianism," and political activism are all directed against forces inimical to liberty.

The ideology of the radical right contains several anarchistic ideas. The most important and obvious one has already been suggested: emphasis on individual freedom. Freedom is a moral necessity. One can be moral only if he freely decides to act in a certain way; action that is compelled has no moral quality. Man "lives between good and evil, beauty and ugliness, truth and error, and he fulfills his destiny in the choices he makes. No social institution, not even the conglomerate of institutions we call 'society,' can make the least of these choices."[43] Virtue "is made inaccessible to the coerced citizen, wherever and to the degree that the state compels his action. His actions may look like virtuous actions, but they are the actions of an automaton and cannot be truly virtuous, because being unfree to reject virtue, he is unfree to choose it."[44] Government has passed social legislation that so severely regiments society that freedom, the condition for moral action, has almost been eliminated. If there is a need for reform, it should be reform not of social institutions (there has been too much of this already) but of the moral individual; this is the American way.

It is bad enough that the liberals have reduced the sphere for free individual decision. It is even worse when one realizes that they possess no firm moral convictions of their own, that they recognize no objective ethical standard. They are corrupted by pragmatism, relativism, positivism, subjectivism, materialism, and nihilism, and can see no aim higher in life than economic security and ignoble happiness.[45] They fashion a society in this image wherein men are directed to "do well"—and surrender dreams of higher ideals.

If the domination of government is dispensed with or reduced, the individual must be prepared to live by his own standards. For anarchists and for the radical right ethics therefore takes on an added dimension of importance. Life in accordance with ethical rules is the inescapable alternative to life in subjection to political rules. The individual himself, must recognize and choose an ethical code, must adopt it and make it his. It may be grounded in nature or in God; in either case it provides a more satisfactory order to man's life than can a meddlesome state. He now responds in conscience to his deepest inner convictions rather than to the external commands of whatever government happens to be in power.

If men are to live together, there must be some consensus on these ethical principles. Anarchism and the radical right both believe there is such a consensus, although they disagree on what it is. The radical right claims that these ethical principles are found in the traditions of Western civilization, while anarchism tends to find them in the natural endowments of man. Anarchism tends to be more optimistic about man's inherent goodness, while the radical right stresses his limitations or "original sin." But on the major points anarchism and the radical right are in perfect agreement: without a tutelary government the individual can be guided only by moral law; with a tutelary government the individual is not free to respond to it.

Statism

The strongest force against individual freedom is the government. Since 1932 there has been an unmistakable trend toward enlarging the scope of governmental control. The Democratic Party takes "credit" for this and is still pledged to ambitious programs of social improvement. The Republican Party has also destroyed, or sought to destroy, individual freedom. Under the control of liberals or moderates it nominated Wendell Willkie in 1940 and Thomas

Dewey in 1944 and 1948; neither of these men was concerned with reversing the trend. In 1952 and 1956 the Republicans won with a candidate who was hardly distinguishable from a Democrat and who "consolidated" the socialism of his predecessors. Richard Nixon, who lost in 1960 and won in 1968, has no views at all. Barry Goldwater's statement is a classic:

> I have little interest in streamlining government or in making it more efficient, for I mean to reduce its size. I do not undertake to pro-mote welfare, for I propose to extend freedom. My aim is not to pass laws, but to repeal them. It is not to inaugurate new programs, but to cancel old ones that do violence to the Constitution, or that have failed in their purpose, or that impose on the people an unwarranted financial burden. I will not attempt to discover whether legislation is 'needed' before I have first determined whether it is constitution-ally permissible. And if I should later be attacked for neglecting my constituents' 'interests,' I shall reply that I was informed their main interest is liberty and that in that cause I am doing the very best I can.[46]

Only Goldwater in 1964 and Ronald Reagan, who hoped for the nomination in 1968, are firmly committed to the task of reducing the power of the government and its interference in the lives of individuals.[47]

It would require volumes to list the ways in which the govern-ment reduces individual freedom. More than one radical rightist has expressed sentiments similar to those of Proudhon quoted pre-viously.[48] Most of the government's interference is unnecessary. The function of government is simply to protect the nation from its external enemies and to preserve life, liberty, and property at home. It does not require thousands of laws to fulfill this simple function. Laws recognize "rights" that do not exist while destroying those that do. Man has the right to be protected in the free use of his life, liberty, and property; he does not have the right to certain of the rewards a collectivist state might choose to dispense.

The social programs supported by the government would seem to serve humane ends. But whether a citizen is to have security in his old age, medical care, low-cost housing, or even an education for his children—all these are his responsibility alone. Social legis-lation encourages irresponsibility for the many while unfairly penal-izing the productive few. It encourages people to believe that society owes them all the good things in life. Recipients of relief are not questioned enough or penalized for having children out of wedlock; they become more and more unreasonable about what constitutes "suitable" work. Poverty programs thus support the lazy and the promiscuous. And social welfare utterly stifles the generous impulses of voluntary benevolence. "Every person of good will wants to see other men better off—better housed, better fed, better educated, and so on. But he has grave doubts about the propriety or the effectiveness of the means employed by the welfare staters. And when it comes to taking care of the unfortunate, *every lover of liberty believes devoutly in voluntary gifts and charity*. But he objects to the imposition of a 'pseudo-charity' by government on unwilling givers as immoral and uneconomic—injurious alike to the recipients and to the forced contributors." [49] Public power, public mental health, farm subsidies, urban renewal, and fluoridation should be viewed with great suspicion. The Tennessee Valley Authority should be sold to private business. Codes of "Fair Employment Practices" should be opposed in the various states. "Right to work" laws, since they weaken the trade unions, should be supported.

The hyperactivity of government is paid for by crushing taxes. The tax burden is borne disproportionately by those with higher incomes. The entire radical right favors reduction of the income tax, most of it favors elimination of the graduated tax, and some of it favors the repeal of the Constitutional amendment authorizing income tax laws. The attitude the radical right takes against the seizure of property by an insatiably greedy state is very similar to the attitude of the individualist anarchists of the United States. The universal anarchist demand that a worker should not be robbed of the fruits of his labor also is relevant here.[50]

The wealth appropriated by the state makes possible the establishment of a vast bureaucratic apparatus, staffed by unproductive officials whose duty it is to interfere with personal freedom in every area of human life. This bureaucracy is wasteful and corrupt. Admiral Ben Moreell, founder of the Americans for Constitutional Action, spoke in 1963 of the "Robin Hood government that promises to rob the rich to pay the poor and, when there are not enough rich left to pay the bills, robs rich and poor alike to pay Robin Hood. . . ." [51] The radical right can point to the inefficiency and waste in such cherished projects as the Post Office, TVA, Federal housing, and poverty programs. M. Stanton Evans can quote critics from the liberal establishment itself on the follies of the big bureaucracies that direct them.[52] Frank S. Meyer writes: "The only ground on which conservatives have to stand is a moral and spiritual criticism of the essential inhumanity of socialism and welfarism: the levelling that, by reducing the person to a statistical number, degrades all man, whatever their capacity or position; the ignominious removal of responsibility for his future and his family from the hands of individual man into the hands of an all-probing bureaucracy; the steady attrition of all separate and rooted centers of power and the massive growth of a single bureaucratic center of state power which from day to day gains more and more control over all the avenues of thought and life." [53]

Another common criticism of the Federal bureaucracies is that they are staffed by intellectuals and/or professional managers instead of men who actually possess the necessary technical knowledge and experience. Federal "businesses" are run by men with no background in business, men who have never had to show a profit or "meet a payroll." Farm agencies are run by men who have never operated a plow. The Justice Department is run by men who have never argued a case in court. And the armed services are directed by civilians who have never led an army; that generals and admirals are so little heeded in matters of grand strategy is the cause of much that is tragic in America's position today.[54]

The policy of the radical right is to work for the reduction of the power of the Federal government and an increase in the power of local government. The authority of the states must be interposed between Washington and the people. The United States Constitution has been corrupted. It intended to set up a *federation* of autonomous states. The founding fathers knew that the cause of freedom would better be served by decentralizing authority. Much that has been done by the Federal government in the last century and a half has been unconstitutional. Even Abraham Lincoln, the first Republican President, acted unconstitutionally when he refused to permit the Southern states to secede. While the anarchist perceives the state as an unnecessary evil, the radical right perceives it as a necessary evil. Since power will always exist in this world, it should be divided "in order that those who hold it may balance each other and the concentration of overweening power be foreclosed." [55] The best that any government—national, state, or local—can do is protect the freedom of the individual from invasion by others.

The whole development in America is heading toward state socialism. The radical right, preferring the economics of *laissez-faire* and taking Ludwig von Mises, F. A. Hayek, and Henry Hazlitt as its oracles, regards every interference with the free market as socialistic. The moderates concede that many of the sponsors of social legislation are not socialists but insist that they contribute to a trend that, if not reversed, will lead to full socialism. The extremists make little distinction between a regulated economy and socialism. Some may view the trend in America as being consciously directed by *bona fide* socialists in league with Communists. Liberals, whether socialists, fellow travelers, dupes, or Communists, cannot be expected to be "hard" on Communism. Their goals and the Communists' are too similar: control of the economy by the government under the banner (sincere or hypocritical) of "the general welfare." "Social security and the health of the aged will stay political footballs. They will tend to socialize the minds of the people and condition us mentally and materially for more socialism." [56]

The liberal argument that certain individual freedoms in the area of economics must be given up in order to win greater freedom in other areas is invalid. Freedom is a style or habit of human action; if it is carved up, it cannot be expected to survive. Loss of freedom in earning and spending an income will be reflected in all areas of life. Even the freedoms to speak and to worship are reduced, sometimes to meaninglessness, when the individual is made to serve in a vast bureaucratic economy from the cradle to the grave: Content in his security, he loses the habit of speaking out for what really concerns him, and he has nothing to pray for. Ironically, he is in a collective that does not even require him to be concerned for others. "The plain fact is that the welfare state is destroying the character of a large portion of the American people. . . . The only way to relieve suffering and provide for the unfortunate . . . is voluntary Christian charity." [57] One of the "certain eternal truths" affirmed in the "Sharon Statement" at the founding of the Young Americans for Freedom is: "That the market economy, allocating resources by the free play of supply and demand, is the single economic system compatible with the requirements of personal freedom and Constitutional government, and that it is at the same time the most productive supplier of human needs." William F. Buckley, Jr., wrote: "Let the individual keep his dollar—however few he is able to save—and he can indulge his taste (and never mind who had a role in shaping it) in houses, in doctors, in education, in groceries, in entertainment, in culture, in religion; give him the right of free speech or the right to go to the polling booth, and at best he contributes to a collective determination, contributes as a rule an exiguous voice. Give me the right to spend my dollars as I see fit—to devote them, as I see fit, to travel, to food, to learning, to taking pleasure, to polemicizing, and, if I must make the choice, I will surrender you my political franchise in trade, confident that by the transaction, assuming the terms of the contracts are that no political decision affecting my sovereignty over my dollar can be made, I shall have augmented my dominance over my own affairs." [58]

Democracy

The radical right is no more comforted than were anarchists by the fact that much of the authority exercised by the state against the individual has its foundation in democratic processes. Tyranny of the majority over the minority is no better than any other kind of tyranny. That others deprive *me* of *my* freedom does not mean that I must regard the deprivation as legitimate. The radical right does not have a romantic trust and confidence in the wisdom of the masses. The all but unanimous opposition to redistricting on the "one man, one vote" principle indicates no support for a fundamental principle of democracy.[59] Robert Welch in his famous address on "Republics and Democracies" quoted several writers on the evils of democracy: Cicero, Edmund Randolph, Alexander Hamilton, Samuel Adams, James Madison, T. B. Macaulay, Immanuel Kant, Benjamin Disraeli, Ralph Waldo Emerson, Oscar Wilde, G. K. Chesterton, and others.[60] Democracy is not merely imperfect; it is fraught with positive dangers.

Most spokesmen of the radical right believe that the *form* of government is much less important than its *quality*. The measure of the latter is the degree to which a government permits citizens to lead their own lives. The principle of individual self-rule is more important than any particular system of government. An enlightened monarchy can provide more freedom than a busy democracy.

The American form of government, the rightists all insist, is a republic, not a democracy. The suffrage requirements were intended to be set up by the several states—as each sees fit. In this conception of a republic the restrictions against the government are far more important than its powers. Welch writes of "those certain unalienable and divine rights [that] cannot be abrogated by the vote of a majority any more than they can by the decree of a conqueror. The idea that the vote of a people, no matter how nearly unanimous, makes or creates or determines what is right or just becomes as absurd and unacceptable as the idea that right and justice are simply whatever a king says they are." [61]

The Supreme Court has failed to protect Constitutional government. It has accepted legislation that goes far beyond the delegated powers of Congress. It has permitted more and more power to go from the Legislative to the Executive branch of the Federal government.[62] It has stood by while powers reserved to the states by the Constitution have passed on to Washington. It has rewritten the Constitution by imposing on the states the "one man, one vote" principle in electoral districting. It has adopted a ridiculously expanded interpretation of the "equal protection" clause of the Fourteenth Amendment, which it not only employed in the redistricting decision but in the segregation and prayer decisions as well. Where will it end? "If you really set about making people equal, there is no stopping place." [63] These failures of the Supreme Court have inspired the radical right to demand impeachment, Congressional reform of the Federal court system, or a Court of the Union.[64]

Conspiracies

Spokesmen of the radical right, like the anarchists of old, suspect the existence of conspiracies dedicated to the elimination of their views or their persons. One conspiracy, moreover, is composed of some of the same powerful forces that frustrated the anarchists. Domestically these forces include cultivated men of wealth, intellectuals, and clergymen.[65] The difficulty the radical right experiences in bringing its message to the people, in changing their minds, in educating the populace to the accelerating loss of freedom in American society, and in nominating and electing "conservative" candidates is attributed to the control of all the mass media by "liberals" (or worse).[66] Just as campus reformers complain that the radicals get all the coverage, the "conservative" maintains that the left gets it all. When the members of the YAF seek to restrain the SDS, they are dismissed as "vigilantes." In a pamphlet called "The Death of Freedom of Speech" Hargis expressed fear that "by January 1, 1969, there will not be a single anti-Communist or Conservative broadcast on the air." [67] Many of the publications of the radical right have been victimized by a "conspiracy of silence." The term "the Establishment" carries just as much opprobrium when used by the radical right (as it frequently is) as it does when it is used by anarchists, old and new. Like the anarchists, the radical right has its martyrs: Senator McCarthy, for whose untimely death the left-wingers were held partly responsible; Maj. Gen. Edwin A. Walker, who was forced to resign from the army in 1961 and who narrowly missed assassination in 1963; and John Birch himself, the first American killed in "World War III."

Internationally, the conspiracy working against the radical right is the old foe of Bakunin and all other anarchists: Marxist-Leninist Communism. This international movement has already destroyed the freedom of half the people of the world [68] and will harm America whenever and to whatever extent circumstances permit.[69] "Washington has been taken over!" proclaims Welch. "By which we mean that Communist influences are now in full working control of our Federal Government." [70] Meyer puts it more moderately: "It must be understood that Liberalism weakens the fiber of society, but that Liberals are not, as are Communists, conscious enemies, conspiratorially organized for the conquest of world power." But the evidence "would seem to show that it is categorically impossible for Communism to be defeated under Liberal leadership." [71] Since the days of the Popular Front, liberals have not perceived foreign and domestic Communism to be an enemy in quite the same way as Fascism. They welcomed Castro (at first) as a staunch "anti-fascist" and Mao Tse-tung as an "agrarian reformer." [72] Today, they are afraid to criticize left-wing revolutionists because they do not want to be guilty of "McCarthyism"! Thus, according to the radical right, the left has not been very perceptive.

There is a difference of opinion among the spokesmen of the radical right on precisely how well the "Communist conspiracy" is succeeding. The extremists, such as Welch, may call important American officials "conscious agents"; moderates, such as Buckley, may instead speak of "an ineffectually anti-Communist Liberal." Between the two designations are such terms as "Comsymps," "fellow-travelers," and "dupes." [73] Our foreign policy may be *planned* by the Communists or it may stem from sympathy with some of their aims, an absence of anti-Communist principles ("soft on. . ."), or cowardice in the face of a possible nuclear war. The extremists are more fearful of domestic Communism than of foreign, while the moderates are more fearful of foreign Communism than of the domestic brand.

Negativism

Anarchists are well known for their negativism: "Down with the government, down with taxation, down with the churches!" The radical right is also characteristically negative. It opposes not only most of the social change that has occurred since 1932 but many events that were permitted to happen before then. The election of Andrew Jackson, for example, was a disaster. The change to the direct method of electing Senators was a mistake. The ideas of John Dewey should never have become influential in American education. This social program should be dismantled; that law should be repealed. Both anarchism and the radical right are negative toward those forces that, in their opinion, have infringed upon individual liberty. To be negative toward statism is to be positive toward human freedom.[74]

Direct Action

There is yet another significant similarity between the anarchists and the leaders of the radical right. Although the latter, as has been seen, are avid politicians, they are also willing to employ the direct tactics so loved by the anarchists. They will employ the existing political channels and apparatus, but often display a certain impatience and even contempt for established methods. Ordinary courtesies and niceties sometimes must be discarded; legal restrictions occasionally must be ignored or violated.

The practice of character assassination, so common among the McCarthyites,[75] Birchers,[76] the Christian Crusade, and the Circuit Riders, is closer to "direct action" than it is to normal political action. This practice gets government officials, school principals, and college professors fired. The radical right has organized boycotts against merchants who stock commodities manufactured in "Iron Curtain" countries or in nations that trade with Red China. The famous "card parties" of the Birchers create direct pressure.[77] When the John Birch leadership asked its people to protest a story in *Ladies' Home Journal* ("The Children's Story"), which was (erroneously) believed to be pro-Communist, the magazine received over two thousand letters. Businessmen who speak out in favor of such "un-American" enterprises as the United Nations or the North

Atlantic Treaty Organization may receive angry letters and threats from extremists. Educators are frequently harassed for adopting textbooks alleged to contain pro-Communist material. Robert De Pugh, leader of the Minutemen, defended the supersecrecy of his organization this way: "Minutemen feel if their identities are unknown they will be in a better position to obtain information on the infiltration of school systems by Communists and subversives." [78]

The Young Americans for Freedom demonstrates a leaning toward direct action, especially in its anarchist faction. Some members have favored open defiance of the military draft and have burned facsimiles of draft cards (Goldwater had opposed the draft). The libertarians have also favored repeal of drug laws ("Everyone has the right to go to hell in his own fashion"). Their underground newspapers are as vigorously and impolitely critical of the new left as the new left newspapers are of them. At the national YAF convention in 1969 in St. Louis the shouted slogan was "Sock it to the Left!" This convention, almost as chaotic as that of the SDS in Chicago, did pass one resolution with overwhelming support: Active resistance (lawsuits, injunctions, physical confrontation) against radical groups that seek to disrupt the universities. "Let college administrations understand," concludes the resolution, "that unless they provide protection for enrolled students and qualified recruiters, the Young Americans for Freedom will henceforth provide that protection." [79] The national college director of the YAF is Phillip Abbott Luce, formerly active in the SDS.

Even the political ends sought are often pursued in non-political organizations. There is in the radical right a distrust for both major political parties and their ancillary organizations—a distrust that was deepened rather than dispelled by the election of 1964. In July 1964 Kent Courtney, founder of the Conservative Society of America and publisher of the *Independent American,* demanded the nomination of Goldwater and the subsequent purge of the liberals from the Republican Party. Although the organizations of the radical right are often shrouded in secrecy, they seek to impose their doctrines on the American voters and political parties in as direct and vigorous a way as possible.

There is a serious ambiguity in the theory of government held by spokesmen of the radical right. On the one hand, they are distrustful of democratic government, and seek support for the individual against the masses in the restrictions imposed by the Constitution and the Supreme Court. On the other hand, they often fail to respect certain substantive and procedural rights of the individual when popular causes (*e.g.*, anti-Communism) are at stake. The almost fanatical zeal they can mount for their programs of direct action can be explained only by assuming that they are fully convinced they are speaking for the great bulk of Americans ("the Silent Majority"?). They are, as it were, messiahs in bringing control of the country back to the people to whom it really belongs. Impatient with the Constitutional cloaks with which the liberals wrap themselves, they offer instead a kind of "direct democracy" through which the authentic voice of America can speak. This populist fervor, expressing itself in mass petition and disgust with established governmental machinery and officials, is at odds with the "indirect democracy" of the Constitutional republic that the rightists exalt in other places.

Propaganda and Education

This phenomenon has a parallel in the thought of the anarchists. They too opposed democracy and sought ways to limit it. The new society they advocated was to reflect directly the actual feelings of the people, unfiltered by political forms and organization. For both the radical right and anarchism distrust of government is the one constant. It is this distrust that makes them both reject democratic *government* while appealing to the *demos against* government. The people do ill when they have a government that directs the life of society; they do well when they wrest government from the hands of that directive minority. The unsolved problem for both anarchism and the radical right is: How can the popular will achieve its positive goals in society without utilizing the power of government?

The chief mission of the radical right is to educate (or reeducate) the American people. Society is so bad that even *successful* political action is not enough. More is required than simply replacing liberal government officials with "conservative" ones. Although the education of voters may be a means for achieving political victories, it is even more the case that political activity is a means for education. The radical right is not seeking anything so prosaic as taking over the government. It seeks to transform the fabric of society itself, to restore the ancient wisdom and virtue to a people gone wrong. Like the anarchists, spokesmen for the radical right write books,[80] pamphlets,[81] and newspapers, and conduct seminars and radio and television programs in order to alter the minds of the people. When this has been accomplished, the political problems will take care of themselves. Education for a way of life ultimately takes precedence over politics. "As you look more and more carefully into the hopes that have been bred, and the disappointments that have followed, through the political performances of . . . twenty years, you come increasingly to realize the wisdom of the old advice: 'Put not your faith in politicians.' We shall have to use politicians, support politicians, create politicians, and help the best ones we can find to get elected. I am thoroughly convinced, however, that we cannot count on politicians, political leadership, or even political action except as part of something much deeper and broader to save us." [82] The columnist of the *National Review*, Frank S. Meyer, expressed the same idea: "The skills and techniques of political organization have their place in our society, but they are only secondary auxiliaries for a movement whose duty it is radically to transform the consciousness of an age." [83] The vision must be articulated and disseminated before it is enacted.

Harding College in Searcy, Arkansas, whose president is George S. Benson, has been called the "academic seat of America's Radical Right." [84] On the campus is the headquarters of an organization called the National Education Program, also headed by Benson, which provides newspaper columns, film strips, movies, pamphlets, study guides, and books to institutions and organizations all over the country. These "educational materials" defend fundamentalist Christianity and *laissez-faire* economics, and criticize liberalism, socialism, and Communism. The NEP also produces radio and television programs. "Freedom Forums" designed to educate business and educational leaders are held on the campus and elsewhere. Benson himself is a supporter of the John Birch Society and believes that the Communists have infiltrated all important segments of American society. The Manion Forum, with headquarters in South Bend, Indiana, has also been a prodigious "educator" for the radical right, having distributed millions of printed items, radio and television speeches, tapes, and film strips. Both the NEP and the Manion Forum have been generously supported by business corporations, large and small.[85]

In the mission of "educating" people to the true nature of Communism, it is important that the teachers be reliable. "In gaining access [as speakers] to many college campuses, Red conspirators have promoted the fraudulent idea that in order to learn about communism a person must listen to a Communist. The exact opposite is true. One does not learn about communism by listening to a Communist because the Communists are cunning liars, and their speeches give a completely false image of communism."[86] The use of ex-Communists is sound because they know "at first hand" the evils of the system.

Finally, the radical right extremists, like the anarchists, have a devotion to principle that makes them reject compromise. Reform is not enough; only thoroughgoing change will suffice. Ideologically they are confidently "correct." Specific solutions to particular problems are not required because they would do very little good; the fundamental illnesses of society would remain. This is another reason for being skeptical of the claim to "conservatism" made by many members of the radical right. "The right wing tolerates no compromises, accepts no half measures, understands no defeats. In this respect, it stands psychologically outside the frame of normal democratic politics, which is largely an affair of compromise."[87] If the people believed only a small fraction of what the radical right tells them about the structure, officials, and policies of the government, schools, and churches, they would indeed be in a revolutionary state of mind. The right's dogmatic insistence on the truth of its position is frequently accompanied by a reluctance (or inability) to discriminate. The extremist Dan Smoot writes: "I wondered, when I was a member of the FBI Commie Squad, why those who oppose Communism were vilified and slandered. I learned the reason. It was because people were blindly following the philosophy of the New Deal, which stands for the total transfer of power from the individual to the Federal Government under the claim of using the power beneficently. This is the same philosophy of the Fair Deal, the New Frontier, and Modern Republicanism. . . . It is also the basic philosophy of Communism, Fascism, and Nazism."[88]

To summarize: The ideology of the radical right bears significant resemblances to the theory of anarchism in its individualism, its suspicion of conspiracy, its negativism, its "direct action," and its commitment to propaganda-education. At the same time there are fundamental differences between the ideas of the radical right and those of anarchism.

CRITICAL COMMENT

Very few viewpoints have been criticized so often, so thoroughly, and so well as that of the radical right. Because it is a challenge to the conservative-liberal consensus, it has been attacked by defenders of the *status quo*. Because it has attracted millions of voters and contributors (and potentially millions more), it has provoked into print political writers, who cannot afford to ignore its appeal. Since its target so often includes intellectuals and professors (especially Harvard professors), the response from these very articulate people has been massive. The "establishment" has indeed met the intellectual and political challenge of the radical right.

Common Criticisms

It is not the intention here to add to the vast critical literature, but merely to present a short list of the common (and sound) criticisms made of the radical right. (1) Failure to discriminate. The differences between the welfare state and socialism, between socialism and Communism, are significant. To blur these distinctions is to do a great disservice to social thought. (2) Ignorance of the enemy. The knowledge of Communist theory is very superficial—especially among those rightists who offer seminars in the subject. The knowledge of the activity of domestic Communists is very faulty also; the Communists have not "infiltrated" in nearly the strength and scope that the radical right claims. (3) A different kind of disloyalty. Intemperate attacks on the government, its officials, and American social institutions seriously damage public confidence, thereby weakening the power of these institutions and individuals to serve America's interests. (4) Inadequate documentation. Personal and political charges against individuals are seldom proved. (5) Emotionalism. The high degree of heat is often at the expense of light; useful communication disappears in an atmosphere of passionate rhetoric. (6) Propaganda. The appeal to fear is not legitimate; it causes people to panic and to seize on oversimplified "solutions." If the radical right actually believes in all the "conspiracies" it talks about, its members are foolish or paranoid; if it does not, it is unprincipled. (7) Dogmatism. While it is a fine thing to have strong opinions, people who believe in human fallibility and human pride should have more reticence! (8) Intolerance. Adherents of unpopular views should not be penalized by law or public opinion for holding them. (9) Uncompromising attitude. Serious ideological dissent has a place in society, but compromises must be made from time to time for the benefit of society as a whole. (10) Discourtesy. This quality, so prevalent in the student left, abounds also in the radical right. Disagreement becomes a personal matter, thus barring cooperation on common problems. (11) Propensity to *ad hominem* attacks. The background, virtue, and present position of a statesman or writer have nothing to do with the soundness of his argument. Any reasoned position must be examined on its own merit, rather than rejected for personal reasons. (12) Misplaced emphasis on rights. Some rights are more important than others, but the right, for instance, to retain all of one's income must rank lower than the right, for instance, to be protected from public libel. Certain civil rights, such as due process, are rather consistently undervalued. (13) Poor historical sense. Measures like the "New Deal" legislation have not brought us to socialism; they have saved us. Some of the men who have been pilloried as "leftists" have done the country a great service in fighting radicalism. (14) Static economic theory. *Laissez-faire* liberalism has demonstrated its inadequacy. If collectivism is not the answer, another one must be found. The answer is not found in the economic writing of the radical right. (15) Personal conceit. The economic success that many members of the radical right have enjoyed is not always in perfect proportion to such sterling personal qualities as diligence, imagination, and virtue. To attribute success purely and simply to these qualities and derive a concept of radical individualism from it is to misread the actual situation and to ignore the factors of luck, inheritance, "sharp practice," and, above all, the conditions for commerce preserved and enhanced by government legislation. (16) Lack of social concern. To point out the apparent lack of benevolence and brotherhood in the radical right is to commit the *ad hominem* fallacy. But it *is* relevant to state that no social or political program can be adequate unless it takes into account the needs of the less fortunate citizens: the sick and the aged, the poverty-stricken, and those racially persecuted. (17) Distrust of planning. Many social problems are so vast and so complicated that they can be solved only by deliberate and coordinated planning by several governmental units and agencies. To let matters drift (the pollution problem, for example) is to invite disaster. (18) Attenuated individualism. The individualism of the radical right usually takes the form of denouncing governmental control over private lives, especially in the area of economics. But individualism has a positive dimension also; it suggests originality, creativity, and challenge to public opinion. The rightist has read only part of Mill's *On Liberty;* he tends to be a conformist and to insist on conformity from others. (19) Rejection of democracy. If the majority is not to rule, this leaves only the minority. What is the basis for preferring the latter? Are the Westerners wiser than the Easterners, the farmers more virtuous than the city-dwellers? (20) Confusing Constitutionalism. The members of the radical right claim to be strong supporters of the Constitution, but are sometimes reluctant to extend Constitutional protection to their enemies. The radical right defends a strict reading of the Constitution and opposes the attempts of President, Congress, Supreme Court, and people to "violate" it on behalf of the general welfare or in pragmatic response to social conditions. But interpretation and application are required in any case. Who will make these determinations? Robert Welch, Clarence Manion, William F. Buckley, Jr.? According to what principles? Finally, the radical right believes that the American Constitution is the most perfect governing instrument devised and often tries to imagine what the founding fathers intended when they wrote a particular clause. Yet, of all groups in America, it has been most assiduous in proposing Constitutional Amendments such as those forbidding spending for "general welfare," prohibiting American troops from serving on certain foreign soils, redefining treason and its punishments, and repealing the income tax. Most of them seem ridiculous and not in the spirit of the original document. (21) Exclusive patriotism. It is a fine thing to be patriotic, but it is not fair to impugn the patriotism of others who have a different vision of what America should be. (22) Unimaginative foreign policy. Reliance on force is outmoded. Ways must be discovered of preserving the interests of the United States without resorting to force. (23) Irresponsible foreign policy. The foreign policy recommended by the radical right is simple and direct. It is conceivable that use of bold and forceful action is an effective way to preserve the nation's security. But the radical right acts irresponsibly when it rejects out of hand the many alternatives to its aggressive policy: diplomatic relations with the Soviet Union, participation in the UN, NATO, International Trade Organization, UNESCO, UNICEF, and USIA, and carefully calculated programs of foreign aid, etc. (24) Christian fundamentalism. While rejecting responsible scholarly interpretations of the Bible, many elements of the radical right make their own political interpretations that are, to say the least, questionable. In any case it is unfair to impose "Christian" views on the many Americans who do not profess Christianity. It is also unfair (and unconstitutional) for the government to impose any theistic bias on the people in its dealings with them. (25) Anti-intellectualism. Consistent attacks on intellectualism *per se* weaken the confidence of the people in the role of reason as a means to truth. If reason is discarded, passion and prejudice must fill the gap. "In your heart you know he's right" is self-contradictory. (26) "Conservatism" without tradition. Many members of the radical right, especially the extremists, are as ignorant of the conservative tradition as those of the student left are of *their* tradition. If they want to call themselves "conservatives," they should have a deeper knowledge of the rich and varied Western civilization (or at least the Colonial American civilization) they wish to conserve. Their program often looks more like a populist expression of lower-class resentment at threatened changes than a call to return to the ancient verities. Are the forerunners of the radical right Edmund Burke and James Madison or are they Father Coughlin and Gerald L. K. Smith?

Individual Freedom

It is not the intention in this discussion to link the radical right with popular movements in America's past, to explain why its adherents react as they do to contemporary problems, or to find conditioning causes in membership in certain ethnic groups or social and economic classes. These are tasks for historians, sociologists, and psychologists—and they have already done their work.[89] Here we will simply analyze some central ideas of the radical right and the unwarranted length to which they have been carried.

Many of the fundamental beliefs of the radical right are sound and valuable: emphasis on individual freedom, recognition of the enemies of freedom, rejection of Communism, commitment to objective values, and willingness to set forth an ideology. The radical right should not be criticized for the basic views it holds but for the immoderate manner in which it holds them. Its theorems are sound; only its corollaries are invalid.

(1) Emphasis on individual freedom. The importance of freedom is recognized by virtually all political systems from communism to fascism. No one can be against freedom. There are disagreements, however, because people mean different things by the term "freedom" and/or prize some freedoms over others. "Freedom" for some (*e.g.*, Hegelians and Christians) means an inner ability (or compulsion) to respond to divine law; for some (*e.g.*, democrats) it means the authority or right of an individual, equal to that of everyone else, to make political policy or choose political leaders; for some (*e.g.*, anarchists) it means the right to lead one's own life without

direction from society. On the relative importance of various freedoms in the third sense of the word, some (*e.g.*, Manchester liberals) place economic freedom high on the list; others (*e.g.*, socialists) give freedom from want a high place; some others (*e.g.*, liberals) prize freedom of speech and religion most highly.

The radical right, like anarchism, emphasizes the importance of the individual to determine his own conduct. The rightist persuasively argues that man's dignity and moral integrity require that he author his own actions and be responsible for them. The rightist does not like to be told that he is permitted to be free in *some* areas, but is under constraint in others. Who gave whom the right to constrain anyone anywhere? Like the anarchist, the rightist wants freedom "across the board." He is entirely justified in taking a negative stance against all government controls, against all collective decisions on how he should act, against all bureaucratic officials who meddle. As an individual, man is responsible only to his own conscience.

But since men live in societies, this regard for freedom can only be a stance—a *prima facie* rejection of controls, a "wise prejudice" in favor of autonomy. In society one soon learns that what Peter gets, Paul cannot have. If I have the freedom to kill, someone else will not have the freedom to live. If I have the freedom to retain my inherited fortune, someone else will have less freedom to build up his own. The issue of freedom in society thus raises the question: *Who* is to have freedom? Moreover, freedom can be provided in some areas only by inhibiting it in other areas. The freedom to have an inexpensive education is possible only because the freedom to retain all one's income is infringed. Freedom of press is infringed for the sake of freedom from public libel. The issue of freedom in a society thus raises an additional question: *What* freedoms are to be supported?

The radical right, quite properly, is for freedom in the abstract. Very little justification for this is required. It is not so easy, however, to answer (and defend that answer) the question *Who* is to have *what* freedoms? But the radical right *assumes* answers to them. It selects the freedoms *it* prizes and illegitimately endows them with the unqualified goodness attributed to freedom in general.

Sometimes these selected freedoms are defended by appealing to moral or religious authorities: "men *ought* to have these freedoms." Sometimes they are defended by appealing to the intentions (or presumed intentions) of the founding fathers. Sometimes they are defended by appealing to the protection afforded by the Constitution. And sometimes they are defended by an *ad populum* appeal to what the masses of good Americans "really" want. But the defense is nearly always of freedom *per se,* not of a particular selection from a host of complicated and interrelated possibilities.

Everyone has (and should have) his own conception of what freedoms are important and valuable. Who has the authority to make the selection that shall for a time serve as *public* policy? Only one thing is clear: the radical right does not have it. In a republic the choice is made by a constitutional document as interpreted by appointed courts. In a democracy the choice is made by popular referenda or popularly elected officials. In a democratic republic the choice is made by both. That is what government is all about. If one does not want the choice made at all, he is an anarchist. If he is willing to entrust the choice to political procedures, he is an "archist." If he wants to make the choice for society *himself,* he is a member of the radical right.

Enemies of Freedom

(2) Recognition of the enemies of freedom. The radical right has a vivid conception of conspiracies against freedom. This is a very valuable attitude to have, although the term "conspiracy" is perhaps too strong and emotion-laden. But it does make sense to speak of "enemies of freedom." While it is difficult to measure the quantity of freedom in any group, it is true that some societies have more freedom than others. The scope and frequency of actions dictated by one's own vitally based objectives can vary, say, from a social club to a concentration camp. Just as there are parents who tend to over-control their children, there are corporations that tend to "program" the conduct of their employees and college administrations that impose rules of dress and social behavior on the student body. In democratic societies there are "planners" who would regiment the daily conduct of citizens without providing compensating freedom elsewhere. In all societies there are hosts of special interest groups that try to get legislation passed, ostensibly on behalf of the public interest but actually to augment their own freedoms at the expense of others. There are mass media of communication that attempt to constrain men's minds and refashion their tastes. There are even forces in society that seek to deny some people certain important freedoms because of race or religion. Finally, certain forms of gov-

ernment (*e.g.,* fascism and communism) make serious incursions against freedom in general. The worst deprivation of freedom is to deny a person equal right as a voter to help determine what freedoms a society will espouse. In short, the enemies of freedom are those who seek to reduce the net amount of freedom in society or to assign a share of it to one part of the population at the expense of others. The radical right does well when it recognizes these enemies and distrusts them.

Once again, however, the radical right goes too far. It goes too far in the way it deals with these enemies of freedom. It does not make sense to deprive enemies of freedom of those freedoms a given society is pledged to protect. Any regime can tolerate its friends. The genius of the American system is to be able to tolerate its foes. Bad as it is to persecute a Marxist or to ban Communist literature, it is even worse when, as so often has been the case, the target of abuse has never been proved to *be* a Marxist or the suppressed book a Communistic one. The zeal of the radical right, grounded as it is on the proper instincts, runs amuck.

The radical right also errs in making too inclusive a judgment on who the enemies of freedom are. It has been suggested that the real targets of the radical right are not the Communists at all. McCarthy, for example, was not "out to get" the Communists but to discredit liberals and socialists. Liberals and socialists are *not* enemies of freedom in anything like the way that Communists are. Liberals and socialists work through the regular channels of democratic government. They recognize, as Communists do not, the basic freedom of individual citizens to make public policy and to elect their officers. Citizens thus have equal voices in determining which freedoms will be enhanced and which will be reduced. The radical right makes the fatal mistake of viewing a *readjustment* of prevailing freedoms as an attack on freedom itself. The liberals and socialists are not *enemies* of freedom so much as they are defenders of freedoms that do not happen to be highly cherished by the radical right. The radical right, prizing *economic* freedoms so highly, regards *their* diminution as loss of freedom *per se.* It cannot outvote the liberals, so it abuses them.

(3) Rejection of Communism. The radical right is correct in perceiving Communism to be an enemy of freedom and in rejecting it for that reason. Communism deprives its people of the right to govern themselves and of all important civil liberties. It drowns their economic, artistic, and scientific individuality in a monolithic state. It is by intent and in fact a totalitarianism.[90]

Domestically, the Communists did have some influence in governmental, educational, and labor organizations in the thirties and forties. Well organized and ideologically sophisticated, they wielded influence disproportionate to their numerical strength. Always adhering slavishly to the Moscow line, American Communists were more loyal to an international revolutionary movement under Stalin than they were to the United States or to democracy. America was betrayed by spies who gave important military secrets to the Soviet Union. The liberals, fearful of fascism, were inclined to be "soft" toward these totalitarians of the left. Unfamiliar as it was with much of the Marxist-Leninist-Stalinist philosophy, the radical right did recognize in Communism an implacable opposition to the most basic and cherished freedoms of the Western world.

The enemy at home is also the enemy abroad. Communist countries aid our foes and harm our friends. Since the time of Lenin, America has been called a capitalistic imperialist nation and efforts have been made to destroy our "economic control" over underdeveloped countries in order that they may be subjected to something even worse. Subject people in Hungary and Czechoslovakia have been kept under Russian control—in obvious frustration of their own wishes. The Soviet Union and Red China have given arms to the regimes of North Korea, North Vietnam, Cuba, and the Arab nations in order that they too may stay in power—and extend their rule over other peoples. With every advance of Communism, America encounters more states opposed to its interests and hostile to the freedoms our people hold dear. Whatever one may say about America's motives or the imperfections of its own society, the unmistakable fact is that international Communism seeks to mobilize the forces of the world against it. The survival of the United States as a democratic republic depends upon the effectiveness of the stance it takes against Communism at home and abroad. This is no phantom enemy.

How does the radical right deal with this domestic and foreign enemy? Domestically, it tends to emulate the enemy's methods. There is nothing sacred about our economy; it is our democracy and civil liberties which must be preserved. The radical right fails to distinguish between Communists actively engaged in treason or conspiracy and those who happen to espouse a Marxist philosophy. In failing to distinguish Communism from other leftist orientations, it scatters its fire across the whole spectrum instead of concentrating it against the real enemy. Never having found *one* Communist in an important decision-making position in the government (Alger

Hiss will *not* qualify), it yet continues to talk about the presence of "conscious agents" in Washington. Instead of approaching the Communist theory studiously and reasonably, it purveys sensationalist oversimplifications; it seeks to arouse fear rather than understanding. It presents two contrasting ideologies, ours and theirs, one perfect and the other horrible. Failing to recognize that the Communist Party in America is weaker today than it has ever been, it continues to say that the day of the takeover ("someone will knock on your door in the middle of the night. . . .") is fast drawing near. It makes Communism the scapegoat for everything it does not like and (to change the metaphor) cries wolf whenever trouble occurs. Concern for Communism thus loses its impact, and people come to believe that, since it didn't *really* infiltrate the Girl Scouts or control the NAACP, it doesn't exist at all. And most seriously of all, the obsession with Communism prevents its victims from seeing the problems of this nation realistically and in their true light. They see everything through panic-tinted glasses.

The presence of so many hostile nations has aggravated the nationalism to which Americans are prone. We see ourselves as the world's lone defender of truth and light and prepare for a showdown in Dodge City at High Noon. Finding Communism utterly unsuitable to our tastes, values, and traditions, we see it similarly unacceptable anywhere in the world. Because economic and political liberty has served us well, we see it as the only solution for all societies everywhere, no matter how poor or corrupt they may be. The radical right (and others) have trained us to believe that the victory of Communism in a rice paddy on the other side of the world is an affront to America. No one knows whether "coexistence" is possible, but surely Eisenhower was right at least once, when he said, "Nuclear war is unthinkable."

In summary, the radical right is correct in saying that Communism is to be rejected, but the consequence of this realization does not have to be national hysteria.

Positive Commitment

(4) Commitment to objective values. The radical right professes a belief in the objectivity of moral, esthetic, and religious values. One can and should say: "X is good. It is not good because I or my society *say* it is good; it is good in its own right. Since it is good, it

should be respected and promoted." Another way to express this objectivity is, in the manner of Immanuel Kant, to state that there are moral laws to which sentient beings are subject. They issue their commands without promise of reward and require devotion to duty for duty's sake. There is a difference between moral actions and immoral ones, between virtue and vice, between a good life and a bad one. This difference is grounded in something permanent in the universe itself; it is not a function of social mores, success in action, or personal taste. To find the normative principles and to adhere to them is the mission of the thoughtful and conscientious man.

Much has happened in modern times to cause skepticism in these matters. The great advances in natural science have weakened religion, which commonly sponsors transcendent values. Social science has discovered fundamental differences in the value structures of various societies. Is one's conscience simply a result of the particular culture which conditioned it? The work of Freud and others in psychology shows that men act in response to feelings rather than thought, and that our justifications are more rationalistic than rational. In philosophy, which should be concerned with such things, we find three dominant schools of thought, all of which reject objectivity: (1) Pragmatism. Value, like truth, is made, not discovered. The idea that guides us truly is true; that which gives us satisfaction is satisfactory. Truth and morals dissolve together in a willful quest for subjective values. The gospel of success in action implies that what works for *you* is true and that what is good for *you* is good. Truth, which once meant correspondence between idea and reality, now means correspondence between intention and result. (2) Logical Empiricism. Since value judgments can be neither validated nor invalidated, directly or indirectly, by sense observation, they are cognitively meaningless. But they may evince a feeling on the part of the speaker. "X is good" means "X—hurrah!" "Y is right" means "I want you to do Y." The subject matter of ethics thus becomes *statements,* and philosophical activity consists in analyzing the feelings of those who make them. (3) Existentialism. Values are created by human beings as they create their own "essence." To seek refuge in external sources is cowardly. Man is cursed with freedom; he must in good faith legislate his own morals.

The radical right senses a loss of confidence in the old values. It is justified in lamenting a trend in which moral obligation gives way to moral nihilism. When society confuses "the desirable" with "the desired," it has indeed lost its bearings.

But once again the radical right overgeneralizes. Some teachers do present these "modern" ideas with no alternative options, but most do not. Some intellectuals are without religious or ethical commitment, but most are not. Many of those who stress the role of passion in our lives do so in order to give a balanced account of human nature; the rational and spiritual aspects are seen in a somewhat different perspective. The permissiveness of educational leaders is not necessarily an invitation to students heedlessly and mindlessly to "do their own thing," but is a demand for conscious and deliberate speculation on values: "The unexamined life is not worth living." The hope is that the individual will responsibly *choose his own set of values* and commit himself to them because he has recognized them to be worthy. This is better than conditioning students to give lip service to values imposed from on high, for the same reason that sincerity is better than hypocrisy.

The response of the radical right to subjectivism is excessive. The radical right will brook no objection to the "value system" it holds. It is certain—and intolerant. Often the "value system" is so defective, so inhuman, so patently a product of social conditions itself, so "half-baked," that one will rebel against the whole enterprise of objective morality. Or, if the system has redeeming attributes, the behavior of its adherents may be so inconsistent with it that the young person becomes cynical. The way to meet the moral crisis is not to impose a bad ethic, but to practice a *good* one, and in the meantime to encourage the young to study the highest insights of the past and present in the hope that they will find something that satisfies their idealism and inspires their lives. And always one must recognize that there is room in the world of ethical thought for honest men to disagree.

(5) Willingness to set forth an ideology. It is indeed refreshing to encounter on the social scene a movement that is not content to find a comfortable place for itself somewhere in the liberal-conservative center. The radical rightist, like a good umpire, "calls 'em as he sees 'em." There is no compulsion to fit into a consensus, to overlook a violation, to "endure a moment and see injustice done." The role of the critic, the dissenter, requires courage, and any society which is not to stagnate needs such people. Too often voters have been presented with "competing" political platforms which differ only in emphasis, and with bland candidates who avoid mak-

ing *political* issues out of crucial social issues. Goldwater *was* a choice, not an echo.

It is, however, unfortunate that many of the ideas with which the radical right challenges the establishment are not really new ideas, but some of the very ones that got McKinley elected. And it is also unfortunate that the tactics employed by those who disseminate these ideas are often mean and nasty.

In defending the resort to ideology by the radical right, one should add a provision. While suggestions for fundamental changes should be given a fair hearing, these changes should not be such as to *disrupt* society. They should never be accepted totally and irrevocably. This is what both the radical left *and* the radical right need to learn from conservatism. A certain continuity must be preserved. A victory, therefore, for a new ideology should not mean ruin for 45 percent of the population, exile for all the previous leaders of the establishment, and the instant enactment (at last) of utopia. A victory should mean, instead the beginning of a new trend, the tentative heading in a different direction, some new wine in the old wineskins (or new wineskins for the old wine). The radical right often has something else in mind.

NOTES

[1] "He would seem to be asking only for derisive laughter when he puts himself forward as a conservative." Frank S. Meyer, *The Conservative Mainstream* (New Rochelle, N. Y.: Arlington House, 1969), p. 34.

[2] He (and others) "write books showing how you can be a Conservative and yet agree with the Liberals about everything not demonstrably unimportant." Willmoore Kendall, *The Conservative Affirmation* (Chicago: Henry Regnery Company, 1963), p. 140.

[3] "As conservatives picked up the pieces after the wreckage of the 1960 election, some of them recalled the old saying from John Gay's Fables: 'An open foe may prove a curse / But a pretended friend is worse.' Amen!" Clarence Manion, *The Conservative American* (New York: The Devin-Adair Co., 1964), p. 105.

[4] Meyer, p. 84.

[5] See Harry and Bonaro Overstreet, *The Strange Tactics of Extremism* (New York: W. W. Norton & Company, 1964), p. 72.

[6] "The pseudo-conservative is a man who, in the name of upholding traditional American values and institutions and defending them against more or less fictitious dangers, consciously or unconsciously aims at their abolition." Theodor W. Adorno *et al., The Authoritarian Personality* (New York: Harper & Row, 1950), p. 676.

[7] See M. Stanton Evans, *The Future of Conservatism* (New York: Holt, Rinehart and Winston, 1968), pp. 12, 41, and elsewhere.

[8] Meyer, p. 236.

9 Other "apostles of discord" not regarded as part of the radical right are George Lincoln Rockwell, Conde McGinley, Elizabeth Dilling, Westbrook Pegler, James Oviatt, Lyrl Van Hyning, John Kasper, *et al.*

10 See, for example, G. Edward Griffin, *The Fearful Master: A Second Look at the United Nations* (Belmont, Mass.: Western Islands, 1964).

11 Meyer, p. 119.

12 "Just the fact that we are fighting the Communists somewhere is a tremendous step forward after years of retreat under the slogan of 'coexistence.'" *Ibid.*, p. 382.

13 See Kent and Phoebe Courtney, *Disarmament: A Blueprint for Surrender* (New Orleans: Conservative Society of America, 1963).

14 "Our leaders are not Communists but they have consistently failed to grasp the elementary logic of Communist nuclear blackmail, with the result that we have found ourselves without any strategy whatever—not even enough strategy to enforce a doctrine we felt capable of enforcing one hundred and forty years ago." "But if in fact we seek to avoid war: and the surest way to avoid war is to assert our willingness to wage it, a paradox that surely is not so complex as to elude the understanding of professional students of the drama." William F. Buckley, Jr., *Rumbles Left and Right* (New York: G. P. Putnam's Sons, 1963), pp. 78, 80.

15 Meyer, p. 375.

16 *Ibid.*, p. 376.

17 *Ibid.*, p. 384.

18 Quoted in Arnold Forster and Benjamin R. Epstein, *Danger on the Right* (New York: Random House, 1964), p. 124.

19 "Students are fed up with the terror tactics of the New Leftists and the wishy-washy, knee-jerk liberalism of the administrators who would rather hide under their desks than take any significant action against those people trying to burn down their offices." Phillip Abbott Luce, "The Battle for the Media," *Human Events* 29:46 (November 11, 1969), p. 13.

20 Meyer, p. 217.

21 John R. Coyne, Jr., *National Review* 21:39 (October 7, 1969), p. 1025.

22 Harvey H. Hukari, Jr., "How to Combat Campus Radicals," *Human Events* 29:46 (November 15, 1969), p. 12.

23 The packet, distributed by The Movement To Impeach Earl Warren, included in addition to the petition addressed to the Congress: speeches by Senator James O. Eastland, Welch's "classical" essay on the differences between republics and democracies, and Rosalie M. Gordon's book, *Nine Men Against America: The Supreme Court and Its Attack on American Liberties* (Belmont, Mass.: Western Islands, 1965 [1958]).

24 The most successful petition was sponsored by Robert Welch in *American Opinion* (1967). It called for all members of Congress to oppose "giving aid in any form, directly or indirectly, to our Communist enemies." This, in the first instance, includes food, and in the second, includes the satellite countries as well as Russia. We are *at war* with Communism in Vietnam; to help Hanoi in any way is treason. See Robert Welch, "The Truth About Vietnam" and "More Truth about Vietnam"; Wallis W. Wood, "Vietnam: While Brave Men Die" (*American Opinion*, 1967). The August 1969 *Bulletin* of the John Birch Society

reported that 1,402,622 signatures on 84,956 petitions had been delivered to 52 members of Congress on July 28, 1969.

25 Robert Welch, *The Blue Book of the John Birch Society* (Belmont, Mass.: Western Islands, 1961), p. 94.

26 For an annotated list of radical right periodicals, see Robert H. Muller, *From Radical Left to Extreme Right* (Ann Arbor, Mich.: Campus Publications, 1967).

27 Welch, pp. 81–82.

28 Evans, p. 223.

29 See, for example, Evans' chapter "Those 27 Million," in *ibid.*, pp. 187–201.

30 The third party candidacy of George Wallace in 1968 attracted many radical right voters. But Wallace does not fit the radical right requirements as well as did Barry Goldwater. Wallace's racism was too overt. But more important, in domestic matters in Alabama he had been too liberal; he had sponsored too many expensive welfare programs.

31 See Forster and Epstein, p. 218.

32 See William F. Buckley, Jr., and Brent Bozell, *McCarthy and His Enemies* (Chicago: Henry Regnery Company, 1954).

33 See Overstreet, p. 94. Billy James Hargis lamented the fact that the National Council of Churches collected almost $25 million in 1968. "What a magnificent waste of money!" "Protestant laymen who put their tithes and offerings into denominations affiliated with the NCC will stand before the judgment seat of God without excuse for their support of this antichrist, ecumenical outfit." *Christian Crusade* 21:7 (July 1969), p. 8.

34 Carl McIntire, *Servants of Apostasy* (Collingswood, N. J.: Christian Beacon Press, 1955), p. 325.

35 Billy James Hargis, *Christian Crusade* 21:5 (May 1969), p. 4.

36 In fairness to the old anarchists, it should be said that much that is taking place in the sexual revolution would be rejected by *them* also. Much that is defended as "liberating" and natural is, in the view of the old anarchists, unnatural, debased, and sick.

37 Welch, pp. 146–147.

38 See Overstreet, pp. 196–197.

39 See *National Review* 21:39 (October 7, 1969), pp. 996–997.

40 "As you know, it is my usual practice to garnish even the most minor assertion with a wagon load of evidence. But I now take the position . . . that to add to the obvious facts that the 'Civil Rights movement' was not only planned by the Communists, but was begun, is staffed, and is conducted by the Communists— and has only one real purpose: the destruction and Communization of America— would be an unforgiveable redundancy." Alan Stang, "The King and His Communists," p. 46, reprint from *American Opinion* (October 1965).

41 Evans, p. 179n.

42 It is, according to the radical right, an easy matter to show that domestic Communists do constitute a "clear and present danger" to the system that guarantees freedom.

43 Meyer, p. 34.

44 *Ibid.*, p. 45.

45 "The impact of the views and attitudes of the intellectual leadership has

affected and distorted the forms in which traditional truths are held and understood by the American people. . . ." *Ibid.*, p. 60.

46 *The Conscience of a Conservative* (New York: MacFadden Books, 1961), pp. 23–24.

47 Karl Hess, former speechwriter for Barry Goldwater and now an anarchist of the new left, wrote a famous article in which he tried to show the anarchism present in both extremes. " 'When the histories are written,' you [Goldwater, 1968] said, 'I'll bet that the old right and the New Left are put down as having a lot in common and that people in the middle will be the enemy.' That's right. They do and they are. . . . You were quite correct in your perception: liberals are fatheads. The only thing worse than a big government is a bigger one!" In defense of the militancy of the black liberation movement, Hess quoted the famous line he wrote to Goldwater: "Extremism in the defense of liberty is no vice and moderation in the pursuit of justice is no virtue." Karl Hess, "An Open Letter to Barry Goldwater," *Ramparts* 8:4 (October 1969), p. 29.

48 See above, pp. 71–72.

49 Ben Moreell, *The Admiral's Log II* (Philadelphia: The Intercollegiate Society of Individualists, 1960), pp. 188–189.

50 The radical right, like anarchism, is also concerned with protecting a sound currency, although labor is not necessarily its basis. But inflation, created by heavy government spending, does erode the wealth that labor has created.

51 Moreell, p. 188.

52 Evans, pp. 94–97.

53 See Meyer, p. 187.

54 There is a rough parallel in the private sector. Business leaders are no longer those who own their own business and control it. They are professional managers or administrators. A man who has never built an automobile or manufactured steel may be hired as chief executive by a great automotive or steel company. Things have gotten so complicated that an owner of extensive property can no longer direct his own enterprise.

55 Meyer, p. 41.

56 *Human Events*, January 1962.

57 *Ibid.*, April 1962.

58 William F. Buckley, Jr., *Up from Liberalism* (New York: McDowell, Obolensky, 1959), pp. 180–181.

59 "In the voting for the Tennessee State Senate, one-third of the electorate nominated two-thirds of the legislators. In almost every state of the Union one could point to similarly glaring disproportions—though none so astounding as in California, where the single state senator from Los Angeles represents 6,038,-771 persons, while a colleague from a rural area represents 14,294 persons, a ratio of 422.5 to 1. In forty-four states, less than forty per cent of the population can elect a majority of the state legislators; in thirteen states, fewer than a third of the voters can elect a majority." *The Radical Right*, Daniel Bell, Ed. (Garden City, N. Y.: Anchor Books, 1964), p. 28.

60 See Robert Welch, *The New Americanism* (Belmont, Mass.: Western Islands, 1966), pp. 89–114.

61 *Ibid.*, p. 113.

62 To place all the power in the hands of the President and to vote on him every four years is to transform the American system into a "plebiscitory democracy."

63 *National Review* 21:45 (November 18, 1969), p. 1157.

64 Such a Court, established by Constitutional amendment and composed of the fifty chief justices of the states' supreme courts, would be able to overrule decisions of the United States Supreme Court.

65 "You need not be taken in by the solemn whisper that the Establishment has a president, an executive committee, a constitution, by-laws, and formal membership requirements, to believe that there do exist people of varying prestige and power within American Liberaldom; that we speak here of the intellectual plutocrats of the nation, who have at their disposal vast cultural and financial resources. . . ." Buckley, *Rumbles Left and Right*, p. 30.

66 More moderate expressions of this belief in conspiracy were: (1) Nixon's farewell to members of the press in 1962 when he said that they would no longer have Richard Nixon "to kick around"; (2) The analysis of Goldwater's defeat in 1964 as largely brought about by the hostility of the press; (3) Vice President Agnew's speech of November 13, 1969, against "irresponsible" handling of news by the television networks; (4) The attempt by the Justice Department in 1971 to prevent *The New York Times* and other newspapers from printing material from the classified "Pentagon Papers."

67 The reason: The FCC might enforce the so-called "fairness doctrine" and fine stations that do not inform individuals or groups attacked and provide time for a reply. In a chapter titled "Utilizing the Enemy's Techniques," he advised readers how this threat could be met. See Billy James Hargis, *The Death of Freedom of Speech* (Tulsa: Christian Crusade Publications, 1967).

68 The loss of China to Communism is acutely felt. See John T. Flynn, *While You Slept: Our Tragedy in Asia and Who Made It* (Belmont, Mass.: Western Islands, 1965 [1954]).

69 See James Burnham, *The Web of Subversion: Underground Networks in the U. S. Government* (Belmont, Mass.: Western Islands, 1965 [1954]).

70 See Overstreet, p. 71. Other such expressions: Billy James Hargis boasted that the "Christian Crusade was the first organization to prove that the Communists had a *master music plan* to use rock-and-roll and folk music to recruit youth to immorality and unpatriotic action. . . ." (*Christian Crusade* 21:5 [May 1969], p. 15.) "How can we account for our present situation [in the struggle against world Communism] unless we believe that men high in this Government are concerting to deliver us to disaster? This must be the product of a great conspiracy, a conspiracy on a scale so immense as to dwarf any previous such ventures in the history of men." Joseph R. McCarthy, *America's Retreat from Victory: The Story of George Catlett Marshall* (Belmont, Mass.: Western Islands, 1965 [1951]), pp. 135–136. "I am convinced that the Council in Foreign Relations, together with a great number of other tax-exempt organizations, constitutes the invisible government which sets the major policies of the federal government; exercises controlling influences on governmental officials who implement the policies; and, through massive and skillful propaganda, influences Congress and the public to support the policies. I am convinced that the objective of this invisible government is to convert America into a socialist state and then make it a unit in a one-world socialist system." Dan Smoot, *The Invisible Government* (Belmont, Mass.: Western Islands, 1965), p. xi.

71 Meyer, pp. 81–82.

72 For an interesting account of how the liberals were deceived by Castro, see Buckley, *Rumbles Left and Right*, pp. 60–70.

73 "The theft of our atom secrets—the fruits of American technical ingenuity—
were made possible by a naive tolerance of Communists and their front organizations, of the saccharine vagaries of fellow travelers and prostituted
liberals. Unless we learn the art of self-defense in international terms, we will
have the suicide of Western civilization on our conscience." Charles A. Wil-
loughby, *Shanghai Conspiracy* (Belmost, Mass.: Western Islands, 1965 [1952]), p.
248.

74 M. Stanton Evans is not afraid to take the negative tone in elections. People
will vote *against* things at least as often as they vote *for* them. In a chapter
called "The Power of Negative Thinking" (*op. cit.*) he showed how such an
approach can and does win elections.

75 For an excellent defense of Senator McCarthy by a moderate of the radical
right, see Frank S. Meyer's column, "The Meaning of McCarthyism" in *National
Review* (June 14, 1958) and printed in *op cit.*, pp. 187–193. McCarthy expressed
himself "existentially, if not analytically."

76 Robert Welch outdid Senator McCarthy. In a long letter about Eisenhower,
called "The Politician" and distributed privately in the fifties, Welch called the
President, a "dedicated, conscious agent of the Communist conspiracy." The
manuscript was toned down and published in 1962. "In the third stage the
Communists have installed in the Presidency a man who, for whatever reasons,
appears *intentionally* to be carrying forward Communist aims. . . . With regard
to this third man, Eisenhower, it is difficult to avoid raising the question of
deliberate treason." Most of Eisenhower's associates and appointees are also attacked. For example: "For many reasons and after a lot of study, I personally
believe Dulles to be a Communist agent who has had one clearly defined role
to play; namely, always to say the right things and always to do the wrong ones."
It should be mentioned that Welch presents his beliefs as personal and not
necessarily those of the membership of the John Birch Society. Robert Welch,
The Politician (Belmont, Mass.: Robert Welch, 1963), pp. 279, 223.

77 Cards stating "Always Buy Your Communist Products At _____" would
be "planted" on the shelves of offending stores where they would be found by
shoppers. In several cities local ordinances have been passed requiring stores to
purchase licenses before selling "Communist products."

78 See Overstreet, p. 251.

79 See *The Alestle*, September 26, 1969, pp. 21–24.

80 The radical right even has its own bookstores, which not only stock printed
materials but have on hand petitions to be signed, lists of speakers available in
the area, and notices for meetings and rallies. Examples: Betsy Ross Bookshop
(Los Angeles), Anti-Communist Bookstore (Fort Lauderdale, Florida), and Pro-
Blue Patriotic Book Store (Torrance, California).

81 Some typical *Tax Fax* pamphlets: "The Poverty Racket" ("Has LBJ's Job
Corps become a breeding ground for criminals?"), "Beware the A.C.L.U." ("Is
the American Civil Liberties Union a Communist front?"), "Communist Infiltration of Anti-Poverty War" ("How the Communists plan to use your income
tax dollars to finance their subversive activities."), "Let Our Children Pray"
("How to reverse the Supreme Court's atheistic decision which bans prayer in
schools."), and " 'Selling Out' Our Soldiers in Vietnam . . . for a Profit!" *Tax
Fax* pamphlets are issued by the Conservative Society of America (New Orleans)
under Kent and Phoebe Courtney, who also edit *The Independent American*.

82 Robert Welch, quoted in Forster and Epstein, p. 21.

83 Meyer, p. 78.

84 Forster and Epstein, p. 87.

85 This is an obvious difference from the anarchists!

86 Billy James Hargis, *Christian Crusade* 21:5 (May 1969), p. 9.

87 Richard Hofstadter, "Pseudo-Conservatism Revisited: A Postscript (1962)." See Bell, p. 102.

88 Dan Smoot, quoted in Forster and Epstein, p. 134.

89 See, for example, the work of Daniel Bell, Richard Hofstadter, David Riesman, Nathan Glazer, Peter Viereck, Talcott Parsons, Alan F. Westin, Herbert H. Hyman, and Seymour Martin Lipset in *The Radical Right*. These men are all of the liberal-conservative center and are past or present professors at universities on the Eastern seaboard.

90 See Gerald Runkle, *A History of Western Political Theory* (New York: The Ronald Press Company, 1968), pp. 523–542.

10

Existentialism

PHILOSOPHY OF FREEDOM

The unifying principle in all existentialist thought is that the individual man gives meaning and direction to his life and his world by means of the specific acts he chooses to perform. The existentialists also agree among themselves on several other principles: philosophy is concerned with practical matters; the method of phenomenology is indispensable; existence is more fundamental than essence; man is free. But there is great disagreement among them on the nature of the existential situation and the resources that man brings to it. Søren Kierkegaard, for example, stresses the primacy of individual feelings, while some of his philosophical successors view man's predicament in more rationalistic terms. Martin Heidegger is hopeful of formulating a philosophical theory of being, while Karl Jaspers, though retaining a Kantian rationalism for the world of experience, is skeptical. Jean-Paul Sartre, an atheist, calls man a "useless passion" and is repelled by the absurdity in the non-human universe; Gabriel Marcel, a Christian, perceives divine intention in the world and denies that man is utterly without guidance.

So we are faced once again with the task of dealing with a school of thought that has a discernible and essential unity but also has many spokesmen whose views are often in conflict with one another. Because the existentialist philosophy is technical and subtle, we will select one of its adherents for most of the attention in the hope that this will serve the cause of coherence. Because of the extensiveness of his writings, the relative clarity of his thought, and the fame of his name, we have chosen Sartre.

Being For-itself and In-itself

Sartre makes a fundamental distinction between two realms of being: being-in-itself (*être-en-soi*) and being-for-itself (*être-pour-soi*). The first is object, the second is subject. The first is non-conscious, the second is conscious. The first is a plenitude, the second is a nothingness.

In the phenomenon we find the two kinds of being co-present. Consciousness must have an object and the in-itself is meaningful only in consciousness. The phenomenon is the in-itself as it appears to the for-itself. "Consciousness considered apart is only an abstraction; but the in-itself has no need of the for-itself in order to be; the 'passion' of the for-itself only causes *there to be* in-itself. The *phenomenon* of in-itself is an abstraction without consciousness but its *being* is not an abstraction." [1] The phenomenon, however, is "transphenomenal" and presumably can endure without a *particular* for-itself. Sartre does not wish to talk about a real world beyond the phenomena. Unlike Kant and certain dualists, he has no interest in positing a noumenal world or objects apart from perception. As far as man is concerned, the real world is composed of the phenomenal objects of experience.[2]

Sartre thus seeks to establish an alternative to objectivism (or realism), in which all objects exist independently of consciousness, and subjectivism (or idealism), in which all objects are states of mind. "To say that consciousness is consciousness of something is to say that it must produce itself as a revealed-revelation of a being which is not and which gives itself as already existing when consciousness reveals it." [3] A favorite paradoxical statement of Sartre's is: The for-itself "is a being which is not what it is and is what it is not." [4]

The being-for-itself knows the being-in-itself by negating it. "Every negation is determination." [5] It excludes meanings in order to invest meaning. And it can invest meaning only by reflecting on itself as perceiving qualities or essences. And it can perceive a quality only by reflecting on itself as the internal negation of that quality. "In order for its determination as the nothingness of being to be full, the for-itself must realize itself as a certain unique manner of not being *this* being." [6] "The necessary condition for our saying *not* is that non-being be a perpetual presence in us and outside of us, that nothingness haunt being." [7]

The for-itself achieves consciousness by "nihilating" that to which it is opposed. It knows the in-itself by interposing nothingness between itself and the object. "The irreducible quality of the *not* comes to add itself to that undifferentiated mass of being in order to release it." [8] "Man is the being through whom nothingness comes to the world. . . . This *nothing* is human reality itself as the radical negation by means of which the world is revealed." [9] It creates a universe for itself by hollowing out objects from the opaque and baffling given. Nothingness is a condition for the appearance of being—and appearances constitute reality. "Nothingness lies coiled in the heart of being like a worm." [10] In short, the existing for-itself acts in a creative way to make a meaningful world, and it does so by means of its own nothingness and "naughting" function.[11]

To the extent that the person does so act, he expresses his subjectivity and things in the phenomenal world become objects *for him*. The in-itself possesses only as much reason as the subject can project into it. This formulation may sound more subjective than Sartre would wish it to be. Strictly speaking, the consciousness does not in any way *construct* the object; it does not transfer and "objectivize" certain elements found in its own subjectivity. " 'There is' being because I am the negative of being, and worldliness, spatiality, quantity, instrumentality, temporality—all come into being only because I am the negation of being. These add nothing to being but the pure, nihilated conditions of the 'there is'; they only cause the 'there is' to be realized." [12] The action of making a phenomenon consists of overlaying the being of the in-itself with nothingness. The phenomenon is simply the in-itself *plus* nothing! Actually, the action is more constitutive of the for-itself than of the in-itself. While the for-itself seems to have a passion "to lose itself in order that the affirmative 'world' might come to the In-itself," [13] the for-itself can establish itself only *in terms of* the in-itself! [14]

The basic character of the in-itself as senseless, pointless, and absurd is never far below the surface. Sartre conveyed this idea in a famous passage in a novel:

> So I was in the park just now. The roots of the chestnut tree were sunk in the ground just under my bench. I couldn't remember it was a root any more. The words had vanished and with them the significance of things, their methods of use, and the feeble points of reference which men have traced on their surface. I was sitting, stooping forward, head bowed, alone in front of this black, knotty mass, entirely beastly. . . . Existence had suddenly unveiled itself. It had lost the harmless look of an abstract category: it was the very paste

of things, this root was kneaded into existence. Or rather the root, the park gates, the bench, the sparse grass, all that had vanished: the diversity of things, their individuality, were only an appearance, a veneer. This veneer had melted, leaving soft, monstrous masses, all in disorder—naked in a frightful, obscene nakedness. . . . The chestnut tree pressed itself against my eyes. Green rust covered it half-way up; the bark, black and swollen, looked like boiled leather. . . . Absurdity was not an idea in my head, or the sound of a voice, only this long serpent dead at my feet, this wooden serpent. Serpent or claw or root or vulture's talon, what difference does it make. . . . Knotty, inert, nameless, it fascinated me, filled my eyes, brought me back unceasingly to its own existence. In vain to repeat: "This is a root"—it didn't work any more. I saw clearly that you could not pass from its function as a root, as a breathing pump, *to that,* to this hard and compact skin of a sea lion, to this oily, callous headstrong look. . . . The root, with its colour, shape, its congealed movement, was . . . below all explanation.[15]

So the narrator of the story is nauseated by the unintelligibility of being-in-itself. It is too much *(de trop).*

Human Freedom

Counterposed against all this is man's freedom. Man's freedom was implied above in his knowledge of the real world. He detaches himself from being-in-itself in order to question, to limit, to constitute. In this free action he remakes his world and himself. "Knowing is an absolute and primitive event; it is the absolute upsurge of the For-itself in the midst of being and beyond being, in terms of the being which it is not and as the negation of that being and a self nihilation." [16] In the act of knowing, as in any other act, man can produce an act that no prior state can determine; he is able to effect in himself a "break with being." "Every nihilating process must derive its source only from itself. . . . Every psychic process of nihilation implies, then, a cleavage between the immediate psychic past and the present. This cleavage is precisely nothingness." [17]

All human actions are free. They are, in the strict sense, uncaused—even when motivated. Ends and motives are themselves decided *by* acts. "Causes and motives have meaning only inside a projected ensemble which is precisely an ensemble of non-existents. And this ensemble is ultimately myself as transcendence; it is Me in so far as I have to be myself outside of myself." [18] The self cannot cause anything, because its essence is made and altered from moment to moment; it is always something other than what can be said of it. Man is free in his volitions and his emotions; they are all ways of being one's own nothingness. My feeling of fear, for example, "is free and manifests my freedom; I have put all my freedom into fear and I have chosen myself as fearful in this or that circumstance." [19] No rationalistic, materialistic, or mechanistic explanation of man's actions can destroy his freedom. Since freedom comes from nothingness, it is beyond the power of all "external" factors. There is always a *break* with the given, a rupture in being, a disengagement toward an end that does not yet exist.

While being-in-itself is mere plenitude and positivity without potentiality ("it is what it is"), being-for-itself discerns lack, constitutes lack, and experiences lack. It can have possibilities, development in time. It alters its world as it alters the essence of its personal self.[20] It strives to surpass the present reality of world and self. "Without the world there is no selfness, no person; without the person, there is no world. . . . The world [is] mine because it is haunted by possibles and the consciousness which *I am;* it is these possibles as such which give the world its unity and its meaning as the world." If one felt no lack in the present, he would fall back into "being" and become identical with it. "The Future as the future presence of a For-itself to a being drags being-in-itself along with it into the future." [21] Sartre imagines a tennis game in which he occupies various positions on the court, his movements designed to unite himself with a future state and to merge with it.[22] Sartre's best summary statement on lack and temporality is this: "The Future is the ideal point where the sudden infinite compression of facticity (Past) of the For-itself (Present), and of its possible (a particular Future) will at last cause the Self to arise as the existence in-itself of the For-itself." [23]

One of the slogans of existentialism is that existence precedes essence. Man is not created with a human nature such that his actions flow naturally and necessarily from it. His essence is not given him by God or nature; it is made by him in action.[24] He does brave deeds, so he is brave. He thinks philosophical thoughts, so he is philosophical. "To be ambitious, cowardly, or irritable is simply to conduct oneself in this or that manner in this or that circumstance." [25] Thus his self takes on attributes. A free existent has created its own essence. The "project toward self" (which is what constitutes selfness) is never finished. The free being has a "constantly renewed obligation to remake the *Self*." [26] What kind of a self will it create? The act is always *beyond* the self. The essence that was made in the past never explains the act performed in the future. One's actions are not even determined by what he has made himself to be. Hence anguish. Anguish "is constituted when consciousness sees itself cut from its essence by nothingness or separated from the future by its very freedom." [27]

Ethics

In anguish, the individual becomes conscious of his freedom. Anguish must be distinguished from fear. Fear applies to what other beings in the world may do to him; anguish applies to what he may do to *himself*. One may fear artillery fire but feel anguish at how he may act when under fire. Fear applies to man as an object in a determined world; anguish characterizes man as a subject free to act in this way or that. All sorts of possibilities are open. The individual must reject them all but one; he engages himself in that one, and it remains his course of action only as long as he sustains it. Neither his desire successfully to traverse a mountain path, his horror of falling, his habit of prudence, nor his conviction that suicide is wrong can in themselves prevent him from leaping from the precipice. He is not determined either to perish or to survive; he is free to do either. Nothingness once again "insinuates itself" between objects of consciousness and the act.

Recognition and adherence to ethical values do not relieve the anguish that is part of acting and of making the self. There are no values fixed by God or enshrined in external ethical systems. Freedom itself is the unique foundation of value. "*Nothing,* absolutely nothing, justifies me in adopting this or that particular value, this or that particular set of values. . . . In this world where I engage myself, my acts cause values to spring up like partridges." [28] It is from the values created that the world derives its significance, action its point, and self its essence. "Nothing can ensure me against myself, cut off from the world and from my essence by this nothingness which I *am*. I have to realize the meaning of the world and of my essence; I make my decision concerning them—without justification and without excuse." [29]

Sartre speaks of the "serious man" who seeks to conceal his freedom from himself. Such a man loses himself in his affairs, assumes that values are *in* objects, and that he must accord both affairs and objects a certain respect and respond to them in a certain way.[30] Some men seek refuge in psychological or physical determinism, some in divine predestination. They appeal to their environment, to their origins and upbringing. They mask their anguish by disclaiming responsibility. They act "in bad faith" by locating the causes for their actions outside themselves, in a fixed and operative essence ("self-determinism"), or in a combination of the two. They refuse to carry the burden of their freedom. But this freedom cannot be put down. No one is free not to be free; everyone is "condemned to be free." [31] He may make his choices hesitantly and indecisively, but the mode of choice is itself a choice. One is free to try to conceal his freedom from himself, but his success will be only provisional. Anguish will break through. "I flee in order not to know, but I can not avoid knowing that I am fleeing; and the flight from anguish is only a mode of becoming conscious of anguish. This anguish, properly understood, can be neither hidden nor avoided." [32]

Man did not ask to be born and is no more responsible for his birth than for any other fact. He did not ask to be free or responsible for his actions, but he is not free to be not free and he is not responsible for his responsibility. But he is responsible for his deeds. "The responsibility of the for-itself is overwhelming since he is the one by whom it happens that *there is* a world; since he is also the only one who makes himself be, then whatever may be the situation in which he finds himself, the for-itself must wholly assume this situation with its peculiar coefficient of adversity, even though it is insupportable. He must assume the situation with the proud consciousness of being the author of it, for the very worst disadvantage or the worst threats than can endanger my person have meaning in and through my project; and it is on the ground of the engagement which I am that they appear. It is therefore senseless to think of complaining since nothing foreign has decided what we feel, what we live, or what we are." [33]

Limitations to Freedom

To say that man is free is not to say that he is always effectual, that he always succeeds. The factual situation always imposes limitations. One may not be free to accumulate a fortune, cure a disease, climb the mountain, or stop a war. "Success is not important to freedom." [34] One may not be free to escape from prison, but he is free to choose to try to escape. Sartre discusses various kinds of limitations. One theme is common to all of them: they *confirm* the existence of freedom. "The resistance which freedom reveals in the existent, far from being a danger to freedom, results only in enabling it to rise as freedom. There can be a free for-itself only as engaged in a resisting world. Outside of this engagement the notions of freedom . . . lose all meaning." [35] Jaspers calls them "boundary situations." What are these limitations?

(1) My Place. My birth in Japan limits my freedom to be a physician in Kansas City. While it is impossible for me to be a native of any country but Japan, I am free to seek to be a physician in Kansas City by overcoming all the obstacles that stand in the way. (2) My Past. That I have been trained as a surveyor will have some bearing on my action in the present. "No free surpassing can be effected except in terms of a past." But the meaning that the past is to have for me is decided by myself. I determine precisely what bearing it is to have by projecting myself into the future by my choice of my present action. (3) My Environment. What I can do will be limited by the "instrumental things" around me, by their particular "coefficients of adversity and utility." But here again freedom asserts itself. I may embark on easy or difficult projects. I always feel resistance in my environment and freely choose the implements which may help me overcome it. (4) My Fellow Man. Because there are other people in the world, things will exist as instruments for *their* ends as well as for my own. Success in their projects may be incompatible with success in mine. They may encompass me in surroundings carrying their meanings instead of my own; they may have the power to forbid me certain actions. "Evidently it must follow, someone will say, that my freedom escapes me on every side; there is no longer a *situation* as the organization of a meaningful world around the free choice of my spontaneity; there is a *state* which is imposed upon me." [36] Sartre answers [37] that one is not free to choose the society in which he is to live, but is free to act in *whatever* society he finds himself in. He can refuse to function as an object in someone else's world, he can disobey prohibitions, he can ignore directions. He may finally choose death. The fact of other persons is, however, a serious limitation on my freedom. It is imposed on me by *their* freedom, and it is not lightly to be dismissed. (5) My Death. I know that my death is inevitable; it is the final limitation on my freedom. One usually does not know

when death will come—he is like a condemned man uninformed of the date of his own execution who watches other prisoners being marched off to theirs.[38] Death cannot be considered as the chord that resolves everything at the end of the melody. I cannot plan what I wish to accomplish in a full life, then wait for death in old age after I have completed everything. At any moment death may interrupt the project in which I have engaged myself, and my efforts will have been for naught. Since my whole life is in suspense, death, being an end only in the sense of arbitrary termination, cannot give life a final meaning; it would seem to *remove* all meaning from life. "I can neither discover my death nor wait for it nor adopt an attitude toward it, for it is that which is revealed to me as undiscoverable, that which disarms all waiting, that which slips into all attitudes. . . . Death is a pure fact as is birth; it comes to us from outside and it transforms us into the outside." [39] But, says Sartre, death is merely a situation-limit *to* my freedom, not a qualification *within* my freedom. When I am dead, just as when I am an object in another's world, I am no longer present as a free subject. "The freedom which is *my freedom* remains total and infinite. Death is not an obstacle to my projects; it is only a destiny of these projects elsewhere. And this is not because death does not limit my freedom but because freedom never encounters this limit." [40]

We have already encountered the absurdity of being-in-itself. We are now led to a similar characterization of being-for-itself. It too is *de trop*. "It has the feeling of its complete gratuity. . . ." Facticity "simply resides in the for-itself as a memory of being, as its unjustifiable presence in the world." [41] Not only does it seek to flee from anguish, it undertakes an additional double flight—from the world and from the self. It flees the present in order to escape from the past of world and self; it disengages itself from the *this* in order to establish a *that* in the future. But the self and the world of the future are not complete and must be surpassed. "We run after a possible which our running causes to appear, which is nothing but our running itself, and which thereby is by definition out of reach. We run toward ourselves and we are—due to this very fact—the being which cannot be reunited with itself. In one sense the running is void of meaning since the goal is never given but invented and projected proportionately as we run toward it." [42] More succinctly: "I flee the being without foundation which I was toward the founding act which I can be only in the mode of the *I would be*." [43] There is meaning to this, however. The meaning is the running itself. "Possibility is the meaning of the for-itself." [44]

OTHER PEOPLE

The Look

The for-itself, as we have seen, always views the world as *his* world and endows it with meanings relative to his purposes. He is a subject; it is an object. While I am sitting in a park, the view which I enjoy is *my* view. The bench serves me, the trees shade me, the breeze refreshes me. From my position as subject, I am in command of the situation. I see a passerby whom I assume to be a person, a human being rather than a shadow or a puppet. He sits down with a newspaper. I may vaguely conjecture that he has consciousness and is a free being like myself. I am quite content to believe that he is another person. But I am not threatened, for I still apprehend him, like the benches and the trees, as an object. His meaning, like theirs, derives from my purposes and my interests. If it occurs to me that he has projects of his own, that "my" things have meaning in *his* universe, I begin to get somewhat uneasy. Is it possible that this *object* has stolen part of my world from me? "The appearance of the Other in the world corresponds . . . to a fixed sliding of the whole universe, to a decentralization of the world which undermines the centralization which I am simultaneously effecting." [45] But I do not panic. He is still "simply a little particular crack in my universe. At the heart of this solid, visible form he makes himself a particular emptying." [46]

Now let us suppose that the Other suddenly turns from his newspaper and *looks* at me. I am devastated. I become an object for him. His subjectivity is now in command. My world flows toward the Other, and I along with it. My freedom escapes me. I as a subject have become alienated from my self.[47] My person is simply an object, along with all the others, in *his* world. The hemorrhage in my world that occurred when I first saw him and idly speculated that he might be a person is no longer internal, self-contained. It is complete. I have a world no longer; I now function as a thing for the Other who regards me.[48]

The individual experiences the presence of other individuals as *shame*. In shame one *lives* the situation of being looked at. The look, when directed upon me, is not perceived as an objective event in the world but is experienced as a form of self-revulsion. I am touched to the quick. I am ashamed that I am as the other sees me:

powerless, devoid of freedom. The subject who sees me has been substituted for the object seen by me. The experience of shame is the same as the one we have when we have been noticed in a vulgar gesture or looking through a keyhole.[49] I am seen in an awkward posture behaving in a contemptible way for ignoble ends. I am that ridiculous figure whom the Other has *caught* peeking through a keyhole. This shame may be more understandable than the shame experienced in the park, but the essential point is that in both, subjectivity has been converted to objectivity. Shame can be experienced by the man "caught" watching a Shakespearean tragedy as well as the one watching a burlesque show. Shame is "the apprehension of myself *as a* nature although that very nature escapes me and is unknowable as such. Strictly speaking, it is not that I perceive myself losing my freedom in order to become a *thing,* but my nature is over there, outside my lived freedom—as a given attribute of this being which I am for the Other." [50]

In a sense I am *enslaved* by the Other, who fixes me in his world. His is the center of freedom, not mine. He qualifies me by passing value judgments on me. What use he will make of me I do not know. I know only that I am afraid, that I am in danger.[51] "This danger is not an accident but the permanent structure of my being-for-others. . . . Through the Other's look I *live* myself as fixed in the midst of the world, as in danger, as irremediable. But I *know* neither what I am nor what is my place in the world, nor what face in this world in which I am turns toward the Other." [52] The Other possesses the secret of what I am. For *me* to know the subject that enslaves me would require me to view him as an object—which would, of course, release me from slavery.

Release from slavery is, of course, always possible in principle. I can *recover* myself by making the Other an object. He will still retain subjectivity in a way—as a hollow box has an inside. I will remain "inside his world, but since he is now an object, his possession of me is purely interior and without efficacy.[53] The affirmation of my freedom by making the Other *my* object is what Sartre calls arrogance. Like shame, arrogance is an authentic response to the fact of other beings in the world.

Pride, however, is not authentic. Pride is a reaction to shame, a way of masking shame. The person looked at perceives (or imagines that he perceives) a *favorable* appraisal from the Other. He resigns himself to being an object and is proud that he is an estimable object. He accepts these qualities conferred upon him by the Other and encourages the feelings of love or admiration the Other may have for him. Pride (or vanity) is a form of bad faith. One alienates his freedom in order to be objectively good in the eyes of others. A free self should never take pride in himself, no matter how attractive he is perceived to be.[54]

One lives always under the threat of the Other. The "Other-as-object" may at any time become "Other-as-subject." "Being-for-others is a constant fact of my human reality, and I grasp it with its factual necessity in every thought, however slight, which I form concerning my self." [55] Distances and perspectives may vary, but *they* are always there. The presence of the Other need not be felt through a single, dramatic look; it may be felt in a steady and undifferentiated way by anyone who knows that he dwells in a society.

I as a subject may be generous and understanding toward the Other-as-object. His being, after all, is real—he is a concrete object. I may recognize his transcendence and accord him a derived kind of subjectivity. He too is engaged in projects, in surpassing his present.[56] He appears as "a center of autonomous and intramundane reference"—in *my* world.[57] But Sartre offers a word of caution: "The Other-as-object is an explosive instrument which I handle with care because I foresee around him the permanent possibility that *they* are going to explode and with this explosion I shall suddenly experience the flight of the world away from me and the alienation of my being. Therefore my constant concern is to contain the Other within his objectivity, and my relations with the Other-as-object are essentially made up of ruses designed to make him remain an object." [58] Only the dead are forever objects.

That I am always for others (millions of potential Others) proves the existence of myself as a being with essence. I am always in doubt as to what precisely this essence is. Lest this sound too Hegelian, Sartre insists that the true being of the for-itself cannot logically be derived from the being of the for-others any more than the conventional being of the for-others can be derived from the being of the for-itself. But my being is both for-itself and for-others. "Selfness is reinforced by arising as a negation of another selfness [that is, by being an object to another subject] and . . . this reinforcement is positively apprehended as the continuous choice of selfness by itself as *the same* selfness and as *this very selfness*." [59] Sartre goes on from this to a very complicated analysis showing how selves receive their essences from themselves and others in complex reversals and refinements of object-subject relations. We will not follow him in this discussion.

Love and Masochism

The relations between persons are not the simple unilateral relations we find between, say, a person and a table. They are reciprocal and fluid. And they obtain in a context of conflict. "Conflict is the original meaning of being-for-others." [60] Sartre illustrates this in his discussion of love, language, and masochism ("First Attitude Toward Others") and indifference, desire, sadism, and hate ("Second Attitude Toward Others"). We will briefly indicate something of Sartre's analysis of each of these.

In order to simplify the discussion of *love,* we will substitute for Sartre's terms ("lover" and "beloved") the letters "A" and "B." A loves B. A does not simply wish to possess B as a subject possesses an object. He does not intend to be a tyrant; he is not interested in power and enslavement; he is not satisfied if passion automatically flows from B to himself. What A in his love wants is a special type of appropriation. "He wants to possess a freedom as freedom." [61] He wants freely to be loved, but is not satisfied if B pledges freely to love him for a time. A wants to preside over a free kind of captivity; he wants B to be out of reach but his own. "The lover [A] does not demand that he be the cause of this radical modification of freedom but that he be the unique and privileged occasion of it." [62] Indeed, A is content *himself* to be the object—*provided* that B's freedom loses itself in him. A will be *in* the world provided that he is the "whole world" to B. In such a situation, A would be used as an instrument by B, but because B could have no other projects beyond A, A would be a special kind of instrument. A wishes to be *unsurpassable,* the absolute end of B's freedom. B must be willing (freely) to steal, lie, or even kill for A. A must freely be chosen to be loved by B, the unique and uncontingent object of B's love ("we were made for each other"). A is filled with joy. He is no longer *de trop.* His existence is justified. It is "taken up and willed even in its tiniest details by an absolute freedom. . . ." [63] A, in short, seeks both to be a subject and an object. And, if his love is requited, so does B!

We now must talk about seduction and fascination, which are modes of *language.*[64] Since A wishes to be both subject and object, seduction becomes a very delicate matter. A cannot reveal his subjectivity, for this would eliminate B's freedom—and this, of course, is to be avoided. A tries to present himself to B as "the world"—

the key to its wealth, society, and happiness. A beseiges B, he proposes himself as unsurpassable. A seeks "the consent of [B's] freedom, which [A] must capture by making it recognize itself as nothingness in the face of [A's] plenitude of absolute being." [65] A tries to make himself an object of fascination for B.

What do we have when everything works out? When A's love is requited, when A and B love one another? A mess. "Each of the lovers is entirely the captive of the Other inasmuch as each wishes to make himself loved by the other to the exclusion of anyone else; but at the same time each one demands from the Other a love which is not reducible to the 'project of being-loved.'" [66] A and B are both willing to be objects, but each requires the other to be a subject. This is contradictory. Second: "Each one wants the other to love him but does not take into account the fact that to love is to want to be loved and that thus by wanting the other to love him, he only wants the other to want to be loved in turn." [67] This is an infinite regress. Finally: Lovers are vulnerable at all times to the *look* of third parties, a process in which subjectivity is lost. The lovers and their love become objects in a hostile perspective. That is why lovers seek (but never find) solitude. The first phenomenon accounts for the lover's perpetual insecurity, the second for his perpetual dissatisfaction, and the third for his perpetual shame. Hence the "triple destructibility" of love.

One recourse is to *masochism*. A views his own subjectivity as the obstacle to love, so he tries to lose himself *completely* in the subjectivity of B. He refuses to be anything *but* an object and loves his shame as the profound sign of his objectivity.[68] He no longer requires that he be "the whole world" to B; he is content to be one object among others—not even a *special* instrument for B's use. "Masochism is an attempt not to fascinate the Other by means of my objectivity but to cause myself to be fascinated by my objectivity-for-others. . . . Masochism is characterized as a species of vertigo, vertigo not before a precipice of rock and earth but before the abyss of the Other's subjectivity." [69] But masochism must necessarily fail. It is impossible for one to view *himself* as an object, no matter how much he debases himself. He can only be an object to the *Other*. Furthermore, *he* is the one who chooses to do the ridiculous things he does; he cannot lay down his burden of freedom. "The more he tries to taste his objectivity, the more he will be submerged by the consciousness of his subjectivity—hence his anguish." [70]

288 THE NEW ANARCHISM

"Second Attitude" Toward Others

The first attitude having failed, one may assume the second. I may look at the Other, confront his subjectivity, bring out into the open the struggle between our two freedoms. If I succeed, the Other has now become an object (not a beloved). I ignore his subjectivity, I am blind to his freedom. I am *indifferent* to him except as he may have a function as a waiter, perhaps, or a ticket collector.[71] Granting that indifference may be achieved (some people may go for years without suspecting what the Other is!), Sartre does not believe that it can be experienced as an adequate solution. First, because the danger from the Other still exists and, being unknown, is doubly dangerous. Second, because the burden and responsibility of being free ("this terrible necessity") becomes unmistakable for the indifferent man. Never permitting himself to be an object, he is thrown back solely to his own "unjustifiable subjectivity."

We will not here attempt to present anything like an adequate account of Sartre's analysis of *desire*. "Desire is not only the clogging of a consciousness by its facticity; it is correlatively the ensnare-ment of a body by the world. The world is made *ensnaring;* consciousness is engulfed in a body which is engulfed in the world. Thus the ideal which is proposed here is being-in-the-midst-of-the-world; the For-itself attempts to realize a being-in-the-midst-of-the-world. . . . But desire is not first nor primarily a relation to the world. The world here appears only as the ground for explicit relations with the *Other*. Usually it is on the occasion of the Other's *presence* that the world is revealed as the world of desire." [72] De-sire, like everything else, fails—and not simply because pleasurable satisfaction is the death of desire. In sexual relations, where desire is best exemplified, my desire is to take and appropriate the body of an Other which is saturated with consciousness (due to the caress) and which is itself incarnated with desire. But when I seize her flesh and penetrate her, "my own body ceases to be flesh and be-comes again the synthetic instrument *which I am.* And by the same token the Other ceases to be an incarnation; she becomes once more an instrument in the midst of the world which I apprehend in terms of its situation." [73] The incarnation of flesh of us both dis-appears—mine because of my insistence, hers because of my success. "What I take in my hands is *something else* than what I wanted to take." [74]

This brings us to *sadism*. The "lover" coldly persists, but now the Other is *simply* an "instrumental-object." The sadist, impassioned only by his tenacity and barrenness, seeks to appropriate the incarnation of the Other. He incarnates the Other through violence, using whatever instruments he can (including his own body). He seeks to get hold of the Other's freedom instrumentally, through pain. He will demand proofs that the Other's freedom has been ensnared in the body he possesses. He does not suppress the freedom so much as he forces it to *identify* itself with the tortured and humiliated flesh. The Other "struggles against the expanding flesh and finally freely chooses to be wholly identified with this body; this distorted and heaving body is the very image of a broken and enslaved freedom." [75]

Sadism is, of course, a blind alley. It does not lead anywhere. The body of the Other has become pure instrument, but for what? Certainly not for pleasure or satiation; simple desire would have yielded these. How, now that I have succeeded, do I utilize this flesh? "It *is there*, and it is there *for nothing*." [76] There is also failure on a different level. The freedom of the Other forever eludes the sadist's grasp. The sadist discovers "that he can not act on the Other's freedom even by forcing the Other to humiliate himself and to beg for mercy, for it is precisely in and through the Other's absolute freedom that there exists a world in which there are sadism and instruments of torture and a hundred pretexts for forswearing oneself." [77]

Sadism and masochism are the reefs on which sexual desire founders. Do I appropriate the flesh of the Other or do I submit my flesh to the Other? Desire fluctuates between both perils; " 'normal' sexuality is commonly designated as 'sadistic-masochistic.' " [78] This has a wider significance, as was implied in the discussion of the first attitude toward others. "We can never hold a consistent attitude toward the Other unless he is simultaneously revealed to us as subject and as object, as transcendence-transcending and transcendence-transcended—which is on principle impossible. Thus ceaselessly tossed from being-a-look to being-looked-at, falling from one to the other in alternate revolutions, we are always, no matter what attitude is adopted, in a state of instability in relation to the Other." [79]

Hate arises when all attempts (such as those discussed above) to establish a satisfying relation with the Other are given up as hopeless. The hater wishes to eliminate the existence once and for all of the Other, of the being whose freedom invariably rises up to haunt him. He hates the person who dominates him, who is indifferent to him, who is kind to him, who is good, who is bad. When he hates a particular person, he may hate him as the representative of *all* the Others. He wants his death. But hate too must fail. I cannot kill everyone. And even if I killed that one symbol of all the Others, I do not cancel out the life he was. I cannot recapture what he has alienated: "What I was for the Other is fixed by the Other's death, and I shall irremediably be it in the past." [80] I have been contaminated. And I "will never cease to apprehend [my] dimension of being-for-others as a permanent possibility of [my] being." [81]

Community

We have talked about being-in-itself, being-for-itself, and being-for-others. Is it also possible to talk about "being-with-others"? Is a person ever *in community* with the Other? Sartre considers two possibilities: (1) A plurality of objects in which no one is a subject—a community of beings-for-others. "Us" is a significant term. (2) A plurality of subjects in which no one is an object—a community of beings-for-themselves. "We" is a significant term.

(1) Suppose that two people are confronting one another. One of them is myself. Now a third person comes on the scene. If he looks at *me,* then I in my alienation perceive the other two as forming a community; they are subjects. If he looks at the Other (who is looking at me), an unstable state results which can be resolved only by my alliance with the Other or the Third. If he looks at the Other (at whom I am looking), I may be able to disarm them both by shifting my look to the Third. But suppose the Third arrives and looks at us both simultaneously? We are both alienated and exist as objects in his world. "Our possibilities are equally dead-possibilities *for the Third.*" [82] We are together in an objective, indissoluble whole; we have solidarity. We may fight or we may cooperate—but not as subjects. Whatever we do, we are united as objects in the synthesis of the Third. I am not a single object but am locked in subjection with others. I experience "humiliation and impotence; the one who experiences himself as constituting an *Us* with other men feels himself trapped among an infinity of strange existences; he is alienated radically and without recourse." [83]

Can there in any society be class-consciousness? What common

passion can an oppressed class experience under the rule of an oppressing class (the Third)? The oppressed will have conflicts and
jealousies among themselves, but will experience a collective alienation. The privileges that the oppressors possess make us see our
plight more plainly. "Without the Third, no matter what might
be the adversity of the world, I should apprehend myself as a
triumphant transcendence; with the appearance of the Third, 'I'
experience 'Us' as apprehended in terms of things and as things
overcome by the world." [84] The individual may seek to recover his
freedom *as* an individual. But if class unity does develop, as it will
in certain strongly structured societies, class consciousness will also
develop and aim at "freeing the whole 'Us' from the object-state
by transforming it into a We-subject." [85]

There are, of course, some people who do not wish to save themselves at all—either as individuals or as a class. Such people are
quite willing, for example, "to be submerged in the crowd-instru-
ment by the look of the leader." [86] This is the social correlate of
masochism.

A religious "solution" to the problem of the reality of the "Us"
is to posit the existence of God as the Third in relation to *all* social groups. Humanity must struggle and suffer and seek to develop
its objective potentialities. But the humanity realized, whatever else
it may be, here or in heaven, will never be *ours*.

(2) Do we, as workers engaged in a common task, soldiers marching together in cadence or members of a ruling class, ever achieve
the unification of for-itselfs ("we-subjects")? Sartre admits that we
may experience a common rhythm, but he rules out any genuine
Mitsein. "The subjectivities remain out of reach and radically separated." [87] Behind the fugitive and vague feelings of being with
others, conflict remains. "We should hope in vain for a human 'we'
in which the intersubjective totality would obtain consciousness of
itself as a unified subjectivity. Such an ideal could only be a dream
produced to the limit and to the absolute on the basis of frag-
mentary, strictly psychological experiences." [88]

Merely because the oppressed class feels an "us-unity" does not
imply that the oppressing class must also feel a "we-unity." The
privileged bourgeois does not even think of himself as a member of
an oppressing class! He does not want to think of classes at all, but
rather of a harmony of interests in a national whole. If there are
injustices, let them be rectified! Only when the bourgeoisie are
overthrown will they have class-consciousness—as an "Us-object."

The oppressed class will then be *their* Third! Will the new rulers seek a "we-subject" in their new role? Will they fail? Will they oppress the other with the same singular disregard for their freedom? Will they in bad faith talk about the general welfare? Will they encourage the grotesqueries of social masochism? Sartre did not deal with these questions. If he had, he would probably have given an affirmative answer to them all.

EXISTENTIALISM
AND POLITICS

In Sartre's long major work, *Being and Nothingness,* there is no discussion of politics as such and very little reference to politics at all. Bemused by the existentialist jargon, one might be tempted to say that the politics of nothingness is nothing, and that the implied political outlook of a philosophy about isolated free consciousnesses is anarchism. If man is condemned to be free, he is condemned also to anarchism. But the matter is not so simple. Neither Sartre nor any other prominent existentialist has stepped forward to espouse anarchism.

Before we examine the relationship between existential philosophy and anarchism, we should seek to discover the political theory that its adherents espouse.

We have already encountered Sartre's view that a sense of community, if it is possible at all, is experienced as the "Us-object," never as the "We-subject." We know also that the relation between for-itselfs is one of conflict and that the closer people come to one another, the more likely it is that one of those intolerable attitudes—ranging from love to hate—will develop. Now this person, now that one, is subject and in anguish, or, from the other side, is object and in shame or pride. I must be being-for-itself, but I continually find myself as being-for-others. I consent to be being-for-others, but my shame will not permit me to renounce my freedom. I am always a subject, but my subjectivity is inevitably alienated. The only "solution" seems to be one of theory only: I must be the *only* subject. All other people must be and remain objects in *my* world, shut up there with their dead possibilities. But others might want to be God also, and realistically I know that I cannot prevail. Conflict and struggle return as I engage desperately in a contest I cannot win.

I am in an impossible situation and so is mankind. The situation cries for a political solution—either a positive one or a principled rejection of politics itself. We have to figure out how to live with people or without them; we have to decide on the authority or non-authority that will facilitate the best kind of society. If these are impossible tasks, then political theory is without point and use-less.

In *Being and Nothingness* Sartre briefly examines the claims of liberalism. Liberalism teaches us to respect the freedom of others while cooperating with everyone for humanitarian goals. But this is impossible, for every attitude taken toward others, violent or peaceful, rigorous or gentle, insistent or tolerant, violates the very freedom we profess to respect. In principle we are saying (with Rousseau) that we will *force* the other to be free. We try to enlist his support for our projects but succeed only in making him an object or in arousing his resistance. "Thus respect for the Other's freedom is an empty word." [89] It would thus appear that freedom necessarily will be destroyed by even the most liberal kind of gov-ernment. At the same time, we know that freedom can never be destroyed.[90] The political man will necessarily, then, be either guilty or ineffectual! [91]

Sartre As Critic
of Dialectical Materialism

In a lecture delivered in Paris in 1945 ("Existentialism Is a Hu-manism"), Sartre expressed some political views.[92] He attacked ma-terialism for regarding men as objects. He explained how men invented values and gave meaning to life, going as far as to say: "There is a possibility of creating a human community." [93] He defended a kind of humanism in which man is not considered as an end but as always in the making, a humanism without God, a humanism that portrays man as maker of his own laws in a human universe.

In the discussion that followed the lecture Pierre Naville, a prominent French Marxist, roundly criticized Sartre for what he took to be his political position. Sartre, said Naville, was nothing but an old-fashioned reformist, a revivalist of humanistic liberalism. His emphasis on human freedom and dignity meant that he was only espousing an eighteenth-century theory of a fixed human na-ture. He refused to see the effect on "human nature" of historical

social change, speaking always of the "human condition" instead
of human *conditioning*. Sartre, Naville charged, sees human action
as isolated and uncaused and refuses himself to give directives. He
talks about anguish, forlornness, and despair in order to escape
social responsibility. He says that man must freely involve himself,
but man is already involved. "When pseudo-Marxists or liberals cry
up the dignity of the person above all else, it's because they shrink
from the demands of the present world situation. Likewise, the
existentialist as liberal cries up man in general because he doesn't
succeed in formulating a position that events demand, and the only
positive position we know of is Marxism. It's Marxism that poses
the real problems of the age." [94]

Sartre's answer is very short and does not come to terms with all
the points Naville made. Sartre does challenge Naville on the historical "certainties" he assumes. His best retort is against Naville's
commitment to the concept of causality: "You talk of a statistical
order of causality. That doesn't mean a thing. I wish you'd tell me
clearly and precisely what you mean by causality. The day that a
Marxist explains it to me I'll believe in Marxist causality. When
someone talks to you of freedom, you go about saying, 'I beg your
pardon, there is causality.' You're unable to give an account of this
causality, which has no meaning except in Hegel. What you've got
is a Marxist dream of causality." [95]

Soon after this encounter Sartre published an article in *Les
Temps Modernes* called "Materialism and Revolution." It is critical, not so much of Marx, but of "Marx *through* Neo-Stalinist
Marxism." Once again Sartre attacks materialism: "By what miracle
is the materialist, who accuses idealists of indulging in metaphysics
when they reduce matter to mind, absolved from the same charge
when he reduces mind to matter? Experience does not decide in
favor of his doctrine—nor, for that matter, does it decide in favor
of the opposing one either." [96] The Marxist places himself as an
object in physical nature, then steps back to tell us what it is all
about. He banishes his subjectivity in order to claim, through a play
on the word "objectivity," an impossible kind of all-knowing objectivity. "How could a captive reason, governed from without and
maneuvered by a series of blind causes, still be reason?" [97] The
dialectical aspect of dialectical materialism is also false. According
to Sartre, dialectical action is possible only in the realm of ideas.
Matter is inert and quantitative; it cannot create new syntheses. "It
is incapable of producing anything itself." [98] Nature does not have

a history. Even biological evolution proceeds in a mechanical order, not a dialectical one. Sheer change in time is not history. History "is defined as the deliberate resumption of the past by the present; only human history is possible." [99] Materialists resort to dialectics because mechanical causation will not reveal enough. But the "progress" and "synthesis" they "discover" go beyond anything that science can legitimately deal with. Sartre also scoffs at the principle that the economic base (mode of production) of a society determines its "superstructure." "I have witnessed conversions to materialism; one enters into materialism as into a religion. I should define it as the subjectivity of those who are ashamed of their subjectivity." [100] So the Marxists, not able to live with their materialism (denseness, exteriority, and inertia), escape "by a furtive recourse to idealism." [101] Revolutionary classes are moved by ideas; they respond to new social theories. The new tasks that their "material conditions" are supposed to have "imposed" upon them are carried out, says Sartre, because they want to change their world and will adopt the ideas that most effectively challenge their oppressors. If these ideas are those of dialectical materialism, the ideas achieve a kind of pragmatic truth—until the next revolutionary class comes along. Communist leaders have *faith* in Marxism. They will not permit disagreement within the ranks because it may weaken the cause; but when they can shift to foes outside the ranks, they claim to possess the *truth!* They require the services of scientists and artists, but fear their intellectuality. The intellectual's "dangerous freedom of thought which is an expression of his relative material independence, is countered by the faith of the militant worker who, because of his very situation, *needs* to believe in his leaders' orders." [102] Sartre, with *his* intellectual freedom, refuses to choose a doctrine that destroys thought. The thoughtful man cannot accept a myth—even in order to help the oppressed. Genuine revolutionary hopes do not require a myth. Truth will serve.[103]

Sartre As a Marxist

In 1957 Sartre returned to the Marxist fold in an article called "Marxism and Existentialism." This became part of "Search for a Method," which appeared as the introductory essay in Sartre's *Critique of Dialectical Reason* (1960). In this essay Sartre insisted that philosophy is not only practical, but that its method serves as "a social and political method." [104] Even Descartes' philosophy

cleared the ground for certain social struggles. A philosophy remains efficacious as long as the *praxis* (the purposeful human activity) that engendered it remains alive. "The directed violence of
weapons will overthrow privileges which have already been dissolved in Reason." [105] Marxism still possesses that relevance, for
man has not yet gone beyond the historical moment that Marx
expressed. It is impossible to go *beyond* Marxism—at its best this
would consist of finding something in Marx hitherto missed; at its
worst of returning to pre-Marxism. "Revisionism" is out. Marxism
is a living philosophy and adapts *itself* to new conditions. Kierkegaard discovered the "specificity of human *existence.*" Marx also
realized that man must be judged not by his ideas, but by his actions, the way that he lives—his work and social *praxis*. We understand classes by the work they are engaged in; and we understand
revolutions from their concrete struggles and attainments—all in
the context of a specified economic system. In order to know man in
his real life, we must consider him "first a worker who produces
the conditions of his life." [106] Marx furthermore discovered man's
basic alienation: the objectivization of men in a system of commodities which they make and which controls them.

In spite of all the historical events proving the basic truths of
Marxism, some people, says Sartre, have found that it did not satisfy
their need to understand. What happened? Marxism stopped and
the Soviet Union grew. The Russian leaders, in their great political struggle to build socialism, could not handle a schism between
theory on one side and practice on the other. In order to get on
with the job, they placed doctrinal theory "out of reach"—nothing
was to weaken the ideological struggle! Theory became empty and
practice became unprincipled. "This fixed image of idealism and
violence did idealistic violence to facts. For years the Marxist intellectual believed that he served his party by violating experience, by
overlooking embarrassing details, by grossly simplifying the data,
and above all, by conceptualizing the event before having studied
it." [107] Apologists have called the Soviet intervention in Hungary
a sound and moderate checking of a counter-revolutionary movement. Opponents have called it an act of aggression by the Russian
bureaucracy against a workers' democracy. Neither—according to
Sartre—is correct, and neither version would have resulted from
the application of a living Marxist method. Marxism today has been
frozen into dictates; it is an *a priori* and absolute system of knowledge. Its theoretical bases and dialectical method *could* be applied

to a great many things, but it no longer seems to live *"with history."* [108] Existentialism may revitalize Marxism by addressing itself to concrete experience, by seeking man "everywhere *where he is, at his work, in his home, in the street.*" [109] All the insights of existentialism can be integrated with a Marxist framework. Marxism is still the only philosophy of our time. It will remain the philosophy of our time until everyone achieves "a margin of real freedom beyond the production of life." [110] What the philosophy of freedom will be which takes its place, no one can know. In the meantime, existentialism will assist Marxism in giving a dialectical interpretation to history.[111] As long as Marxism remains a dogmatic metaphysics, it will need existentialism. If Marxism is properly reinvigorated, existentialism will be "absorbed, surpassed and conserved by the totalizing movement of philosophy" and will cease to become a particular inquiry." [112]

Existentialism and Marxism

The Marxism of Sartre is not typical of other existentialists—any more than the existentialism of Sartre is typical of other Marxists. Maurice Merleau-Ponty bitterly attacked Soviet Communism in *Humanism and Terror* (1947) and Albert Camus announced his rejection of Marxism in *The Rebel* (1951). But more important, Sartre's Marxism is incompatible with his own existentialism. The two theories just do not go together. It would be instructive to hear Marx himself, if he could be resurrected, vent his indignation at Sartre's attempt to "revitalize" his theory with concepts that are so at odds with it. In his excellent essay, "Basic Differences Between Existentialism and Marxism," George Novack made the following pertinent points: (1) For existentialism the universe is irrational; for Marx it is not. (2) For the existentialist human behavior is unpredictable and "ambiguous"; for Marx people in general will act in a way determined by their social situation. (3) For existentialism nature is conceived subjectively; for Marx it is wholly objective and materialistic. (4) Existentialism emphasizes human individuality; Marx emphasizes class solidarity. (5) Existentialism says that man is condemned to be free; Marx says that men must achieve their freedom through comprehending and using natural laws. (6) Existentialism holds that actions are good if they are done in good faith; Marx holds that they are good if they assist in the struggle for socialism. (7) Existentialism is pessimistic about man's destiny;

Marx is optimistic.[113] (8) Existentialism holds that alienation is metaphysically inevitable and is a result of the presence of the Other; Marx holds that alienation, being a result of particular social systems, is eradicable.[114]

But to wrench existentialism away from Marxism (or to refuse to permit Sartre to be a Marxist) does not make existentialism in general or Sartre in particular an advocate of anarchism.

EXISTENTIALISM
AND ANARCHISM

Rebels Against the System

From its beginning with Kierkegaard, existentialism has been a philosophy for individuals who, in order to protect their individuality, have rebelled against "the system." They have chosen their particular existence rather than live an essence that society seeks to fasten on them.[115] The existentialist ideal of individuals, not willing to drift, who in their weakness and isolation yet oppose the great forces of government, society, and public opinion, is similar to the anarchist ideal of opposing all invaders of individual sovereignty. Heidegger calls man to authentic existence: do not lose yourself in those patterns of life that society makes available to you. The impersonal "one" (*das Man*) is a cipher: one pays one's taxes, one submits to laws, one obeys the conventions.

The consistent theme of existentialism is that man should avoid being a *thing*, an object. He should not be as an object, for he is a subject. Marcel gives a dismal description of the mass-production worker who is hardly distinguishable from the productive mechanism itself. In order that he may continue to function, his *vital* "functions" must be supervised as well: so much time for meals, so much time for recreation, for sleep, etc. Periodic medical checkups are scheduled, and finally, when the human machine has worn out, it is tossed on the scrap heap.[116] Karl Jaspers also is concerned with the depersonalization of man, which increases with growing industrialization. In the vast interlockings of modern society, with its millions of people, things have to be controlled. Control is achieved by organization, propaganda, and catering to the most common appetites of the masses. There is no room for individuality and spirituality—only tranquillity. Even writers *must* satisfy the needs of the many.[117] Nothing must be permitted to disrupt, for chaos would result and chaos is deadly. "When the titanic apparatus of the mass order has been consolidated, the individual has to serve it." [118] These existentialist ideas have also been espoused by the anarchists.

The note of revolt is often sounded in existentialist literature. Camus makes revolt a key notion in his work. Revolt for him is an existential event, a personal experience rather than a social action. Revolt "says Yes to something within man that is irreducible, and it says No to something outside man which is unacceptable." [119] Revolt will go to great lengths to preserve these values which it finds. The value most commonly found in "metaphysical revolt" is human solidarity. Does metaphysical revolt ever issue into historical revolution? Yes, but not all revolutions exemplify revolt, and revolt does not have to develop into revolution. Camus is pessimistic. Most revolutions affirm values beyond history (thus inhuman); they are conducted inhumanly and produce inhuman societies; they therefore betray revolt through murder and tyranny. So Camus would for the most part, stay with revolt. But revolution is not ruled out. "If revolution seeks to correct social injustice, its first act, when power is seized, should be to guarantee a certain freedom in the midst of its efforts to establish a new justice—otherwise the creation of a new and equally intolerable tyranny becomes inevitable." [120] Camus is not an anarchist, but there is nothing in this short exposition which has not been said by anarchists: deep-seated protest against conditions, solidarity with others, failure of previous revolutions, and agreement of means with ends.

The Dilemma of Freedom

The greatest contribution existentialism can make to anarchism would seem to be its theory of freedom. Anarchism requires the existentialist philosophy—desperately. With all its concern for freedom, anarchism lacks a philosophy of freedom. Anarchism dispenses with political power in order to obtain freedom; it refuses passively to accept external moral and religious standards. Sometimes it also rebels against social conditioning and public opinion. But freedom for anarchism generally seems to mean the likelihood of satisfying one's desires and loosening the restraints that stand in the way of such satisfaction. All this is quite compatible with a deterministic view of human nature.

What significant freedom can be gained if the anarchist retains a deterministic theory of human nature? Certain rather obvious and arbitrary restrictions on freedom may be swept away, but man remains a creature who is caused to act as he does. The fact that the desires, which he now (in theory at least) succeeds in gratifying, are his desires, does not save him. A well-structured society or a diabolically clever government can provide its people with *this* much freedom. To be able to do what you apparently *want* to do is freedom of the most deceptive kind—if these desires are products of an external world. Even if desires and actions are products of the self ("self-determinism"), they fall short of freedom if the self is made to be what it is by outside forces.

Unless anarchism can espouse a philosophical theory of freedom, it is doing no more than *selecting* from outside forces those that will continue to coerce (*e.g.*, the need that other people have for help) and those that will no longer be permitted to coerce (*e.g.*, government). It is by no means unreasonable to evaluate and screen determining factors (although one would be determined in the selecting process itself), but the result would be a tailored version of a determinism, not a free society. This is an endeavor that *anyone,* anarchist and archist alike, could make.

But *existentialist* freedom, since it dispenses with *all* coercion, would seem to be what the anarchists are really after. Make your *own* values, take the responsibility for your own actions, remake your own essence, frustrate past conditioning, "nihilate" being-in-itself, objectify the whole world through your own subjectivity, etc. If government threatens you, "look" at it and will the death of its practitioners.

The difficulty with all of this is that we already *have* the kind of freedom the existentialist talks about.[121] Freedom is not something that, in the manner of the anarchists, we have to struggle for; we already have it! We are condemned to have it. Not even the masochist can succeed in laying down its burden. Sartre may complain about the tyranny of Russian "Marxists," but the fact is that the kind of freedom he is talking about is just as possible (inescapable, rather) under the commissars as in one of Warren's anarchic communities. He may, furthermore, proclaim man's dignity as a "for-itself," but if the sense of freedom is to be recognized as that which cannot be annihilated, a tyrant may give it the nod and continue his oppressive ways. That Sartre should join the Communist movement is not so strange; his philosophy of man is compatible with any political (or non-political) movement.[122] The existentialist's freedom can neither be given nor taken away, while the anarchist's freedom is contingent. We might expect the existentialist and the anarchist to join hands, for they both praise freedom. But the fact is that anarchism, a social philosophy, lacks a theory of freedom; and existentialism, a philosophical position, lacks a political tendency. Historical success for anarchism will have no bearing on existentialism, for people already *had* freedom. Recognition of the truth of existentialism will have no bearing on anarchism, for people would still have to win something the anarchists believe they lack.

What the Existentialist
Can Say to the Anarchist

If it is true that freedom can (must) exist in *any* society, *whatever* its government or non-government, is there anything that existentialism and anarchism can say to each other?

On the hopeful side, the existentialist can say to the anarchist: "You perceive a kind of society in which the more obvious kinds of domination have disappeared. While the opportunities for 'authentic existence' may thereby decrease, the temptations for 'bad faith' will also be less. However, I cannot but sympathize with your hatred of power. I find the notion of the Other empowered with the right of making laws and controlling armed policemen thoroughly unsettling. It may be true that I am blessed with freedom, but certain social situations can nevertheless put me in a very uncomfortable position. I know that factual circumstances cannot, in the strict sense, limit my freedom, but they can contribute to the alienation of myself. After all, to the degree that I am made an object by the Other (their laws, their public opinion, their corporations, their IBM systems), I cease to have freedom. So I think I will join you.

"We may never be a 'we-subject,' but I certainly do not want to be part of an 'us-object.' But whether I join you or not, I approve of your temperament. You do 'engage' yourself. You know (abstractly only, I'm afraid) what you want and you know the many roadblocks placed in your path. I must accord to your courage a grudging admiration. You are willing to act and in your action you will change yourself and your society. You try to mask your *anguish* in embarking on an unjustifiable course of action (which *all* courses of action are), but most of you face up to the *forlornness* of your project (alone, with no God to guarantee success), and the *despair* you experience in the erratic behavior of your companions in the project. Finally, you do manifest in your violence and 'propaganda by the deed' an existentialist response to death. You do not wait for your executioner to come to you in his good time; you go to him in yours. Some of you have indeed lived 'being unto death.' I would rather join you than the Marxists, for they seek 'we-unity' through authoritarianism—which is impossible. I would rather join you than democratic liberals, for they are so 'serious' that they are blind to the *real* seriousness of a social system that links us to other objects in a way that the majority believes serves the *general welfare!* We existentialists can be activists, you know. Many of us were Resistance fighters in occupied France."

The anarchist can say to the existentialist: "Perhaps neither of us knows what freedom is. But I know that I am not free now. It doesn't require much phenomenological analysis to know that. And you, while you say that you are free, chronically complain about alienation. So let's work together and see what happens. You do have to engage yourself in *some* way, you know. Do you want to enhance your own power or that of the Other? If you hang back, I will accuse you of bad faith. So engage yourself, man! Surely you can conceive of a social situation (different from the present one) where the range of your choices would be *wider*. There is freedom and there is freedom. I will grant that one may retain his freedom in a dungeon, but is this the *kind* of freedom you would freely choose? You claim to live for the future by exploiting the present. So conceive of possibilities, engage in projects that will expand your opportunities for freedom in the future. Can you not imagine societies where freedom would express itself more effectually? All this is simple common sense. You have analyzed freedom so thoroughly that you have virtually destroyed it as a meaningful category of human action. Take the brackets away from the phenomenological object. Your true feelings are the same as ours. Openly confirm the value of a society of free men and by your confirmation make it the legitimate ideal for social action!"

Existentialism as a Reductio

A hopeless attitude toward the possibility of existential anarchism might view existentialism as a devastating *reductio ad absurdum* of the anarchist ideology. If anarchism really does espouse a philosophy of freedom, what are its consequences?

The anarchist, regardless of his propensities for collectivism, must perceive himself as an individual, for only individuals can be free. His actions will be his own, without any real support from anyone else. He must be prepared to face the world, struggle against his enemies, and lead his life in the good society—by himself. Dependent on neither his comrades nor a benevolent state, he can draw only upon his inner resources as he chooses his actions. He will experience despair when his comrades (in their freedom) betray him. He will experience dread in his realization that he will have to bear all the responsibilities of his own action. He will experience forlornness in espousing those values he espouses without the certification of an outside authority. In stripping himself of all social controls, he also strips himself of all social help; he will stand naked, armed with nothing but his own integrity. He may wish to cooperate, to experience "mutual aid," to work together with his comrades in producing the material goods of life. But he can count on none of these things. *He* is freed from social control, but so are others. The demise of authority which gave him his freedom has also given others freedom—to isolate him, to plunder him, and finally, perhaps, to subjugate him. The process may have run full circle: he is left only with the philosophical freedom to resist— which is what he had to start with.

What attitudes toward others are open to him? Those offered and analyzed by Sartre constitute a dismal catalog: love, masochism, indifference, desire, sadism, and hate. This may be more dismal than the existence of freedom really requires. But the catalog indicates the perhaps insuperable difficulty of satisfactory social relations between two centers of absolute freedom. If the fundamental relation between free agents is one of conflict, then neither individualistic nor collectivistic anarchism is possible. The first, prizing independence, would always live in *fear* of others; the second, prizing cooperation, would always live in *frustration* by others. In no case could the anarchists develop a legitimate sense of community, for the "we-subject" is impossible. It is impossible simply because a free subject cannot accept another as an equally free subject. Disillusioned by strife and invasion, our group of anarchists might invoke a "social contract" to institute something that would *guarantee* the equality of their freedoms. If solidarity can subsist only in an "us-object," they might seek it by submitting themselves jointly to an Other. Thus power and authority, whether the Third is a constitution, a ruler, or an abstract majority vote, are back.

The philosophy of existentialism, as firmly opposed to authority as is anarchism, provides anarchism with a doctrine of freedom which can only destroy it. Both the existentialist and the anarchist choose freedom, but only the former knows its consequences.

If the anarchists were to be *shown* the consequences, they would not be impressed. The Jews of the Old Testament were told by God of the evils of kingship. They answered, "Nevertheless, give us a king." Similarly, the anarchists will answer the existentialists, "Nevertheless, destroy all kings." If man is doomed always to be free in any case, with all the misery that implies, the anarchists will prefer the kind of "dreadful freedom" where the most obvious frustrations of human hopes have been eliminated. Who knows what new human relationships will arise in a society where institutionalized power is not permitted to exist?

NOTES

1 Jean-Paul Sartre, *Being and Nothingness: An Essay on Phenomenological Ontology*. Hazel E. Barnes, Trans. (New York: Philosophical Library, 1956), p. 622. *L'Etre et le néant: Essai d'ontologie phénoménologique* was originally published in Paris in 1943 by Librairie Gallimard.

2 "All consciousness is positional in that it transcends itself in order to reach an object, and it exhausts itself in this same positing. All that there is of *intention* in my actual consciousness is directed toward the outside, toward the table. . . ." *Ibid.*, pp. li–lii.

3 *Ibid.*, p. lxii.

4 See *ibid.*, p. 79.

5 *Ibid.*, p. 16.

6 *Ibid.*, p. 189.

7 *Ibid.*, p. 11.

8 *Ibid.*, p. 15.

9 *Ibid.*, pp. 24, 181.

10 *Ibid.*, p. 21.

11 Heidegger had earlier sought to analyze nothingness and its naughting function—see *Sein und Zeit* (1927) and *Was ist Metaphysik?* (1929). He also had argued that understanding was projective, that man structures his world in terms of his practical purposes.

12 *Ibid.*, p. 217.

13 *Ibid.*

14 The philosophical complexities of Sartre's position cannot properly be dealt with here. The reader is referred to *Being and Nothingness*. Sartre's own expression of his phenomenology is, in the end, clearer than that of any expositor known to this writer.

15 *Nausea*, Lloyd Alexander, Trans. (New York: New Directions, 1964), pp. 126–129.

16 *Being and Nothingness*, p. 216.

17 *Ibid.*, p. 27. See also pp. 78–79.

18 *Ibid.*, p. 437.

19 *Ibid.*, p. 445.

20 The self has an essence only as the result of its past. Strictly speaking, such a self is not a for-itself, for the latter is always in the living present and unbound by anything it "was." "The Past is a For-itself reapprehended and inundated by the In-itself." *Ibid.*, p. 120.

21 *Ibid.*, p. 127.

22 See *ibid.*, p. 125.

23 *Ibid.*, p. 128. For Heidegger too, the *Dasein* is always ahead of itself. Man *is* his possibilities. Heidegger worked out a theory of time in *Sein und Zeit* which is basic to existentialist philosophy.

24 "Human reality does not exist first in order to act later; but for human reality, to be is to act, and to cease to act is to cease to be." *Ibid.*, p. 476.

25 *Ibid.* The text has "matter" instead of "manner," but this surely is an error.

26 *Ibid.*, p. 35.

27 *Ibid.*

28 *Ibid.*, p. 38.

29 *Ibid.*, p. 39.

30 He practices an ethics "which is ashamed of itself and dares not speak its name. It has obscured all its goals in order to free itself from anguish. Man pursues being blindly by hiding from himself the free project which is this pursuit. He makes himself such that he is *waited for* by all the tasks placed along his way. Objects are mute demands, and he is nothing in himself but the passive obedience to these demands." *Ibid.*, p. 626.

31 See *ibid.*, p. 439.

32 *Ibid.*, p. 43. Heidegger distinguishes "authentic" from "unauthentic existence." In the former the person *decides,* in the face of all risks and uncertainties; in the latter he looks for standards and excuses outside his own conscience. See John Wild, *The Challenge of Existentialism* (Bloomington: Indiana University Press, 1955), pp. 126–132.

33 *Being and Nothingness*, pp. 553–554.

34 *Ibid.*, p. 483.

35 *Ibid.*

36 *Ibid.*, p. 512.

37 We cannot present Sartre's long analysis here, but will indicate part of his answer. We will return to the problem of other people in the second section of this chapter.

38 Sartre himself prefers this analogy: We are like a condemned prisoner bravely preparing himself to make a good showing on the scaffold—only to be carried off by a flu epidemic. See *ibid.*, p. 533.

39 *Ibid.*, p. 545. Heidegger, influenced by Kierkegaard, has a significant discussion of "being unto death" (*Sein zum Tod*) in *Sein und Zeit*. The individual, since death can come at any time, should live authentically at all times instead of losing himself in trivial matters. He should live as if death were always imminent. You cannot postpone existing! Sartre somewhere said that the Resistance fighters were never so free as when they were acting under the threat of death.

40 *Ibid.*, p. 547.

41 *Ibid.*, p. 84.

42 *Ibid.*, p. 202.

43 *Ibid.*, p. 203.

44 *Ibid.*

45 *Ibid.*, p. 255.

46 *Ibid.*, p. 256.

47 My own look "is stripped of its transcendence by the very fact that it is a *look-looked-at.*" *Ibid.*, p. 266.

48 The Look does not have to be, literally, a visual stare. It may consist of any perceptual process and it may be conveyed by a footstep, a photograph, a written report, etc.

49 Sartre calls shame the feeling of an "original fall." We have "fallen" into the world of things and are vulnerable. The biblical story of the fall expresses the same idea. After original sin Adam and Eve knew they were naked and were ashamed. Their nakedness symbolizes their defenseless state as objects; the fig leaf (or clothes) symbolizes the wish to see without being seen—to exist as subjects. See *ibid.*, p. 289. Elsewhere Sartre calls the Look the true meaning of the Medusa myth.

50 *Ibid.*, p. 263. See discussion above of "limits" to freedom.

51 "The fact of the Other is incontestable and touches me to the heart. I realize him through *uneasiness;* through him I am perpetually *in danger* in a world which is *this* world and which nevertheless I can only glimpse" (*ibid.*, p. 275). "This world," of course, is the *Other's* world. I cannot grasp it because it is someone else's world. I can grasp *no* world because I am no longer a subject. I am *in* this world because I am an object in it.

52 *Ibid.*, p. 268. "Being-for-others" is a translation for *être-pour-autrui.*

53 See *ibid.*, p. 289.

54 The feeling of pride contains its own contradiction. The proud man, as object, tries to affect the Other. "I attempt to lay hold of the Other so that he may release to me the secret of my being. Thus vanity impels me to get hold of the Other and to constitute him as an object in order to burrow into the heart of this object to discover there my own object-state. But this is to kill the hen that lays the golden eggs. . . . Freed in spite of myself from my object-state, I remain alone confronting the Other-as-object in my unqualified selfness which I have to be forever without relief." *Ibid.*, p. 291.

55 *Ibid.*, p. 280.

56 But in a different and more concrete (and more degraded) way than myself. As I see him, he is engaged not as a free subject. Engagement-as-object is engagement in the sense of the term in this statement: "The knife is deeply engaged in the wound." See *ibid.*, p. 292.

57 *Ibid.*, p. 295.

58 *Ibid.*, p. 297.

59 *Ibid.*, p. 283.

60 *Ibid.*, p. 364.

61 *Ibid.*, p. 367.

62 *Ibid.*

63 *Ibid.,* p. 371.

64 Language "is originally the proof which a for-itself can make of its being-for-others, and finally it is the surpassing of this proof and the utilization of it toward . . . my possibilities of being this or that for the Other. . . . Seduction . . . is the complete realization of language." *Ibid.,* p. 373.

65 *Ibid.,* p. 372.

66 *Ibid.,* p. 375.

67 *Ibid.,* p. 376.

68 See *ibid.,* p. 378.

69 *Ibid.,* p. 378.

70 *Ibid.*

71 In terms of our ill-fated lovers, A may become indifferent to B and view her only as performing a function for him—*e.g.,* in the kitchen or in bed.

72 *Ibid.,* p. 392.

73 *Ibid.,* p. 398.

74 *Ibid.*

75 *Ibid.,* p. 404.

76 *Ibid.,* p. 405.

77 *Ibid.*

78 *Ibid.,* p. 404.

79 *Ibid.,* p. 408.

80 *Ibid.,* p. 412.

81 *Ibid.*

82 *Ibid.,* p. 417.

83 *Ibid.,* p. 419.

84 *Ibid.,* p. 421.

85 *Ibid.,* p. 422.

86 *Ibid.*

87 *Ibid.,* p. 425.

88 *Ibid.,* p. 429.

89 *Ibid.,* p. 409.

90 "I shall never be able to accomplish anything except to furnish [the Other's] freedom with occasions to manifest itself without ever succeeding in increasing it or diminishing it, in directing it or in getting hold of it." *Ibid.,* p. 410.

91 He will, of course, be both at the same time.

92 The burden of the lecture was not political. Sartre's intention was to give a clear and simple account of the practical principles of the existentialist philosophy.

93 Sartre, *Existentialism,* Bernard Frechtman, Trans. (New York: Philosophical Library, 1947), p. 58.

94 Pierre Naville in *ibid.,* p. 78.

95 Sartre in *ibid.,* p. 89.

96 Jean-Paul Sartre, "Materialism and Revolution," in George Novack, Ed., *Existentialism versus Marxism: Conflicting Views on Humanism* (New York: Dell Publishing Co., 1966), p. 87.

97 *Ibid.*, p. 89.

98 *Ibid.*, p. 91.

99 *Ibid.*, p. 92.

100 *Ibid.*, p. 101.

101 *Ibid.*, p. 103.

102 *Ibid.*, p. 106.

103 The volume edited by George Novack contains three significant answers to Sartre's criticism: Georg Lukacs, "Existentialism or Marxism?" (1947); Roger Garaudy, "False Prophet: Jean-Paul Sartre" (1948); and Herbert Marcuse, "Sartre, Historical Materialism and Philosophy" (1948). To discuss them here would take us too far from the issue.

104 Jean-Paul Sartre, *Search for a Method*, Hazel E. Barnes, Trans. (New York: Vintage Books, 1968), p. 5.

105 *Ibid.*, p. 6.

106 *Ibid.*, p. 20.

107 *Ibid.*, p. 23.

108 *Ibid.*, p. 29.

109 *Ibid.*, p. 28.

110 *Ibid.*, p. 34.

111 Most Marxists did not accept this offer with any great show of enthusiasm.

112 *Ibid.*, p. 181.

113 As Julian Symons put it, the Marxist would rather be "waiting for Lefty than waiting for Godot."

114 See Novack, pp. 317ff.

115 "Existence belongs to the individual thing, the individual which . . . lies outside or at least cannot be reduced to a concept." *The Journals of Søren Kierkegaard,* Alexander Dru, Ed. and Trans. (New York: Oxford University Press, 1938), p. 358.

116 See Gabriel Marcel, *The Philosophy of Existence* (New York: Philosophical Library, 1949), pp. 1ff.

117 Kierkegaard also had contempt for the media: "Indeed if the Press were to hang out a sign like every other trade, it would have to read: Here men were demoralized in the shortest possible time, on the largest possible scale, for the smallest possible price" (p. 490).

118 Karl Jaspers, *Man in the Modern Age,* Eden and Ceder Paul, Trans. (London: George Routledge and Sons, 1951), p. 40.

119 Thomas Hanna, "Albert Camus: Man in Revolt," in George Alfred Schrader, Jr., Ed., *Existentialist Philosophers: Kierkegaard to Merleau-Ponty* (New York: McGraw-Hill Book Company, 1967), p. 431. This paragraph is indebted to Hanna's excellent essay.

120 *Ibid.*, p. 365.

121 Not all existentialists hold that man is necessarily free, but they all hold that freedom is within the reach of everyone now. See Wild, pp. 117ff.

122 It must be confessed, however, that his espousal of certain *philosophical* principles of Marxism remains baffling.

11

Conclusion: Confessions of a Liberal

DISILLUSIONMENT WITH GOOD GOVERNMENT

If there is anything that the anarchists and quasi-anarchists [1] agree upon it is the incompetence of government to deal with the fundamental problems of our times. Poverty exists side by side with affluence. Racial injustice continues. The natural environment becomes increasingly ugly and polluted. Human and material resources are wasted in wars that serve no recognized ends. Public education, a colossal consumer of tax funds, fails to make itself relevant to social issues. Individuals, submerged in huge collectives, are daily threatened by loss of identity. People's lives are so completely directed by powerful and impersonal institutions that they find it far easier to go along with the tide than to take up the burden of freedom. Government is not only incompetent to deal with these and other human distresses, it is involved in the very social fabric which sustains them.

This government that our critics are talking about is not a Bourbon despotism, a fascist dictatorship, a Communist totalitarianism, or a capitalist oligarchy. It is a system of representative democracy. In theory at least, all can vote and all are represented. The system provides methods by which legislators can make laws on behalf of the majority while preserving minority rights. Officials are moved in and out of power in peaceful and orderly ways. The government of the United States, the United Kingdom, and certain other western "democracies," is without question the best government that man has yet devised.

There are two things that good government is committed to do: (1) serve the will of the majority; (2) protect the rights of the minority. Everything that any democratic republican can reasonably argue for must fall into one of these categories. But if one regards governmental action in these categories as *destructive* of significant human ends, he is on his way to anarchism. If the *best* government is necessarily a *bad* government, then government itself is seriously discredited. It is disillusionment with "good" government that makes the individual an anarchist.

If, on the one hand, government serves the majority by acting as its agent for *oppressing* the minority, the incipient anarchist will believe that he would fare better *without* government, that the collective power of the majority must become deinstitutionalized. Why, for example, should he fight a war he doesn't believe in? Pay disproportionate taxes to support social reforms he doesn't need? Support a police force that is uncongenial to his "life style"? Obey a majority regime that reflects a popular bias against his own race? It is always uncomfortable to be outnumbered; it is unendurable when one's foes have the added advantage of an established system of government.

Exercise of the other legitimate governmental function—protection of the rights of the minority—can also drive a man to anarchism. It is obvious that the determination of these rights is a difficult and controversial matter. Even when they are specified in writing (*e.g.*, in a constitution), they are subject to the contingencies of interpretation and application. There is, indeed, virtually nothing that a clever individual cannot oppose because of real or fancied interference with his rights. Thus any individual may argue that the *wrong* rights are being protected at the expense of the *correct* ones. He could for example, argue that the government is excessively protective of certain kinds of property rights or that it is too generous in its respect for the right of non-profit-making organizations to avoid paying taxes. He could question the efforts of government to compel businesses to serve or hire people from certain races. He could oppose the government's indulgence of technical legal rights in judicial procedures. The incipient anarchist, in short, could come to believe that the government's commitment to individual rights in general operates at the expense of his own or the general welfare. So here, as above, he becomes disgusted with government and is willing to take his chances in a more open society. Perhaps, by common consent, society as a whole can solve its problems better when there is no government setting up and protecting a rigid set of arbitrary, technical, and artificial rights.

Of course, in order for one to arrive at genuine anarchism, he would have to reject *both* functions of government. Few ever arrive consciously at such a comprehensive position. But many get themselves into an anarchistic state of mind through disgust with one function or the other. This disgust may be so great that they never ask themselves about the other function. Government has failed *here,* they say, so government is bad.

EMBATTLED LIBERALISM

Where does the liberal stand? The liberal traditionally seeks the well-being of society. He tries to identify problems and to devise rational solutions. He experiments and is guided more by hope for success in the future than by precedents established in the past. He discovered centuries ago that government exists solely to serve the governed and that it is the best single institution for that purpose. He knows that society can utilize its government in a positive way to promote human happiness. And he knows that society can also utilize its government in a negative way to protect the individual from the depredations of his fellows. He sees government as arising from the people it exists to serve. He believes that the people must create their own social goals and choose how they will be pursued, while, at the same time, reserving areas of individual freedom from public direction. He does not underestimate the difficulty of this task. He knows that changes will come and he welcomes change as necessary for progress. But he values orderly transition, peaceful methods, and "due process." The liberal, with his belief in good government, is the opposite of the anarchist.

It is not surprising, then, that liberalism is the favorite target of anarchism and of the quasi-anarchism espoused by the student left, the radical right, and existentialism. Liberalism is the most plausible theory of government-as-good. The theory of government-as-bad cannot be established unless liberalism is refuted. It is easier to attack the actual governments supported and staffed by liberals than it is to attack the theory of liberal government itself. The anarchists were willing to attempt the latter. Many quasi-anarchists prefer to do the former while pretending that they are doing the latter.

The quasi-anarchists are not rejecting government *per se* so much as they are rejecting things that government is doing which it should not be doing and things that government is not doing which it should be doing. In this respect they are like the liberals—who also call government to account. Indeed, many of the new left and the radical right (and some of the existentialists) have at one time been liberals and have used liberal methods. But they became disillusioned and rejected the liberal point of view. They reject liberalism, not because liberalism is "archic" and they are anarchic, for their own programs require governmental action. The student left requires government in order to mount an exhaustive anti-poverty program, purify the environment, support universities that deal with social problems, protect the rights of minority groups, etc. The radical right requires government to protect national sovereignty, insure the safety and wealth of individuals, etc. Even the existentialists require government to protect them from even more comprehensive enemies to their freedom.

The quasi-anarchists of the right and left reject liberalism for two major reasons. The first is that the liberal is not doctrinaire. He is suspicious of panaceas and extreme positions. He does not see things in terms of blacks and whites, but as shades of gray. He is hopeful without being visionary, cautious without being afraid. For these reasons, the liberal cannot possibly accept the radical programs of either right or left. Preferring to "make haste slowly," the liberal is appalled at the grandiose schemes of the extremists and what seems like irresponsible planning. Temperamentally, the liberal—calculating, careful, broad-minded, sober, and knowledgable —is at the opposite pole from the impassioned, single-minded, impatient, and obsessed partisans of the extreme left and right.

The second reason has to do with methods. The gradual, orderly, legal methods of liberalism stand in contrast to the high-pressure, threatening, direct actions of the extremists of the right and left. This intolerance and militancy is what the contemporary extremists share with the old anarchists. Since their cause is so great, holy indeed, just about anything goes. The establishment has forfeited its right to polite and responsible criticism. It is so evil that virtually any effective tactic is justified. The continued existence of orderly government is not as important *at this stage* as acceptance by society of radical demands. All appeals—no matter how outrageous, utopian, or messianic—are in order if the establishment can thereby be shaken.

The liberal is indeed embattled. The radical left regards him as no better than a Goldwaterite and the radical right sees him as the teacher and inspiration of student activists. The existentialists see him as the upholder of a system that converts subjects into objects and are cynical of his claim to respect the freedom of others. The liberal who in the past was honored as a constructive critic of society is now forced into the unfamiliar role of apologist for a rotten one. He has no great vision to place before the people to stir their souls and win their support. His appeals to reason and constitution are tame in a day of circus demonstrations, and his plea for time and planning sounds like temporizing in a day of instant gratification. He is blamed for dozens of the ills he warned about decades ago, and is cruelly regarded as "the establishment." Across the political spectrum he is outnumbered by his enemies, and yet he is expected to make great and decisive changes on the basis of whatever temporary coalitions he can form. He learned his tactics in a different era, but he must act now when the pace of public events makes the thirties seem like a halcyon age.

THE OPTIONS
OF LIBERALISM

The liberal can answer his critics of the right and left. He can show them that emotion is no substitute for reason, that innovation for the sake of innovation is futile. He can continue to strive to find the right balance between positive collective action and the protection of individual differences. He can point out that the anarchism in his critics' methods and outlook can work against them if their causes ever become part of government policy. In any rational debate with his rivals the liberal must necessarily win on points—if for no other reason than that by definition he is reasonable and progressive.

But victory in debate is not nearly enough for the liberal position. Liberalism could win the debate when judged by the gods of reason, justice, and humanity, but lose the support of the society which it is pledged to serve. Liberalism, or its proponents, must also vigorously and promptly *act*. And it must act *more* vigorously and promptly than it was accustomed to in quieter times.

Liberal action is required in the realm of means. Government is not nearly responsive enough to the people to support the contention that this is a democratic republic. Reforms in the way we nominate and elect the President, governors, Senators, and Representatives are long overdue. The seniority system in Congress must go. Redistricting must continue on the basis of the "one man, one vote" principle. Recall provisions should probably be provided for all representative officials. Immoral and venal behavior in political officials should be promptly and decisively dealt with. The whole interrelated "system" of township, city, county, and state government must be radically revamped. The gross inefficiencies and injustices of judicial procedure at all levels must be eliminated. These are just a few of the obvious evils that should be rectified.

In view of the serious deficiencies in the "legal" and "orderly" methods by which society conducts its business, the critic of "direct action" is on shaky ground. While he assails the tactics of the new left and the radical right, he must know that the channels for conventional and respectable tactics are, in their corruption, wastefulness, and unresponsiveness, not much better. He must take firm steps when rebels break the law, disrupt business, and intimidate officials, but he can do it with a much better conscience (and more widespread public support) when he has cleaned his own house.

There is nothing more significant in the liberal position than concern for the means by which changes are made. Since the liberal seeks improvement, and since improvement can occur only through change, all institutions must provide means by which orderly changes can take place promptly, responsively, intelligently, and gracefully. This applies to government at all levels, to business corporations, to universities, and to churches. The methods of the new left and the radical right are contemptible. But given the sanctioned methods presently available, their popularity is understandable. Most people do not have an absolute loyalty in principle to conventional methods. Liberalism properly stands or falls on the adequacy of its methods. Fundamentally, liberalism *is* a method.

The liberal leadership must also act creatively in the realm of ends. Failure to do great things casts suspicion on the efficacy of the methods themselves. It is possible that the old liberals have won their big battles and are just hanging on now, tired from their exertions in the past and somewhat complacent. But the world is moving too fast for such a posture. The concept of unemployment insurance was fine in 1935 but inadequate for 1970. The atomic bomb was useful in 1945 but fatal for 1970. Integration was a step forward in 1954 but will not suffice in 1970. In the forties the concept that the U.S. had to face up to its world responsibilities was a creative idea and a necessary antidote to isolationism; but the old ideas of foreign aid and intervention do not fit the sixties and seventies. Examples could be listed endlessly. The true liberal must regain the initiative. Too often in the last decade he has seen the good causes preempted by emotional extremists who hardly know what they mean and what realistic actions can be taken.

Liberalism must cease being apologetic. It must be willing to take credit for its achievements of the past. The forces of liberalism fired the Jacksonian period when an oligarchy was transformed into a representative democracy. Liberal leadership gave the world the vision of world peace through a League of Nations and a United Nations. Liberals from both parties addressed themselves successfully to the worst problems of the economic depression. It was in a liberal frame of mind that the foes of fascism defeated the military forces of Germany, Italy, and Japan in World War II. In the 1950s liberalism successfully met the threat of McCarthyism and defeated it. The superb record of the Warren Court was a triumph of liberal principles. Liberalism has declared war on poverty and discrimination. Whatever aberrations still exist in this country, liberalism has always stamped its values on American society. Liberalism is self-corrective and always looks to the future. Its tasks are never complete, but it can find inspiration for continuing struggle in its great achievements of the past.

There is one other point: anarchist, new leftist, radical rightist, and existentialist have all insisted that society stop closing in on the individual, and that the individual be left to find in himself the authority for his actions. All have opposed utopias in which men are programmed from the outside. Beyond all the demands society makes on him, there must be an area in which man freely legislates for himself.

This aim is not outside the liberal point of view. Liberalism began when men sought to limit those political and religious forces that would control their private lives and thoughts. Liberalism then began to take a different tack: it sought in a positive manner to guarantee those goods without which man could react only in a day-by-day manner to those forces threatening his basic well-being and security. Some liberals may now believe that their objective is to fashion society in such a way that everyone will necessarily be happy and content. The existentialists know better. Guaranteed social felicity is *not* the objective. The anti-utopias, *1984* and *Brave New World,* can achieve *that.* The objective is to solve those increasingly difficult social problems that stand in the way of a man's discovering himself and his own aims in life. War, pollution, racism, poverty must be conquered in order that men may begin to live authentically. But reform must somewhere have an end. *How* men are to live must be their own affair. Authority, no matter how benign, must somewhere along the line be dispensed with. The true objective of liberalism, in short, is to utilize government in order to produce that freedom which the anarchists thought was possible only by the destruction of government.

NOTES

1 This term is not entirely adequate, but will be used for the sake of brevity to refer to those groups which have been shown above to have points of similarity to anarchism. The student left and the radical right will always be intended, and sometimes the existentialists as well.

Index